CRUSADE PREACHING AND
THE IDEAL CRUSADER

CRUSADE PREACHING AND THE IDEAL CRUSADER

by

Miikka Tamminen

BREPOLS

British Library Cataloguing in Publication Data

A catalogue record for this book is available from the British Library.

© 2018, Brepols Publishers n.v., Turnhout, Belgium

D/2018/0095/83
ISBN: 978-2-503-57725-8
e-ISBN: 978-2-503-57726-5
DOI: 10.1484/M.SERMO-EB.5.113992
ISSN: 1784-8806
e-ISSN: 2295-2764
Printed in the EU on acid-free paper

CONTENTS

Appendices

Abbreviations

AASS	*Acta Sanctorum quotquot toto orbe coluntur, vel a catholicis scriptoribus celebrantur, quae ex Latinis & Graecis, aliarumque gentium antiquis monumentis*, ed. by Johannes Bolland and Jean Baptiste Carnandet, 68 vols (Paris: V. Palmé, 1643–1940)
COD	*Conciliorum Oecumenicorum Decreta*, ed. by Joseph Alberigo (Freiburg: Herder, 1962)
CPI	Christopher T. Maier, *Crusade Propaganda and Ideology: Model Sermons for the Preaching of the Cross* (Cambridge: Cambridge University Press, 2000)
CR	Christopher T. Maier, 'Crusade and Rhetoric against the Muslim Colony of Lucera: Eudes of Châteauroux's *Sermones de Rebellione Sarracenorum Lucherie in Apulia*', *Journal of Medieval History*, 21 (1995), 343–85
JVSP	Jessalynn Bird, 'James of Vitry's Sermons to Pilgrims', *Essays in Medieval Studies*, 25 (2008), 81–113
MGH SS	Monumenta Germaniae Historica, Scriptores (Hannover: Hahn, 1826–)
PCHL	Penny J. Cole, *The Preaching of the Crusades to the Holy Land, 1095–1270* (Cambridge, MA: Medieval Academy of America, 1991)

PL   *Patrologiae Cursus Completus. Series Latina*, ed. by Jacques-Paul Migne, 221 vols (Paris: Garnier, 1844–64)

QBSS   *Quinti belli sacri scriptores minores*, ed. by Reinhold Röhricht (Geneva: J.-G. Fick, 1879)

RHC Occ. *Recueil des Historiens des Croisades: Historiens Occidentaux*, 16 vols (Paris: Académie des Inscriptions et Belles-Lettres, 1844–1906)

RLS   Johannes Baptist Schneyer, *Repertorium der lateinischen Sermones des Mittelalters*, 11 vols (Münster: Aschendorffsche Verlagsbuchhandlung, 1969–90)

SVP   Nicole Bériou and Isabelle le Masne de Chermont, eds, *Les Sermons et la visite pastorale de Federico Visconti archévêque de Pise (1253–1277)* (Roma: École Française de Rome, 2001

UEE   Alexis Charansonnet, 'L'Université, l'Eglise et l'Etat dans les sermons du cardinal Eudes de Châteauroux (1190?–1273)' (unpublished doctoral dissertation, Université de Lyon 2 – Louis Lumière, 2001)

Acknowledgements

I would like to express my gratitude to several persons whose help has been crucial when writing this book. I wish to thank Professor Christian Krötzl, Docent Katariina Mustakallio, and Docent Jussi Hanska, who have offered their generous support and advice throughout the long process. I have always been able to turn to them when in doubt or in need of help. I also want to thank Professor Kurt Villads Jensen, Doctor Christoph T. Maier, and Professor Kirsi Salonen for their thoughtful comments and criticism. I greatly valued their insights and suggestions.

Several colleagues and friends have also contributed to my work by reading parts of the book, by giving practical advice, by discussing various issues, or simply by being there and offering peer support. In particular, I would like to thank Docent Ville Vuolanto, Docent Sari Katajala-Peltomaa, Dr Jussi Rantala, and Dr Jenni Kuuliala for their help. I am also very grateful to Dr Philip Line, who checked the language of the book.

The work has received financial support from the Academy of Finland, the University of Tampere, the Finnish Institute in Rome (Wihuri Foundation Scholarship), and the Ella and Georg Ehrnrooth Foundation. I would like to thank the staff and the residents of the Finnish Institute in Rome, particularly Simo Örmä. The time spent in Villa Lante and in the many libraries of Rome had great importance for the work.

Lastly and most importantly, I want to thank my family and relatives. My parents have encouraged and supported me throughout the process. My wife, Iiria, and our children, Matilda and Aaro, have helped in countless ways and been extremely patient with me during the writing process.

Miikka Tamminen
Kangasala, April 2017

Introduction

Veri Crucesignati

This study explores the creation of the ideal crusader in thirteenth-century society through a focus on crusade sermons and crusade preaching. How was the image of the true crusader constructed in the crusade model sermons of the thirteenth century? In some of the crusade sermons we find the evaluative term 'veri crucesignati', which is used to describe imaginary figures, the true crusaders.[1] The use of such a term suggests that for the authors of the model sermons there could be different kinds of participants in crusades: there could be crusaders of the right kind, true and fitted to the cause, but there could also be false crusaders, untrue and unsuitable. The aim of this study is to reveal those features that, according to the crusade preachers, defined the 'true' crusaders and separated them from the 'false'. How were participants in the crusade movement guided to true crusading in the model sermons?

This is a little-researched area in crusading studies, touched on only briefly by a few modern scholars. Previous studies on crusade preaching and crusade model sermons have concentrated on recruitment for the expeditions.[2] Scholars have examined the many ways in which the crusades were made attractive to possible participants: how the taking of the cross was promoted, how

---

[1] Jacques de Vitry, 'Item sermo ad crucesignatos vel -signandos', *CPI*, p. 114; Guibert de Tournai, 'Ad crucesignatos et crucesignandos sermo primus', *CPI*, p. 189.

[2] *JVSP*, p. 81.

the crusades were explained to Christians who might want to join the movement, and how they were persuaded to take part. However, it is also important to examine the sermons from another viewpoint. The crusade model sermons were not composed solely for the purposes of recruitment. The rubrics of the crusade model sermons also indicate this: some of the sermons are entitled 'ad crucesignatos et crucesignandos', that is, as sermons meant for those intending to become crusaders, as well as for those who have been signed with the cross.

A comprehensive study of crusade sermons is required, where the focus is on the messages intended for those who have already taken the cross. This approach makes possible an examination of the different dimensions of crusade ideology and the values associated with crusading in thirteenth-century society: the qualities which were appreciated and valued by contemporaries and traits which were considered disadvantageous or unavailing in the crusading context. With this approach the expectations, the aspirations, and the concerns of the crusade ideologists with regard to the conduct and the quality of the crusaders may be observed.

Several crusade model sermons from the thirteenth century written by crusade preachers from different parts of Europe are still extant. This study includes a corpus of thirty-six crusade model sermons and two crusade preaching manuals as primary sources. These were written by eight individual authors, of French, English, and Italian origin. The geographical scope of the study, however, extends far beyond these regions, for the model sermons and manuals were meant to be valid everywhere within Western Christendom.[3] The period in question, the thirteenth century, has been described as the 'golden age' of crusading — the time when the crusade movement reached its 'maturity'. This period saw an increase of crusading enemies, the intensification of crusade propaganda, and the full development of many crusading practices.[4] It is thus an ideal period when discussing the creation of the 'true' crusader in crusade ideology and crusade propaganda.

The main purpose of this study is not to focus on the audience of the crusade sermons, nor the intentions or the deeds of the crusaders, but rather on the messages and concepts presented by the authors of the crusade model sermons.[5] I will explore the ways in which the authors of the sermons attempted

[3] Hanska, *'And the Rich Man also died; and He was buried in Hell'*, p. 15; See also d'Avray, *The Preaching of the Friars*, esp. pp. 123–28.

[4] See, for example, Tyerman, *England and the Crusades*, p. 88; Riley-Smith, *The Crusades: A History*, p. 183.

[5] Carolyn Muessig has noted that modern scholars have for the most part viewed the *ad*

to instruct the participants *or* those intending to participate in crusades, and how the crusaders' behaviour, morale, outlook, emotions, and state of mind were moulded by crusade preachers to adapt to the nature of the undertaking, the 'sanctity' of the crusading journey. The approach of the study is comparative and qualitative — the messages of the crusade model sermons are compared and their interrelationship analysed. Throughout this work these messages are contextualized and compared to other contemporary crusade sources. A quantitative approach is applied on occasion to support and substantiate the analysis.

In examining the 'true' crusader, this study deals with ideals and optimums, not with actualities or real-life crusaders. Nevertheless, the crusade preachers' intentions were not to create a utopian crusader — an unattainable goal — but to construct an ideal and present ways in which the participants of crusades could strive towards this ideal. These conceptions of 'true' crusaders were not the only ones that contemporaries might have. Indeed, there could be many different views of 'true' crusaders during the thirteenth century. This study focuses on the views of the authors of the crusade model sermons, who were ecclesiastics, crusade ideologists, and propagandists.

The term 'propaganda' is problematic, but it is nonetheless used by most modern scholars of crusading studies.[6] Some have preferred to use alternative expressions such as crusading 'message' or crusading 'exhortation'.[7] The term is ambiguous and has acquired negative connotations. Propaganda is sometimes described as deceptive, as the intentional distribution of fabrications of truth. This negative interpretation often assumes that propaganda is the conscious telling of lies to the audience, hence that the propagandist does not believe in the veracity of the information given and knows he/she is lying. When viewed neutrally, propaganda is defined simply as the 'communication of ideas designed to persuade people to think and behave in a desired way'.[8] This is the definition adopted in this study: propaganda in this context means deliberate and system-

---

status sermons (which account for many of the crusade model sermons discussed in this volume) from the viewpoint of what the sermons reveal about the intended audiences of the sermons. She has correctly argued that what the *ad status* sermons tell about the preachers and their views is more significant. Muessig, 'Audience and Preacher', esp. pp. 275–76.

[6] See, for example, Richard, *Histoire des croisades*, p. 280: 'propagande — il faut bien employer le mot'. Morris, 'Propaganda for War'; Riley-Smith, *The Crusades, Christianity, and Islam*; Tyerman, *God's War*.

[7] See, for example, *PCHL*.

[8] Taylor, *Munitations of the Mind*, pp. 4–8; See also Menache, *The Vox Dei*, pp. 175–90.

atic communication of messages, which may contain factual or false information, aimed to influence people in a sought-after and purposeful manner.

The principal question — how crusade propagandists constructed the ideal crusader in the model sermons — brings forth additional key questions that this study aims to answer: Could anyone become a 'true' crusader in the opinion of the authors of the crusade model sermons? Did status, wealth, age, or gender have an effect on 'true' crusading during the thirteenth century? How were the ideal crusaders guided to join the movement and how were they instructed to act during the journey? The complex medieval concepts of crusade indulgence and crusading martyrdom are also considered in connection with these problems.

In this study I will argue that for the authors of the crusade sermons, the conduct, attitude, and frame of mind of the participants were not inessential side issues but significant questions, which had both practical and ideological dimensions. The examination will reveal which qualities of the crusaders were considered important in the crusade ideology of the thirteenth century and why these features had relevance. I will challenge some of the existing views expressed in crusade studies and contest suggestions that certain concepts in the crusade ideology of the thirteenth century lacked importance, such as the *imitatio Christi* or the theme of pilgrimage.[9] My hope is that the examination of the crusade model sermons of the thirteenth century, with a focus on ideal crusading, will provide a new and important interpretation of these issues.

This study begins with an introduction to the field of crusade research, where the historiography of the crusades and the most recent research trends are discussed. Particular emphasis will be placed on studies dealing with crusade sermons and crusade preaching. I will also briefly introduce the authors of the crusade sermons and present a general background to the composition of the thirteenth-century crusade model sermons. The primary sources of the study are then introduced. I will explain the choice of sources and describe the complications in identifying and defining crusade sermons.

After this first introductory chapter, this study proceeds with an analysis of the crusade model sermons. It is divided into three main analytical chapters, which are arranged according to different themes. Chapter 2 examines the utilization of biblical themes and models in crusade sermons. The crusading journey was discussed and explained in many different ways by the crusade preachers. The most important frame of reference was naturally the Bible, which pro-

---

[9] For the *imitatio Christi*, see Throop, 'Zeal, Anger and Vengeance', pp. 177–201, esp. p. 198. See the discussion below, pp. 108–39. For the theme of pilgrimage, see Smith, *Crusading in the Age of Joinville*, p. 77. See also below, pp. 237–49.

vided for the authors the main motifs for their sermons. Crusading was interpreted and explained in the sermons by using scriptural themes and by citing moral lessons from both the Old and the New Testament. Biblical accounts of the past and scriptural prophecies of the future were linked to current circumstances and to crusading objectives. The chapter explores how the Bible and biblical figures were used by preachers in the creation of the 'true' crusader.

Chapter 3 examines the relations between God and the crusader. This relationship was a key question for many crusade preachers of the thirteenth century. The authors attempted to explain in the sermons how the crusaders should serve God, how they could acquire a closer relationship with Christ, and the consequences of this service and close friendship. The theme of *imitatio Christi* was used extensively by most crusade preachers. The devotional dimension of crusading and the pious features of the 'true' crusader are studied in detail in the chapter.

Chapter 4 focuses on more earthly issues and examines how the crusaders were guided to deal with questions related to everyday life. The crusade preachers discussed various worldly matters in their sermons and preaching manuals. Earthly wealth, family relations, business affairs, and carnal desires were all questions which needed to be dealt with in the sermons. The pilgrimage tradition provided for the authors a theme which was utilized to illustrate how the 'true' crusaders should make their sacred journey through the world. A final chapter will present the conclusion to the entire study.

Crusade Studies

Crusading is an intricate concept and 'crusade' a difficult term to define. Nine hundred years after the First Crusade, after a wealth of research and centuries of writing crusade histories, historians are still battling with some of the basic questions, including how the crusades should be defined. During the last few decades, scholars have tried to explain the causes for the different crusades and find a definition that would encompass all the different expressions of crusading and all the medieval expeditions, without much success. Ever since Giles Constable wrote his influential article discussing the historiography of the crusades in 2001, crusade historians have been labelled as representatives of different schools of thought according to the ways they have defined the crusades in their studies.[10]

---

[10] Constable, 'The Historiography of the Crusades', pp. 1–22. Constable has revised the

In tracing the development of crusading historiography from the Middle Ages to modern times, Constable pinpointed some of the existing definitions used in crusade studies and the problems which these definitions present. These definitions may be typecast as traditionalist, pluralist, popularist, or generalist viewpoints, depending on their emphasis. The traditionalist approach underlines the significance of Jerusalem to the crusade ideology. Its proponents maintain that only those crusades that were directed to the Holy Land, to liberate Jerusalem and the Holy Sepulchre, were true crusades; other medieval expeditions that have been categorized as crusades were not truly crusades. Many of the important modern scholars from the first half of the twentieth century may be classed as traditionalists, including René Grousset, Steven Runciman, and Hans Eberhard Mayer.[11]

The pluralists, on the other hand, view the crusades as an expression of a certain kind of penitential war with strong ties to the pilgrimage tradition. While the traditionalists underline the destination — that is, the Holy Land and Jerusalem — as a defining feature of the crusade, the pluralists emphasize papal authorization. For them the demands of the pope and his authority are the essential factors in defining the crusades. The pluralist approach expands the scope of crusading both geographically and chronologically. While the traditionalists focus on one area, the Holy Land, and on a relatively short period, the time from the First Crusade to the fall of Acre in 1291, the pluralists research many different areas and take into account centuries of crusading, up until the sixteenth century, or in some cases even further, to modern times. Jonathan Riley-Smith is regarded as the most important representative of the pluralist school.[12]

The popularists, a name introduced by Norman Housley rather than Constable, are regarded as scholars who underline spiritual and psychological aspects in giving definition to the crusades. This school of thought has been

article considerably in Constable, *Crusaders and Crusading in the Twelfth Century*, pp. 3–44. See also Riley-Smith's and Housley's prior remarks and the division made between the traditionalists and the pluralists in Riley-Smith, 'The Crusading Movement and Historians', pp. 1–12; Housley, *The Later Crusades*, pp. 2–3.

[11] Constable, 'The Historiography of the Crusades', p. 12; Housley, *Contesting the Crusades*, pp. 2–3. For the influential studies of Grousset, Runciman, and Mayer, see Grousset, *Histoire des croisades*; Runciman, *A History of the Crusades*; Mayer, *Geschichte der Kreuzzüge*.

[12] Constable, 'The Historiography of the Crusades', p. 12; Housley, *Contesting the Crusades*, p. 3. For a recent study by Riley-Smith, and his views on the development of crusade ideology in the Middle Ages and the exploitation of crusade rhetoric during the imperial and colonial period, see Riley-Smith, *The Crusades, Christianity, and Islam*.

influenced particularly by the French scholars Paul Alphandéry and Alphonse Dupront. In popularism the eschatological aspects of crusading are accentuated. The division between official and popular ideas of crusades, made already by Leopold von Ranke in 1887 and Carl Erdmann in 1935, are emphasized in this approach.[13] Religious enthusiasm, revivalism, and apocalyptic visions are the mental and spiritual background that gave birth to the crusades, according to the popularist viewpoint.[14]

Finally, there is the generalist approach to the crusades, which is the broadest of all the different schools of thought. The generalists regard the crusades as holy wars authorized by God. Various Christian wars fought during the Middle Ages after the First Crusade can be classed as crusades, because these wars were claimed to be fought in order to execute God's will. The ideological justification for the crusades rested in the authority of God. According to this viewpoint, the crusaders were fulfilling God's will and papal approval was not necessary.[15]

Because of the complexity of the crusade movement and the many different medieval expressions of crusade enthusiasm, a case can be made for all four schools of thought: they all have their strengths, but they also have their particular weaknesses as well. The traditionalist approach is well suited for studying the first three major crusades directed to the Holy Land. However, it is extremely difficult to explain or to interpret the great number of medieval sources that mention similar expeditions to places other than the Holy Land from the traditionalist viewpoint. Simply to classify these expeditions as a corruption of the crusade ideology or misguided attempts at crusades that cannot be designated as such seems an oversimplification of what occurred.

The pluralists, on the other hand, can work with the many different kinds of crusades mentioned in medieval sources. However, while pluralism is well suited for the study of expeditions that were directed to various destinations or against many different enemies, this approach too encounters difficulties when trying to explain or analyse the so-called 'popular' crusades. These crusades, such as the Children's Crusade of 1212, lacked papal approval and thus fall outside the definition of the crusade given by the pluralists. There were also

---

[13] Ranke, *Weltgeschichte*, p. 71; Erdmann, *Die Entstehung des Kreuzzugsgedankens*, p. 250.

[14] Constable, 'The Historiography of the Crusades', pp. 12–14; Housley, *Contesting the Crusades*, pp. 5–7. For the views of Paul Alphandéry and Alphonse Dupront, see Alphandéry, *La Chrétienté et l'idée de croisade*; Dupront, *Du Sacré*.

[15] Constable, 'The Historiography of the Crusades', pp. 14–15; Housley, *Contesting the Crusades*, pp. 6–7. Ernst-Dieter Hehl may be considered a generalist. For Hehl's views on crusading, see Hehl, 'Was ist eigentlich ein Kreuzzug?'.

military expeditions during the Middle Ages, such as raids against the Muslims, which were carried out by Christians who had not taken the cross and were therefore not officially *crucesignati*. Nonetheless, the contemporary participants in the 'popular' crusades or the participants in the raids regarded themselves as soldiers of God who, like the *crucesignati*, were fighting against the enemies of God.[16]

The popularists' approach to crusading is the most suitable for studying the 'popular' crusades. The mentality of the masses and the revivalist movements of the Middle Ages can be successfully analysed with this methodology, as Gary Dickson's studies exemplify.[17] However, this viewpoint is the most constricted, the Children's Crusade and the Shepherds' Crusades being the only true expressions of the crusades as defined by the popularists. The approach falls short in explaining the many well-organized, official crusades of the period, which were prepared for years with determination and perseverance and were carried out by the crusaders in a cool-headed manner, rather than in the heat of the moment, in the spirit of revivalism, or in a state of anxiety caused by apocalyptic fears and hopes.

The generalists' approach makes it possible to study the many different kinds of crusades, both the official and the 'popular', as well as the traditional crusades to the Holy Land and those to various other destinations during the later Middle Ages, without leaving any expeditions that could possibly be described as crusades outside the definition. However, the problem with the generalist viewpoint is that it tends to become too broad an approach. Many of the central ideas in the crusade ideology and many of the important expressions of crusading zeal — the taking of the cross, the crusade indulgence granted by the pope, the reverence for the Holy Sepulchre — appear to become insignificant when the definition of crusading adopted includes many expeditions that did not involve these.[18]

The crusade movement and crusade ideology cannot be conceived as immutable — these phenomena are not, at any given point of time, in a static state: rather, the crusade movement evolved through the years, the decades, and the centuries, and there were many different factors contributing to its development. Members of the clergy and the laity, and various institutions and individuals with many different aspirations and ambitions, all influenced the evolution of the crusade movement, and they did so in different situations and on

---

[16] Housley, *Contesting the Crusades*, pp. 8–9.

[17] Dickson, *The Children's Crusade*; Dickson, *Religious Enthusiasm in the Medieval West*.

[18] Housley, *Contesting the Crusades*, p. 13.

different occasions over the years, making both intentional and unintentional contributions. There was no single person or group of people that could control the development. This explains the different approaches in crusade studies and the problems these have encountered. In my opinion a combination of the different schools of thought or a modification of some of the viewpoints is needed when studying an extended period of time, which will include many different kinds of crusades, just as this study does.

A generalist point of view, which takes into account the basic, defining features of the crusades, or a modified pluralist point of view, which accepts that there could be other kinds of crusades than simply those which had papal approval, seem to be the most suitable approaches to the crusades of the thirteenth century. Some modern scholars have attempted to adapt their approaches, both in an effort to avoid being labelled as representatives of one or another school of thought, and to come to terms with the elusiveness of the crusades. For example, the views of two important current scholars who originally approached the problem from opposite ends, Christopher Tyerman and Norman Housley, appear to have become closer to each other in recent studies. Tyerman seems to have moved from the traditionalists' school closer to the generalists' camp, while still acknowledging and emphasizing the ideological fundamentals of the crusade movement, whereas Housley, once a self-confessed 'pure' pluralist, appears to become a modified one, acknowledging the attractions of the generalist approach as well as its shortcomings.[19]

Excessively rigid definitions are impractical for the study of such a nebulous subject as the crusades. However, some definitions must be made. This study may be regarded as taking either a modified pluralist or an atypical generalist approach to the crusades. I view the crusades as penitential, Christian holy wars, which were directed not only to the Holy Land but to various other places also, and which lasted for much longer than the so-called traditional crusading period that ends in 1291. I regard the campaigns against the Albigensians and Lucera Muslims as crusades, and I have included crusade sermons against these enemies as primary sources of this study. Although the crusades most often had papal approval, I recognize that there were instances and expressions of crusading zeal during the Middle Ages, as well as expeditions and other military activities, which can be regarded as crusades, but which for various reasons

---

[19] For the traditionalist views of Tyerman, see esp. Tyerman, 'The Holy Land and the Crusades', and the current views in Tyerman, *God's War*. For Housley's adherence to the pluralist school of thought, see Housley, *The Later Crusades*, p. 2, and for his current modified views, see Housley, *Contesting the Crusades*, pp. 2–13.

lacked papal approval at the time. In my opinion different kinds of Christian and Judaeo-Christian ideas converged in crusade ideology. The crusades were a peculiar mixture of concepts of just and holy wars and traditions of pilgrimage and indulgence.

Studies on Crusade Preaching

The crusades were born out of preaching, as the sermons delivered by Pope Urban II at Clermont in 1095 and during the subsequent preaching tour in France created the crusade movement. The crusade sermons of Urban II have not survived, but there are four accounts of the Clermont sermon, apparently given by eyewitnesses but written from memory several years after the event. Texts and descriptions of three decrees of the Clermont council have also survived, together with six of Urban's letters on the subject, alongside other fragmentary evidence and incidental observations of his preaching. It is therefore possible to make qualified observations about the messages of Urban and the content of his preaching.[20]

Dana C. Munro's study of 1906 is regarded as a classical examination of the crusade preaching of Urban II. Munro examined and reconstructed Urban's crusading messages from a variety of medieval sources.[21] Of the modern crusade historians, Jonathan Riley-Smith and H. E. J. Cowdrey in particular have contributed to our understanding of the content of Urban's sermons and the circumstances of his preaching. The pope stressed the need to liberate Jerusalem and free the Eastern Christians and the Eastern churches. Christians participating in the special pilgrimage would receive an indulgence for their labours.[22]

Crusade preachers had an important role in the inception of both the First and subsequent crusades. Charismatic preachers such as Bernard of Clairvaux, whose preaching was instrumental in the making of the Second Crusade (1147–49), and Foulques de Neuilly, whose revivalist preaching created great fervour during the preparations for the Fourth Crusade (1202–04), were largely responsible for the spreading of the crusade message.[23] The crusade preachers

---

[20] Riley-Smith, *The First Crusade and the Idea of Crusading*, pp. 13–30.

[21] Munro, 'The Speech of Pope Urban II at Clermont, 1095'.

[22] Cowdrey, 'Pope Urban II's Preaching'; Riley-Smith, *The First Crusade and the Idea of Crusading*, pp. 13–30.

[23] For a recent, new assessment on the crusade preaching of Bernard of Clairvaux and further references, see Purkis, *Crusading Spirituality*. See also the collection of essays in Gervers,

did not merely promote the crusades but had a hand in the development of crusade ideology, both intentionally and unintentionally, at times with papal authorization and at times without.[24]

Earlier scholars have also studied the crusade preachers of the thirteenth century and their sermon material. The crusade preachers first attracted the attention of historians during the latter half of the nineteenth century. Crusade model sermons and manuals intended for crusade preachers were examined in short studies.[25] Reinhold Röhricht provided an edition of the manual *Brevis ordinacio de predicacione sancte crucis in Anglia* in 1879 and briefly examined the crusade model sermons in an article in 1884.[26] Some of the thirteenth-century model sermons, including sermons of Jacques de Vitry and Humbert de Romans, were studied by G. Wolfram and A. Lecoy de la Marche in 1886 and in 1890.[27] In 1888, Cardinal Jean-Baptiste Pitra also edited some of the crusade sermons of Jacques de Vitry and Eudes de Châteauroux.[28]

The Second Crusade and the Cistercians. For the preaching of Foulques de Neuilly, see Forni, 'La "Nouvelle Prédication" des disciples de Foulques de Neuilly'; *PCHL*, pp. 87–88.

[24] The popular preaching of Peter the Hermit, or Pierre d'Amiens, for example, has been considered crude and unauthorized by modern scholars, but the visions of revenge and the anti-Semitic ideas which he promoted would prove to be long-lasting sidetracks in crusade ideology. Peter the Hermit had an influential role, alongside Urban II, in the early stages of the crusade movement. He has been described as 'a freelancer', 'a demagogue', and 'a religious charlatan' by historians. Riley-Smith, *The First Crusade and the Idea of Crusading*, pp. 31–34. *PCHL*, pp. 34–36. Peter's preaching and his messages have also been studied by several historians. From the modern historians particularly Morris and Flori have examined Peter's preaching; see Morris, 'A Hermit Goes to War'; Morris, 'Peter the Hermit and the Chroniclers'; Flori, *Pierre l'Ermite et la Première Croisade*. See also an older study by Hagenmeyer, *Peter der Eremite*.

[25] *CPI*, pp. 14–15.

[26] Röhricht, 'Die Kreuzpredigten gegen den Islam'; 'Brevis ordinacio de predicacione', *QBSS*, pp. 1–26.

[27] Wolfram, 'Kreuzpredigt und Kreuzlied'; Lecoy de la Marche, 'La Prédication de la croisade au treizième siècle'. Hermann Hoogeweg's 1894 analysis of the writings of Oliver von Paderborn unfortunately does not include the actual sermons of Oliver, for these have not survived. Hoogeweg, *Die Schriften des Kölner Domscholasters*. See also Hoogeweg, 'Die Kreuzpredigt des Jahres 1224'.

[28] J.-B. Pitra was a French theologian who was appointed as the Cardinal-Bishop of Frascati (Tusculum) in 1879. Pitra edited medieval sermons of his French-born predecessors, which included some of the crusade sermons of Jacques de Vitry and Eudes de Châteauroux, who had been successive cardinals of Tusculum during the thirteenth century. See *Analecta Novissima*, ed. by Pitra, pp. 310–15, pp. 328–33.

Despite this early interest in the thirteenth-century crusade model sermons, in-depth studies of the sermons have been carried out only recently.[29] Penny Cole's 1991 study was a watershed in crusade preaching research. Cole examined the preaching of the crusades to the Holy Land from the First Crusade until the year 1270. Her study included many different kinds of sources related to crusade preaching, including crusade model sermons, manuals for crusade preachers, the *reportationes* of crusade sermons, and chronicle descriptions of crusade preaching.[30] Christoph Maier's study on the crusade preaching of the mendicant friars followed in 1994. Maier's study focused on the involvement in the crusade movement of the two major mendicant orders, the Franciscans and the Dominicans, between the pontificates of Gregory IX (1227–41) and Nicholas IV (1288–92). Like Cole, Maier used many different kinds of sources in his study: papal letters, chronicles, annals, and crusade preaching manuals, as well as the crusade model sermons and the exempla used in the sermons.[31]

Two important articles were published after this by Christoph Maier, in which he examined crusade preaching and the crusade model sermons of the thirteenth century: in 1995, Eudes de Châteauroux's preaching against the Lucera Muslims was explored in an article which also provided critical editions of his three crusade sermons, while in 1997, Philippe le Chancelier's and Eudes de Châteauroux's crusade preaching against the Albigensian heretics was examined.[32] In the same year Nicole Bériou published an article in which she also discussed Philippe le Chancelier's and Eudes de Châteauroux's sermons against the Albigensians.[33] In 2000, Christoph Maier published the study *Crusade Ideology and Propaganda: Model Sermons for the Preaching of the Cross*, which has become a work frequently cited by crusade historians. Maier's study includes seventeen crusade model sermons from the thirteenth and early fourteenth centuries, which have been edited and translated, as well as an insightful, short analysis of the sermons. This work has earned Maier a reputation as 'a leading scholar of crusade preaching in the thirteenth century', to quote Norman Housley.[34]

[29] *CPI*, p. 15.

[30] See also the article by Cole, d'Avray, and Riley-Smith, 'Application of Theology to Current Affairs'.

[31] For a list of the crusade model sermons and the exempla, see appendix 2 in Maier, *Preaching the Crusades*, pp. 170–74.

[32] *CR*, pp. 343–85; Maier, 'Crisis, Liturgy and the Crusade'.

[33] Bériou, 'La Predication de croisade'.

[34] Housley, 'Review: Crusade Propaganda and Ideology', p. 939.

Studies on crusade preaching and crusade model sermons of the thirteenth century have continued to appear throughout the first decade of the new millennium. In addition, new material has been found. The crusade preaching of the early thirteenth century has been examined by Jessalynn Bird. In her unpublished dissertation work, Bird focused on the preaching of the Paris reformers.[35] She has written several articles on crusade preaching and the sermons composed during the promotion of the Albigensian Crusade and the Fifth Crusade, focusing particularly on the preaching of Jacques de Vitry and Oliver von Paderborn. Recently, in 2008, Bird published an article on Jacques de Vitry's sermons intended for the pilgrims and the crusaders, including critical transcriptions of two sermons, which are also utilized in this study.[36]

The sermons of Eudes de Châteauroux, several of which are linked to the crusades, have been studied by Alexis Charansonnet. In 2001, Charansonnet defended his doctoral thesis, 'L'Université, l'Eglise et l'Etat dans les sermons du cardinal Eudes de Châteauroux (1190?–1273)'. This three-part, 1040-page dissertation work includes editions of sixty-five sermons of Eudes de Châteauroux, most of which have been edited by Charansonnet himself. Some of these sermons are also utilized in the current study.[37] Finally, a group of scholars led by Nicole Bériou and Isabelle le Masne de Chermont published a study on the preaching of Federico Visconti in 2001. This study provides critical editions of 106 sermons composed by the Archbishop of Pisa, analysis of the sermons, and biographical information. The two crusade sermons of Federico Visconti edited in the work are also researched here.

This study owes a huge debt to the work done by the above-mentioned scholars, Penny Cole, Christoph Maier, Nicole Bériou, Jessalynn Bird, and Alexis Charansonnet. I have had the advantage of utilizing the critical editions and transcriptions of the model sermons that they have previously prepared in my own study.[38] I have also benefited greatly from their analyses of the model

[35] Bird, 'Heresy, Crusade and Reform'.

[36] Bird, 'The *Historia Orientalis* of Jacques de Vitry'; Bird, 'Innocent III, Peter the Chanter's Circle, and the Crusade Indulgence'; Bird, 'Crusade and Conversion after the Fourth Lateran Council'; Bird, 'Paris Masters and the Justification'; *JVSP*.

[37] I have used in this study the printed version of the unpublished dissertation of Alexis Charansonnet from the year 2001 (Université de Lyon 2). While this book was being prepared for publication it came to my attention that another version of the dissertation with a slightly different pagination had been released by the author; available at <https://tel.archives-ouvertes.fr/tel-00390699/document>. I regret any inconvenience this may cause for the reader.

[38] I am particularly grateful to Christoph Maier for allowing me to make use of his and Nicole

sermons and the conclusions which they have reached. This study aims to further our understanding of the crusading messages expressed in the model sermons of the thirteenth century. Although the sermons have undergone various degrees of previous scholarly examination, this has not exhausted the source material.[39]

There is one particular area which has been overlooked in studies of thirteenth-century crusade model sermons, and which Jessalynn Bird has also identified as a gap in the research. In her recent article, Bird pointed out that the crusade preachers played a role in creating the identity of the crusading armies, sustaining the morale of the crusaders during their journeys, and explaining the goals of the expeditions to the participants. The sermons contain material on these issues that has largely been missed or ignored by modern scholars.[40] In the present study I intend to fill the gap in the research by focusing on this neglected area.

The Authors of the Crusade Sermons

The crusade preachers examined in this study came from different backgrounds and from different parts of Europe. They each held a high position in thirteenth-century society, either in the Roman Church, in the mendicant orders, or in the University of Paris: two of the preachers were cardinals of the Roman Church, one an archbishop, one a bishop, one served as the master general of the Dominican Order, one acted as the Franciscan regent master at Paris, and two were chancellors of the University of Paris.[41] The biographical details of the preachers have been studied previously, and for this reason only a short introduction is included here, with references to further reading.

Bériou's transcriptions of the sermons of Philippe le Chancelier and Eudes de Châteauroux. Maier and Bériou are preparing a further study of these sermons to be published in future. I have also consulted the manuscripts of these sermons in the Médiathèque d'Arras containing Eudes de Châteauroux's sermon: Arras, MS 876, fols 88vb–90rb; and the Bibliothèque municipale d'Avranches containing Philippe le Chancelier's sermons: Avranches, MS 132, fols 243ra–244vb, 248va–250ra, 250ra–251ra, 251ra–252vb, 272rb–273vb. See Appendices II and V.

[39] For example, Maier emphasized that his study on the crusade model sermons was not meant as 'the final word on the subject', but rather as 'first inroads into as yet little explored areas of research'. *CPI*, p. 16.

[40] *JVSP*, p. 81.

[41] Eudes de Châteauroux held a high position in both the Roman Church and the University of Paris. He was the chancellor of the university before becoming the Cardinal-Bishop of Tusculum.

Philippe le Chancelier (*c.* 1160/70–1236) served as the Archdeacon of Noyon, a position he may have held as early as 1202, but certainly by 1211. In 1217, he was made the chancellor of the cathedral of Notre Dame de Paris, that is, the chancellor of the University of Paris in its early stages. Today Philippe is best known for his philosophy and his poetry. He wrote a philosophical work, *Summa de bono*, which had great influence on the thinking of both Albertus Magnus and Thomas Aquinas. He was also a preacher of repute, who has left a large corpus of sermons — 723 incipits of his sermons are listed in Schneyer's *Repertorium*. Philippe le Chancelier's crusade preaching is connected to the Albigensian Crusade in the year 1226. Before his death in 1236, Philippe was also involved in rooting out heresies in northern France.[42]

Jacques de Vitry (*c.* 1160/70–1240) was born in Vitry-en-Perthois, a town near Reims. He studied in Paris and belonged to the circle of students who were taught by the famous teacher Peter the Chanter. In 1210, he was ordained to the priesthood. Jacques was a gifted and celebrated preacher, whose utilization of exempla in the sermons was innovative. In 1213–14, he preached the crusade against the Albigensian heretics. In 1216, Jacques was elected as the Bishop of Acre. He preached the Fifth Crusade against the Muslims and participated personally in the expedition. In 1218–21, he was with the army of the Fifth Crusade in Egypt. After his return to Europe, Jacques continued to preach the crusade against the Albigensians. In 1229, he was made the Cardinal-Bishop of Tusculum (today known as Frascati). Jacques died in 1240 in Rome. He wrote several works. Those dealing specifically with crusades are *Historia orientalis*, the letters which he sent from the Fifth Crusade, and his crusade sermons. During the 1230s, Jacques composed a collection of model sermons, dividing the collection into four categories and creating the first comprehensive collection of sermons *ad vulgares* or *ad status* — sermons arranged according to different social groups.[43]

Roger of Salisbury (*c.* 1185–1247) studied theology at the University of Paris. In 1223 he was a canon of Salisbury and in 1225 a lecturer of theology

---

[42] For further information on the life and works of Philippe le Chancelier, see Bériou, 'Philippe le Chancelier'. For the critical edition of *Summa*, see Philippe le Chancelier, *Summa de bono*, ed by Wicki. For the significance of his philosophy, see also McCluskey, 'The Roots of Ethical Voluntarism'. For Philippe's influence on Albertus Magnus and Thomas Aquinas, see Houser, *The Cardinal Virtues*. See also Traill, 'Philip the Chancellor and the Heresy Inquisition'. For the sermons of Philippe, see *RLS*, IV: *Autoren: L–P*, pp. 818–68.

[43] For Jacques de Vitry, see *Historia Occidentalis*, ed. by Hinnebusch; Sandor, 'Jacques de Vitry'; *CPI*, pp. 8–9; See also the biography written by Funk, *Jakob von Vitry*. For the crusading messages of *Historia orientalis*, see Bird, 'The *Historia Orientalis* of Jacques de Vitry'.

there. In 1244 Roger was elected Bishop of Bath and Wells. He died in 1247 and was buried at Bath. Different kinds of works written by Roger have survived, including commentaries and moral sermons on the Gospels as well as Sunday sermons. Among these works is one crusade sermon that may have been preached during Roger's episcopacy, that is, between 1244 and 1247.[44]

Eudes de Châteauroux (*c.* 1190–1273) had a long and influential career at the top of the hierarchy of the Roman Church. He studied at Paris and preached the crusade against the Albigensians in 1226. Eudes became the chancellor of the University of Paris in 1238, two years after Philippe le Chancelier's death, and after the short chancellorship of Guaird de Laon. As a chancellor of the university, Eudes was involved in the condemnation of the Talmud in 1242–44. In 1244 Eudes was made the Cardinal-Bishop of Tusculum, succeeding Jacques de Vitry in the position. He was in charge of the crusade propaganda in France during the preparations for the Seventh Crusade and travelled as the papal legate to the expedition. In 1248–54 Eudes was with the crusade army first in Cyprus, then in Egypt, and then in the Holy Land. In the 1260s he preached the crusades against the Mongols and the Lucera Muslims. Eudes was a skilled preacher, who has left a sizeable collection of sermons, over 1100 of which have survived.[45]

Humbert de Romans (*c.* 1190/1200–1277) studied at the University of Paris and reportedly qualified in arts and canon law. Humbert joined the Order of Preachers and by 1237 he was the prior of the convent in Lyons. In 1240 he was made the provincial prior of the Roman province and in 1244 the provincial prior of Francia. In 1254 Humbert became the fifth master general of the Dominican Order, retiring in 1263. During his retirement, Humbert wrote several works, many of them as aids to the friars of the order in their preaching task. His crusade sermons are part of the *ad status* — a collection of sermons that belong to a larger work known as *De eruditione predicatorum*. Humbert also wrote a preaching manual, the *De predicatione sancte crucis*, which focused on crusade preaching and which the crusade preachers could carry with them on their preaching tours. He also composed a three-part work for the Second

---

[44] *PCHL*, pp. 168–73; *Fasti Ecclesiae Anglicanae*, ed. by Greenway, VII, 1–6; IV, 84–85.

[45] For the life and the sermons of Eudes de Châteauroux, see *UEE*. See also Charansonnet, 'L'Évolution de la predication du cardinal Eudes de Châteauroux'; *CPI*, pp. 9–10; Iozzelli, *Odo da Châteauroux*; d'Avray, *Death and the Prince*, p. 38. For Eudes's preaching against the Albigensians, see Bériou, 'La Predication de croisade'. For his role in the condemnation of the Talmud and Eudes's sermon for the conversion of Jews, see Behrman, '*Volumina vilissima*'. For the sermons, see *RLS*, IV: *Autoren: L–P*, pp. 394–483.

Council of Lyons in 1274, known as *Opus tripartitum*, of which one part is a crusading apology, a tract written against crusade criticism.[46]

Federico Visconti (*c*. 1200–1277) was born to one of the most distinguished noble families of Pisa. He served as the domestic chaplain of Cardinal Sinibaldo Fieschi, the future Pope Innocent IV, in the 1230s. In 1235–36 Federico made two journeys to France, where he studied at the University of Paris. In 1250–52 he served again as the domestic chaplain of Innocent IV. The relations between the republic of Pisa and the papacy were deeply troubled at the time. In the conflict between the papacy and Frederick II of Hohenstaufen, Pisa had taken the emperor's side, which led to the excommunication of the Pisans, and the city was placed under interdict. During the 1250s, Federico worked hard to repair relations, since he had been appointed as the Archbishop of Pisa in 1253 but could not be consecrated before the interdict was removed. Finally, in 1257 Federico was made Archbishop of Pisa by Pope Alexander IV. Federico held several synods to reform the Pisan church. In 1260 and 1261 he preached crusades against the Mongols and against the Muslims of the Holy Land.[47]

Guibert de Tournai (*c*. 1210–1284) is another highly educated author of the crusade model sermons. Guibert studied and taught at the University of Paris. He appears to have held a master's chair at the university before joining the Franciscan Order in 1235–40. In 1246–48, Guibert probably participated in the preaching campaign in France for Louis IX's first crusade, and he may have participated in the actual expedition; there are some pointers to this, but with the sources currently available to us, it is impossible to verify this. Guibert had close relations to the Capetian royal house: the treatise *Eruditio regum et principum* from the year 1259, for example, was written at the request of Louis IX. Guibert was the regent master of the Franciscans at Paris, possibly in the years 1259–61. He wrote several works, which included educational, historical, and hagiographical writings. The tract named *Collectio de scandalis ecclesiae*, written for the Second Council of Lyons in 1274, has been successfully identified as his work. This tract also mentions the crusades. Guibert's col-

---

[46] For the life and works of Humbert, see Brett, *Humbert of Romans*; *CPI*, pp. 11–12. See also Murray, 'Religion among the Poor in Thirteenth-Century France'; Tugwell, '*De huiusmodi sermonibus texitur omnis recta predicatio*'. Kurt Villads Jensen has provided an edition of the *De predicatione sancte crucis* online. For the *Opus tripartitum*, see Humbert de Romans, *Opusculum tripartitum*, ed. by Brown, pp. 191–98.

[47] For Federico Visconti, see especially *SVP*; Murray, 'Archbishop and Mendicants'; Vauchez, 'Les Origines de l'hérésie cathare'. See also Brentano, *Two Churches*, pp. 194–206.

lection of sermons was very popular during the Middle Ages and contains three crusade model sermons.[48]

The Pastoral Reform Movement

All the authors of the crusade model sermons studied here have in common an academic education in the university at Paris. At some point in their careers the preachers studied at Paris; some continued teaching there and climbed high in the university hierarchy. An important aspect of their shared background was the context of the pastoral reform movement. The so-called pastoral reform originated at the turn of the twelfth and thirteenth centuries at the University of Paris.[49] It focused on correcting the morality of Christians, both ecclesiastics and lay people, as Christian society as a whole was thought to be in need of spiritual reform. The pastoral movement dealt with a variety of issues, among them Christian morality and orthodoxy, religious education, teaching of canon law, preaching, warfare, and marriage.[50]

In the pastoral reform movement the moral doctrine that was studied and taught in Paris was meant to be distributed outside the schools, and the teachings and the ideas were to be transformed from academic discourses to practical courses of action in the everyday life of Christians. This transformation required a vast dissemination of information. The priests and other members of the clergy who were implementing the reform needed to be educated. Thus,

---

[48] *CPI*, pp. 10–11; d'Avray, *The Preaching of the Friars*, pp. 144–46; Roest, *Franciscan Literature*, pp. 384–86. See also the introduction by Ephrem Longpré in the edition of Guibert de Tournai's *Tractatus de Pace* from the year 1925, pp. vii–xliv; Baudry, 'Wibert de Tournai'. For further references and for an interesting discussion on Guibert's letter sent to Louis IX's sister, Isabelle, see Field, 'Gilbert of Tournai's Letter to Isabelle of France'. The claim that Guibert participated in the Seventh Crusade is founded on the argument that he wrote the work *Hodoeporicon primae profectionis Sancti Ludovici Galliarum regis in Syriam*, which appears to have once existed, but which is now lost. See, for example, Golubovich, *Biblioteca Bio-Bibliografica*, p. 219. Le Goff, nonetheless, views Guibert's participation to the Seventh Crusade as 'probable'. Le Goff has also suggested that during the campaign the king and Guibert developed a friendship. Le Goff, *Saint Louis*, p. 409. For the authorship of the *Collectio de scandalis ecclesiae*, see the inaugural dissertation of Bernhard Stroick from the year 1930, Stroick, *Verfasser und Quellen*. See also Throop, *Criticism of the Crusade*, pp. 69–104.

[49] See Jacques de Vitry's own description of Peter the Chanter in *Historia Occidentalis*. Jacques de Vitry, *Historia Occidentalis*, cap. VIII, ed. by Hinnebusch, pp. 94–101. For more information on Peter the Chanter's circle, see Baldwin, *Masters, Princes and Merchants*.

[50] *CPI*, pp. 4–6; *PCHL*, pp. 115–17; Tamminen, 'The Test of Friendship'.

texts and aids were drafted during the thirteenth century to help the clergy in their work — first in absorbing the new ideas and then communicating these to their audiences. These writings and manuals are often called *pastoralia*, which is a wide term used of all the different aids. The *pastoralia* could be theoretical or practical; the instructions could, for example, contain information about pastoral duties, explication of the Christian doctrine, or rudiments of canon law.[51]

The academically educated preachers had a particularly important role in pastoral reform. At the beginning of the thirteenth century, Paris-trained preachers were in charge of communicating the new ideas directly to the clergy and the laity outside university circles. Frequently, the moralist preaching of the pastoral reform would go hand in hand with the preaching of the cross.[52] The moralist reformers' preaching task was inherited by the friars of the mendicant orders, who continued to preach the word of God and voice the ideas of pastoral reform to both secular and ecclesiastical audiences throughout the thirteenth century.[53] During the pontificate of Gregory IX the mendicant orders were also employed in the service of the crusade movement. The use of mendicant friars, both Dominicans and Franciscans, from the beginning of the 1230s, had many benefits. Most importantly, they were trained preachers who had a strict hierarchy and were thus easily controlled by the papacy.[54]

The reform and the revival of preaching, which also began at the end of the twelfth century and continued throughout the thirteenth century, was part of the pastoral reform movement. The preaching aids and the collections of model sermons, particularly the *ad status* sermons, were the product of the pastoral reform.[55] The *ad status* sermon collections were produced for the benefit of various social groups arranged by the status of the audience rather than for a liturgical event. In an *ad status* sermon the problems of a particular group of people, as perceived by the preachers, could be addressed: the moral short-

---

[51] *CPI*, pp. 4–6; Boyle, 'The Inter-Conciliar Period'.

[52] Bird, 'Heresy, Crusade and Reform'; Bird, 'The Construction of Orthodoxy'.

[53] *CPI*, p. 7. See also d'Avray, *The Preaching of the Friars*.

[54] The friars were also prepared to roam, so they could be sent anywhere to spread the crusading message. The local diocesan clergy was thus replaced by the mendicants as distributors of crusade propaganda. The local clergy was not always reliable, as it was susceptible to local influences that might conflict with papal demands. Moreover, the skills of the local clergy responsible for crusade preaching, as well as their knowledge of canon law, might be of a low level. Maier, *Preaching the Crusades*, pp. 3–5.

[55] *CPI*, pp. 5–8. See also Rusconi, 'De la predication à la confession'; d'Avray, *The Preaching of the Friars*.

comings of farmers, for example, could be pointed out in the sermon intended solely for them, and practical guidance and moral solutions could be given on how the farmers might become better Christians, and in particular, how the sins peculiar to their social group could be avoided.

The *ad status* sermon collections were written for many groups of people. Jacques de Vitry, for instance, incorporated in his collection sermons intended for judges and advocates, the poor and the afflicted, the lepers and the infirm, those in mourning, pilgrims, powerful men and knights, townsfolk, merchants and moneychangers, farmers and workers, artisans, sailors and mariners, male and female servants, married people, the widowed, virgins and young girls, and boys and adolescents. Nor were the servants of the Church excluded, as sermons were addressed, for example, to prelates and priests and other clerics, as well as hermits and the members of the military orders. In addition, of course, Jacques de Vitry wrote sermons for crusaders and those intending to become crusaders, and it is these with which this study is largely concerned.[56]

Many of the crusade sermons of this study are from the *ad status* collections. The experienced preachers who composed the model sermon collections intended them to work as examples or manuals for others. The model sermons provide a unique insight into 'medieval mentalities'. David d'Avray has called medieval preaching 'a sort of distillation' of society.[57] The model sermons give us a glimpse of the popular ideas of a specific time and region condensed into manuscript form. By their nature the model sermons reflect popular opinions and common ideas of the society in which they were produced. The model sermons were created in order to help other preachers, the inexperienced, the less educated, the busy, or simply the lazy, in their work. The model sermons were written to match the level of knowledge and understanding of their intended users — the common preachers.[58]

In addition to this, the authors of the model sermons had to take into account the conditions, expectations, beliefs, and attitudes of those to whom the sermons would be preached. In other words, the model sermons had to correspond to the world view of the intended audience. The preachers who composed the sermons had to use familiar imagery and digestible language. Ideas that were too controversial or images that were beyond comprehension would work against the intentions of the preacher and condemn the model to oblivion. To gain popularity and to attract the widest possible audience the

---

[56] See *RLS*, iii: *Autoren: I–J*, pp. 212–20. See also Muessig, 'Audience and Preacher', p. 266.

[57] D'Avray, 'Method in the Study of Medieval Sermons', p. 7.

[58] Hanska, *'And the Rich Man also died; and He was buried in Hell'*, pp. 21–22; *CPI*, p. 16.

authors of the model sermons had to operate at a rather general level. Reference to the problems of a specific locality or use of images intelligible only to a particular group of people had to be avoided. The themes presented in the model sermons were meant to be acceptable and comprehensible throughout Latin Christendom.[59]

David d'Avray has drawn a parallel between medieval preaching and modern mass communication. Medieval sermons reached large crowds of people and spread ideas and information across wide tracts of Europe. This mass communication can be divided into different forms: the revivalist preaching may be conceived as mass communication as event, similar to the short-term advertising campaigns of modern times; a long-term, cumulative influence on people's attitudes could also be achieved through preaching, which may be regarded as mass communication as system.[60] In crusade preaching both types of mass communication occurred. An example of revivalist preaching is the preaching of Peter the Hermit and Foulques de Neuilly.[61] The crusade sermons incorporated in the sermon collections had a long-lasting effect and influenced both preachers' and the audiences' opinions and assumptions about the crusades for a long time. These sermons had an effect on people's views in many different regions, where the models were utilized time and again over the decades and centuries, and may thus be considered as mass communication as system.

The model sermons are a difficult source material. They were originally distributed in a written form and they are also preserved as such, but they were meant to be delivered orally. The model sermons may thus be called 'oral literature' — a form of literature that was initially written down but subsequently

---

[59] Hanska, 'And the Rich Man also died; and He was buried in Hell', pp. 15, 21.

[60] D'Avray, 'Method in the Study of Medieval Sermons', pp. 8–10.

[61] There are also other examples of revivalist crusade preaching, such as that of the peasants named Nicholas and Etienne de Cloyes during the Children's Crusade of 1212. The revivalist movement, often called the Children's Crusade, is a complex affair for historians: in the descriptions of the crusade, historical events and myths are deeply intermingled. According to the legends, two peasants, Nicholas from Cologne in Germany and Etienne de Cloyes in France, preached the journey to Jerusalem and caused upheaval in these regions. The preachers as well as the participants are in some accounts described as juveniles. See Dickson, *The Children's Crusade*. For a medieval account, see, for example, the description in *Chronica Regiae Coloniensis*, where the youngest participants are claimed to be six years old. 'Chronica Regiae Coloniensis Continuatio prima', ed. by Waitz, MGH, SS, 24, pp. 17–18, esp. p. 17: 'multa milia puerorum a 6 annis et supra usque ad virilem etatem, invitis parentibus, cognatis et amicis retrahentibus, quidam aratra vel currus quos minabant, alii pecora que pascebant, vel si qua alia habebant pre manibus, relinquentes, subito unus post alium currentes, crucibus se signaverunt'.

spoken, and which would ultimately reach large numbers of the illiterate.[62] This creates some difficulties in the interpretation of these sources, in that we do not know how these sermons were eventually delivered for the ultimate audience; were model sermons preached as a whole, were only parts of them preached, or were they never preached?

Spreading the Message

During the thirteenth century, many crusading practices developed, and crusading became more organized than before. Pope Innocent III's pontificate (1198–1216) is regarded as particularly important in the evolution of the movement. During this pontificate, the redemption and commutation of crusading vows were institutionalized, an elaborate system of crusade taxation and collection of crusading funds was created, and various liturgical practices were introduced which were to aid the crusades.[63] Innocent III studied at Paris and was tutored by Peter the Chanter. Innocent's pontificate has been described as a period of 'pastoral revolution', or the time of 'pastoral concern'. The pope pronounced three major crusades; the Fourth Crusade, the Albigensian Crusade, and the Fifth Crusade.[64] His views on reform and crusades were to have a great impact on the development of crusade ideology and the crusade preaching of the thirteenth century.

Innocent III regarded preaching as the most important of the duties belonging to the pastoral office. Preaching was also crucially important for the crusade movement. The promotion of crusades depended largely on crusade preaching.

[62] D'Avray, 'Method in the Study of Medieval Sermons', p. 17.

[63] Innocent III's pontificate has been studied thoroughly by modern historians. His views on crusades and the development of the crusade movement during his reign have been scrutinized in several studies. See, for example, the many articles discussing Innocent III and the crusades in Sommerlechner, *Innocenzo III*. For Innocent III and the crusades, see Roscher, *Papst Innocenz III. und die Kreuzzüge*; Moore, *Pope Innocent III*. See also Maier, *Preaching the Crusades*, pp. 1–3; Maier, 'Crisis, Liturgy and the Crusade', pp. 633–34; Tyerman, *England and the Crusades*, p. 86. For further information on the pontificate of Innocent III, see Bolton, *Innocent III*. The close association between crusading and liturgical events was another invention of Pope Innocent III. For this, see Maier, 'Mass, the Eucharist and the Cross'.

[64] Katherine Jansen, for example, has described this as the 'pastoral revolution', while Christoph Egger has described the time as the 'revival of pastoral concern'. Jansen, *The Making of the Magdalen*, pp. 104–05; Egger, 'The Growling of the Lion and the Humming of the Fly', esp. p. 32. For Innocent's views on preaching and his sermons, see Innocentius III, *Between God and Man*, trans. by Vause and Gardiner.

Innocent III wished to have better control over the movement, which meant, above all, better control over crusade preaching. It was important to determine what was said about the crusades and who said it. During Innocent's pontificate, the great preaching tours of the twelfth century were replaced with diocesan preaching: the bishops and those appointed by them were to take care of the crusade preaching locally. The benefit was that even the remotest areas heard the crusading message. Innocent also wanted to select his own preachers to help the bishops in their task. Accordingly, the pope created a network of crusade propagandists, who could travel as individual legates or as groups with legatine powers to different regions targeted for the promotion of crusades.[65]

Medieval crusade preaching was carried out in different ways and on diverse occasions. The crusade sermons were preached not only from the pulpit to a congregation inside the church, but also from platforms constructed in open fields to large crowds of people. Preaching the cross might be the sole purpose of the gathering, but it could be promoted during tournaments or in the town square without any prior arrangement. The travelling crusade preachers could muster people from two, three, or even more parishes to hear their preaching. These occasions might become great events, which could also be timed to coincide with the feast of a patron saint of a particular town where the preaching was carried out, or some other important feast day.[66] In these public events peer pressure affected people's behaviour, which compelled people who had not gone to them with the intention of taking the cross to do so. This was utilized by the crusade preachers of the thirteenth century. The stimulating example provided by someone taking the cross was regarded as so significant that some crusade preachers allegedly took 'actors' or people who were instructed to take the cross first with them, whose example the rest might then follow.[67]

In 1213, Innocent III took further measures to control crusade propaganda. In his encyclical *Quia maior* he carefully spelled out how the prospec-

---

[65] The local knowledge of dialect and customs could also be made use of, and there would be no dispute over jurisdiction between the bishop and a crusade preacher coming from outside the region. *PCHL*, pp. 84–89.

[66] Riley-Smith, *The Crusades, Christianity, and Islam*, pp. 36–37.

[67] Earlier, Pope Urban II appears to have used this method: after the Clermont sermon the Bishop of Le Puy stepped forward to take the cross, which he assumed from the pope on bended knee, while a cardinal shouted out from the background 'God wills it!', after which the rest of the audience knew how they ought to behave. Baldric de Dol, *Historia Ierosolimitana*, ed. by Bongars, p. 88; Tyerman, *The Invention of the Crusades*, pp. 69–70; Tyerman, *Fighting for Christendom*, p. 129.

tive crusade ought to be promoted by the preachers, detailing also the liturgical instructions that ought to be included in the promotion. The encyclical was sent to various parts of Europe, so that almost all the provinces gained a copy of it, thus ensuring that the crusading message was uniform. Finally, in the constitutions of the Fourth Lateran Council of 1215, many clauses of the encyclical were repeated in the decree *Ad liberandam*. The pattern set by these ideological contributions of Innocent III was followed by later popes, crusade ideologists, and crusade propagandists of the thirteenth century.[68]

Primary Sources

Eleven out of the thirty-six crusade model sermons studied here belong to *ad status* sermon collections. These include the sermons of Jacques de Vitry, Guibert de Tournai, and Humbert de Romans.[69] Some of the crusade sermons of Eudes de Châteauroux, as well as the sermon of Roger of Salisbury, may also be classed as *ad status* sermons, although they belong to collections of miscellaneous sermons. To take one example, as revealed in the title of Eudes's collection of sermons in Arras — *Sermones venerabilis patris Odonis episcopi Tusculani et sunt de diversis casibus* — the sermons in this collection are not specifically arranged by the social status of the recipients, but the collection contains various sermons of different themes intended for different audiences and in different circumstances. It includes sermons *de diversis casibus* and also sermons *de communi sanctorum*.[70]

Crusade preaching could be directed to small groups of people, such as to the nobles at the royal court or to the clergy inside a church. The cross might be preached on the various feast days. There was no specific liturgical date for

---

[68] The crusade decree of the Fourth Lateran Council, *Ad liberandam*, was followed closely in the crusade decree of the First Council of Lyons (1245), the *Super cruciata*, during the pontificate of Innocent IV. Gregory IX's crusading bull *Rachel suum videns* also had great influence on the crusade ideology of the thirteenth century. See *PCHL*, pp. 158–65. See also Purcell, *Papal Crusading Policy*, and the appendix, where the crusading decrees of 1215 and 1245 are compared. See the decrees in *COD*, pp. 210–11, 243–47. For the encyclical *Quia maior*, see *PL*, CCXVI, cols 817–22.

[69] See Appendices III, VI, and VIII.

[70] See the title in the collection of Eudes de Châteauroux's sermons in the Médiathèque d'Arras, Arras, MS 876, fol. 1ʳ. The collection of Eudes's sermons in Paris in the Bibliothèque nationale de France has the title *Sermones venerabilis patris Odonis episcopi tusculani et sunt de tempore per totum circulum anni*, *UEE*, II, 672–75.

the preaching of the cross, but crusades were often promoted during Lent and the feast days of the Invention of the Cross or the Exaltation of the Cross.[71] Crusade model sermons were also appropriate for other occasions such as the celebrations of saints' days. Eudes de Châteauroux appears to have preached one of his crusade sermons on the feast of the Conversion of St Paul, and Philippe le Chancelier's two crusade sermons could also be preached during this feast.[72] Guibert de Tournai mentioned that one of his crusade sermons could provide sermon material for any saint's day.[73] According to the different rubrics of Roger of Salisbury's crusade sermon, this could be preached to crusaders or on Good Friday or on the fourth Sunday after the octave of Epiphany.[74]

The diversity of crusade preaching creates some difficulties in interpreting, recognizing, and classifying crusade sermons. Eudes de Châteauroux's sermons provide a good example of the complications encountered. His numerous sermons include some which defy precise definition: for instance, some of them may be categorized as either crusade sermons or other sermons, such as the two sermons for the remembrance of Robert d'Artois and other nobles from the year 1251–54. These sermons can be classed simply as anniversary sermons for the dead, but they were originally preached during the Seventh Crusade to audiences that seem to have comprised mainly crusaders, and they were composed in remembrance of dead crusaders. Thus crusading is an essential aspect of these anniversary sermons. The sermons justify crusading, explain the current defeats, encourage crusading in the future, and were originally preached to crusaders, which would thus make them crusade sermons.[75]

On the other hand, among Eudes's collection of sermons are some that discuss crusading victories or crusading defeats, but which appear not to have been preached to current or prospective crusaders. An example is the Sunday sermon that Eudes delivered at the papal curia in 1266 after the news of the fall of Safed had reached the Italian peninsula. This could be regarded either as a sermon presenting crusade ideology and explaining crusading disaster, which would

---

[71] Maier, *Preaching the Crusades*, pp. 108–09.

[72] See Appendices II and V.

[73] Guibert de Tournai, 'Ad crucesignatos et crucesignandos sermo primus', *CPI*, p. 176.

[74] Roger of Salisbury, '*Ascendente* Ihesu *in naviculam*, et cetera. Istud potest esse thema ad crucesignatos vel in die Parasceves', *PCHL*, p. 167.

[75] Eudes de Châteauroux's anniversary sermons for those who died at Mansurah have been edited by Cole, *PCHL*, pp. 236–43.

make it a crusade sermon of sorts, or simply as a Sunday sermon dealing with a specific subject.[76]

The complications of identifying and defining crusade model sermons need to be acknowledged. At the same time, excessively inflexible definitions are to be avoided, simply because they might lead to the exclusion of important crusade sources. The strength of the evidence of the current study derives from the use of a wide range of sermons written by several different authors. In addition to the *ad status* sermons, this study includes many different feast day sermons. The following criteria were used to define which crusade model sermons were appropriate for selection as the primary sources of this study: the sermons explored here were intended as model sermons for the crusaders or intending crusaders, or were preached to promote or explain crusading during the preparations for an expedition or during an actual campaign to crusaders, to intending crusaders, or to the supporters of a crusade, during the period between 1216 and 1277.

This span of more than sixty years is an important period in the evolution of the crusade movement. The many significant changes introduced during the papacy of Innocent III and the decisions made in the Fourth Lateran Council were followed through by Innocent's successors. The period includes several major crusades, two conducted by Louis IX, as well as many other crusade expeditions against various enemies in different regions. The period is also marked by the extended struggle between the papacy and the Hohenstaufen.[77]

The earliest of the sources is a crusade preaching manual, the *Brevis ordinacio de predicacione sancte crucis*, written *c.* 1216. This work has often been credited to Philip of Oxford, but the authorship of the manual is highly dubious.[78] The last of the crusade model sermons that can be placed in some specific

---

[76] Eudes de Châteauroux, 'Sermo eadem xix dominica quando primo audita fuit captio Sapheti et trucidatio illorum qui ibi erant', Roma, AGOP, MS XIV, 34, fols 176va–178rb.

[77] In addition to Louis IX's two crusades, the Seventh and Eighth Crusades, there were numerous other expeditions during the period, such as the renewed Albigensian Crusade of 1226–29, the crusade of Frederick II in 1228–29, the crusade of James I of Aragon to Mallorca in 1229–31, the crusade of Jean de Brienne to Constantinople in 1231, the crusade against the Stedinger in Germany in 1232–34, and the Barons' Crusade of 1239–41. The struggle between the papacy and the Hohenstaufen during the thirteenth century involved, particularly, popes Gregory IX, Innocent IV, Alexander IV, Urban IV, and Clement IV. For the conflict, see Abulafia, *Frederick II*. See also Runciman, *The Sicilian Vespers*.

[78] For the manual, see 'Brevis ordinacio de predicacione', *QBSS*. For the attribution of the *Brevis ordinacio* to Philip of Oxford, see, for example, Powell, *Anatomy of a Crusade*, p. 52. For opposing views, see *PCHL*, pp. 110–11; Maier, *Preaching the Crusades*, p. 114.

historical context are the sermons of Eudes de Châteauroux against the Lucera Muslims, from the year 1268/69. However, Eudes de Châteauroux's, Federico Visconti's, and Humbert de Romans's model sermon collections were compiled or edited during the late 1260s and 1270s. Eudes's second edition of model sermons was composed at the end of the 1260s, and he worked on a third edition before his death in 1273, while Federico's crusade sermons are from the beginning of the 1260s, but the collection was finished after his death in 1277. Humbert de Romans's crusade model sermons belong to his larger work, the *De eruditione predicatorum*, which was written between the years 1266 and 1277. The rest of the crusade sermons of this study appear to have been written down before 1277; hence this is the terminus year for the book.[79]

The criteria that define the crusade model sermons of this study exclude as primary sources such sermons as the Sunday sermon delivered at the papal curia in 1266 or Eudes's sermons delivered after Charles of Anjou's victorious crusade against Manfred of Hohenstaufen, also preached in 1266, as well as his sermons after the victory over Conradin of Hohenstaufen in 1268.[80] These sermons, although clearly connected to crusades, were not meant as model sermons for crusaders or to be delivered to an audience of current or prospective crusaders, whereas the three sermons against the Lucera Muslims are included among the primary sources, because these appear to have been preached while the crusade was under way to an audience which seems to have included current or prospective crusaders, possibly even to Charles of Anjou himself.[81]

This study includes seventeen crusade sermons composed by Eudes de Châteauroux. The large number is explained by Eudes's extraordinary involvement in many different crusades and the vast collection of his sermons that have survived. Four of these sermons are well-defined crusade model sermons with clear reference to crusading in the rubrics of the sermons.[82] Another four sermons are more ambiguous in nature, but may still be safely defined as crusade sermons. These include the three sermons against the Lucera Muslims

---

[79] *CPI*, pp. 9–12; See also Appendices II–VIII. Guibert de Tournai's crusade sermons appear to have been written down in 1263–68. The sermons were included in a larger work known as *Rudimentum doctrinae*, added to its fourth part *De modo addiscendi*. *PCHL*, p. 195; Field, 'Gilbert of Tournai's Letter to Isabelle of France', p. 60.

[80] Iozzelli, *Odo da Châteauroux*, pp. 182–206; *UEE*, ii, 884–96, 970–73, 976–79.

[81] *CR*, pp. 343–85, esp. p. 354.

[82] The well-defined sermons are titled *Sermo de cruce et de invitatione ad crucem*, *Sermo ad invitandum ad accipiendum crucem et ad confortandum crucesignatos*, *Sermo de invitatione ad crucem*, *Sermo ad invitandum ad crucem*. See Appendix V.

and one against the Albigensians.[83] Eudes was in charge of the crusade propaganda for the Seventh Crusade in 1245–48, and he was the appointed legate on the expedition of 1248–54.[84] He appears to have preached three sermons for the feast of St George during this period. The earliest of these sermons was preached in 1246 or 1248 in France for intending crusaders and those who had already taken the cross.[85] The two later feast day sermons for St George seem to have been preached to the crusaders during the expedition, in Cyprus in 1249 and in Damietta in 1250.[86]

Eudes seems also to have preached three sermons for the feast of the Holy Relics of Sainte-Chapelle during this period. The first was preached in 1248 at the consecration of the chapel. The consecration was postponed, so that it would take place right before Louis IX's departure for the Seventh Crusade.[87] The two other sermons for the feast of the Holy Relics appear to have been preached by the legate during the crusade, the first possibly in 1249 in Egypt and the second in 1251 in the Holy Land.[88] Eudes also promoted the coming crusade in France, possibly in 1248, during the feast of the Conversion of St Paul. In addition to the seven feast day sermons, the two anniversary sermons for the remembrance of Robert d'Artois are included among the primary sources of this study, since all these appear to have been preached to crusaders during the Seventh Crusade.[89]

---

[83] Appendix V.

[84] For the career and the sermons of Eudes de Châteauroux, see esp. *UEE*, vols I–II.

[85] Charansonnet has dated this sermon to the year 1246 by eliminating other possible dates. The year 1248 is also possible. *UEE*, I.1, 119–27, esp. p. 120 n. 94.

[86] The dating of the second sermon is more certain than the previous one. Eudes mentions the dedication of a church in which the sermon was given during the feast of St George in April: 'beatus Georgius cuius honore et nomine ecclesia ista est fundata'. Eudes de Châteauroux, 'De sancto Georgio sermo', *UEE*, II, 738. This is most likely a church in Cyprus, where the crusade army stayed for the winter season (1248–49), sailing from the island to Egypt in May 1249. For the dating of the second sermon, see *UEE*, I.1, 215–21. The third sermon appears to have been preached after the disaster of Mansurah (February 1250), but before Louis IX and Eudes departed to the Holy Land (May 1250). The feast of St George coincides with the captivity of the king. Eudes's third sermon is brief, but has a sense of urgency; it makes a reference to the Mamluks, but does not mention the coup d'état of 2 May 1250; it seems likely that the sermon was preached in April (24) in 1250 in Damietta for the Christian refugees and crusaders in the city. *UEE*, I.1, 233–36. Charansonnet's study provides editions of all three sermons, *UEE*, II, 700–705, 737–41, 747–49.

[87] Housley, *Fighting for the Cross*, pp. 280–81; *UEE*, I.1, 170–78.

[88] *UEE*, I.1, 220, 224–27, 264–67.

[89] See Appendix V.

Eudes's sermon for the feast of Thomas Becket, which also appears to have been preached during the preparations for the crusade, is not included in the primary sources, as the subject of the sermon is not the crusade, although the references made to the coming campaign are noted in this study.[90]

Eudes de Châteauroux's sermons were written down systematically: Eudes provided two editions of his sermons written in his own scriptorium, and a third one was also in the making in the early 1270s. The manuscript tradition thus gives some clues as to when the sermons were first composed and when they were revised and edited. All the sermons linked to the Seventh Crusade belong to the first edition of Eudes's sermons, which was edited before 1261.[91] Alexis Charansonnet has studied Eudes's sermon material extensively. The sermons, which he has convincingly linked to the promotion of the Seventh Crusade or to the actual expedition, contain internal evidence that appears to point to the crusade, which is in turn supported by the evidence of the manuscript tradition. Some of the dates and years specified for Eudes's sermons are more certain than others: the date of the sermon preached for the feast of the Holy Relics of Sainte-Chapelle, in 1248, for example, appears quite certain, whereas the other two sermons preached for the feast of the Holy Relics during the campaign are less easily dated.[92]

---

[90] There are references to the Seventh Crusade made in the sermon; however, this does not appear as a crusade sermon but rather as a sermon discussing the relations between clergy and laity. Eudes focuses his attention in the sermon on the conflict between the barons of France and the clergy. The secular lords had rebelled against the clergy and the papacy over rights of jurisdiction and fiscal policy. Louis IX had backed the barons' revolt and sent an ambassador to Pope Innocent IV, who protested against the violations made by the clergy and the impoverishment of the Church in the Kingdom of France — the Church's goods were taken away from the kingdom and outsiders were made rich, according to the ambassador. These political difficulties were further tangled up with the struggle between the papacy and the Hohenstaufen. In 1246 Frederick II was preparing to attack the pope in Lyons with a strong army, but Louis IX intervened. Eudes de Châteauroux seems to have preached several sermons defending the papal policies and the rights of the Church, in which he reprehended the secular lords for the rebellion. The sermon for the feast of Thomas Becket appears largely to belong to this historical context. *UEE*, i.1, 127–48. Le Goff, *Saint Louis*, p. 168. See also Matthew Paris's account of the ambassador's message, Matthew Paris, *Chronica majora*, ed. by Luard, pp. 99–113.

[91] For the dating of Eudes's sermons, see *UEE*, vols i–ii, esp. ii, 636–71; Charansonnet, 'L'Évolution de la predication du cardinal Eudes de Châteauroux', pp. 114–24; *CPI*, pp. 10, 76. Eudes was working on a third editions of his sermons; however, his death in 1273 prevented the completion of this.

[92] *UEE*, i.1, 220, 224–27, 264–67.

Five crusade sermons composed by Philippe le Chancelier are also analysed in the book. All of these sermons were preached in the year 1226 against the Albigensian heretics. Three of the sermons can be placed in quite a precise historical context, in the different phases of the build-up to the crusade, because of the information in the rubrics of the manuscript held in Avranches. The rubrics mention that the sermons were preached 'to scholars' and that they were delivered 'between Epiphany and Purification at the time when King Louis took the cross against the Albigensians', after which more details are followed for each sermon.[93] The Troyes manuscript presents these sermons as model sermons for 'the signing of the cross against the Albigensians' and also provides details in the rubrics of the contents list of the sermon collection: for example, the third sermon is presented as a sermon about 'the ways of giving thanks after the reconciliation between the prelates and the princes'.[94]

The fourth sermon of Philippe le Chancelier appears to have been preached to King Louis VIII and other crusaders in 1226. This is revealed by a rubric of Philippe's sermon *Dicit Dominus ad Moysen*, which once existed in a manuscript held in Vitry-le-François. The rubric stated that the sermon was preached *In concilio Bitt. ad cruce signatos, presente rege*.[95] Philippe's sermon thus seems to have been delivered first at the council at Bourges in 1226, where Louis VIII was with his crusading army ready to set out for the Albigensian Crusade. Yet the two surviving copies of Philippe's sermon do not place the sermon in its original context. These copies have been revised and edited, so that the ser-

---

[93] Philippe le Chancelier, 'Sermo scolaribus inter Epiphaniam et Purificationem tempore quo rex Ludovicus assumpsit crucem in Albigenses, de dolore et signis doloris ecclesie sancte matris nostre et infirmitate et causis doloris et remediis contra dolorem et quid sit clipeum levare', Avranches, MS 132, fol. 248ᵛᵃ; Philippe le Chancelier, 'Sermo de eodem, quomodo apparuit potentia Dei et sapientia et bonitas in eo quod mutavit voluntatem regis et principum prius contradicentium ad assumendum crucem, quod factum est per tria suffragia supradicta, scilicet elemosinam, ieiunium et orationem, et nota v psalmos qui intitulantur ab oratione', Avranches, MS 132, fol. 250ʳᵃ; Philippe le Chancelier, 'Sermo de eodem, de gaudio quod rex et principes assumpserunt crucem; quod sic altare et que oblationes et quomodo concordant que facta sunt in Purificatione', Avranches, MS 132, fol. 251ʳᵃ.

[94] Philippe le Chancelier, 'De agendis gratiarum actionibus post reconciliacionem prelatorum et principum cum assumerent cruces contra Albigenses se offerentes Deo', Troyes, MS 1099, fol. 1ʳ; Maier, 'Crisis, Liturgy and the Crusade', pp. 644–45.

[95] According to the *Catalogue général des bibliothèques publiques de France*, there was in Bibliothèque de Vitry-le-François a manuscript numbered 69 that had the title '*Omelie et sermones magistri Philippi, cancellarii Parisiensis*'. Fol. 139 of the manuscript had the rubric indicating the presence of Louis VIII. See *Catalogue général*, pp. 35–36; Maier, 'Crisis, Liturgy and the Crusade', pp. 650–51; *CPI*, pp. 22–23; Bériou, 'La Predication de croisade', p. 102.

mon, as it appears now, is presented as a model sermon for the feast day of the Exaltation of the Cross.[96] The fifth sermon of Philippe was preached during a procession which was held to support the Albigensian Crusade. The sermon was delivered in Paris, at St Victor on 21 August, the Friday after the feast of the Assumption of the Virgin.[97]

This study includes four crusade sermons of Humbert de Romans that belong to his *ad status* collection and were intended for the preaching of different kinds of crusades.[98] Humbert's crusade preaching manual, *De predicatione sancte crucis*, is also explored and is included among the primary sources. This handbook is an invaluable source of information when examining crusade ideology and propaganda of the thirteenth century. It was written in the late 1260s; the manual may have a connection to Louis IX's second crusade, the Eighth Crusade, which was in the making at the time. Crusade manuals have many similarities with crusade model sermons. Both were intended to give guidance for crusade preachers and provide material for crusade sermons. Humbert's manual includes advice and examples for the crusade preachers. It contains crusading ideas, justifications for the movement, anecdotes, exempla, models which could be used as such in the crusade sermons, a list of relevant biblical passages, and formulaic invitations to take the cross.[99]

The book also discusses four crusade sermons of Jacques de Vitry. Jacques incorporated two crusade model sermons into his *ad status* collection. However, there are also two other *ad status* sermons included in the primary sources of this study, which are sermons intended for pilgrims. These two sermons have been studied before, mainly in the context of pilgrimages within Europe or to the Holy Land. Jessalynn Bird, however, has recently suggested that the sermons should be viewed in the crusading context. Bird has convincingly connected the sermons to the Fifth Crusade.[100] Jacques composed his sermon col-

---

[96] Maier, 'Crisis, Liturgy and the Crusade', pp. 650–51; *CPI*, pp. 22–23; Bériou, 'La Predication de croisade', p. 102.

[97] Philippe le Chancelier, 'Sermo in die veneris infra octabas Assumptionis beate Virginis apud Sanctum Victorem in processione pro rege Ludovico quando erat ante Avinionem, quomodo tota spes nostra debet esse in cruce et beata Virgine et quomodo Christus multiplex pependit pro nobis ut nos ad simile provocaret', Avranches, MS 132, fol. 243ra; Maier, 'Crisis, Liturgy and the Crusade', p. 652; Bériou, 'La Predication de croisade', p. 102.

[98] See Appendix VI.

[99] Humbert de Romans, *De predicatione sancte crucis*; citations throughout are to the edition by Jensen. For studies on the manual, see Brundage, 'Humbert of Romans and the Legitimacy of Crusader Conquests'; Cole, 'Humbert of Romans and the Crusade'.

[100] *JVSP*, pp. 81–88. Bird has also provided transcriptions of Jacques's sermons in her

lection approximately a decade after the Fifth Crusade, in the 1230s. During the composition of the collection, he appears to have reworked many of his old sermons. The two sermons have also been revised, and they are presented in the *ad status* collection as sermons meant specifically for pilgrims. However, many of the passages of the sermons appear to have been intended for both crusaders and pilgrims. Jacques uses the term 'crucesignati' several times in the sermons and utilizes the terms 'peregrini' and 'crucesignati' often as synonyms.[101]

Of all the crusade preachers examined in this study, Jacques de Vitry used most consistently, in various writings, the term 'pilgrim' in a crusading context. Jacques referred to the crusaders as pilgrims in his crusading history, the *Historia orientalis*. In his hagiographic account of Marie d'Oignies, Jacques applied the term 'pilgrimage' when he referred to the Albigensian Crusade. And in his letters from the Fifth Crusade, Jacques called the crusaders pilgrims several times.[102] It would not be inconsistent for Jacques to include aspects of crusading in his sermons intended for pilgrims. This would in fact be characteristic of him, as pilgrimages to the Holy Land and the crusades were deeply intertwined in Jacques's thinking.

The internal evidence in Jacques's sermons for the pilgrims, besides the blunt references to the *crucesignati*, often points to the crusading context. Jacques, for example, develops the theme of suffering in his sermons to the ultimate end — dying for Christ. This would seem quite an extreme point to be incorporated into customary sermons meant for ordinary pilgrims. Pilgrims visiting different local or remote shrines, although facing many dangers on their journey, including the possibility of losing their lives, were traditionally not expected to seek death while making the pilgrimage. Dying for Christ and earning martyrdom were much more common themes in sermons or other texts describing or promoting the crusades. Jacques himself discusses these issues in a similar way in his sermons for the knights of the military orders.[103] Indeed, Jacques's two ser-

study, which are utilized in the present study. Jacques de Vitry, 'Ad peregrinos, thema sumpta ex epistola ad Galathas iii', *JVSP*, pp. 88–94; Jacques de Vitry, 'Ad peregrinos. Thema sumpta ex Zacharias ultimo', *JVSP*, pp. 94–102. The sermons are titled in the Troyes manuscript simply as 'Sermo ad peregrinos' and 'Item sermo ad peregrinos'. See Jacques de Vitry, 'Sermo ad peregrinos', Troyes, MS 228, fols 151rb–152va; Jacques de Vitry, 'Item sermo ad peregrinos',Troyes, MS 228, fols 152va–154rb.

[101] Jacques de Vitry, 'Ad peregrinos, thema sumpta ex epistola ad Galathas iii', *JVSP*, p. 93; Jacques de Vitry, 'Ad peregrinos. Thema sumpta ex Zacharias ultimo', *JVSP*, pp. 96–97, 102.

[102] Jacques de Vitry, *Historia orientalis*, ed. by Donnadieu; Jacques de Vitry, *Vita Maria Oigniacensi*, *AASS*, v, 565; Jacques de Vitry, *Epistola*, IV, ed. by Huygens, p. 106.

[103] Jacques de Vitry, 'Ad peregrinos, thema sumpta ex epistola ad Galathas iii', *JVSP*, p. 92:

mons for the pilgrims appear to correlate strongly with these and with his sermons for the crusaders generally.[104]

In his sermon for the pilgrims, Jacques also uses an exemplum of a noble knight who was about to go 'beyond the sea' and who had to leave his family behind. Again, the wording, as well as the scene of the story and the content of the exemplum, all appear to belong to the crusading context, which Guibert de Tournai seems also to have acknowledged when he incorporated this exemplum into his own sermon — not his sermon intended for the pilgrims, but the sermon meant for the crusaders.[105] It is possible that parts of Jacques's sermons for the pilgrims were preached to crusaders during the preparations for the Fifth Crusade or the actual campaign. The sermons offer guidance to the crusader pilgrims, a term used by some scholars,[106] and as such they are extremely valuable for the purposes of this study. Jacques's aim in the sermons is to advise the crusaders and pilgrims on how they should act and behave during their journey.[107]

'Sancti igitur cum necesse habent mori, desiderant mortem suam vendere et preciosam facere ut ex illa sibi vitam eternam comparent. Alii autem qui pro Christo non moriuntur, moriendo non merentur. Unde cum omnis mori oporteat, melius est mortem lucrari quam perdere. Mortem lucrantur qui in Domini servitio moriuntur'. In both sermons for the pilgrims and the sermons for the knights of the Temple, Jacques explained that there was no reason to fear death while in the service of Christ. Death should be prepared for, for in death the pilgrims and the knights would earn their reward. See below, p. 194.

[104] *JVSP*, p. 88.

[105] Jacques de Vitry, 'Ad peregrinos, thema sumpta ex epistola ad Galathas iii', *JVSP*, p. 91: 'Unde de quodam milite nobili legimus quod iturus ultra mare fecit adduci ad se filios parvulos quod valde diligebat, et cum eos diu aspiciens amplexaretur, dixerunt famuli eius: "Dimittite parvos istos et abeatis, quare multi nos expectant ut vos deducant." Quibus ille. "Idcirco filios meos coram me adduci feci ut, excitato affectu ad ipsos, cum maiori angustia mentis pro Christo relinquam illos, et ita magis merear apud Dominum."' Guibert follows this closely in his crusade sermon. Guibert de Tournai, 'Ad crucesignatos et crucesignandos sermo tertius', *CPI*, p. 202: 'Unde legimus de quodam nobili milite, quod iturus ultra mare fecit adduci ad se filios parvulos, quos valde diligebat. Et cum eos diu aspiciens amplecteretur, dixerunt ei famuli eius: Dimitte pueros istos et recedatis, quia multi vos expectant, ut vos deducant. Quibus ille: Ideo coram me filios meos adduci feci, ut excitato affectu ad eos cum maiori angustia mentis reliquam eos pro Christo et ita magis merear apud Deum'. The significance given to the cross in Jacques's two sermons for the pilgrims also points to the crusading context. In the crusade sermons the importance of the sign of the cross was underlined, and many of its different features were explained for those signed with it.

[106] See, for example, Folda, *Crusader Art in the Holy Land*, p. 44.

[107] Jacques de Vitry's sermon against the Albigensians from the collection of *Sermones feri-*

Guibert de Tournai composed three crusade model sermons, which belong to his *ad status* collection and are included in the primary sources of this study. Guibert also composed one sermon for the pilgrims, which is not included in the primary sources. Guibert utilized Jacques's sermons for the pilgrims in his own sermon, but this is difficult to connect to any of the crusades or to an audience of crusaders. Unlike Jacques's sermons to pilgrims, Guibert's sermon cannot be fitted into the crusading context, to some specific circumstances, or to a particular expedition. Guibert does not use terms that point directly to an audience of crusaders, such as the term 'crucesignatus', but has purposely, it seems, avoided using these terms while borrowing from Jacques's sermons. Hence, Guibert's sermon for the pilgrims is used only as a secondary source in this book.[108]

There are also two crusade sermons composed by Federico Visconti and one composed by Roger of Salisbury that are included in the primary sources of this study. Federico Visconti's sermons are from a collection of sermons which was composed as a historical record of the archbishop's preaching. These sermons, as they have been written down, are close to 'live' sermons: they have been edited, but are not heavily reworked models; they do not contain material for several sermons and are not abbreviated models, but appear as sermons that were once preached. The compilation indicates when, where, and to whom they were delivered, as well as often providing information on the language in which the sermons were delivered, that is, whether they were preached in Latin or in the vernacular.[109]

---

ales et communes is, however, excluded from the primary sources, even though the sermon probably contains a vestige of the material that Jacques once used while preaching the crusade against the heretics in the 1210s or 1220s. This model sermon, in the form in which it has been preserved, is a treatise written against the Cathars. The sermon refutes the heresy and provides justifications for the repression of the Albigensians. It is not a model sermon meant for the crusaders or intending crusaders, nor was it preached in the preserved form to crusaders during a crusade. I would like to thank Carolyn Muessig for her kind help and advice, and for allowing me to consult the transcription of 'Sermo 25' from the collection *Sermones feriales et communes* that she has prepared. Muessig has also discussed the sermon in Muessig, 'Les Sermons de Jacques de Vitry sur les cathares'.

[108] For Guibert de Tournai's sermon for the pilgrims, see Guibert de Tournai, 'Ad peregrinos', Assisi, MS 501, fols 129ʳ–131ᵛ.

[109] *CPI*, pp. 19–20. The two crusade sermons of Federico Visconti were preached at the beginning of the 1260s to an audience of Pisan clergy: see Federico Visconti, 'Quando idem dominus predicavit crucem litteraliter clero pisano de mandato domini Pape', *SVP*, pp. 543–51; Federico Visconti, 'Quando idem dominus predicavit [crucem] respondendo nuntiis

Reportationes of crusade sermons from the beginning of the thirteenth century have also survived, which are preserved in the collections of sermons in Paris, but are not included in the primary sources.[110] These crusade sermons are not conventional model sermons, as they were originally written down by anonymous observers, 'reporters', who recorded the sermons. The *reportationes* are accounts of 'live' sermons that were once delivered. We do not know how faithfully the anonymous observers recorded the sermons, how accurate they were in writing down the information, or how well they understood the messages put forth by the preachers. In most cases we also lack knowledge of who preached the sermons and in what circumstances.[111]

The Model Sermons

The model sermons must be distinguished from 'live' sermons. With model sermons questions arise about the performance of the sermon and the way their messages were communicated. The thirty-six crusade model sermons studied here vary greatly in these respects. The sermons have been composed in different ways, and they have survived in different types of collections. In the case of some of the sermons the rubrics of the models tell us the time and the place when the sermon was first delivered, as with some of the sermons of Philippe le Chancelier and Federico Visconti. In fact, one of Philippe's crusade sermons provides an excellent example of how a 'live' sermon could be transformed into a model sermon, where the crusade theme has been dissipated and the model reworked as a feast day sermon.[112]

Tartarorum in clero pisano', *SVP*, pp. 551–55. In the manuscript of the latter sermon there is a red cross drawn in the title of the sermon, indicating the word 'crucem'. See Firenze, MS Plut. 33 sin. 1, fol. 41va.

[110] The are six *reportationes* of crusade sermons in Paris, BnF, MS nouv. ac. lat. 999, fols 169va–170ra, 188ra–189ra, 199ra–va, 233rb–vb, 240ra–va, 240va–241ra; *CPI*, pp. 20–21; Bériou, *L'Avènement des maîtres*, I, 58–69. There are also two *reportationes* of crusade sermons in Paris, BnF, MS lat. 14470, fols 281rb–283vb. See Jessalynn Bird's transcription of these two sermons in Bird, 'The Victorines, Peter the Chanter's Circle, and the Crusade'. For the *reportationes* in general, see Bataillon, 'Sermons rédigés, sermons reports'; Bériou, *L'Avènement des maîtres*, I, 73–131.

[111] One *reportatio* mentions in the rubrics that the sermon was delivered by Jean d'Abbeville. *PCHL*, p. 222. Another sermon seems to have been delivered by Pietro Capuano. The *reportationes* appear to have been written in 1210–20. Bériou, *L'Avènement des maîtres*, I, 58–69; *CPI*, p. 20; Bird, 'The Victorines, Peter the Chanter's Circle, and the Crusade', pp. 16–17.

[112] *CPI*, pp. 19–24.

We usually know the intended audience of the *ad status* sermons directly, which is not the case with most medieval sermons arranged according to the liturgical calendar.[113] The *ad status* sermons proclaim at the outset of the model the particular group of people to whom the sermon should be preached. However, the identification of the audience of crusade model sermons as crusaders often tells us very little, since a group of crusaders or prospective crusaders might include various distinct social groups, such as ecclesiastics, scholars, knights, or townspeople. In many cases it is also impossible to know whether the model sermons were ever preached by the author of the model to a 'live' audience, although it is safe to assume that the preacher's own experiences of delivering 'live' sermons influenced the composition of the models.[114] In some cases we can determine from internal evidence that the sermons, or parts of them, were preached by the authors themselves in specific circumstances, as with some of the sermons of Eudes de Châteauroux.

Many of the crusade sermons preserved in the *ad status* collections have been reworked by the authors, often in such a way that if there was once an original 'live' sermon the traces of it have been lost. Some of the *ad status* crusade sermons would not have been very effective had they been preached in the form we know them, such as the sermons of Jacques de Vitry or Humbert de Romans. Jacques's crusade model sermons include too much information and too many examples to weld into one sermon. Indeed, these seem to have been intended to provide material for several different crusade sermons. On the other hand, the model sermons of Humbert de Romans are quite abbreviated. They are didactic, short, and to the point, without any effort to produce eloquent passages which might be used by preachers. The preachers using these models needed to mould them to suit their own particular circumstances.[115] The preachers had to select those parts of the models and the themes presented by the authors which they thought would be most useful for their own purposes. Jacques de Vitry supplied many themes from which the preachers could choose, while Humbert de Romans adduced the most important points that needed to be addressed.

The crusade model sermons analysed in this book may be roughly divided into three types of model sermons: abbreviated, extended, and plain model sermons.[116] Jacques de Vitry's two crusade sermons may be viewed as extended

[113] Muessig, 'Audience and Preacher'.

[114] *CPI*, p. 19.

[115] *CPI*, pp. 27–31.

[116] See Maier's division of the three types of crusade model sermons, *CPI*, p. 32.

sermons. In fact, these model sermons come close to being crusade preaching manuals. Jacques's extended sermons are much longer than plain model sermons, and they contain exempla, subthemes, and various arguments for the preachers to use in their own sermons, as do the crusade preaching manuals.[117]

The majority of the crusade model sermons I discuss belong to the third type, to the category of plain model sermons. These sermons are structured so that those using the models could preach them more or less in their extant form. The preachers using these model sermons could make minor modifications to the models as appropriate to the target audience, or they could translate the model into the vernacular, but they could also, if they so wished, follow the model sermon to the letter from beginning to end.

There are differences between some of the plain model sermons examined in this study, even among the sermons of individual authors. Eudes de Châteauroux's different crusade sermons, for example, would require varying amounts of work from the preachers using them. Some of Eudes's sermons have been reworked so that the original crusading enemy has been obscured and the sermons could be easily used against a variety of enemies; other model sermons are quite specific in their description of the enemy and the circumstances of the crusade in question, such as the three crusade sermons against the Lucera Muslims.[118] Preachers using the sermons against the Lucerans as models for their own crusade sermons would have to make a considerable number of changes, to borrow passages from here and there, or to follow only the structure of the models. Also, some of Eudes's crusade sermons from the Seventh Crusade, such as the anniversary sermons for Robert d'Artois or the sermons for the feast of the Holy Relics, which are plain model sermons, would serve better as models for the sermons for the dead or feast day sermons than as model sermons for the promotion of crusades.

Treatises for preaching, the *artes praedicandi*, were also written during the thirteenth century. These treatises were examples of *pastoralia*, designed to educate and guide preachers in the composition of sermons. The authors of the crusade model sermons used some of the techniques and rhetorical tools dis-

---

[117] See Jacques de Vitry, 'Sermo ad crucesignatos vel -signandos', *CPI*, pp. 82–99; Jacques de Vitry, 'Item sermo ad crucesignatos vel -signandos', *CPI*, pp. 100–127; Humbert de Romans, *De predicatione sancte crucis*.

[118] Eudes de Châteauroux, 'Sermo de rebellione Sarracenorum Lucherie in Apulia', *CR*, pp. 376–79; Eudes de Châteauroux, 'Sermo de rebellione Sarracenorum Lucherie', *CR*, pp. 379–82; Eudes de Châteauroux, 'Sermo de rebellione Sarracenorum Lucherie', *CR*, pp. 382–85.

cussed in the preaching guides. In the *artes praedicandi* the construction of sermons was also carefully explained, for the structure was believed to have great importance for both audience understanding and memory of the messages of the sermon and in enabling the preacher to memorize it. The sermons were to have a lucid structure and division, at times with subdivision that separated different parts of the sermon into logically organized sections.[119]

The crusade model sermons discussed in this volume are structured in different ways. Three principal ways of structuring the overall argument of the crusade model sermons may be identified as structuring by theme, by distinctions, and by comparisons.[120] These three ways of structuring could also partly overlap in the sermons — the sermons structured by theme, for example, could include comparisons and distinctions. The authors who structured their model sermons by theme utilized a chosen biblical passage or a particular theme throughout the sermon, developing many different arguments and messages from this. The model sermons could have a protheme, a principal theme, and several subthemes. Jacques de Vitry and Federico Visconti, for example, started both of their crusade model sermons with a protheme, which was then followed with a main theme.[121]

Several of the authors of the crusade sermons, such as Guibert de Tournai and Humbert de Romans, used distinction as a structuring method in their models.[122] This scholastic method focused on a specific term, which was used

---

[119] Thomas of Chobham, who was one of the pioneers of writing treatises for preaching, for example, regarded division as an important element in the construction of sermons. For Thomas of Chobham's *Summa de arte praedicandi*, see Thomas de Chobham, *Summa de arte praedicandi*, ed. by Morenzoni, esp. cap. 7, 2.1.3, pp. 284–85; For the *artes praedicandi*, see Gilson, 'Michel Menot et la technique du sermon médiéval'; Charland, *Artes praedicandi*; Roberts, 'The *Ars Praedicandi* and the Medieval Sermon'; *CPI*, p. 34.

[120] *CPI*, pp. 34–50.

[121] Jacques de Vitry developed his crusade sermons using a principal theme, as well as additional themes, and divided the sermons into different sections, also utilizing exempla. Jacques's crusade sermons are an example of model sermons structured by theme. See Jacques de Vitry, 'Sermo ad crucesignatos vel -signandos', *CPI*, pp. 82–99; Jacques de Vitry, 'Item sermo ad crucesignatos vel -signandos', *CPI*, pp. 100–127. Federico Visconti structured his two crusade sermons with a short and a longer protheme, followed by the main theme, and used distinction as a rhetorical tool. See Federico Visconti, 'Quando idem dominus predicavit crucem litteraliter clero pisano de mandato domini Pape', *SVP*, pp. 543–51; Federico Visconti, 'Quando idem dominus predicavit [crucem] respondendo nuntiis Tartarorum in clero pisano', *SVP*, pp. 551–55.

[122] *CPI*, p. 46.

to distinguish different levels of meaning and which created different structural levels in the sermon, as well as giving overall unity to the entire sermon. In his first crusade model sermon, Guibert de Tournai, for instance, created a two-part structural division for the whole sermon from the terms 'sanctus' and 'signum'.[123] Humbert de Romans also structured one of his sermons with the term 'peregrinatio', dividing his sermon into three parts, where he explained the differences between 'general' and 'special' pilgrimages, and the 'prerogative excellence' of crusade-pilgrimage.[124]

The authors of the crusade model sermons used many different kinds of comparisons as rhetorical tools in their sermons, such as illustrative stories, metaphors, allegories, and similitudes, which helped them to explain various aspects of the crusades. These comparisons could also give an entire sermon its structure. Eudes de Châteauroux often constructed the arguments of his crusade sermons from comparisons which he drew from the Old Testament.[125] Eudes found parallels with different biblical stories and contemporary events in his sermons against the Lucera Muslims and the Albigensian heretics, as well as those preached during the Seventh Crusade.[126]

The manuals intended for crusade preaching had structures of their own, which naturally differed from those of the crusade model sermons. The *Brevis ordinacio de predicacione sancte crucis* is divided into four parts: the opening chapter, the chapter *De circumstanciis crucis*, followed by the chapters *De carne et eius deliciis* and *De vocacione hominum ad crucem*. Each section begins with short introductory remarks that explain the main subject under consideration and then proceeds to details and specific examples. The whole work is structured so that it would be easy to use by the crusade preachers utilizing the manual. The themes of the *Brevis ordinacio* are explained in a straightforward and easily comprehensible manner. The theological considerations are represented lucidly and reasserted with numerous biblical examples.[127]

---

[123] Guibert de Tournai, 'Ad crucesignatos et crucesignandos sermo primus', *CPI*, pp. 176–91.

[124] Humbert de Romans, 'Ad peregrinos crucesignatos', *CPI*, pp. 210–15.

[125] The overall argument of Eudes's sermon against the Mongols is structured by comparison between the crusade and the biblical war against the forces of Nicanor. Eudes de Châteauroux, 'Sermo de invitatione ad crucem', *CPI*, pp. 144–51.

[126] See, for example, Eudes de Châteauroux, 'Sermo de rebellione Sarracenorum Lucherie in Apulia', *CR*, pp. 376–79; Eudes de Châteauroux, 'Sermo contra hereticos de Albigensibus partibus', Arras, MS 876, fols 88vb–90rb; Eudes de Châteauroux, 'Sermo ad invitandum ad accipiendum crucem et ad confortandum crucesignatos', *UEE*, II, 733–36.

[127] 'Brevis ordinacio de predicacione', *QBSS*, pp. 1–26.

Humbert de Romans's manual, the *De predicatione sancte crucis*, is a longer tract, which is also arranged systematically. Humbert's manual has a structure that is well thought out and which has a clear purpose. The *De predicatione sancte crucis* is divided into forty-six chapters and two sections: the first part comprises themes for crusade sermons (Chapters 2–26), while the second includes a list of relevant biblical passages which might be used in crusade sermons and information and advice for the crusade preachers (Chapters 27–46).[128]

Humbert begins the treatise with an introduction, where he explains how the handbook ought to be used. He advises the preachers to divide their crusade sermons into short passages and to use formal invitations to take the cross when they preached. These are marked in the margin in the manual. Humbert also maintains that hymns, such as 'Veni sancte spiritus', 'Veni creator spiritus', 'Vexilla Regis', or 'Salve crux sancta', ought to be sung at events where crusades were preached. According to Humbert, the manual provided all sorts of material for crusade preachers and it benefited both experienced and inexperienced preachers. The preachers utilizing Humbert's work could apply the arguments as he presented them in their sermons, or modify them; they could select from the variety of different themes and messages for their own crusade sermons, or the more experienced preachers could simply seek inspiration from the manual.[129]

Of the thirty-six crusade model sermons studied here only four were preached or meant to be preached specifically against the Muslim enemies of the Holy Land.[130] This astonishingly small number becomes less surprising if we also include sermons against the Muslims in other places with a clear connection to the Holy Land in the number. During the thirteenth century, major crusades were directed to destinations other than the Holy Land, especially Egypt, for strategic reasons. It was believed that these crusades would aid in the recovery of the Holy Land, and the model sermons preached for them can be classed as sermons directed against the Muslims in general — both those threatening the Holy Land and those dwelling in other places — but the primary goal of these crusades was the liberation of the Holy Land. There appear to be sixteen to sev-

---

[128] Humbert de Romans, *De predicatione sancte crucis*; *PCHL*, p. 212; Maier, *Preaching the Crusades*, p. 115.

[129] Humbert de Romans, *De predicatione sancte crucis*, cap. i.

[130] Three of Eudes de Châteauroux's sermons from the Seventh Crusade seem to have been preached in the Holy Land, after the failure of the Egyptian expedition. These sermons deal, however, mostly with the crusading disaster and do not focus on the Muslim enemy. One of Federico Visconti's sermons appears to have been preached against the Muslim enemies in the Holy Land. See Appendices II–VIII.

enteen crusade model sermons which were preached, or parts of them may have been preached, during the Fifth or the Seventh Crusade. Humbert de Romans's preaching manual was also meant to give information and examples which were to be used in the promotion of a Holy Land crusade as was the English crusading manual, the *Brevis ordinacio de predicacione sancte crucis*. However, both manuals could also be used in the preaching of other crusades.[131]

Many of the crusade sermons of this study are difficult to link to any specific enemy or to any specific crusade, as they have been written as model sermons for the preaching of the cross in general.[132] Nonetheless, the rubrics of some of these sermons reveal the purposes they were meant for. One sermon is meant to be preached against Muslim enemies anywhere, another is meant for both crusaders and pilgrims and thus has a connection to the Holy Land, and a third sermon is directed against various enemies, including the enemies of the Holy Land.[133] There is also internal evidence in the model sermons that may give us a hint of the kind of crusade the sermon may have been meant for. Two of Guibert de Tournai's sermons, for example, specifically discuss Jerusalem or the Holy Land, which suggests that these parts may have been intended for promotion of a Holy Land crusade.[134]

Using this broader method of assessment, we have twenty to twenty-one crusade model sermons and two crusade manuals that were preached or meant

---

[131] Jacques de Vitry's two sermons for the pilgrims appear to have a connection to the Fifth Crusade to Egypt. Jacques's sermons for the crusaders also contain several internal references that point to the Holy Land, and parts of the sermons may have been preached during the promotion of the Fifth Crusade. Eleven of Eudes de Châteauroux's sermons appear to have been preached during the promotion of the Seventh Crusade to Egypt or during the actual expedition. Three of these sermons appear to have been preached in the Holy Land. Roger of Salisbury's crusade sermon was preached during the 1240s, and it may have been part of the promotion of the Seventh Crusade in England. See the Appendices.

[132] The sermons of Guibert de Tournai, for example, belong to this group. In these sermons the rubrics do not indicate the intended enemies and whereas Jacques de Vitry is known to have participated in the Fifth Crusade, it is uncertain whether Guibert personally participated in an expedition. He may have been on the Seventh Crusade and promoted this in France. See above, pp. 17–18 n. 48; Appendix VIII.

[133] These three crusade sermons belong to Humbert de Romans: 'Ad peregrinos crucesignatos', 'In predicatione crucis contra Sarracenos', and 'De predicatione crucis in genere quocumque'. See Appendix VI.

[134] Guibert de Tournai, 'Ad crucesignatos et crucesignandos sermo primus', *CPI*, p. 186; Guibert de Tournai, 'Ad crucesignatos et crucesignandos sermo tertius', *CPI*, p. 208. One of Humbert de Romans's sermons also mentions specifically the Holy Land: Humbert de Romans, 'In predicatione crucis contra Sarracenos', *CPI*, p. 228.

to be preached against the Muslim enemies of the Holy Land, for the aid of the Holy Land, or for those travelling to the Holy Land. There are also two crusade sermons that appear to have been preached against the Mongols in the early 1260s. These sermons were preached when the Mongols were perceived as enemies who threatened the Holy Land.[135] Thus, the total number of crusade model sermons against the enemies of the Holy Land may be assessed as twenty-two to twenty-three sermons.

Of the thirty-six crusade model sermons, seven are specifically preached or meant to be preached against heretics.[136] One of the crusade sermons may have been preached against the Ghibellines during the conflict between Guelf and Ghibelline factions in Italy in the 1260s, but this is far from certain.[137] Three of the crusade model sermons were preached against the Muslim community of Lucera. They too thus belong to the prolonged struggle between the papacy and the Hohenstaufen. During the 1260s the papacy was engaged in a conflict against the descendants of Frederick II. The Church's champion Charles of Anjou fought first against Manfred of Hohenstaufen and then against Conradin of Hohenstaufen over the rule of the *Regno*.[138]

A quarter of the crusade model sermons of this study were preached against enemies other than the Muslims of the Holy Land. Seven or eight of the sermons were preached against Christian enemies and two against the Mongols. The rest of the crusade sermons were either preached against the Muslim enemies in the Holy Land, in Egypt, or in Italy, or they have no clearly specified enemy. Of all the authors of the crusade model sermons, Eudes de Châteauroux appears to have preached against the greatest variety of crusading opponents: the Albigensian heretics, the Muslims in Egypt, the Holy Land, and Lucera, and the Mongols, and possibly the Ghibellines too.[139]

---

[135] Federico Visconti, 'Quando idem dominus predicavit [crucem] respondendo nuntiis Tartarorum in clero pisano', *SVP*, p. 552; Eudes de Châteauroux, 'Sermo de invitatione ad crucem', *CPI*, p. 146.

[136] See Philippe le Chancelier's sermons in Appendix II; the sermon of Eudes de Châteauroux, 'Sermo contra hereticos de Albigensibus partibus', Arras, MS 876, fols 88vb–90rb; and the sermon of Humbert de Romans, 'In predicatione crucis contra hereticos', *CPI*, p. 222.

[137] Eudes de Châteauroux, 'Sermo ad invitandum ad crucem', *CPI*, p. 166. *UEE*, ii, 669.

[138] The Kingdom of Sicily was often called the *Regno*, 'the kingdom', to distinguish it from the Holy Roman Empire. This emphasized the fact that Frederick II ruled both a universal empire and a territorial monarchy. Abulafia, *Frederick II*, pp. 2–3, 408–35.

[139] Appendix V.

It is important to bear in mind that the crusade sermons of this study were meant as model sermons and that most of them were deliberately reworked so that the sermons could be utilized on different kinds of occasions. Eudes de Châteauroux, for example, may have cut down the direct references to enemies in his sermons against the Mongols and the Ghibellines. In the model versions of these sermons, the Mongols are mentioned only once, and the Ghibellines are not mentioned at all, which leaves very much open the question of whether the *Sermo ad invitandum ad crucem* was initially preached against them or not. By this method, the sermons which were originally intended for the preaching of crusades against the Mongols could be easily turned into sermons against the Muslims and vice versa.

Chapter 2

The Crusader and the Bible

The Shield of Joshua

> *The Lord said to Joshua:*
> *Lift up the shield that is in your hand towards the city of Ai,*
> *for I will deliver it to you.*[1]

The Old Testament patriarch Joshua and the wars he waged were favourite themes of the crusade preachers, utilized repeatedly to justify or to explain the crusades. Philippe le Chancelier opened his first crusade sermon against the Albigensian heretics in 1226 with the Bible passage where God urged Joshua to lift up his shield and go to war. Philippe also continued on the biblical theme in his next two crusade sermons.[2] The crusade manual *Brevis ordinacio de pred-*

---

[1] Philippe le Chancelier, 'Sermo scolaribus inter Epiphaniam et Purificationem', Avranches, MS 132, fols 248va–250ra: '*Dixit Dominus ad Josue: Leva clipeum, qui in manu tua est, contra urbem Hay, quoniam tibi tradam eam*'. Jos. 8. 18.

[2] Philippe le Chancelier, 'Sermo scolaribus inter Epiphaniam et Purificationem', Avranches, MS 132, fols 248va–250ra; Philippe le Chancelier, 'Sermo de eodem, quomodo apparuit potentia Dei', Avranches, MS 132, fol. 250ra: '*Non contraxit Josue manum, quam in sublime porrexerat, tenens clipeum, donec interficerentur omnes habitatores urbis Hay* etc. *et fecit eam tumulum sempiternum*'; Philippe le Chancelier, 'Sermo de eodem, de gaudio quod rex et principes assumpserunt crucem', Avranches, MS 132, fol. 251ra: '*Tunc edificavit Josue altare Domino in monte Ebal de lapidibus inpolitis, quos ferrum non tetigit et obtulit holocausta super eum Domino*'. Jos. 8. 18, 26, 28, 31. Transcribed by Maier and Bériou.

icacione sancte crucis made use of the same biblical passage, as did Eudes de
Châteauroux in his crusade sermon against the Albigensian heretics.[3] Eudes,
in fact, used the stories of Joshua in several of his crusade sermons preached
against various enemies in the period from the 1220s to the end of the 1260s.[4]
Joshua is also mentioned in Humbert de Romans's crusade manual several
times with references to both wars against the cities of Jericho and Ai and the
crossing over Jordan.[5]

Joshua was incorporated early on into crusade ideology, as a model which
the crusaders could follow. Pope Urban II is said to have compared the leaders of the First Crusade to Moses and Joshua.[6] Pope Honorius III continued
the tradition by describing the leader of the Fifth Crusade, the papal legate
Pelagius, as another Joshua (in a letter sent to the legate in 1219).[7] Joshua was
an important biblical figure in the crusade propaganda and a particularly significant figure to the Capetian royal house.

The Capetians based their visions of sacred kingship on parallels drawn
between Old Testament kings and the Capetian monarchs. Joshua, David,
Solomon, and Josiah were regarded as prefigurations of the French kings. The

---

[3] 'Brevis ordinacio de predicacione', *QBSS*, pp. 1–26; Eudes de Châteauroux, 'Sermo contra
hereticos de Albigensibus partibus', Arras, MS 876, fol. 89vb.

[4] Eudes de Châteauroux, 'Sermo contra hereticos de Albigensibus partibus', Arras, MS 876,
fol. 89vb; Eudes de Châteauroux, 'De sancto Georgio sermo', *UEE*, ii, 739, 741; Eudes de
Châteauroux, 'Sermo de invitatione ad crucem', *CPI*, p. 148; Eudes de Châteauroux, 'Sermo de
rebellione Sarracenorum Lucherie', *CR*, pp. 379–81.

[5] Humbert de Romans, *De predicatione sancte crucis*, cap. ii, xv, xxii, xxvi, xxvii, xliiij.

[6] Baldwin I of Jerusalem was referred to as 'a powerful leader, similar to Joshua' on his tomb-
stone. Gaposchkin, 'Louis IX, Crusade and the Promise of Joshua', esp. p. 256. Erdmann, *Die
Entstehung des Kreuzzugsgedankens*, p. 107. Fulcher de Chartres, *Historia Hierosolymitana*, lib.
II, cap. LXIV, 8, ed. by Hagenmeyer, p. 614: 'Dux validus patriae, consimilis Iosue'. See also
Katzir, 'The Conquest of Jerusalem, 1099 and 1187', esp. p. 107.

[7] Honorius III, 'Ad Pelagium', ed. by Bouquet, p. 691: 'Quare, sicut alter Josue, populum
Domini corrobora et conforta, sustinens et sustinere docens difficilia quaeque animis indef-
essis, ut opus Dei, quod laudabiliter incoepisti, ipso auctore, valeas feliciter consummare'.
Gaposchkin, 'Louis IX, Crusade and the Promise of Joshua', p. 256. Joshua's importance as a
model for the crusaders has been acknowledged by several scholars; see, for example, Erdmann,
Die Entstehung des Kreuzzugsgedankens, p. 107; Katzir, 'The Conquest of Jerusalem, 1099 and
1187', esp. p. 107. Recently, however, this significance has also been questioned. Douglas S.
Earl has suggested that Joshua and his wars have been misread as a text of conquest by scholars
and that the book of Joshua was 'not central' to either 'the justification or the preaching of the
Crusades'. This conclusion is a clear misinterpretation of the crusade sources. Earl, 'Joshua and
the Crusades', esp. p. 23.

Capetians were depicted as successors to the biblical leaders, as the last kings before the end of time, with their own role in salvific Christian history.[8] Both Philippe le Chancelier's and Eudes de Châteauroux's crusade sermons, which make extended use of the wars of Joshua, were connected to the crusades of the Capetian kings — to Louis VIII's and Louis IX's crusades — and Eudes's sermons also to the crusades of Charles of Anjou, the son of Louis VIII.[9]

Crusade preachers and the ecclesiastics who associated contemporary monarchs with the biblical kings could have different intentions. On the one hand, the association could be made as an encouragement and as an attempt to guide kings and princes to 'good' Christian rulership.[10] On the other hand, ecclesiastics could give support and foundation to royal claims of sacral kingship. In Eudes de Châteauroux's crusade sermons both are in evidence. In a sermon preached for the feast of the Holy Relics of Sainte-Chapelle at the consecration of the chapel in 1248, just before the Seventh Crusade set out, Eudes associated Louis IX with the Old Testament patriarch Joshua. By this association, Louis too became a leader for a chosen people, the French, and in particular the crusaders, just as Joshua had been for the Israelites. Although he was not a monarch himself, Joshua was conceived of as an ideal model for the crusader kings. Indeed, in the stained-glass windows of Sainte-Chapelle, he is depicted as a king with a crown on his head.[11] Joshua's military achievements against the enemies of God, and the fact that he had conquered the Holy Land, made him a perfect example for the crusading monarchs to follow.

Sainte-Chapelle was commissioned to house the holy relics of the Passion of Christ, which Louis IX had purchased from Baldwin II, the Latin Emperor of Constantinople, in 1238–41.[12] In his sermon, Eudes mentioned some of these

[8] Gaposchkin, 'Louis IX, Crusade and the Promise of Joshu', pp. 245–48. Le Goff, *Saint Louis*, pp. 388–401. For general information on the Capetian dynasty, see Bradbury, *Capetians*.

[9] The Angevins drew similar parallels between themselves and the Old Testament kings. The grandson of Charles of Anjou, Robert of Naples, for example, was described as a fine king 'like another Joshua', who would subdue Jericho with his wisdom and power. Kelly, *New Solomon*, p. 270.

[10] Guibert de Tournai, for example, tried to give guidance to Louis IX in his *Eruditio regum et principum*. This tract belongs to the tradition of 'the Mirrors of the Princes' and was written for the king in 1259. Guibert depicted in three letters the necessary qualities of a good king, utilizing examples from Antiquity and from both the Old and the New Testament. The Old Testament kings David, Solomon, and Josiah were among these examples. Guibert de Tournai, *Eruditio regum et principum*, ed. by Poorter. See also Le Goff, *Saint Louis*, pp. 409–17.

[11] Gaposchkin, 'Louis IX, Crusade and the Promise of Joshua', pp. 245–47.

[12] For these relics, see Frolow, *La Relique de la Vraie Croix*, pp. 427–30.

important relics: the Crown of Thorns, a piece of the Holy Cross, the Holy Nails, the *sudarium*, that is, the shroud of Christ, a piece of a stone from the Holy Sepulchre, the Holy Sponge, and a piece of iron from the Holy Lance. Eudes compared these relics to the twelve stones that the twelve men chosen by Joshua had picked up from the river Jordan.[13] He also linked the Passion relics of Louis IX to the Ark of the Covenant. The relics were a sign of God's love and his new alliance with the Christian people. This love was something which the infidels, the Saracens, or the Jews could not understand.[14]

A section of the stained-glass windows of Sainte-Chapelle was dedicated to Joshua, where he was depicted as a crusading prince. The biblical story of Joshua and the Israelites' battles in the Holy Land were presented in the images as a narrative of holy war that preceded Louis IX's crusade.[15] One of the images in a stained-class window portrays Joshua bearing the Ark of the Covenant over Jordan. Eudes's reference to the twelve stones in the sermon continued and extended the story depicted in the window. The twelve stones were an allusion both to the recently acquired relics and to the prospective crusade; the Passion relics were a contemporary equivalent of the Ark of the Covenant.[16] In the biblical story, Joshua and the Israelites had crossed Jordan with the Ark when Joshua was on his way to conquer Jericho and the rest of the Holy Land. When the priests were carrying the Ark over Jordan, the river stopped flowing and the Israelites walked on dry ground. The twelve stones were a reminder of this miracle that God had worked for his chosen people.[17]

According to the typological interpretation, these past events could be considered as precedents of contemporary ones: Louis IX was fulfilling his task in

---

[13] Eudes de Châteauroux, 'Sermo in festo reliquiarum sancte capelle regis Francie', *UEE*, II, 731: 'De numero horum testimoniorum sunt hec sancte relique, sancta corona, crux, clavi, sudarium, sepulchrum, spongia, ferrum lancee, et alia, sicut duodecim lapides quos filii Israel de Iordane extrauerunt testimonium perhibent quod ipsi Iordanem sicco uestigio transierunt'. Jos. 4. 1–5.

[14] Eudes de Châteauroux, 'Sermo in festo reliquiarum sancte capelle regis Francie', *UEE*, II, 729–32, esp. p. 731.

[15] The images have been analysed by several scholars and a detailed interpretation of them suggests that Joshua was depicted as a crusading leader. For analysis of the stained-class windows, see, for example, Gaposchkin, 'Louis IX, Crusade and the Promise of Joshua', p. 247; Jordan, *Visualizing Kingship in the Windows of the Sainte-Chapelle*; Folda, *Crusader Art in the Holy Land*, pp. 234–36.

[16] Gaposchkin, 'Louis IX, Crusade and the Promise of Joshua', pp. 253–55; Brenk, 'The Sainte-Chapelle as a Capetian Political Program', pp. 195–213, esp. p. 207.

[17] Jos. 3. 15–17, 4. 6–8.

salvific history, as a successor of Joshua. The French people were God's chosen people. Louis had brought the relics of the Passion to the new Jerusalem, to Paris, just as Joshua had brought the Ark of the Covenant to the Holy Land.[18] Louis's forthcoming crusade would complete the narration. The king would cross the sea, just as Joshua had crossed Jordan, and conquer the Holy Land just as the Israelites had conquered it before him. God wanted this to happen.

The Passion relics were the sign of God's love for his new chosen people and a reminder of his miracles, just as the Ark had been a sign of God's love for the Israelites and the twelve stones a reminder of his miracle in the crossing of the river. However, as Eudes argued in his sermon, these relics were a sign of much greater love than the one God had shown for the Israelites: the Israelites were given manna for forty years, the sea was divided for them, they were taught and instructed by God; but for the Christians, God gave his own son, so he would wear the Crown of Thorns, be crucified, pierced, and buried. Christians ought to try to repay this great love the best they could.[19] With this comment, Eudes implied that Christians could show their gratitude and their own love for Christ by taking the cross and joining the coming crusade.

In these passages of the sermon, Eudes was careful to mention the different features of the Passion of Christ, the relics of which Louis IX had just acquired. The crown was referred to in the sermon as well as the piercing, because the piece of the lance was among the relics; the crucifixion was referred to, for Louis had bought the nails that had been used to fasten Christ to the cross as well as a piece of the cross itself; and burial was mentioned, because the stone of the Sepulchre had also been acquired. The sermon, the newly purchased holy relics, and the recently made images in the stained-class windows must have made a powerful impression on those present at Sainte-Chapelle in 1248: all the different components spoke the same language, telling of the love and the sacrifice of Christ, the salvation of all Christians, and the sacred kingship of the Capetians. By these means — through the sermon, the images, and the relics — Louis IX's and his fellow crusaders' role in sacred history was communicated to the audience.

---

[18] *UEE*, I.1, 176–77. For the typological indentification of Louis IX with Joshua, see Gaposchkin, 'Louis IX, Crusade and the Promise of Joshua', pp. 246–47, 250–55.

[19] Eudes de Châteauroux, 'Sermo in festo reliquiarum sancte capelle regis Francie', *UEE*, II, 732: 'Multo maius enim fuit quod filius Dei pro nobis spinis uoluit coronari, crucifigi, lanceari, sepeliri et signum maioris dilectionis quam quod Dominus populum israeliticum quadraginta annis manna pauit, coram eis mare diuisit, eos docuit et instruxit. [...] Et ideo ea debemus corde intentissimo perscrutari et ea habere pre oculis ut nos inflamment ad amorem Dei et inducant nos et stimulent ut ei uicem pro nostro modulo rependamus'.

Eudes shared Louis IX's visions of the conquest of the earthly Jerusalem. In the sermon, the legate lent his support to the Capetian royal programme, at the same time promoting the upcoming crusade.[20] In his two other sermons for the feast of the Holy Relics, both of which were preached during the crusade, Eudes made several references to the Passion relics. Some of the relics appear to have been taken along with the army on the Seventh Crusade. The relics served as a reminder of the love of Christ and the friendship between him and the crusaders during the campaign. Like the Ark of the Covenant, the Passion relics would be carried to the Promised Land by the servants of God. The remembrance of the love of Christ and the alliance between Christians and God were important, both after the initial success and in the time of crisis: the second sermon of Eudes for the feast of the Holy Relics from 1249 appears to have been preached in Egypt after the taking of Damietta, and the third sermon for the same feast in 1251 in the Holy Land after the defeat of Mansurah. The Passion relics were a cause of happiness and reminded the crusaders that the glory of victory belonged to Christ and eventually to all Christians, but the relics also brought comfort to the crusaders as they waited for reinforcements far away from home, or struggled to come to terms with a crusading failure.[21]

Ai and Jericho Revisited

The most specific identification between Joshua and a crusade leader was made by Eudes de Châteauroux not in the sermons from the Seventh Crusade, but in his sermons preached against the Lucera Muslims. The Lucera Muslims had been transported from Sicily to the mainland by Frederick II of Hohenstaufen in the 1220s–1240s. This was a fairly large community of about fifteen thousand to twenty thousand people. Frederick II made the decision to remove the Muslim communities from Sicily in order to subdue the chronic rebellions in the island. The resettlement was meant to isolate the Muslims far away from possible allies. Pope Honorius III seems to have accepted the idea of transferring the Sicilian Muslims to the mainland in the late 1220s, but already in the 1230s Pope Gregory IX began to express concern about the situation

---

[20] Eudes de Châteauroux, 'Sermo in festo reliquiarum sancte capelle regis Francie', *UEE*, II, 731.

[21] Eudes de Châteauroux, 'Sermo in festo sanctarum reliquiarum', *UEE*, II, 742–46; Eudes de Châteauroux, 'Sermo in festo sanctarum reliquiarum', *UEE*, II, 763–66. For the timing of the sermons, see Appendix V.

in Apulia. In 1255, during Pope Alexander IV's crusade against Manfred, an attack against Lucera was carried out, but this expedition came to nought.[22]

In the crusade model sermon from the year 1268, Eudes described Louis IX's brother, Charles of Anjou, as 'our Joshua', who battled against the Muslims of Apulia. Eudes explained to his audience of current and prospective crusaders that the war against Jericho from the biblical past was a parallel to the current situation in Apulia: just as God wanted the Israelites to crush their enemies in Jericho, so he wanted the Christians to crush their enemies in Lucera. Charles of Anjou, as the Joshua of the Christians, was destined to defeat Lucera, 'another Jericho', where the Muslims had armed themselves against all Christians, as the Canaanites inside Jericho had armed themselves against the Israelites.[23]

The precise identification between Charles and Joshua in Eudes's model sermon justified the crusade against the Lucera Muslims, confirmed God's support, and promised victory for the crusade. Joshua's leadership provided an important model for the crusade preachers, a biblical example that could be used to guide the crusading leaders. The leaders, the sermon asserts, should conduct themselves on the journey as their predecessor in the biblical prefiguration did. Like Joshua, the crusading leaders needed to be pious and pure, and they should always obey God's commands.

Joshua's biblical enemies also had significance in the crusading context. The events surrounding the conquests of the cities of Jericho and Ai were referred to in several of the model sermons. Both Philippe le Chancelier and Eudes de Châteauroux used biblical identifications to illustrate to their audiences about who

---

[22] Matthew Paris includes a short report of the attack. Matthew Paris, *Historia Anglorum*, ed. by Madden, p. 345: 'Dominus papa Alexander Octovianum cardinalem destinavit cum maximo exercitu ad destruendam civitatem Nucheram [Lucera], cum Memfredo rege ibi latitante'. *CR*, pp. 343–85, esp. p. 354. See also Taylor, *Muslims in Medieval Italy*, p. 41; Taylor, 'Muslim–Christian Relations in Medieval Southern Italy'.

[23] Eudes de Châteauroux, 'Sermo de rebellione Sarracenorum Lucherie', *CR*, p. 379: 'Hec ystoria parabola est instantis temporis: Dominus dedit terram Apulie nostro Iosue, id est domino Karolo. In hac terra erat quasi altera Iherico, Lucheria, habitatio et refugium Sarracenorum, quibus erat munita et armata contra omnes Christianos non tam modo Apulie sed etiam tocius regni Sicilie'. Jos. 7. 11–14. In his critical study, Douglas S. Earl has also noted Eudes's reference to Joshua but has regarded the sermon as 'unusual and atypical'. Earl has argued that although Eudes did make a passing allusion to the Israelites' crossing of the Jordan this theme was not developed further, while the other crusade preachers did not really utilize the model of Joshua at all. Earl, 'Joshua and the Crusades', p. 33. Earl has, however, used only selective evidence in reaching these conclusions. Eudes de Châteauroux did in fact develop the theme of crossing the Jordan in several of his crusade sermons from the Seventh Crusade, as discussed above.

the crusaders were fighting against. They linked the Albigensian heretics to the people of Ai and compared their sins to the sins of the Canaanites. Eudes quoted a biblical passage to explain how Joshua dealt with the people of Ai, explaining that he did not draw back his hand that held the shield until all the inhabitants of Ai were killed. He associated the heretics to the Canaanites with Jerome's interpretation of what Ai meant.[24] Ai was interpreted as a question of life or life in the valleys, which Eudes connected to the filth of heresy.[25]

Philippe le Chancelier also utilized Jerome's interpretation of Ai in his crusade sermon, linking the heretical wickedness of the Albigensians and their sins of avarice and lust to the sins of the inhabitants of Ai.[26] Philippe justified the war in Languedoc with the biblical example and connected the Albigensian Crusade to the larger question of the recovery of the Holy Land. Philippe viewed the ancient conquest of Ai as a prefiguration of the contemporary conflict in Languedoc and an example which the Christians should follow. The Israelites had to conquer Ai before they could conquer the Promised Land. This precondition was as valid now as it was in biblical times. In the contemporary context Ai meant the lands of the Albigensians. The Christians had to conquer these lands before they could go on to liberate the Holy Land. If they did not proceed in this order, they could have no success in the recovery of the Holy Land.[27]

---

[24] Eudes de Châteauroux, 'Sermo contra hereticos de Albigensibus partibus', Arras, MS 876, fol. 89vb: 'Josue vero non contraxit manum quam in sublime porrexerat tenens clipeum, donec interficerentur habitatores Hay. Hay interpretatur vita vallium, id est peccatum hereseos, quo retento omnia retinentur, et per quod obturatur unititur intercidere, quia hoc interciso civitas ecclesie non potest stare, et per hoc apparet immanitas sceleris hereseos'. Jos. 8. 26. Transcribed by Maier and Bériou.

[25] Hieronymus, *Liber interpretationis*, ed. by de Lagarde, p. 126: 'Ahi quaestio vel vallis siue vivit'. Bertrand de la Tour also used this theme in his crusade sermon and utilized Jerome's interpretation. To Bertrand, this meant that it was a question of life, for it was certain to God that the people of Ai would die, but they were not sure if they would live. Bertrand de la Tour, 'Item alia de eodem', *CPI*, p. 246: 'Unde bene interpretatur Hay "questio vite", quia, cum sit certum aput Deum de eorum morte, apud ipsos dubium est si vivant'.

[26] Philippe le Chancelier, 'Sermo scolaribus inter Epiphaniam et Purificationem', Avranches, MS 132, fol. 249[vb]: 'Hec levanda est contra urbem Hay, que interpretatur *questio vite*, id est contra hereticam pravitatem, que querit ut suffocet vitam spiritualem, et que est fides iuxta Abacuc ii: *Iustus mens ex fide vivit*, sicut venenum impetit cor, ubi vita, interpretatur eciam *vita vallium*, quia lascivia est, ad quam fluunt omnes sordes, luxurie et avaricie, quia propter hec duo hereses adinveniuntur, quod notatur ii Pet. ii: *Multi sequuntur eorum luxurias, per quos via veritatis blasphematur, et in avaricia fictis verbis negociantur*'. Hab. 2. 4, II Pet. 2. 2–3. Transcribed by Maier and Bériou.

[27] Philippe le Chancelier, 'Sermo scolaribus inter Epiphaniam et Purificationem', Avranches,

In another crusade sermon, Philippe used the same biblical passage as Eudes de Châteauroux, reminding his audience that Joshua did not draw back the hand that held the shield until all the people of Ai were slain.[28] For Philippe's audience of scholars this did not mean the actual, physical extermination of the Albigensian heretics, but the spiritual killing of the heresy through the intercessory means available to the ecclesiastics supporting the crusade from afar. In Philippe's interpretation Joshua's shield symbolized the faith and the three powerful, spiritual weapons which the ecclesiastics could employ: prayers, almsgiving, and fasting. Scholars participating in the crusade against the heretics on the home front should not cease in their efforts but continue relentlessly to fight against heresy with acts of intercession.[29]

The crusaders and the supporters of the movement, for Philippe, should not rest until their God-given task was completed, just as the Israelites under the command of Joshua had not rested. The enemies that Joshua faced were important in explaining the 'type of enemy' that the crusaders were fighting against. Joshua had fought and defeated the Canaanites, the enemies of God, as the enemies of faith, which seemed to guarantee success for the crusading armies: as the heirs of Joshua and as the new chosen people fighting against the old enemy, the crusaders were entitled to the same success as their Old Testament predecessors, as long as they succeeded in emulating them morally and spiritually. However, if they failed in this, Joshua's battles also provided an example of what might follow from their shortcomings.

Avaricious Achor and the Crusader's Cupidity

In Joshua's wars there had been an example of behaviour displeasing to God, with which the crusaders could be instructed. This example was utilized by several authors of the crusade model sermons. Jacques de Vitry used it repeatedly in his writings and in several of his crusade sermons. In a sermon intended

---

MS 132, fol. 250ʳᵃ; Maier, 'Crisis, Liturgy and the Crusade', p. 654.

[28] Philippe le Chancelier, 'Sermo de eodem, quomodo apparuit potentia Dei et sapientia', Avranches, MS 132, fol. 250ʳᵃ. Jos. 8. 26.

[29] Philippe le Chancelier, 'Sermo de eodem, quomodo apparuit potentia Dei et sapientia', Avranches, MS 132, fol. 250ʳᵃ: 'Sicut dictum est, clipeus triangularis tria suffragia significat: oracionem, elemosinam et ieiunium, de quibus dictum est: *Leva clipeum, qui est in manu tua*, sicut ergo fecit Josue, scilicet quod *non contraxit manum, donec* etc. Sic et nos non cessemus ab hiis tribus, donec negocium fidei perfecte promoveatur, per quod interficiantur *omnes habitatores urbis Hay*'. Transcribed by Maier and Bériou. Jos. 8. 18. Maier, 'Crisis, Liturgy and the Crusade', p. 647.

for the pilgrims and the crusaders, Jacques warned that the Christians ought not go into battle trusting in their strength, or go in an impure spiritual state, for then they would be easily and quickly beaten, as the biblical story of Achor illustrated.[30]

Achor or Achan was an avaricious man in the ranks of Joshua's army who stole some of the riches of the Canaanites during the conquest of Jericho, and in so doing disobeyed God's specific orders.[31] God did not allow Joshua and the Israelites to conquer Ai before this theft had been expiated.[32] In his sermon for the crusaders and pilgrims, Jacques used the allusion to Achor to ensure that the crusaders would fight in a proper state of mind — piously — and for the proper reasons. They should not try to gain spoils or other worldly things for themselves while fighting for God.

Jacques de Vitry encountered first-hand the problems caused by the distribution of spoils gained by crusading. In 1219, during the Fifth Crusade, there was a dispute over how treasure should be divided among the crusaders after the capture of Damietta. Jacques complained in a letter sent to Pope Honorius III that some of the crusaders were no more than 'thieves and robbers, pilgrims in name only', 'hateful to God, disobedient to the lord legate', and 'blinded by the cupidity of Achor'.[33] These crusaders were impostors, not true pilgrims, that is,

---

[30] Jacques de Vitry, 'Ad peregrinos. Thema sumpta ex Zacharias ultimo', *JVSP*, p. 99: 'Hi igitur qui de viribus suis presumunt vel cum peccato mortali ad proelium vadunt cito et de facili coruunt. Unde in Iosue vii. Non poterit stare coram hostibus suis Israel, quia pollutus est anathemate Iherico'.

[31] In the manuscripts of the crusade sermons 'Achor' is the most common form used of the person in question. In the edited versions of the Vulgate, both the so-called Clementine Vulgate and the Stuttgart Vulgate, the form is 'Achan'. In the medieval manuscripts, 'Achar' is also used. See, for example, a twelfth-century Biblia Latina in Troyes, MS 27 (vol. II), fol. 8ᵛᵇ. Jos. 7. 1. In this study I have used the form 'Achor', in line with the form used in the sources, even though this may create some confusion with the modern spelling. However, there is a wordplay here with the terms 'Achan' and 'Achor', which is the main reason why I have chosen to follow strictly the form used in the sources.

[32] Jos. 7. 1–25.

[33] Jacques de Vitry, *Epistola*, VI, ed. by Huygens, p. 127: 'Invenimus autem in civitate pauca valde victualia, aurum vero et argentum et pannos sericos cum vestibus preciosis et aliam multam supellectilem reperimus in civitate. Sed quoniam multi fures et latrones et nomine solo peregrini, deo odibiles, domino legato non obedientes, sicut Achor cupiditate excecati, in exercitu nostro supra modum tunc temporis errant, Sarraceni vero maximam partem pecunie partim in terra absconderunt, partim in fluvium proiecerunt, vix ad utilitatem communitatis quadringentorum milium bizantiorum precium colligere et inter nostros dividere potuimus. Idcirco murmur et scandalum non modicum, rixe et contentiones exorte sunt in populo insipienti et

not true crusaders on a penitential, spiritual journey, but greedy men who tried to gather up all the riches of the city for themselves. Jacques was so irritated over the conduct of the crusaders that he returned to the subject in a subsequent letter to the pope. The crusaders, who were guilty of avarice and theft like Achor in Jericho, spent their money on gambling, harlots, and riotous living.[34]

Jacques further utilized the theme in his sermon intended for the brothers of the military orders. He instructed the knights to lay aside all luxuries and extravagance, which belonged to the secular life. With the example of Achor, he pointed out that the knights should renounce 'the gold of earthly wisdom, the silver of lucrative eloquence, and the garment of worldly life, the scarlet, that is, the sins stained with blood'.[35] If the knights refused to give up these vanities they would be on a par with Achor and would suffer the punishment he suffered.[36]

Eudes de Châteauroux also used the story of Achor in his sermon against the Lucera Muslims. He made minor modifications to the biblical account to make the story more appropriate for the current circumstances. In Eudes's version of events Jericho was cursed, which led Achor to sin, whereas in the biblical account, Achor had sinned, after which the curse was placed on the Israelites. This was removed by eliminating Achor, his family, and his goods. In Eudes's sermon, Jericho corresponded to Lucera and therefore this had to be eliminated, which would remove the curse.[37] In his sermon, Eudes illustrated the nature of the curse of Lucera in vivid terms. The religious pollution which

---

indisciplinato'. See also Gaposchkin, 'Louis IX, Crusade and the Promise of Joshua', p. 264.

[34] Jacques de Vitry, *Epistola*, VII, ed. by Huygens, p. 135. Jacques's companion in the crusade and another famous crusade preacher, Oliver von Paderborn, also tells in his history, the *Historia Damiatina*, that the legate of the Fifth Crusade, Pelagius, had used the example of Achor as a deterrent during the crusade: Oliver says that Pelagius made everyone swear that the spoils of the conquered city would be divided justly, and that those crusaders who did not honour the agreement would be anathematized. These 'transgressors' would 'forever remain disgraced like Achor'. Oliver also noted that 'the *concupiscence of the eyes* had made many men thieves' during the conquest of Damietta. Oliver von Paderborn, *Historia Damiatina*, ed. by Hoogeweg, p. 238: 'Transgressores perpetuo remanebunt infames cum Achor, qui furatus est de anathemate Jericho, computandi. Verumtamen *concupiscentia oculorum* plures fures fecit'. 1 John 2. 16.

[35] Jacques de Vitry, 'Sermo ad fratres militaris insignitos charactere militiae Christi', Troyes, MS 228, fol. 132[va]: 'Et multi hodie retinent aurum sapientiae secularis, argentum eloquentiae lucrativae, et pallium conversationis mundane, coccineum, id est, peccatis cruentatum'.

[36] Jacques de Vitry, 'Sermo ad fratres militaris insignitos charactere militiae Christi', Troyes, MS 228, fol. 132[va].

[37] *CR*, p. 362.

spread from the city — the smell of Lucera and the burning torches of the
Muslims — polluted the Christian neighbourhood.[38]

According to Eudes, the crusade preachers had brought down the walls
of Jericho with their trumpets, that is, with their words, which was an allusion to the walls of Lucera, which the Muslims had themselves destroyed after
the Battle of Benevento in 1266 in accordance with the peace treaty they
had made.[39] This achievement was later vitiated by greedy Christians, in the
opinion of Eudes. In the sermon, he criticized openly the administration of
Charles of Anjou for its negligence in dealing with the problem of Lucera.
Charles had defeated Manfred at Benevento, which had ended Hohenstaufen
rule in Italy, but he had made a treaty with Manfred's Muslim subjects. This
had apparently been done against papal wishes and allowed the Muslims to
continue to reside in Lucera, on condition that the fortifications of the city
were demolished and the royal treasure of Manfred, as well as other rewards,
were given to Charles.[40]

In his crusade sermon Eudes linked these events and the arrangements made
by the agents of Charles of Anjou to the sin of Achor. Charles's advisors had
been lured into the sin of cupidity by the treasures of the Lucerans, which had
saved the infidels. Like Achor, who stole from Jericho, some of the Christians
in Charles's court had 'stolen' from other Christians. The Muslims had not been
expelled or destroyed by Charles's forces, because the infidels were able to buy
their freedom with bribes, gifts, and false promises. The king was given bad
advice and counselled not to destroy Lucera on the grounds that the Muslims
living in his lands could one day prove useful to him.[41]

---

[38] Eudes de Châteauroux, 'Sermo de rebellione Sarracenorum Lucherie', *CR*, pp. 379–80:
'Vasa enim castrorum, id est instrumenta bellica posita in excelsis, id est in castris excelsis, loca
circa se posita destruunt atque vastant et vicinos suos impugnant, sic luna in excelso posita ea
que infra se sunt, perturbat ventis, pluviis et grandinibus, sic hec Lucheria Sarracenorum totam
viciniam suam usque ad hoc tempora perturbavit predis et incendiis devastavit. Huius etiam
Lucherie odor, id est fama, usque ad remotos pervenit'. Eudes's references to the burning torches
and instruments of war may point to the Lucera Muslims' use of Greek fire. *CR*, p. 363.

[39] *CR*, p. 363.

[40] *CR*, p. 363. 'Andreae Ungari descriptio victoriae a Karolo Provinciae comite reportatae',
ed. by Waitz, MGH, SS, 26, p. 580: 'Qui iubente rege muros omnes, turres et alias municiones,
quascumque circa vel infra villa suam habebant, destruentes fossata que replentes, ad obtinen-
dam graciam regiam miserunt ei auri et argenti donaria preciosa, reddentes se in manus illustris
regis Karoli'.

[41] Eudes de Châteauroux, 'Sermo de rebellione Sarracenorum Lucherie', *CR*, pp. 380–81:
'Sed, proh dolor, ibi nichilominus remanserunt Sarraceni et eos sub protectione sua; aliqui

The sin of Achor and consequences of this sin appear to have been a popular theme and in common use by the crusade preachers of the thirteenth century. Humbert de Romans also referred to the example provided by Achor in his manual for the crusade preachers. According to Humbert, it was necessary for the crusaders to abstain from sinning. The sins of one man could have devastating results for the whole army, as the biblical story illustrated.[42] Achor was closely associated to the sin of cupidity during the thirteenth century. The name 'Achor' was interpreted to mean 'disturbance', 'disaster', and 'tumult'.[43]

Pope Innocent III had used similar argumentation in the crusading context during the Fourth Crusade. The pope reprimanded the Frankish barons and condemned the conquest of Zara, in a letter of 1203.[44] Innocent warned the

cupiditate illiciti sicut Achor et filii sui furati sunt de anathemate lherico, *pallium cocineum valde bonum ducentos siclos argenti regulam quoque auream quinquaginta siclorum*. Isti Sarraceni velut anathema eiciendi erant omnino a terra, ut nullus omnino remaneret, sed quidam capti cupiditate auri et argenti et pannorum preciosorum protexerunt eos, allegantes utilitatem quam rex poterat habere de eis, si in terra sua remanerent'. Jos. 7. 21. There may be some confusion in this passage: the scribe appears to have missed something when he wrote down this sentence of the sermon; words or phrases appear to be missing. *CR*, p. 380, nn. kk, ff. See also Jacques de Vitry, 'Sermo ad fratres militaris insignitos charactere militiae Christi', Troyes, MS 228, fol. 132ᵛᵃ.

[42] Humbert de Romans, *De predicatione sancte crucis*, cap. xliiij: 'Non solum enim propter peccatum multitudinis vel etiam paucorum ymo etiam in unius interdum totus confunditur exercitus. sicut patet Josue. viij. de peccato Achior'. Humbert also referred to Achor in his *Opus tripartitum*. Humbert de Romans, *Opusculum tripartitum*, cap. xvii, ed. by Brown. p. 198.

[43] In the crusade sermons, the avaricious person is usually named 'Achor'. In the Bible, the person is also referred to as 'Achar'. 1 Par. 2. 7. '*Filii Charmi: Achar, qui turbavit Israel, et peccavit in furto anathematis*'. 'Achor' is also the name of the valley in which Achan or Achor was stoned to death and he and his sons and daughters, as well as all his possessions, were burnt. Jos. 7. 24–25. There is a wordplay on these different names in the book of Joshua: the classical Hebrew root for the word 'Achar' means 'break', 'disturb', and 'destroy'. 'Achor' may point to a similarly spelled verbal root, which means 'make taboo', 'bring disaster', and 'destroy'. The use of both names, Achan and Achar, is understood by viewing Achar as an epithet that derives from the original name Achan and is used to refer to the disastrous fate of the person in question. Hess, 'Reflections on Translating Joshua', pp. 125–42, esp. pp. 129–30. See also Hess, 'Achan and Achor'. The crusade preachers were not unaware of these allusions. Eudes de Châteauroux, for example, relied on St Jerome's interpretation of the names mentioned in the book of Joshua. The *Liber interpretationis Hebraicorum nominum* was standard reading material for medieval preachers. Jerome explained in his work that 'Achor' meant 'disturbance or tumult'. 'Achor turbatio vel tumultus': Hieronymus, *Liber interpretationis*, ed. by de Lagarde, p. 89.

[44] The conquest of Zara, orchestrated by the Venetians in 1202, was the first diversion of the infamous Fourth Crusade. In 1204 the crusaders captured Constantinople from the Greeks. The original intended goal was to recapture Jerusalem by attacking Egypt. For the Fourth

crusaders that they would perish and flee, as the Israelites did during the conquest of Ai, if they did not get rid of the sin and the sinners among them. The sin
of Achor had angered God, and the Israelites were 'immediately slain by the men
of Ai'.[45] Innocent tried to guide the crusaders of the Fourth Crusade to a more
pious frame of mind with the example of Achor and exert his authority over the
obstinate leaders of the army. The *crucesignati* ought to have a penitent outlook
on their journey. They should try to rectify the situation and the mistakes made
earlier. The pope emphasized that God did not let the Israelites conquer Ai until
they had killed Achor and 'all that had been his were consumed by fire'.[46]

The example of Achor was utilized by the crusade preachers in various ways.
The story of the theft in Jericho was a warning to all crusaders: if they sinned
against God, they would be punished, as Achor was. The sinners would bring
disaster and disrupt the holy work of the crusaders. The story also served as a
reminder to the crusaders that they should lay aside earthly ambitions, luxuries, and extravagance, and that they should be careful not to commit the sin
of avarice. In the service of Christ, the crusaders should be pious, humble, and
modest. They should not try to acquire riches for themselves as Achor did. If

Crusade, see, for example, Queller and Madden, *The Fourth Crusade*. This theme was utilized
already during the twelfth century to instruct the crusaders while on the journey. During the
Third Crusade, when the army of Frederick I Barbarossa was at Nish, the Bishop of Würzburg
reprehended the marauding crusaders and gave a sermon in which he guided the Christian soldiers with the example of Achor. *Historia de Expeditione Friderici Imperatoris*, ed. by Austriensis
and Dobrowsky, p. 36: 'Qui episcopus inter cetera hoc sermone exorsus est: pollutus est populus
anathemate, non ero cum eis, nisi mundentur, illud videlicet innuens et proponens de anathemate furti ierichontini Achaz, quando unius peccato universus populus corruit'. For the crusade
of Frederick I Barbarossa, see also Loud, *Crusade of Frederick Barbarossa*.

[45] Innocentius III, *Regestorum sive epistolarum*, CII, in *PL*, CCXV, col. 108; in the edition of
Migne the term 'Achan' is applied: 'Nam in libro Josue legitur, quod, cum Achan, filius Charmi,
pallium coccineum valde bonum, et ducentos siclos argenti, regulamque auream quinquaginta
siclorum de Jerico anathemate rapuisset, iratus est Dominus Israeli. Unde cum adversus Hai
ascendissent tria millia pugnatorum, statim terga vertentes percussi sunt a viris urbis Hai, et
corruerunt ex eis triginta et sex homines; persecutique sunt eos adversarii de porta usque ad
Sabarim, et ceciderunt per prona fugientes'. However, in the manuscript version of the register
the term 'Achor' is again used: Innocentius III, Reg. Vat. 5, fol. 93ʳ.

[46] Innocentius III, *Regestorum sive epistolarum*, CII, in *PL*, CCXV, col. 108. This was an
attempt to persuade the crusaders to keep their oath and to do restitution as they had promised:
the crusaders of the Fourth Crusade were to surrender or compensate for the possible profits
gained in the raid of Zara. This allowed the King of Hungary to have satisfaction over the loss
of the city and its goods. The crusaders also needed to repent their actions, depart from the
unrepentant, when they could, and purge themselves to become suitable participants of the holy
undertaking.

they did this, the treasures they unlawfully seized would be stained with blood. The crusaders should always obey the commandments of God, who had specifically ordered the Israelites not to take anything from Jericho. Similarly, the popes, and the crusade preachers who followed papal instructions, repeatedly ordered the crusaders not to try to amass riches for themselves while on crusade. If the crusaders violated the orders given to them, if they transgressed against the laws of God, they would suffer like Achor. This is not to say that the crusaders could not win treasures for themselves, but this should not be their primary intention. They should not act out of avarice, and when they distributed the spoils they should carefully listen to the advice of the crusading clergy or the pope.[47]

With the story of Achor, the crusade leaders could also be guided to follow the example of Joshua. Like Joshua, the crusade princes and kings needed to encourage their soldiers to renounce all sins and to conduct themselves with dignity while on the expeditions. If some of the crusaders sinned, the leaders should be as determined as Joshua was in getting rid of the sinners and any material gains from sinful acts, so that the crusade could be successful. Crusading failure was explained with the example of the defeat at Ai. If the crusaders did not obey the preachers or papal instructions and resorted to looting, they would suffer defeat by their enemies. But if the crusaders who had sinned were to repent their actions and purge themselves as the Israelites did in the valley of Achor, they would receive a second chance. After the conquest of Zara on the Fourth Crusade, they had the chance to continue and defeat their enemies, and in Apulia they had the opportunity to make another crusade against the Lucera Muslims after the first had been cut short.

The Dream of Judas Maccabaeus

The biblical story of the Jewish uprising against the Seleucid Empire in the second century BC in Judea had considerable relevance for Christian people throughout the Middle Ages. The revolt, led by the Maccabaean family, Mattathias and his five sons John, Simon, Judas, Eleazar, and Jonathan, was a famous and an oft-repeated narrative that appeared in medieval accounts of

[47] During the Fifth Crusade disputes and fights occurred over the spoils after the capture of Damietta. Jacques de Vitry complained in a letter that the crusaders did not listen to the legate's advice on how the gold, silver, silk, and other possessions ought to be divided amongst them. Jacques de Vitry, *Epistola*, VI, ed. by Huygens, p. 127.

various types.[48] Judas was a particularly revered figure of the Maccabaean family. He was regarded by medieval knights as a holy warrior, whose chivalric piety was to be imitated.[49] A fourteenth-century knight and a crusader, Geoffroi de Charny, held the opinion that 'the excellent knight Judas Maccabaeus' was 'strong, skilful, unrelenting in effort', and 'handsome above all others'.[50]

By the beginning of the thirteenth century, allusions to the Maccabaean wars and warriors had become standard topoi for crusade preachers.[51] Pope Urban II had associated the first crusaders' expedition with the wars of the Maccabees (in the Clermont sermon in 1095).[52] The first crowned king of the crusader kingdom of Jerusalem, Baldwin I, was also described in the inscription of his tomb as a 'second Judas Maccabaeus'.[53] Many of the preachers examined in this study utilize the Maccabaean exemplars in their model sermons. The emphasis varies from a mere citation of a convenient passage from the book of the Maccabees to a lengthy argument or a theme of the entire crusade sermon.[54]

In the *Sermo ad crucesignatos vel -signandos*, Jacques de Vitry attempted to raise enthusiasm for the crusade movement by referring to the Maccabees. In his model sermon Jacques asked where the kind of courage which the Maccabees

[48] Dunbabin, 'The Maccabees as Exemplars', esp. p. 32; Morton, 'The Defence of the Holy Land', esp. p. 278. The Vulgate Bible includes the first two books of the Maccabees out of the four.

[49] MacGregor, 'The Ministry of Gerold d'Avranches', esp. p. 236.

[50] In his famous book, the *Livre de chevalerie*, Geoffroi maintained that Judas was 'a splendid example' for all knights and the men-at-arms, 'whom one would like to resemble as closely as possible'. Geoffroi de Charny, *Livre de chevalerie*, ed. and trans. by Kaeuper and Kennedy, pp. 162–63: 'tres bon chevalier Judas Machabeus, [...] il fu fors, appers et penibles; il fu beaus entre touz autres et senz orgueil; il fu preux, hardis, vaillans et bien combatens [...]. comme c'est uns tres beaus exemplaires a toute chevalerie et a genz d'armes [...]. Et qui bien aviseroit et penseroit a la vie es biens et es bons faiz de ce bon saint chevalier dessus dit et que l'en vousist retraire et resembler le plus pres que l'en pourroit de sat res bonne vie et condicions, seurement pourroit l'en tenir et fermement que yceus qui ainsi voudroient leur vie et leurs estaz gouverner ne pourroient ne devroient faillir de venir a tres haute honnour de chevalerie'.

[51] Morton, 'The Defence of the Holy Land', p. 289.

[52] Guibert de Nogent, *Gesta Dei per Francos*, in *RHC Occ.*, IV, 138: 'Si Machabaeis olim ad maximam profuit pietatis laudem, quia pro cerimoniis et Templo pugnarunt: et vobis, o milites Christiani, legitime conceditur, ut armorum studio libertatem patriae defendatis'.

[53] *Corpus Inscriptionum Crucesignatorum Terrae Sanctae*, ed. by Sandoli, p. 57: 'REX BALDEWINVS: IVDAS ALTER MACHABEVS'.

[54] See also Jacques de Vitry's description of Baldwin de Bourgh and his kinsmen from France, who became soldiers of Christ and 'like another Maccabaeus' fought for God in the Holy Land and enlarged the limits of Christendom. Jacques de Vitry, *Historia*, ed. by Moschus, p. 61.

had shown in the past was to be found nowadays. Where was the zeal to serve God, the strength of the Maccabees, and where were the moans and anxieties of Mattathias?[55] By asking these questions Jacques implied that the Christians ought to find in themselves the pious qualities and the zeal that the Maccabees had once possessed, and suggested that they should defend the Holy Land with the same determination and devotion to God that the Maccabees had when they defended the land.

Guibert de Tournai also incorporated a reference to the Maccabees in his crusade sermon. Guibert recalled the victory that the Maccabees achieved over their enemy, the forces of Nicanor. He stressed that the Jews had fought for God and God had helped the Maccabaean warriors in difficult times. He linked the crusaders' struggle to the Maccabaean wars and maintained that the Christians' war was equally justified and that the crusaders too fought for God's sake.[56] Similar ideas, or ideas that went even further, had already been presented during the First Crusade. In his history of the First Crusade, Guibert de Nogent argued that if the Maccabees, who had fought for circumcision and over swine meat, were helped by God, how much more the Christians, who shed their blood for Christ's sake, purified the churches, and propagated the faith, deserved to be helped by God.[57]

Humbert de Romans referred to the Maccabaean warriors only once in his crusade model sermons. However, the importance of Maccabaean exemplars for Humbert becomes clear in his work *De predicatione sancte crucis*. In the manual for crusade preachers Humbert includes a list of biblical texts, *themata* well suited for crusade preaching. A high proportion of these texts — seventeen out of the total of 103 from the Old Testament — are from the books of Maccabees. Humbert also made repeated references to the Maccabees, particularly to Judas Maccabaeus, in his manual.[58]

---

[55] Jacques de Vitry, 'Sermo ad crucesignatos vel -signandos', *CPI*, p. 94.

[56] Guibert de Tournai, 'Ad crucesignatos et crucesignandos sermo primus', *CPI*, p. 182: '*Dato signo adiutorii Dei* commiserunt Iudei *cum Nichanore et maiorem partem exercitus eius vulneribus debilem factam fugere compulerunt*. Nota ergo quod Iudeis in arcto constitutis apparuit signum de celo, quo viso sese recollegerunt et hostes vicerunt, sicut faciunt milites, quando vident signum regis'. II Mcc. 8. 23–24.

[57] Guibert de Nogent, *Gesta Dei per Francos*, in *RHC Occ.*, IV, 206–07: 'Et si Machabaeis olim, pro circumcision et carne porcina pugnantibus, evidens apparuisse legitur coeleste suffragium, quanto amplius his debuit qui, pro repurgio ecclesiis adhibendo et statu fidei propaganda, fusi sanguinis Christo detulere servitium!'

[58] Humbert de Romans, *De predicatione sancte crucis*, cap. xxvii; see also, for example, cap. vi, xvi. Cole, 'Humbert of Romans and the Crusade', pp. 164–65.

Of the crusade preachers examined in this study, Eudes de Châteauroux made the most extensive utilization of the Maccabaean theme, using it in several of his sermons. Eudes opened the *Sermo de invitatione ad crucem* with a passage from II Maccabees. He reminded his audience of a dream that Judas Maccabaeus saw on the eve of the Israelite war against Nicanor. In the dream, Judas was urged to take the 'holy sword as a gift from God' and defeat the enemies of Israel. Again, Eudes compared the Old Testament war to the contemporary situation, when the Mongols posed a threat to the Christians, at the beginning of the 1260s.[59] Just as in biblical times, when Nicanor and the heathens attempted to destroy God's people, now the Mongols wanted to destroy the Christians.[60] This comparison made it clear where each side stood in the conflict: the Mongols were a representation of the ancient heathen enemy who were naturally the enemies of God and the enemies of Christians. God fought alongside the crusaders even as he had fought alongside the Israelites.

The sermon portrays Judas Maccabaeus as the ideal warrior. However, Eudes de Châteauroux does not represent Judas as a knight with outstanding martial skills or a man more handsome than others. These were not the characteristics that made Judas an ideal soldier from the crusade preachers' point of view. The focus of the sermon is on spiritual matters rather than the soldierly qualities of the Maccabaean warriors. According to Eudes, Judas Maccabaeus armed his soldiers not with material weapons, but with great words and knowledge of the celestial vision that he possessed. The shield and lance were dispensable, earthly instruments, while the golden sword, which the Lord gave to Judas in the dream, was a gift from God, a spiritual weapon parallel to the crusaders' cross.[61]

The example provided by Judas Maccabaeus helped Eudes de Châteauroux to explain to the crusaders how they should view their task as God's soldiers. Eudes's audience seems to have initially been composed mainly of members of the nobility, which is indicated by repeated positive remarks about them.[62] In the sermon, Eudes specifically states that God expects the nobles to lead his cru-

---

[59] Eudes de Châteauroux, 'Sermo de invitatione ad crucem', *CPI*, p. 144: '*Accipe sanctum gladium, munus a Deo, in quo deicies adversarios populi mei Israel*'. II Mcc. 15. 16. For the dating of the sermon, see Appendix V.

[60] Eudes de Châteauroux, 'Sermo de invitatione ad crucem', *CPI*, pp. 144–46.

[61] Eudes de Châteauroux, 'Sermo de invitatione ad crucem', *CPI*, p. 144: '*Singulos autem illorum armavit non clipeo et hasta et munitione sed sermonibus optimis et exhortationibus exposito digno fide sompnio per quos universos letificavit*'. II Mcc. 15. 11–16.

[62] Eudes de Châteauroux, 'Sermo de invitatione ad crucem', *CPI*, p. 146.

sading army, because they have proved themselves worthy of the task on previous occasions.[63] Eudes directs his messages to the nobles and argues that the cross is offered especially to the *milites* who, like 'noble birds', form the Lord's army.[64]

Judas was a fine example for the crusading nobles, as during the Middle Ages he was conceived to have been a noble knight. In the sermon, Eudes wanted to point out to the knights that in the service of God, spiritual matters counted. As crusaders the knights should not care too much about their numbers, their weapons, or knightly honours. They should regard the crusader's cross as the most important weapon in their armoury. This sign showed that the knights fought for God and God fought with them. As knights of God, the crusaders should be pious and have the same zeal for God as Judas Maccabaeus had had.

Common to all the accounts of the Maccabees in the crusade sermons is the effort to bring out the piety and the great fervour of faith which the Israelites had shown in their revolt against the pagan oppressors. This zeal is something that the Christians should imitate by taking the cross and carrying it with them on their expeditions. The crusade preachers wanted to underline that the crusades were spiritual campaigns, not wars like any other, but journeys made on behalf of God. In these campaigns the warriors should transform themselves from bloody men of war to pious men of God. The cruelties and the brutality of conventional war should be abandoned. God's war was fought with the zeal of faith, and their weapons were words and visions, the sign of the cross, and 'the golden sword'. Although the warriors were expected to shed blood and kill on the expeditions, they ought to do this out of devotion, piously and humbly, which would give them victory.

The leaders of the Maccabees, Mattathias and Judas, as well as Simon and Jonathan, had all been high priests of the Jews. This priestly office held by the leaders of the revolt made the Maccabaean exemplars even more apposite models for the crusaders. The leaders were religious men, unyielding in their religious beliefs, uncompromising in their rites, who held fast to their faith and fought justly with God on their side. The preachers demanded from those who had taken the cross a spiritual transformation: the crusaders were meant to become quasi-ecclesiastics, religious men.[65] Jacques de Vitry, for

[63] Eudes de Châteauroux, 'Sermo de invitatione ad crucem', *CPI*, p. 148: 'Et Dominus vult ut nobiles sint duces exercitus sui et quod ipsi liberent populum Christianum de manibus Tartarorum. [...] quia dominium semper remanebit penes nobiles'.

[64] Eudes de Châteauroux, 'Sermo de invitatione ad crucem', *CPI*, p. 146: 'Ipsi enim velut aves nobiles ad vocationem Domini veniunt, faciunt ei exercituum et equitationem'.

[65] *JVSP*, p. 82; Tyerman, *The Invention of the Crusades*, p. 20.

example, appears to have wanted to mould the crusaders into warriors akin to the brothers of the military orders, the monastic knights. While on a crusade, the men of war should be as firm in their faith as the high priests of the Maccabees had been. The crusaders should have the morale and devotion of religious men, just as they had many special privileges of the religious.

Like the examples of Joshua and Achor, the Maccabaean episode also provided a deterrent to disruptive behaviour. Eudes de Châteauroux utilized this example in his *Sermo de invitatione ad crucem* in an effort to convince his audience of knights to resist evil. During the thirteenth century, the crusade preachers had to account for an ever-increasing catalogue of crusading failures. The Christian position in the Holy Land had been steadily deteriorating for decades, and there had been major disappointments such as the loss of Edessa in 1144 and the fall of Jerusalem in 1187.[66] Eudes, perhaps more than any of the other crusade preachers, wrestled with the problem of crusading failure in his sermons.[67] Like Jacques de Vitry, he had personal experience of a failed crusade, and as the legate of the army was forced to explain the disaster to the survivors of the expedition. Four of his sermons from the Seventh Crusade deal with questions resulting from the failure in war.[68] Later, in 1266, Eudes contemplated further these issues in a sermon given after the fall of Safed.[69]

---

[66] Some territories were recovered during the Third Crusade of 1189–92 and the German crusade of 1197–98, but the situation remained difficult for the Latins of the East. See, for example, Tyerman, *God's War*, pp. 268–301, 354–74, 448–73, 492–93.

[67] Other preachers also dealt with crusading failures in their writings, but not as extensively as Eudes. Both Humbert de Romans and Guibert de Tournai wrote treatises for the Second Council of Lyons in 1274, where they addressed problems related to crusading. In particular, Humbert discussed the causes of crusading failures and contemporary criticism in his tract the *Opus tripartitum*. Humbert pointed out that some claimed that God did not want Christians to win, indicated by the many crusading failures. However, he refuted the claim by stating that the critics did not understand God at all and explained that the failures might just as well signal God's contentment with the efforts of the crusaders. Humbert de Romans, *Opusculum tripartitum*, XVII, ed. by Brown pp. 197–98.

[68] Eudes de Châteauroux, 'Sermo de sancto Georgio', *UEE*, II, 747–49; Eudes de Châteauroux, 'Sermo in anniversario Roberti comitis Attrabatensis et aliorum nobilium qui interfecti fuerunt a Sarracenis apud Mansuram in Egipto', *PCHL*, pp. 235–39; Eudes de Châteauroux, 'Sermo de eodem anniversario', *PCHL*, pp. 240–43; Eudes de Châteauroux, 'Sermo in festo sanctarum reliquiarum', *UEE*, II, 763–66.

[69] Eudes de Châteauroux gave a sermon in the papal curia after the news of the capture of Safed and the massacre of Christians there had reached the West in 1266. Eudes also opened this sermon with a quotation from the second book of the Maccabees. '*Adaperiat cor vestrum in lege sua et in preceptis suis et faciat pacem. Exaudiat orationes vestras et reconcilietur vobis nec*

The concerns of Eudes de Châteauroux, as well as many of the other crusade preachers, focused on the sins of the Christians and more specifically on the sins of the crusaders. The crusade preachers tried to explain in their sermons how the sinfulness of the participants in the crusade movement might have an effect on the success of the expeditions. In the *Sermo de invitatione ad crucem*, Eudes explained that the crusaders would win, in any event, when they went on crusades. He quoted further his opening passage from the book of the Maccabees: 'with which [the golden sword] you will defeat the opponents of Israel, my people'. Eudes expressed his hope that this passage might be taken literally. The crusaders could be victorious and defeat their enemies, as was promised. However, the victory might also be a spiritual one, since all the crusaders had renounced their sins and thus gained spiritual benefits. A barrier that prevented military victory and conquest was the sins of men. God was separated from people because of their sins. The crusaders would always win, if their sins did not become an obstacle.[70]

Eudes found a convenient example from II Maccabees to back up his argument. The Maccabaean warriors had suffered a defeat against their enemies during the revolt, and many were slain. When Judas Maccabaeus and his men came to collect the bodies of those who had died, they found out why God had forsaken them. Eudes quoted the relevant biblical passage in his sermon — 'Under the tunics of the dead they found offerings to idols' — and explained that this sin made it clear to everyone why they had lost.[71] The passage was cleverly chosen, for the sin of idolatry was strictly condemned during the Middle Ages. This was regarded as the worst of crimes, usually associated with the enemies of the crusaders, implicitly the Muslims.[72] In the sermon, Eudes went on to

---

vos deserat in tempore malo': Eudes de Châteauroux, 'Quando primo audita fuit captio Sapheti et trucidatio illorum qui ibi erant', Roma, AGOP, MS XIV, 34, fols 176va–178rb. II Mcc. 1. 4–5.

[70] Eudes de Châteauroux, 'Sermo de invitatione ad crucem', *CPI*, pp. 150–51: 'Per peccata enim separatur Deus ab hominibus et recedit ab eis'.

[71] Eudes de Châteauroux, 'Sermo de invitatione ad crucem', *CPI*, p. 150: '*Invenerunt sub tunicis interfectorum de donariis idolorum*, omnibus ergo manifestum est factum ob hanc causam eos coruisse'. II Mcc. 12. 40.

[72] Idolatry was considered as the worst crime of the human race by the early church fathers. In the Middle Ages Islam was also linked to this crime. See, for example, Tertullianus, *De Idololatria*, ed. by Reifferscheid and Wissowa, pp. 30–58; see also Van Der Nat, 'Observations on Tertullian's Treatise on Idolatry'. For Augustine of Hippo's views on idolatry, see Augustine's letter to Publicola, *Epistola XLVII*, in *PL*, XXXIII, cols 184–87. For the association of Islam with idolatry, see Tolan, *Saracens*, pp. xx, 105–06, 109, 119–20, 126; Bray, 'The Mohammetan and Idolatry'; Daniel, *Islam and the West*, pp. 309–13. See also Humbert de Romans, *De predicatione sancte crucis*, cap. ii.

urge both the current and the prospective crusaders to cast aside all their sins, so they might be victorious in battle and not suffer the fate of the idolatrous Maccabaean soldiers.[73]

Pope Innocent III also referred to Judas Maccabaeus and the idols found on the dead Maccabaean warriors in a letter instructing the barons of the Fourth Crusade to renounce all sins and to avoid the excommunicated Venetians as much as possible.[74] The Maccabaean idols guided the crusaders to obedience and to respect of the Christian law. The crusaders should not break the rules or commit sins, but they should always follow God's commandments, for, as God's soldiers, they needed to follow God's will. They needed to fight with God, for proceeding into the battle without him and with their sins on their conscience they would fail. Eudes explained this in his sermon by stating that, 'without you [God] we shall be able to do nothing'.[75]

From Patriarchs to Prostitutes

A wealth of biblical persons appear in the crusade model sermons. The figures could signify different things and carry different meanings in different sermons: for instance, to Philippe le Chancelier, the Virgin Mary was the embodiment of continence and temperance,[76] while for Jacques de Vitry, she was a figure in an exemplum of a vision in which she gave her son for everyone who took the cross.[77] The range of biblical persons varied from one end to the other. Prophets, patriarchs, and kings, such as Eliseus, Abraham, and Solomon, were often referred to, but killers and thieves, such as Cain and Achor, were also suitable figures to be incorporated into the crusade sermons.

The most frequently mentioned, besides the ones examined above, are Old Testament leaders Moses and David. Federico Visconti explained the sign of the crusader's cross with the typological identification of Moses and Christ, using this theme in both of his crusade sermons.[78] According to Federico, the crusaders

---

[73] Eudes de Châteauroux, 'Sermo de invitatione ad crucem', *CPI*, pp. 150–51: '*Abiciatis ergo, karissimi, peccata, vos qui crucem accipistis vel assumere intenditis!*' ɪɪ Mcc. 12. 39–40.

[74] Innocentius III, *Regestorum sive epistolarum*, CII, in *PL*, CCXV, col. 108.

[75] Eudes de Châteauroux, 'Sermo de invitatione ad crucem', *CPI*, p. 150: '*Ait Moyses: Si non tu ipse precedis, ut educas nos de loco isto*, quasi dicat: Sine te nichil poterimus facere'. Ex. 33. 15.

[76] Philippe le Chancelier, 'Sermo de eodem, de gaudio quod rex et principes assumpserunt crucem', Avranches, MS 132, fols 252ʳᵇ–252ᵛᵃ.

[77] Jacques de Vitry, 'Sermo ad crucesignatos vel -signandos', *CPI*, p. 98.

[78] Federico Visconti made use of the biblical story where the Israelites fought against

signed with the cross would overcome their enemies, the Tartars (the Mongols), as well as other barbarous nations, just as Moses overcame the Amalekites with his hands raised in the form of the cross.[79] Philippe le Chancelier also utilized the image of Moses with raised hands in his crusade sermon against the Albigensians, as did Humbert de Romans in his crusade manual.[80]

Moses is represented in the crusade sermons as a spiritual leader whose wisdom could be imitated, whose advice — given to the Israelites during their journey to the Promised Land — could prove useful to the crusaders on their journey,[81] as a prefiguration of Christ,[82] or as a model whose piety and deeds the supporters of the crusade movement could follow.[83] David is utilized in a

---

the Amalekites. During the struggle, Moses went to a hilltop to pray and lifted up his hands. Whenever Moses lowered his hands, the Israelites began to lose the battle, but as he lifted his hands and held them up, the Israelites began to win. This was interpreted as a prefiguration of Christ on the cross. Federico Visconti, 'Quando idem dominus predicavit crucem litteraliter clero pisano de mandato domini Pape', *SVP*, p. 548: 'Hinc Moyse orante in monte, extensis brachiis et manibus in formam crucis, vincebat populus Dei, [...] quia et Christo orante expansis in cruce manibus superavit populus christanus'. Ex. 17. 8–13. The preachers often utilized the typological interpretation of the Bible in their sermons, drawing parallels between persons or events of the Old Testament and the persons of the New Testament, or comparisons to contemporary persons and events. Roger of Salisbury, for example, made a typological identification between Eliseus and Christ in his crusade sermon.

[79] Federico Visconti, 'Quando idem dominus predicavit [crucem] respondendo nuntiis Tartarorum in clero pisano', *SVP*, p. 554: 'orent cum Moyse in monte, [...] quod Deus dirigat Israel, idest christianos videntes nunc Deum per fidem, tandem in future per speciem, et vincatur Amalech, idest Tartari et barbarice gentes, quia *si quis cultor est Dei, hunc exaudit Deus*'. Ex. 17. 10–12, John. 9. 31.

[80] Philippe le Chancelier, 'Sermo scolaribus inter Epiphaniam et Purificationem', Avranches, MS 132, fol. 249ra: 'sic enim vincebant filii Israel cum Moyses orabat et alii pugnabant et sicut de Moyse dicitur [...] quod levabat manus in oratione'. Ex. 17. 11. Transcribed by Maier and Bériou; Humbert de Romans, *De predicatione sancte crucis*, cap. iii. Guibert de Tournai also used the story in his *Collectio de scandalis ecclesiae*, ed. by Stroick, p. 40.

[81] Eudes de Châteauroux, 'Sermo de invitatione ad crucem', *CPI*, p. 150; Eudes de Châteauroux, 'De sancto Georgio', *UEE*, ii, 702; Eudes de Châteauroux, 'Sermo in festo sanctarum reliquiarum', *UEE*, ii, 763.

[82] Federico Visconti, 'Quando idem dominus predicavit crucem litteraliter clero pisano de mandato domini Pape', *SVP*, p. 548; Federico Visconti, 'Quando idem dominus predicavit [crucem] respondendo nuntiis Tartarorum in clero pisano', *SVP*, p. 554; Philippe le Chancelier, 'Sermo scolaribus inter Epiphaniam et Purificationem', Avranches, MS 132, fol. 249ra, fol. 249vb.

[83] Philippe le Chancelier, 'Sermo de eodem, quomodo apparuit potentia Dei', Avranches, MS 132, fols 250vb–251ra; Philippe le Chancelier, '*Dicit Dominus ad Moysen*', Avranches, MS 132, fols 272rb–272va.

similar manner in the sermons. Humbert de Romans viewed David as a king who rose up against the evildoers, and maintained that 'our David', the crusaders' David, was Christ.[84] The crusaders themselves could also be compared to David. After the defeats of Mansurah and Fariskur, Eudes de Châteauroux paralleled King Louis IX with King David. David had mourned for the deaths of Saul and Jonathan just as Louis mourned for the deaths of the crusaders. He also drew a more general comparison between David and the French kings who, like the biblical king, had piously fought for the Church.[85] David's victory over Goliath could also be compared to the victory on the cross.[86]

The piety and the prayers of both Moses and David could be imitated by the supporters of the crusade movement. Philippe le Chancelier underlined this in one of his crusade model sermons intended for the scholars who were to help the crusade army fighting against the Albigensians from the home front.[87] Philippe argued that 'a prayer was a defence against all inconveniences' and that the scholars should pray in imitation of David and Moses and follow the example provided in their prayers. David's prayers in particular were to be replicated, for David was attacked by the tyrant Saul and his own son, Absalom, just as the Church was attacked by external and internal enemies, foreign nations and the Albigensian heretics respectively.[88] David also set an example of the right

[84] Humbert de Romans, 'In predicatione crucis contra hereticos', *CPI*, p. 226: 'Quis consurget michi adversus malignantes aut quis stabit mecum adversus operantes iniquitatem? Et nota quod istud olim dictum a David rege modo dicitur a nostro David Ihesu Christo'.

[85] Eudes de Châteauroux, 'Sermo in anniversario Roberti comitis Attrabatensis et aliorum nobilium qui interfecti fuerunt a Sarracenis apud Mansuram in Egipto', *PCHL*, p. 235: 'Legitur quod David audita morte regis Saul et Ionathe filii eius et aliorum nobilium qui cum eis interfecti fuerunt [...]. Sicut causam plangendi habuit David et filii Iuda propter predictum casum et nos specialiter de regno Francie cuius reges consueverunt pii esse sicut David, et debellare inimicos ecclesie sicut David Goliam debellavit et multos alios'. II Reg. 1. 17–18.

[86] Federico Visconti, 'Quando idem dominus predicavit crucem litteraliter clero pisano de mandato domini Pape', *SVP*, p. 550.

[87] Philippe used the example of five Psalms that are described as prayers, three of which are entitled prayers of David and one as a prayer of Moses. Philippe le Chancelier, 'Sermo de eodem, quomodo apparuit potentia Dei', Avranches, MS 132, fols 250vb–251ra. Ps. 16. 1, 85. 1, 89. 1, 141. 1. One of the five Psalms is entitled 'the prayer of the poor man'. Ps. 101. 1.

[88] Philippe le Chancelier, 'Sermo de eodem, quomodo apparuit potentia Dei', Avranches, MS 132, fols 250vb–251ra: 'oratio enim est defensio contra omnia incommoda quedam autem sunt [...]. Alia sunt que sustinemus vel ab extraneis vel a domesticis, et quia David sustinuit infestacionem a Saul, extraneo inimico suo, et a filio uteri sui. Ideo duplex psalmus sic intitulatur: *Oratio David, Oratio David*. Orandum est igitur nobis, quia carnis sustinemus insultus, quia angustias patimur matris, quia dolendum de peccatis aliorum, quia a gentibus ut extraneis mater

attitude and state of devotion for those praying and assisting the crusade from afar. He should be emulated in his meekness, mercifulness, faithfulness, and humility, as well as Moses, who was 'the meekest of all men'.[89]

Moses's brother Aaron is also mentioned in many of the crusade sermons. Both Moses and Aaron were suitable models, particularly for the crusading clergy. Moses was the spiritual leader of the Israelites during their journey from Egypt, and Aaron was a priest. Philippe le Chancelier utilized both of these biblical figures extensively in crusade sermons intended for a clerical audience.[90] Eudes de Châteauroux also built one of his sermons on the figures of Moses and Aaron. This sermon was preached for the feast of the Holy Relics, possibly in the Holy Land in 1251.[91] In the sermon, Eudes drew a typological comparison between Aaron and the pope, as well as other ecclesiastics. He maintained that the ecclesiastics, the pope, the patriarchs, and the archbishops always had to remember the Passion of Christ.[92] This was their duty, and as pastors of their flock they also needed to urge Christians to remember the Passion.

The sermon for the feast of the Holy Relics was preached after the crusading catastrophe in Egypt and dealt with difficult questions caused by the defeat, as do all of Eudes de Châteauroux's sermons from this crusade preached after the defeat of Mansurah in 1250. Eudes's intention was to remind the Christians of

---

ecclesia infestatur et ab hereticis ut propinquis'. Transcribed by Maier and Bériou.

[89] Philippe le Chancelier, 'Sermo de eodem, quomodo apparuit potentia Dei', Avranches, MS 132, fol. 251ra: 'Et attende, quod omnes quinque psalmi intitulantur: a David et a Moyse, quia uterque prevaluit in tribus virtutibus, que competunt orationi, scilicet fidelitas, mansuetudo, humilitas. De David dicitur in Ysa. lv: *Misericordia David fidelis*, et in Psalmo: *Memento Domine David et omnis mansuetudinis eius*. De Moyse dicitur, Numeri xii, quod erat *mitissimus inter omnes homines*'. Isa. 55. 3, Ps. 131. 1, Num. 12. 3. Transcribed by Maier and Bériou.

[90] Philippe le Chancelier, 'Sermo scolaribus inter Epiphaniam et Purificationem', Avranches, MS 132, fol. 249vb. In the sermon, Philippe explained that Aaron signified 'fasting or abstinence': 'Aaron sacerdos, qui immolat victimas, recte significat ieiunium sive abstinenciam, per quam Deo immolamur'. Transcribed by Maier and Bériou. Philippe also opened one his crusade sermons with a biblical passage: '*Dicit Dominus ad Moysen: Dic Aaron: Tolle virgam tuam et extende manum super aquas Egypti et super fluvios et rivos et super paludes et omnes lacus ut vertantur in sanguinem, et sit cruor in universa terra Egypti, tam in ligneis vasis quam in saxeis*'. Philippe le Chancelier, '*Dicit Dominus ad Moysen*', Avranches, MS 132, fol. 272rb. Ex. 7. 19–20.

[91] See Appendix V.

[92] Eudes de Châteauroux, 'Sermo in festo sanctarum reliquiarum', *UEE*, II, 763: 'Sed quare preceptum fuit hoc Aaron, qui erat summus sacerdos? Quia et si omnes Christiani memores esse debeant passionis dominice, maxime sacerdotes et tanto magis quanto maiori gradu potiuntur. Unde et Dominus papa, patriarche et archiepiscopi crucem deferunt ante se ut semper habeant pre oculis Dominum suspensum in cruce'.

the love of God, of the fact that Christ had suffered for all of them and his sufferings were not fruitless. This was to encourage those who were downcast after
the defeat, those who felt that God had deserted them. Eudes wanted them to
recall what was important, what they needed to remember in the face of adversity. The crusaders had to keep their faith and continue on the chosen path.
They would gain their reward for all the pain they had suffered.[93]

Many of the biblical figures mentioned in the crusade sermons, when utilized as behavioural models for the 'true' crusaders, were actually additional
examples of the model provided by the figure of Christ. St Paul was a good
example for the crusaders, because he had succeeded in imitating Christ and
following him with perfection.[94] As prefigurations of Christ, Moses and David
had the same qualities: humility, gentleness, and fidelity. They were linked to
self-sacrifice, suffering, salvation, and victory. The love of Christ surfaced in
a variety of the biblical figures mentioned in the sermons as something that
guided and protected the crusaders on their journey, and the crusaders should
try to imitate and express this love towards fellow men and God.[95]

On the other hand, some of the biblical figures were associated with vices and
were used by the preachers to explain the consequences of sin to the crusaders.
These included notorious scriptural persons such as Eve, Amalek, and Judas, who
were examples of how not to behave. Christians should join the crusade movement and be signed with the sign of God; sinners, who followed the example of
Cain, would be signed with the sign of the devil.[96] The utilization of these infamous biblical persons depended on what the preacher wanted to convey to the
audience. Some stories and some figures were utilized by all crusade preachers in
a uniform manner. The prostitute Rahab, for example, was a positive model in
all the sermons which mention her. Rahab appears as an example of a penitent
saving herself with the scarlet string during the conquest of Jericho, just as the
crusaders saved themselves with the sign of the cross by going on a crusade. This
story underlined the protective and saving powers of the crusaders' cross.[97]

---

[93] Eudes de Châteauroux, 'Sermo in festo sanctarum reliquiarum', *UEE*, ii, 763–66.

[94] Eudes de Châteauroux, 'Sermo in conversione sancti Pauli et exhortatio ad assumendam crucem', *CPI*, p. 138.

[95] See, for example, Eudes de Châteauroux, 'Sermo in conversione sancti Pauli et exhortatio ad assumendam crucem', *CPI*, p. 130; Eudes de Châteauroux, 'Sermo ad invitandum ad accipi-endum crucem et ad confortandum crucesignatos', *CPI*, pp. 152, 154; Guibert de Tournai, 'Ad crucesignatos et crucesignandos sermo primus', *CPI*, p. 180.

[96] Guibert de Tournai, 'Ad crucesignatos et crucesignandos sermo secundus', *CPI*, p. 196.

[97] Jacques de Vitry, 'Item sermo ad crucesignatos vel -signandos', *CPI*, p. 102: 'Orate igitur

Biblical Figures versus Crusading Heroes

Humbert de Romans mentioned in his crusade preaching manual a good number of biblical persons and stories with which crusade preachers could promote
expeditions or explain crusading. The bulk of biblical themes in Humbert's
list are from the Old Testament: out of the 142 *themata* suitable for crusade
sermons, 103 are from the Old Testament, while only 39 are from the New
Testament.[98] There is variation in the use of biblical citations according to the
taste of individual authors. Eudes de Châteauroux, for example, was keen to use
Old Testament stories, while Roger of Salisbury used more New Testament citations in his crusade model sermon than Old Testament, like Federico Visconti
in his two crusade sermons.[99]

Humbert explained in the preaching manual how the biblical figures
should be utilized in crusade preaching. The preachers using the manual could
emphasize the magnitude of the biblical person in question, or his exemplary
actions: persons such as Christ or actions of Eleazar Maccabaeus who gave an
example of 'fortitude to young men'. Or, crusade preachers could emphasize
the biblical message of the story, for example, suffering evil patiently or labouring for God.[100]

In the crusade model sermons, biblical persons are much more common models for the crusaders than crusading heroes of the past. Eudes de

Dominum, ut hodie crucis Christi funiculo de cavernis suis peccatores foras educantur. Hic est
enim funis coccineus per quem Raab liberata est aliis pereuntibus; sicut hiis diebus pereuntibus
duris et obstinatis alii funiculo crucis ad Christum trahuntur'. Guibert de Tournai, 'Ad crucesignatos et crucesignandos sermo primus', *CPI*, p. 188; Eudes de Châteauroux, 'Sermo de rebellione Sarracenorum Lucherie', *CR*, p. 379; Philippe le Chancelier, '*Dicit Dominus ad Moysen*',
Avranches, MS 132, fol. 273ᵛᵃ. Rahab was saved along with all her kin and possessions during the
conquest of Jericho, for she had helped the Israelites. Her house was left unharmed, and it was
recognized from the scarlet cord hanging in the window. Jos. 2. 21, 6. 23, 25.

[98] Humbert de Romans, *De predicatione sancte crucis*, cap. xxvii; Cole, 'Humbert of Romans
and the Crusade', p. 164.

[99] Roger of Salisbury cited the New Testament twenty-two times in his crusade sermon and
the Old Testament fourteen times. Roger of Salisbury, '*Ascendente* Ihesu *in naviculam*, et cetera',
PCHL, pp. 227–31; Federico Visconti cited the New Testament fifty-two and the Old Testament
twenty-four times in his first crusade sermon. In his second sermon the New Testament was
cited six and the Old Testament five times. Federico Visconti, 'Quando idem dominus predicavit crucem litteraliter clero pisano de mandato domini Pape', *SVP*, pp. 543–51; Federico
Visconti, 'Quando idem dominus predicavit [crucem] respondendo nuntiis Tartarorum in clero
pisano', *SVP*, pp. 551–55. See also the biblical index provided by Maier in *CPI*, pp. 272–77.

[100] Humbert de Romans, *De predicatione sancte crucis*, cap. xvi. ii Mcc. 6. 28; Jac. 5. 10.

Châteauroux makes a reference to 'the ancient nobles of the kingdom of Francia' who went on the First Crusade, suspecting that God would compare and equate them with the crusaders of the Seventh Crusade.[101] Humbert de Romans also referred in his sermon to the example provided by the crusaders who had gone before to the Holy Land. According to Humbert, this was one of the reasons why people should join the crusades against the Saracens.[102] However, other preachers made little use of the heroes of the First or subsequent crusades, and without the information provided by the two preaching manuals one could easily make the assumption that earlier crusaders were insignificant figures for the crusade preachers.

In the crusade preaching manuals, crusading heroes of the past are mentioned as examples which the future crusaders could imitate. In the manual *Brevis ordinacio de predicacione sancte crucis*, the heroes of the First Crusade are mentioned by name, and Jacques d'Avesnes, a participant of the Third Crusade, is presented as a model which others could emulate.[103] Stories from the recent historical past, 'real-life' examples, are also incorporated into the final part of the *Brevis ordinacio*. These include short accounts of different expeditions, such as the Battle of Hattin, the Albigensian Crusade, and the Fourth Crusade, and descriptions of famous crusaders, such as Enguerrand de Boves and Hugh of Beauchamp.[104] In this last section of the manual, there are also short 'punch lines' in French, which suggest that the intended audience of the manual was mainly the members of the English aristocracy, who understood French.[105]

---

[101] Eudes de Châteauroux, 'Ad invitandum ad accipiendum crucem et ad confortandum crucesignatos', *UEE*, ii, 734: 'Sic potest dici de hiis qui modo iter arripiunt transmarinum. Comparabit eos Dominus et equabit illos antiquis nobilibus qui de regno Francie exeuntes Anthyochiam et terram Iherosolimitanam acquisierunt'.

[102] Humbert de Romans, 'In predicatione crucis contra Sarracenos', *CPI*, p. 228.

[103] 'Brevis ordinacio de predicacione', *QBSS*, p. 20. Jacques de Vitry also praised the first crusaders and mentioned some of their names and heroic deeds, as well as the heroes of the Third Crusade, presenting them as examples for the prospective crusaders in his crusading history, the *Historia orientalis*. Jacques de Vitry, *Historia orientalis*, XVI, XVII, XVIII, XIX, XX, XXI, CII, ed. by Donnadieu, pp. 164–254, p. 458.

[104] 'Brevis ordinacio de predicacione', *QBSS*, pp. 18–26.

[105] Tyerman, 'Who Went on Crusades to the Holy Land?', p. 15. Christopher Tyerman has noted that the manual was 'designed' for a wealthy, aristocratic audience. It is worth noting, however, that after the Norman conquest of England, French was a common language often used in legal transactions, as well as in the schools and the universities of England, and during the thirteenth century it was a language which the wealthy burghers and other townspeople, who wished to upgrade their social status, learnt and understood. Also, the languages used in

Humbert de Romans also urged the crusade preachers using his manual to utilize the example provided by famous crusaders in their sermons. Humbert suggested that the preachers could inspire people to take the cross by noting how the deeds of the past crusaders are remembered and depicted on the walls of nobles' palaces. The preachers could also recall the deeds of Charlemagne and Godfrey of Bouillon, or the example of the kings of France and England, Philip II Augustus and Richard I, and Emperor Frederick I, who had all taken the cross.[106] Humbert may have mentioned all of the three leaders of the Third Crusade deliberately and with consideration, even though Frederick I died before reaching the Holy Land. The crusade preachers utilizing the manual could choose only one of the leaders, if they so wished and the circumstances required it. For the French crusaders Philip II Augustus's deeds could be remembered, for the German the deeds of Frederick Barbarossa, and for the English the deeds of Richard I. Charlemagne and Godfrey of Bouillon, on the other hand, were distinguished figures whose noble deeds, piety, and service as soldiers of Christ were recognized throughout Western Christendom.[107]

Humbert's manual lists renowned crusaders and famous Christian leaders such as Constantine so that the crusade preachers could also combat criticism of the crusade movement and the allegations made by the 'anti'-crusaders, who claimed that the repeated failure of the expeditions showed that they were not the will of God. In their sermons the preachers could present multiple examples of past expeditions that had been extremely successful. Crusade preachers could utilize anecdotes from the First Crusade, mention the recapture of Acre during the Third Crusade, describe the victorious wars waged under the banner of the cross, or remind their audience that many Christians had won the crown of martyrdom by fighting for God.[108] Humbert also praised the preaching of Peter the Hermit and Urban II in his manual, representing these as zeal-

---

the *Brevis ordinacio*, or the languages in the crusade model sermons, do not necessarily mean that these were the languages in which the preaching was actually carried out. It was important that those who utilized the manual or the model sermons could understand the language, and for this reason Latin was usually employed. The information in the models could be translated in the actual sermons. For the use of French, or Anglo-Norman, in medieval England, see, for example, Trotter, *Multilingualism in Later Medieval Britain*.

[106] Humbert de Romans, *De predicatione sancte crucis*, cap. xvi.

[107] Certain noble and royal figures, particularly the heroes of the First Crusade such as Godfrey of Bouillon, were recognized and idealized crusaders in medieval accounts. Folda, *Crusader Art in the Holy Land*, p. 53. For Charlemagne, see below, pp. 102–08.

[108] Humbert de Romans, *De predicatione sancte crucis*, cap. xvi, x, xxvi, xxx, xxxvi, xxxvij; Humbert de Romans, *Opusculum tripartitum*, cap. xii, xvii, ed. by Brown, pp. 192–93, 197–98.

ous men who had voiced the will of God and signed an enormous amount of people with the cross.[109] Both Peter and Urban could serve as examples for the crusade preachers themselves of how the preaching of the cross could be carried out effectively.

Certain near-contemporary crusaders may have also seemed dangerously flawed for some of the crusade preachers, making them poor models. Richard I of England, for example, was a famous crusader, but he was criticized heavily by his contemporaries as well as by later generations for his taste for adventure, his desire to test his own prowess, and his lack of commitment to the recovery of Jerusalem.[110] Jacques de Vitry gave a conflicted picture of Richard in his *Historia orientalis*: on the one hand, Richard had crusading success and was recognized for this, but on the other hand, he was subject to the faults of pride and envy and constantly bickered with the French king.[111]

The authors of the model sermons may have wanted to avoid mentioning some of the famous crusaders of the past by name in their model sermons so as to avoid any possible controversy. This, added to the fact that biblical stories and biblical figures have traditionally provided the source material for sermons, nowadays as in the Middle Ages, explains the preference for these models rather than near contemporary ones. Nonetheless, it is likely that the crusade preachers would have followed the advice given by Humbert de Romans and made use of famous crusaders in their sermons when the circumstances favoured this. If the preachers, for example, were preaching the cross to noble crusaders whose family had a well-known tradition of going on crusades, or were preaching the cross in the palaces, where the deeds of earlier crusaders were portrayed on the walls, they would have made the most of these conditions.

Biblical Prophecy

The biblical past provided a historical background for the crusades. The authors of the model sermons could draw comparisons with the ancient wars fought by the Israelites or moral lessons from the teachings of the patriarchs or Christ. Biblical prophesies provided a view to the future, which was equally important.

---

[109] Humbert de Romans, *De predicatione sancte crucis*, cap. x, xxxix.

[110] Markowski, 'Richard Lionheart'.

[111] Jacques de Vitry, *Historia orientalis*, XCIX, ed. by Donnadieu, p. 444, CI, pp. 454, 456: 'Venantes enim propriam gloriam et que sua sunt, non que Iesu Christi querentes, invicem detrahendo et invidendo, letificaverunt inimicos suos, magnam autem christianorum populo confusionem induxerunt'.

Scriptural prophesies were utilized by the crusade ideologists and propagandists from the beginning of crusading. The crusaders were seen as agents of God who worked against the devil or fought the Antichrist, whose advent was predicted in the Bible. The crusaders regarded the two cities described in many of the prophesies — the heavenly and the earthly Jerusalems — as their main destinations.[112]

The concurrent journey of the crusaders towards the two cities also converged in medieval apocalyptic visions. The visions of the end had some variation in different crusading campaigns and at different times. In many versions the crusaders' pilgrimage to Jerusalem meant the unification of the two cities: by liberating the earthly Jerusalem the crusaders fulfilled ancient prophesies and helped to transform the earthly city into the heavenly one, a millennial kingdom of Christ or his representatives. The leaders of the First Crusade, for example, asked Pope Urban II, in a letter sent from Antioch in 1098, to come and join the expedition so as to expedite its completion, for by attending the pope would 'open the gates of both Jerusalems, liberate the Lord's sepulchre, and further exalt the Christian name above every other'.[113]

According to many apocalyptic traditions, before the final battle between the forces of Antichrist and Christ, Jerusalem would be ruled by Christians. The authors of the crusade model sermons utilized these traditions and employed different kinds of prophetic writings in their sermons. The figure of the Antichrist was linked to the crusaders' enemies. Guibert de Tournai stated in his crusade sermon that the enemies of the crusaders were marked with 'the dragon of cupidity and the eagle of ambition', which were 'the signs of the Romans', 'the Antichrist and the beast in the Apocalypse'. These were the symbols, with which 'the soldiers of the devil are signed'.[114] In his crusade preaching

---

[112] See, for example, Morris, *Sepulchre of Christ and the Medieval West*, p. 276.

[113] The letter, sent by Bohemond of Taranto, Raymond of Toulouse, Godfrey of Bouillon, Robert of Normandy, Robert of Flanders, and Eustace of Boulogne, is edited by Hagenmeyer, *Kreuzzugsbriefe*, no. XVI, pp. 161–65, esp. p. 164: 'et portas etiam utriusque Hierusalem nobis aperies et Sepulcrum Domini liberum atque Christianum nomen super omne nomen exaltatum facias'. For apocalyptical elements in crusade ideology, see Delaruelle, *L'Idée de croisade au moyen âge*. For the meaning and construction of Antichrist, see Hughes, *Constructing Antichrist*. For the one-thousand-year reign, see Apc. 20. 4–6.

[114] Guibert de Tournai, 'Ad crucesignatos et crucesignandos sermo primus', *CPI*, pp. 182–84: 'Hoc autem est signum regis Ierusalem, ad litteram scilicet crux rubea in albo panno, Christi scilicet passio in corde mundo, non draco cupiditatis vel aquila ambitionis, que sunt signa Romanorum, immo signantur milites dyaboli, verius antichristi et bestie in Apo'.

manual, Humbert de Romans described the Saracens as the 'many Antichrists', which were predicted in the Bible to come at the last hour.[115]

The successive cardinals of Tusculum, Jacques de Vitry and Eudes de Châteauroux, were particularly well acquainted with prophetical works in the crusading context. Both participated in crusades or in the promotion of crusades, where prophecies, apocryphal texts, and revelations pervaded the mood. During the Fifth Crusade, in the spring of 1221, apocalyptic hopes took hold of the crusaders stationed in Egypt. The crusaders, among them Jacques de Vitry, were trapped inside Damietta, unable to decide whether to go on the offensive, wait for the reinforcements, or accept the truce offered by the sultan al-Kamil. During this difficult period, they found several prophetical writings in the captured city, which were studied and quickly translated from Arabic into Latin.[116]

Jacques de Vitry wrote a letter to Honorius III informing the pope of the recently discovered texts and discussing them at length. Jacques also provided excerpts and details of the texts in the letter. The texts included a book entitled *Revelationes beati Petri apostoli a discipulo eius Clemente*, and *excerpta de historia gestorum David regis Indorum, qui presbyter Iohannes a vulgo appellatur*, as well as an unnamed book written by 'a certain astrologer, whom the Saracens regard a great prophet'.[117] The prophetic writings circulated in the camp during the Fifth Crusade, and the papal legate Pelagius had one of the texts read out aloud to the army.[118] The prophecies predicted the destruction of the law of the Saracens: 'as it [Islam] had begun by the sword, so it would perish by the sword'.[119]

These prophesies should not be viewed too cynically by modern readers, even though some of the texts or passages of the texts were clearly written shortly before their 'discovery'. The writings were not mere tools of manipulation by the leaders of the army. The leaders certainly used the texts, some ancient and

---

[115] Humbert de Romans, *De predicatione sancte crucis*, cap. xxvii: 'Et sicut audivistis quia cum Christo veniet nunc ante antiChristi facti sunt multi scilicet saraceni'. 1 John 2. 18.

[116] Jacques de Vitry, *Epistola*, VII, ed. by Huygens, pp. 134–53.

[117] Jacques de Vitry, *Epistola*, VII, ed. by Huygens, p. 150: 'Hunc autem quidam eorum astrologus, quem prophetam magnum Sarraceni reputant'.

[118] The crusaders' taking of Damietta, 'the city surrounded by waters', was also foretold in the texts. In one of the prophecies that has survived from the crusade, the *Prophetia filii Agap*, even the legate Pelagius seems to have been accurately described as 'a man lean of face and tall in stature'. 'Prophetia filii Agap', *QBSS*, p. 218: 'Et ducet eos quidam vir macer vultu, statura prolixus, ad cuius imperium omnes stabunt'.

[119] Jacques de Vitry, *Epistola*, VII, ed. by Huygens, p. 151: 'Predixit autem inter alia multa quanto tempore lex eorum permanere deberet et que sicut gladio inceperat, ita gladio peritura erat'.

others more recent, but the prophesies were in a sense part of the natural and typical language of the crusades. Crusade ideologists and propagandists continually resorted to prophetical visions and to scriptural and apocryphal predictions when they explained the premises and the goals of the movement to the crusaders.[120] The crusade movement was born in this ambience. Both the leaders and the common crusaders were attuned to hearing divine messages about their future. Jacques de Vitry investigated the prophetical writings himself during the Fifth Crusade and was convinced that these were genuine. Jacques was also very enthusiastic about the predictions and made use of prophesies in his own writings, the crusade sermons and the historical works.[121]

The Angel of Revelation

One of the most popular prophetic quotations used in the crusade model sermons was from Revelation 7. 2: 'I saw an angel from the sunrise, carrying the sign of the living God'. This verse was used by Jacques de Vitry, Eudes de Châteauroux, and Guibert de Tournai.[122] The prophecy was utilized in varying ways by the three preachers: Guibert structured his sermon with a distinction from the term 'saint', which he developed with the help of the biblical quotation; Jacques divided the principal theme into two parts, which he discussed further with short additional quotations from the Bible; Eudes used the initial verse, which he associated to a distinction of the term 'cross', and divided this distinction into four main parts.[123]

Each author linked the prophecy to the sign of the cross and the Passion of Christ. The sign of the living God, carried by the angel, corresponded in their interpretation to the cross of Christ. This sign of the living God was the same sign with which the crusade preachers marked the crusaders. God had first signed Christ with the sign when he was crucified, so that he could save mankind and be the first to carry the banner of the cross.[124] Guibert de Tournai

---

[120] Powell, *Anatomy of a Crusade*, pp. 178–79.

[121] Jacques de Vitry, *Epistola*, VII, ed. by Huygens, pp. 150–53.

[122] Jacques de Vitry, 'Sermo ad crucesignatos vel -signandos', *CPI*, p. 82; Eudes de Châteauroux, 'Sermo ad invitandum ad crucem', *CPI*, p. 166; Guibert de Tournai 'Ad crucesignatos et crucesignandos sermo primus', *CPI*, p. 176.

[123] Jacques de Vitry, 'Sermo ad crucesignatos vel -signandos', *CPI*, pp. 82–88; Eudes de Châteauroux, 'Sermo ad invitandum ad crucem', *CPI*, pp. 166–74; Guibert de Tournai 'Ad crucesignatos et crucesignandos sermo primus', *CPI*, pp. 176–79.

[124] Jacques de Vitry, 'Sermo ad crucesignatos vel -signandos', *CPI*, pp. 82–88; Eudes de

explained in his sermon that the sign of the cross was correctly called a sign, since it signified many different things: it was a sign of direction, which guided the Christians at the crossroads of life; it was a sign of distinction with which the soldiers of Christ were signed in battle; it was a sign of victory, with which the crusaders defeated their enemies; it was a sign of recollection, which helped Christians to remember the Passion of Christ; and it was a sign of reward, with which the crusaders entered paradise.[125]

The authors each interpreted the quotation from Revelation according to their own view, placing slightly different meaning or emphasis on different parts of the passage in their sermons. The 'sunrise' was construed to mean the Holy Virgin by Eudes de Châteauroux, for 'the sun is born in the sunrise' and 'the sun of truth and justice', that is, Christ, was born from the Virgin.[126] Jacques de Vitry also connected the 'sunrise' to Christ, but explained that just as the sun slowly rises at dawn, so too Christ slowly enlightens the world.[127] Guibert de Tournai linked the term 'sunrise' to the term 'saint' and interpreted both terms in the context of a saint's life. According to Guibert, the 'sunrise' meant the virtues of the saint 'growing into perfection'.[128]

The identification of the angel mentioned in the biblical passage, the sixth angel of Revelation, was a matter of some debate during the thirteenth century. Both Jacques de Vitry and Eudes de Châteauroux connected the angel to Christ in their crusade sermons, which was the conventional interpretation. However, the meaning and the character of the angel intrigued many, particularly the followers of the Calabrian Abbot Joachim of Fiore and the so-called spiritual Franciscans. Joachim of Fiore had first identified the sixth angel of Revelation as a spiritual leader in his influential book, the *Liber Concordiae*. According to Joachim, 'a new leader' would ascend from 'Babylon', which in this case meant Rome. Joachim identified the angel of Revelation as 'a universal pontiff of the New Jerusalem', which was a clear reference to a pope in Rome.[129]

Châteauroux, 'Sermo ad invitandum ad crucem', *CPI*, pp. 166–74; Guibert de Tournai 'Ad crucesignatos et crucesignandos sermo primus', *CPI*, pp. 176–79.

[125] Guibert de Tournai 'Ad crucesignatos et crucesignandos sermo primus', *CPI*, pp. 180–86.

[126] Eudes de Châteauroux, 'Sermo ad invitandum ad crucem', *CPI*, p. 168.

[127] Jacques de Vitry, 'Sermo ad crucesignatos vel -signandos', *CPI*, p. 86.

[128] Guibert de Tournai 'Ad crucesignatos et crucesignandos sermo primus', *CPI*, p. 178.

[129] Joachim of Fiore, *Liber Concordiae novi ac veteris Testamenti*, bk. IV, pt. 1, ch. 45, p. 402: 'ascendet quasi novus dux de Babilone, universalis scilicet pontifex nove Ierusalem, hoc est sancte matris ecclesie; in cuius typo scriptum est in Apocalipsi: "Vidi angelum ascendentem ab ortu solis, habentem signum dei vivi"'.

After Joachim's death, in 1202, the abbot's writings continued to fascinate read-ers, above all his devoted followers, often called the Joachites, who interpreted and developed Joachim's controversial ideas further. Some were considered to have gone too far by their contemporaries, as the case of Gerardo da Borgo San Donnino illustrates.

Gerardo was a young Franciscan friar who was sent to Paris to study the-ology in the late 1240s. During his stay in Paris, Gerardo decided to write a book, which the Franciscan chronicler Salimbene di Adam later described as 'a foolish thought'. The two men had met and, according to Salimbene, Gerardo appeared otherwise to be a fine young man, but he was 'too obstinate' in his view of the teachings of Joachim and could never be persuaded to change his mind.[130] Gerardo cited the Pseudo-Joachist prophecy, the *Super Hieremiam*, to Salimbene and predicted that the crusade that Louis IX was preparing would end in catastrophe: the king would be captured, the crusaders would be defeated, and a plague would kill many.[131]

In 1254, Gerardo da Borgo San Donnino's book, the *Liber introductorius in evangelium eternum*, had caused a scandal in Paris, and the papacy also had to react. In the *Evangelium eternum*, Gerardo commented on Joachim's idea of history, which was divided into three different *status*, and made a radical interpretation of it. According to Gerardo, the third and final *status* of history would arrive in 1260. This would signify the end of the Church of the second *status*. Joachim's writings would replace both the Old and the New Testament, for 'the spirit of life had left the two testaments in around the year 1200'.[132] For Gerardo the angel of Revelation carrying the sign of the living God symbol-ized St Francis. The spiritual preachers, that is, the mendicant friars, would in Gerardo's view be the new apostles who would deliver the new 'Eternal Gospel' to the Christians.[133]

---

[130] Salimbene di Adam, *Cronica fratris*, ed. by Holder-Egger, MGH, SS, 32, pp. 236–37: 'Alius erat frater Ghirardinus de Burgo Sancti Donini, qui in Sicilia creverat et in gramatica rexerat, et erat morigeratus iuvenis, honestus et bonus, hoc excepto, quod nimis fuit obstinatus in dictis Ioachym et similiter proprie opinioni inseparabiliter adhesit. [...] frater Ghirardinus Parisius missus fuit, [...] et excogitavit fatuitatem componendo libellum et divulgavit stultitiam suam propalando ipsum ignorantibus fratribus'.

[131] Salimbene di Adam, *Cronica Fratris*, ed. by Bernini, pp. 236–37.

[132] 'Protocoll der Commission zu Anagni', ed. by Ehrle, p. 99: 'Quod circa MCC. annum incarnationis dominice exivit spiritus vite de duobus testamentis, ut fierit evangelium eternum'.

[133] 'Protocoll der Commission zu Anagni', ed. by Ehrle, pp. 99–105, 131–33. See also Tierney, *Origins of Papal Infallibility*, pp. 62–63.

The complete work of Gerardo has not survived, but the protocol of Anagni provided by the papal commission which investigated the *Evangelium eternum* gives us a fairly good idea of its contents.[134] Eudes de Châteauroux, who had just returned to Europe from the Seventh Crusade in 1254, was appointed by the pope to lead the investigation. Eudes and the two other commissioners inspected carefully the writings of both Joachim of Fiore and Gerardo da Borgo San Donnino. The investigation resulted in the condemnation of Gerardo's work by Pope Alexander IV in 1255.[135]

The Franciscan Order quickly disassociated itself from Gerardo's views, condemning his interpretation of Joachim's teachings and the work *Evangelium eternum*. However, the Pseudo-Joachist prophecies continued to have a great influence among the Franciscans. Franciscan intellectuals and minister generals such as John of Parma and Bonaventure identified the angel of Revelation as the founder of the Franciscan Order.[136] There were some who disagreed, such as the Franciscan friar Alexander Minorita, who identified many different angels from Revelation, but made no connection with St Francis.[137] However, after the 1240s St Francis was increasingly linked to the sixth angel of Revelation among the Franciscans, and 1260 was viewed by many as the year of the coming of the Antichrist.

John of Parma, the minister general of the Franciscan Order, and Humbert de Romans, then acting as the master general of the Dominican Order, also made a joint public declaration during the crisis over the 'Eternal Gospel' in 1255, where they defended both orders. In the encyclical, the mendicant friars were described as spiritual, angelic men, 'illuminators' who brought light into darkness. The two orders were represented as 'the two Cherubim' spreading their wings over the people. Utilizing prophetical and apocalyptic images, and citing Revelation, the two masters portrayed the Franciscan and Dominican

---

[134] 'Protocoll der Commission zu Anagni', ed. by Ehrle, pp. 99–142.

[135] Reeves, *The Influence of Prophecy in the Later Middle Ages*, pp. 60–61; Whalen, *Dominion of God*, pp. 177–83.

[136] Reeves, *The Influence of Prophecy in the Later Middle Ages*, p. 176; Whalen, *Dominion of God*, p. 189.

[137] For Alexander Minorita the sixth angel of Revelation was Emperor Constantine. Other putative apocalyptic angels were the emperors Justin and Justinian, Pope Calixtus II, Charlemagne, and even a crusader-angel, Godfrey of Bouillon, whom the Franciscan friar identified as 'the mighty angel' of Revelation 18. Alexander Minorita, *Expositio in Apocalypsim*, ed. by Wachtel, pp. 112, 153, 157, 162, 197, 299, 310, 384–85, 408–09; Lerner, 'The Medieval Return to the Thousand-Year Sabbath', p. 60.

orders as the 'two witnesses of Christ who, clothed in sackcloth' were 'already preaching and bearing testimony of the truth'.[138]

The references to the sixth angel of Revelation made in the crusade model sermons indicate some concern with this popular apocalyptic theme of the period. Jacques de Vitry's crusade sermon predates the crises and the association made between St Francis and the sixth angel. However, both Guibert de Tournai's and Eudes de Châteauroux's remarks about the angel may be viewed in this context. Guibert was a member of the Franciscan Order, and his approach followed the popular line of thought among the Franciscans, which gave new symbolic meaning to the angel of Revelation. Guibert, however, avoided making explicit association between St Francis and the angel in his crusade sermon.

Guibert explained in the sermon that the passage from Revelation was suitable for crusade preaching as well as for preaching on any saint's day.[139] He connected the sixth angel of Revelation to sainthood and argued that this angel could be interpreted to mean any saint. In the sermon Guibert attempted to assure his audience of the validity of his viewpoint. According to Guibert, the biblical passage read 'another angel' ascended from the sunrise, meaning that this angel should not be viewed as a reference to Christ. Guibert pointed out that 'the first angel is Christ' and 'the second angel', which was another angel, was a saint who would be sent as a messenger into the world.[140]

Eudes de Châteauroux, who had intimate knowledge of both the views of the spiritual Franciscans and the content of the *Evangelium eternum*, made the exact opposite interpretation in his crusade sermon. Eudes acknowledged that the Bible verse states 'I saw another angel' and that the angel signified a messenger, but according to him, it was quite clear that this angel was Christ. Eudes had a ready explanation to counter the arguments made about the other angel: St John the Evangelist saw many angels, and before noting that he saw 'another angel' from the sunrise, he had described some of them. Thus, the use of the word 'another' was appropriate at this point. In the sermon, Eudes spelled it out as clearly as he could, so that there would be no confusion: St John did mean Christ, the Son of God, whom God had sent as a messenger of peace into the world, when he described the sixth angel of Revelation.[141]

---

[138] 'Salvator saeculi', ed. by Wadding, pp. 380–81: 'Hi sunt duo testes Christi, qui saccis amicti iam praedicant, et testimonium perhibent veritati'. Apc. 11. 3.

[139] Guibert de Tournai, 'Ad crucesignatos et crucesignandos sermo primus', *CPI*, p. 176.

[140] Guibert de Tournai, 'Ad crucesignatos et crucesignandos sermo primus', *CPI*, p. 178.

[141] Eudes de Châteauroux, 'Sermo ad invitandum ad crucem', *CPI*, p. 168.

Despite these differences of opinion with the main details of the biblical passage, the overall theme from Revelation was used in much the same way by the authors of the crusade model sermons. The prophecy announced that during the apocalypse the four angels, whose duty was to devastate the land, would not do their work before those who were faithful to God were signed on their foreheads and saved from the devastation. This biblical prediction was used in an identical way to explain why Christians ought to become crusaders. The true servants of God would be signed with the cross, and this sign would be a mark of their virtue. The sign would protect the crusaders. It would be a shield against evil and the powers of Satan. Ultimately, the sign of the cross would make the crusaders victorious and would save their souls.[142]

The reverse side of this inducement to take the cross was a stark warning: those who would not become crusaders would not be signed by God, and they would perish in the havoc caused by the four angels. Jacques de Vitry explained that these four were in fact demons, 'angels of Satan' who were allowed to 'devastate the land, the sea and the trees' which meant the sinners of the world, the lazy, the slack, and the idle. These people who refused to go crusading would be 'exposed to the devil', and they would suffer 'the intolerable' punishment for their sins in hell.[143]

Many crusade preachers chose a similar biblical passage from Ezekiel to underline the redeeming powers of the crusader's cross and the eternal damnation of those who would not be signed with it. The authors of the model sermons cited the prophet Ezekiel and explained that the letter *thau*, which was marked by the decision of God on the foreheads of those in Jerusalem who would not be killed, was equivalent to the sign of the living God that was marked on the foreheads of those who would not be killed by the four angels.[144]

The crusader's stigmata, a theme used by many crusade preachers, was also linked to this apocalyptic crusading imagery.[145] Many chronicles of the First

---

[142] Jacques de Vitry, 'Sermo ad crucesignatos vel -signandos', *CPI*, pp. 82, 88–92; Eudes de Châteauroux, 'Sermo ad invitandum ad crucem', *CPI*, pp. 168–70; Guibert de Tournai, 'Ad crucesignatos et crucesignandos sermo primus', *CPI*, pp. 176–87. Apc. 7. 2–3.

[143] Jacques de Vitry, 'Sermo ad crucesignatos vel -signandos', *CPI*, p. 90.

[144] Jacques de Vitry, 'Sermo ad crucesignatos vel -signandos', *CPI*, p. 86; Eudes de Châteauroux, 'Sermo ad invitandum ad crucem', *CPI*, p. 172; Guibert de Tournai, 'Ad crucesignatos et crucesignandos sermo primus', *CPI*, p. 180; Federico Visconti, 'Quando idem Dominus predicavit crucem litteraliter clero pisano de mandato domini Pape', *SVP*, p. 548; Philippe le Chancelier, '*Dicit Dominus ad Moysen*', Avranches, MS 132, fol. 273ᵛᵃ; Philippe le Chancelier, 'Sermo in die veneris infra octabas Assumptionis beate Virginis', Avranches, MS 132, fol. 244ʳᵃ. Ez. 9. 4.

[145] See below, pp. 133–43; see also Tamminen, 'The Crusader's Stigmata'.

Crusade mentioned crusaders who were marked with the stigmata, the sign
of the cross that appeared to be divinely imprinted on the foreheads of those
who had first taken the cross.[146] This heavenly mark was also found on the
skin of dead crusaders who had drowned during the First Crusade, an incident
reported also by Humbert de Romans in his crusade preaching manual.[147] The
crusader's stigmata continued the same apocalyptic theme that emphasized the
powers of the cross and linked it to the signs of God mentioned in the biblical
prophecies, the sign of the living God and the letter *thau*, which would save
true Christians from devastation at the end of time.

The Eggs of Asps and the Webs of Spiders

The extended conflict between the papacy and the Hohenstaufen was char-
acterized by different kinds of prophetic visions, which were actively propagated by both parties involved. In the pro-papal camp, Frederick II and his
offspring were often described in biblical terms as the precursors of the devil or
the Antichrist, as figures described by the prophets to bring destruction to the
world.[148] The pro-imperial camp employed similar methods and equally grim
descriptions, Hohenstaufen propagandists linking both scriptural prophecies
and apocalyptic numbers such as the figure 666 to their papal enemies.[149]

Eudes de Châteauroux's three model sermons against the Lucera Muslims
and one that was probably originally preached against the Ghibellines belong to

[146] Fulcher de Chartres, *Historia Hierosolymitana*, lib. I, cap. VIII, ed. by Hagenmeyer,
pp. 169–70: 'nam cum corpora iam mortua qui circumstabant pro posse collegissent, repertae
sunt in carnibus quorundam super spatulas scilicet cruces insignitae. nam quod in pannis suis
vivi gestaverant, competebat, Domino volente, in ipsis servitio suo sic praeoccupatis idem signum victoriosum sub pignore fidei permanere'. Guibert de Nogent, *Gesta Dei per Francos*, vii,
cap. 32, in *RHC Occ.*, iv, 250–51; Ekkehard von Aura, *Hierosolymita*, cap. x, in *RHC Occ.*, v,
19; Raymond d'Aguilers, *Historia Francorum qui ceperunt Iherusalem*, cap. xiv, in *RHC Occ.*,
iii, 272: 'sex vel septem de nostris pauperibus a paganis capti et interfecti sunt: hi autem omnes
defuncti cruces in dextris habuerunt humeris'. Constable, *Crusaders and Crusading in the
Twelfth Century*, pp. 67–68; Purkis, *Crusading Spirituality*, p. 35.

[147] Humbert de Romans, *De predicatione sancte crucis*, cap. xxxix.

[148] Rist, *Papacy and Crusading in Europe*, pp. 191–95. See also Abulafia, *Frederick II*,
pp. 366–47; Kantorowicz, *Kaiser Friedrich der Zweite*.

[149] In the 'Anonymi de Innocentio IV. P. M. antichristo libellus', ed. by Winkelmann,
pp. 20–22: 'Innocencius enim papa sexcentos sexaginta sex secumdum glosam et racionem
designat [...]. Et omnia signa, que sancti de antichristo secundum sacram scripturam ponunt,
spiritualiter intellecta i.e. ut Christo et doctrine eius maxime contraria, Innocencio pape quarto
conveniunt et ideo verus antichristus esse non dubitetur'.

this historical context.[150] One of Guibert de Tournai's crusade sermons or parts of the model may also have been initially preached against the Hohenstaufen.[151] All of these sermons are rich in prophetical language and apocalyptic images. In the sermons against the Lucera Muslims, Eudes made use of his vast knowledge of the Pseudo-Joachist writings and borrowed themes from works such as the *Super Hieremiam*, the *De Oneribus Prophetarum*, and the *Super Prophetas*, known also as the *Super Esaiam*.[152]

Eudes may have also drawn inspiration and information directly from two political treatises produced already in 1245. These influential treatises, the *Iuxta vaticinium Isaiae* and the *Aspidis ova ruperant*, are often attributed to Cardinal Raniero Capocci of Viterbo and his circle. The writings carried many of the themes that were used against Frederick II in the 1240s and would be used against his successors in the decades to come. The themes included vivid imagery from the Revelation, the association of the figures of the dragon and the basilisk to Frederick II, the insinuations made about religious pollution, and specific accusations made against the emperor of heresy, of insulting the rights of the Church, of harming innocent Christians, of siding with the Muslims, of accepting gifts from them, and of enabling them to violate Christian women. These different themes in the texts established a clear connection between Frederick II and the Antichrist or Lucifer.[153]

In 1250, however, the combination of two popular ideas involving the Antichrist — the association made between the emperor and the Antichrist and the Joachite interpretation of the year 1260 as an apocalyptic year of the Antichrist — suffered a blow with the untimely death of Frederick II. The confusion which followed is apparent in the prophetical writings of the period.

[150] See Appendix V.

[151] See Appendix VIII.

[152] The tract known as the *Super Esaiam* should more aptly be called the *Super Prophetas*, as suggested recently by David Morris. The title *Super Prophetas* would follow the medieval manuscript tradition more faithfully, unlike the title *Super Esaiam* that derives from the printed, corrupt edition of the year 1517 and is somewhat misleading. Morris, 'The Historiography of the *Super Prophetas*'.

[153] The *Iuxta vaticinium Isaiae* and the *Aspidis ova ruperant*, together with the papal letters issued by Gregory IX, set the rhetorical tone for the conflict that would dominate the final struggle between the papacy and the Hohenstaufen in the 1250s and 1260s. Cardinal Raniero of Viterbo was a fierce opponent of Frederick II, and he has been regarded as an instrumental figure in the propaganda campaign against the emperor in the 1240s. Lerner, 'Frederick II, Alive, Aloft, and Allayed', p. 360; Abulafia, *Frederick II*, pp. 356–59. For political treatises, see 'Iuxta vaticinium Ysaie' and 'Aspidis ova ruperant', ed. by Winkelmann, pp. 709–21.

There appeared to be many uncertainties after Frederick's death: Had the emperor really died, was he still living, or would he return from death? How should Frederick's death be viewed in relation to the previous prophecies made about him? In the Pseudo-Joachite prophecies these questions were met with a convenient citation from Revelation: 'the beast that was and is not'. With this biblical passage the ambiguities surrounding the emperor's death were cleverly exploited.[154]

The connection between the emperor and the Antichrist quickly passed from Frederick II to his sons. In the Pseudo-Joachite prophecies references were made to Henry VII, Conrad IV, Manfred, Conradin, and even Enzio. Much depends on interpretation, but Manfred appears to be described as 'the eighth beast' with 'the seven horns' in the *Super Prophetas*.[155] The matter of the Lucera Muslims, which was left unsettled after both Frederick's death in 1250 and Manfred's death in 1266, was also discussed in the prophetical writings. The *Super Hieremiam* predicted that Frederick II would injure the Church and would use 'the horns of the unclean nations' against it, probably a reference to the Lucera Muslims. The willingness to use Muslim fighters in the service of the Hohenstaufen armies that fought against Christian armies was an offence that caused anger and was condemned repeatedly in the pro-papal tracts. The *Super Prophetas* also prophesied that the Lucera Muslims would be 'humbled or wiped out, in part by bath [baptism], in part by steel [crusade]'.[156]

In his crusade sermons, Eudes skilfully used the vocabulary and imagery of the anti-Staufen prophecies and identified the predictions as referring to Conradin of Hohenstaufen, the Lucera Muslims, and their opponent Charles of Anjou. For Eudes, as for so many of his contemporaries, Frederick II was the dragon of the Revelation.[157] Eudes followed the example provided in the treatise *Aspidis ova ruperant* and built one of his sermons against the Lucerans on the biblical passage from Isaiah, 'they have broken the eggs of asps and have woven the webs of spiders. He that shall eat of their eggs shall die, and that which is brought out shall be hatched into a basilisk'.[158]

---

[154] 'Sibilla Erithea Babilonica', ed. by Holder-Egger, esp. p. 334: 'sonabitque in populo: "Vivit" et "Non vivit".'; 'De Oneribus Prophetarum', ed. by Holder-Egger, esp. p. 182; 'Super Prophetas' [Super Esaiam], fol. 59ᵛ. Apc. 17. 8.

[155] 'Super Prophetas' [Super Esaiam], fol. 59ᵛ.

[156] 'Super Prophetas' [Super Esaiam], fol. 59ʳ.

[157] Eudes de Châteauroux, 'Sermo de rebellione Sarracenorum Lucherie', *CR*, p. 384.

[158] Eudes de Châteauroux, 'Sermo de rebellione Sarracenorum Lucherie', *CR*, p. 382. Isa. 59. 5.

This biblical citation was in frequent use in the prophetical and political writings of the period. In the treatise *Aspidis ova ruperant* the prophecy was interpreted as a prediction about a long line of Hohenstaufen rulers, where 'Henry and Philip of the branch of the schismatic Frederick [Barbarossa]' were viewed as those who had broken the asps' eggs, and 'he who was fostered by the Church, the young Frederick [Frederick II]', was interpreted as signifying the one who had 'grown up a basilisk' and had 'killed many birds'.[159]

In the crusade sermon, Eudes explained that Conradin of Hohenstaufen was in fact 'the basilisk' mentioned in the passage. This he demonstrated with a play on words: the Latin word 'regulus' for basilisk could be interpreted to mean 'a little king', a diminutive of the word 'rex', just as Conradin meant 'little Conrad'. The Greek word for king, 'basilios', could also be brought into the mix and turned into a Latin diminutive 'basilicus'. All of these words pointed to the same conclusion in Eudes's reasoning: Conradin was the basilisk, 'the king of the serpents'.[160] This little king was the last of the Hohenstaufen, to whom the biblical prophecy had referred all along.

Eudes explained in detail in the sermon what the popular verse from Isaiah meant. The 'asps' were the Lucera Muslims who had 'broken their eggs', that is, rebelled. This was the period, the particular moment that was prophesied in the Bible. The prediction of Isaiah was now being fulfilled. The Lucera Muslims' rebellion was not happening by chance, but all was taking place according to the prophet's vision: the rebellion was a manifestation 'of premeditated and preordained malice'.[161] This was an important point made early in the sermon, because it allowed Eudes to place both the Muslims and the crusaders in their respective roles in the historical event, which appeared to be unfolding according to the divine plan. The crusaders were the soldiers of God fighting against evil. The duty of true Christians was to combat the forces of the Antichrist and the devil.

[159] 'Aspidis ova ruperant', ed. by Winkelmann, p. 717: 'Aspidis ova ruperant iuxta prophetam, Heinricus videlicet ac Philippus, de germine scismatici Friderici, et qui confotus est ab ecclesia, Fridericus iunior surrexit in regulum, qui nitolento sue iussionis flatu peremit plurimas aves volantes ad celum'.

[160] Eudes de Châteauroux, 'Sermo de rebellione Sarracenorum Lucherie', *CR*, p. 384: 'Predicti autem Sarraceni maledicti et eorum complices ad hoc fecerunt, ut factum suum erumpat in regulum, id est ut iste Corradinus fiat regulus, id est rex serpentum, qui et in Greco basilicus appelatur. Basilios enim Grece, rex Latine'.

[161] Eudes de Châteauroux, 'Sermo de rebellione Sarracenorum Lucherie', *CR*, p. 382: 'Primo ostenditur in hiis verbis quod ista rebellio et proditio non evenerunt casu fortuito nec ex improviso sed ex premeditata et preordinata malitia'.

In the sermon, Eudes further explained how the biblical prophecy ought to be interpreted: why the Lucera Muslims should be viewed as the asps, what the webs of the spiders actually were, and what it all meant for the crusaders and for the Christians in general. According to Eudes, the Muslims were the asps because they did not listen to the Christian preachers trying to convert them and because of their excessive love of earthly things. Traditionally the asps represented 'worldly desires' in Christian, allegorical thought. Augustine of Hippo had described the asps mentioned in the Bible as creatures that lived in caves, who had one ear to the ground and blocked the other, so that they could not be lured out.[162] Eudes quoted the relevant biblical passage, Psalm 57, in his sermon and maintained that the asps of Lucera kept one ear pressed to the ground and blocked the other ear with their tail. The Saracens preferred to live in their cave of sins, and the preaching of the missionaries fell on deaf ears.[163]

Philippe le Chancelier used similar metaphors, and indeed the same biblical passage, in his crusade sermon against the Albigensian heretics. In his sermon preached in 1226, Philippe declared that the asps' eggs stood for 'the depravity of heresy'. Heresy was 'the worst kind of whore', who had 'laid her eggs in the hope that she may prevail'. Philippe feared that heretical beliefs would survive and would spread from the Languedoc region to other parts of Christendom through the weakness of the Christians. The crusaders and the supporters of the crusade movement should stay firm and fight against the heretics and heretical beliefs with both temporal and spiritual weapons.[164]

In a similar way, Eudes described the threats posed by the Lucera Muslims to all Christians. The asps hatched their poisonous plans, enjoyed carnal pleasures,

---

[162] Augustinus, *Sermo CCCXVI*, 'In solemnitate Stephani martyris', in *PL*, xxxviii, col. 1432: 'Sicut enim dicuntur aspides, quando incantantur, ut non prorumpant et exeant de cavernis suis, premere unam aurem ad terram, et de cauda sibi alteram obturare, et tamen incantator producit illas'.

[163] Eudes de Châteauroux, 'Sermo de rebellione Sarracenorum Lucherie', *CR*, p. 382: 'Aspides iste Sarraceni de Lucheria, de quibus pre aliis Sarracenis verissime dicitur illud quod in Psalmis legitur: *Illis secundum similitudinem serpentis sicut aspidis surde et obturantis aures suas que non exaudiet vocem incantantium*. Ipsi enim predicatores habuerunt et diversis temporibus eos tamen numquam audire voluerunt sed potius aures suas obturaverunt. Dicitur enim quod aspis unam aurem affigit terre, alteram cauda obscurat, ne vocem incantantis audiat, sic dicti Sarraceni terrenis adherentes nolunt audire vocem Christi'. Ps. 57. 5–6.

[164] Philippe le Chancelier, 'Sermo de eodem, quomodo apparuit potentia Dei', Avranches, MS 132, fol. 250ᵛᵃ: 'meretrix pessima heretica pravitas, iam ova sua posuerat sperans per defectum nostrum se posse prevalere'. Transcribed by Maier and Bériou.

and multiplied in their caves. Their eggs were planted and the spiders' webs were cast, which meant various dangers for the Christians, some of which had already materialized, some of which were waiting to happen, including rebellion, the persecution of the innocent and the vulnerable, the corruption of the weak and the sinister, the attempt to subjugate or to exterminate all Christians. On top of all this, there was the threat of pollution.[165]

In the pro-papal tracts and the Pseudo-Joachite prophecies the religious pollution caused by the Hohenstaufen and their Muslim allies was often discussed. Isaiah provided a biblical passage appropriate for these descriptions as well. In both the *De Oneribus Prophetarum* and the *Super Prophetas*, Isaiah 13 was cited and 'the dark mountain', 'the moon', and 'the stars' described in the biblical prophecy were linked to corruption, pollution, and destruction.[166] Eudes used similar terms and allusions, without specifically quoting the biblical passage, while describing the religious pollution to the ecclesiastical lands caused by the Lucera Muslims.[167] The theme of pollution was exploited by Eudes already in 1226 in the sermon preached against the Albigensian heretics.[168] With references to natural phenomena, the landscape, or weather conditions such as clouds, rain, wind, and hailstorms, or descriptions of low valleys and dark mountains, Eudes visualized the polluting effects of both the Muslims of Lucera and the heretics of southern France.[169]

References to biblical prophecies are found in all of the crusade model sermons and the crusade manuals of this study. The most commonly used passages are from Isaiah and Revelation. Isaiah 13. 2 was, for example, also used by Jacques de Vitry, Humbert de Romans, and Guibert de Tournai. Both Jacques and Guibert made use of the passage 'lift up the sign on the dark mountain' and connected this to the sign of the cross that the crusaders lifted up when

---

[165] Eudes de Châteauroux, 'Sermo de rebellione Sarracenorum Lucherie', *CR*, p. 383: 'Ova istarum aspidum fuerunt eorum venenosa et arguta consilia, quibus non ex insperato neque semel sed ab antiquis temporibus et pluries cogitaverunt iugum Christianorum abicere et eos sue subicere servituti vel exterminare omnino'.

[166] 'De Oneribus Prophetarum', ed. by Holder-Egger, pp. 172–73; 'Super Prophetas' [Super Esaiam], fol. 28^{r–v}. Isa. 13. 2.

[167] Eudes de Châteauroux, 'Sermo de rebellione Sarracenorum Lucherie', *CR*, p. 379–80.

[168] Eudes de Châteauroux, 'Sermo contra hereticos de Albigensibus partibus', Arras, MS 876, fol. 89vb.

[169] See also the allusion made to the 'pestiferous mountain' from Jeremiah that Eudes utilized in his *Sermo in depositione regis vel imperatoris* delivered in 1245 in Lyons. Eudes de Châteauroux, 'Sermo in depositione regis vel imperatoris', *UEE*, II, 649–54. Jer. 51. 25.

they took the cross and left on their expeditions.[170] Humbert, like Eudes, linked the prophecy to the sins of the Muslim enemies, to Muhammed and his followers.[171]

The utilization of biblical prophecies allowed the crusade preachers to justify crusading, to connect contemporary events to specific passages from the Bible, and to explain the consequences of taking up action or of inactivity. The preachers illustrated that the crusaders were fulfilling God's intentions while they participated in the expeditions. God's scheme was progressing as planned and as predicted by holy men. The crusaders were presented as vitally important components in the grand plan. The prophecies encouraged true Christians, the crusaders, to take decisive action and fight against God's enemies. Eudes summed up his prophetical sermon against the Lucera Muslims with further citations from Isaiah and urged Charles of Anjou, whom he interpreted as the 'weaned child' of Isaiah 11, to put his hand into 'the nest of the basilisk'. Charles should act as was predicted in the prophecy. The hole of the asps and the nest of the basilisk, which signified Lucera, should be destroyed by his hand, by the crusaders, in accordance with the revelations made in the Bible.[172]

---

[170] Jacques de Vitry, 'Item sermo ad crucesignatos vel -signandos', *CPI*, p. 104: 'Super montem calliginosum levate signum, exaltate vocem, levate manum, ingrediantur portas duces'; Guibert de Tournai, 'Ad crucesignatos et crucesignandos sermo tertius', *CPI*, p. 200.

[171] Humbert de Romans, *De predicatione sancte crucis*, cap. xxvii: 'Super montem caliginosum, scilicet Machometum cum suis, leuate signum et exaltate vocem, leuate manum, et ingrediantur portas duces'.

[172] Eudes de Châteauroux, 'Sermo de rebellione Sarracenorum Lucherie', *CR*, pp. 384–85. Isa. 11. 8.

The Crusader and God

In the Service of God

The relations between God and the crusaders, or Christ and his soldiers, were key issues for the authors of the crusade model sermons discussed in multiple different ways in the sermon material. The authors of the crusade sermons made clear that it was God's will that the Christians would take the cross and go crusading. The crusades were represented as holy wars that were fought on behalf of God and Christ. The ultimate justification and authorization for the wars came from the highest possible authority — from God. God's will, wisdom, power, and goodness might appear in the decisions of his servants as they wanted to become crusaders. It was God who persuaded the Christians to become crusaders. God might change the kings' and the princes' minds and instil them with a desire to take the cross.[1]

The resolution to take the cross and become a crusader was the best decision one could make. According to the crusade preachers, it was as if both parties, man and God, were in an inebriated state. The deal was so attractive that it seemed as if God was drunk when he proposed it. The crusaders would gain paradise for almost nothing.[2] The crusaders might also seem to be drunk when they voluntarily decided to become crusaders and leave all their loved ones

---

[1] Philippe le Chancelier, 'Sermo de eodem, quomodo apparuit potentia Dei', Avranches, MS 13, fol. 250ra.

[2] Jacques de Vitry, 'Item sermo ad crucesignatos vel -signandos', *CPI*, p. 118; Guibert de Tournai, 'Ad crucesignatos et crucesignandos sermo tertius', *CPI*, p. 208.

behind, as the King of France, Louis IX, his brothers, the knights, and the common people seemed to be when they left for the Seventh Crusade, according to Eudes de Châteauroux.[3]

The crusades were represented as an exchange of gifts between the two close friends, the Redeemer and the crusader. The crusaders could prove their faith by crusading and build a closer relationship with Christ by fighting for him. Christ had a central position in the crusade ideology. The crusaders were urged to liberate Christ's tomb and his patrimony, the Holy Land, where Christ was born and where he had worked for the salvation of all Christians. The crusaders attempted to recover the Holy Sepulchre and cleanse it from pollution. All the crusaders fought on Christ's behalf and out of love for him, no matter how they fought or where the expeditions were directed. These features were communicated carefully and determinedly by the authors of the crusade sermons to their audiences of crusade preachers and crusaders.

God's Will — the Crusader's Own Volition

In the crusade model sermons, God was described as asking for the aid of all his faithful servants. This request of God was voiced by the preachers to the people. Those who were about to take the cross should listen only to advice given to them by the crusade preachers, for they were expressing the will of God, given to them by papal mandate. This was an important ideological point made by the authors, which had also been stressed by Pope Urban II in the Clermont sermon. Urban, in his sermon, appears to have followed closely the guidelines of just war defined by Augustine of Hippo.[4] In his writings, Augustine had considered the circumstances under which Christian warfare was justifiable. The criteria put forward by Augustine were later reduced to three essential principles: just cause, legitimate authority, and right intention. Just war must have a righteous cause. It must be a defensive act or one aiming to recover usurped possessions. The war must be sanctioned by a legitimate authority, and those engaged in the violence of war must have right intentions.[5]

---

[3] Eudes de Châteauroux, 'Sermo in festo sanctarum reliquiarum', *UEE*, II, 745: 'Sic Dominus inebriavit hiis temporibus regem Francie, fratres eius, miliciam et populum eiusdem regni ut de eis faciat voluntatem. Nisi enim fuissent inebriati, crucem non assumpsissent'. Eudes used the biblical theme of the sweet wine of Lebanon from Osee 14 as the opening passage of the sermon, from which the apparent 'drunkenness' of the crusaders derived. Os. 14. 8.

[4] Tyerman, *God's War*, p. 34; Riley-Smith, 'Crusading as an Act of Love'.

[5] For Augustine's theory of just war, see Mattox, *St. Augustine and the Theory of Just War*; Markus, 'Saint Augustine's Views on the "Just War"'. See also Fonnesberg-Schmidt, *Popes and*

Humbert de Romans deliberated on the justifications for the crusade at length in his *De predicatione sancte crucis*. Humbert viewed it as vital for the movement that the crusade preachers would understand the principles of the crusade ideology and could convince sceptical Christians or those influenced by the 'anti'-crusaders that the expeditions were just wars. At the end of his manual Humbert incorporated a short account of Urban's sermon.[6] Humbert also explained the justifications of crusades carefully at the beginning of his manual, dividing these into three essential points. Humbert followed Augustine's and Urban's criteria and argued that the crusades were just wars because the crusaders fought against the Saracens, who were not innocent people, but 'extremely guilty'. The crusaders also fought for good reasons, not out of pride, avarice, or vainglory, but for the defence of the faith and for justice. The crusades had been declared by a legitimate authority.[7]

Some of the preachers also emphasized that they were acting according to the wishes of the Roman pontiff when they promoted crusades. One of Federico Visconti's crusade sermons mentions outright in the rubrics of the sermon that it was preached at the instigation of the pope.[8] In their sermons both Jacques de Vitry and Guibert de Tournai underlined that the pope, as the vicar of Christ and as the spouse of the Church, gave the crusade indulgence to all those who took the cross and helped the Holy Land by means of the powers vested in him by God.[9] Eudes de Châteauroux also declared in his crusade sermons that the

---

the Baltic Crusades, p. 9. For medieval discussions about just war, see also Russell, *The Just War in the Middle Ages*. According to Urban II, the armed pilgrimage that he proposed in 1095 was sanctioned by celestial authority, that is, God, and it was voiced by an earthly authority, the pope. The war had just cause, as it was both a defensive act on behalf of the Eastern Christians and one aiming to recover lost possessions, since the Muslims had seized the Holy Land from the Christians, and the pilgrims fighting against the enemy in the East had pure intentions as they fought for God and Christians, not for themselves.

[6] Humbert de Romans, *De predicatione sancte crucis*, cap. xxxix, De verbis Urbani pape. See also cap. x, De primaria crucisignationis inuentione; cap. xvi, De exemplis antiquorum que inducunt ad bellum contra saracenos. Humbert's manual exists in short and long versions. In some of the versions, there is included at the end of the tract an account of Urban's sermon by Baldric de Dol. Cole, 'Humbert of Romans and the Crusade', pp. 160, 169–74; *PCHL*, pp. 216–17. For Baldric's account of the Clermont sermon, see Baldric de Dol, *Historia Ierosolimitana*, ed. by Bongars, pp. 86–88.

[7] Humbert de Romans, *De predicatione sancte crucis*, cap. ii.

[8] Federico Visconti, 'Quando idem dominus predicavit crucem litteraliter clero pisano de mandato domini Pape', *SVP*, p. 544.

[9] Guibert de Tournai, 'Ad crucesignatos et crucesignandos sermo tertius', *CPI*, p. 208: 'Hinc est quod hodie aperitur thesaurus glorie celestis, et ipse dominus papa, qui sponsus est ecclesie,

pope had called upon the Christians to fight against God's enemies.[10] Humbert de Romans maintained that the holy Mother Church went to war against the enemies of God, and the Church was supported by divine authority in this undertaking.[11]

With these references the crusade preachers could assure their audiences that those who decided to take the cross would gain their reward, as promised by the pope himself. The pope gave legitimacy to the undertaking. His was a lawful authority that enabled him to declare a crusade and offer the indulgence as a reward. The 'true' crusaders would participate in a crusade announced by the pope: the crusade was not a war like any other, declared by secular lords or charismatic figures who did not possess any rights to offer spiritual rewards or indulgences. During the thirteenth century, there were popular revivalist movements, for example, the Children's Crusade and the Shepherds' Crusades, which were condemned by clerical commentators because they lacked papal approval. The participants in these crusades could not be regarded as 'true' crusaders, for the pope had not authorized their actions.[12] The shepherds and the peasants who followed the obscure 'Master of Hungary' in 1251, during the Shepherds' Crusade, were considered 'false' crusaders, for they were acting without lawful mandate from the pope.[13]

Many of the crusade model sermons do not mention the pope at all. However, this is because the sermons are model sermons, which were designed to suit all kinds of crusades. As the actual crusade sermons were delivered, the preachers

obligat bona sponse sue et ex plenitudine potestatis, quam habet sicut Christi vicarius, offert tam largas indulgentias accipientibus crucem et succurentibus Terre Sancte'. Jacques de Vitry, 'Item sermo ad crucesignatos vel -signandos', *CPI*, p. 112.

[10] Eudes de Châteauroux, 'Sermo ad invitandum ad crucem', *CPI*, p. 172: 'Ad hoc enim nos huc venimus missi a summo pontifice, ut per assumptionem crucis signentur et distinguantur servi Dei a servis diaboli et ut stipendia recipiant Domini et ut a gladio pene eterne non occidantur'. See also Eudes de Châteauroux, 'Sermo de rebellione Sarracenorum Lucherie', *CR*, p. 380.

[11] Humbert de Romans, 'De predicatione crucis in genere quocumque', *CPI*, p. 220: 'sancta mater ecclesia auctoritate divina suffulta movet bellum contra tales propter tales et tales causas fidei'. In his manual Humbert also declared that unjust wars lacked authority, but that the crusades were just wars, because these had both human and divine authorization. Humbert de Romans, *De predicatione sancte crucis*, cap. ii.

[12] Dickson, *Religious Enthusiasm in the Medieval West*, pp. 2–3, 14–20; Dickson, *The Children's Crusade*, pp. 17–35.

[13] For the Shepherds' Crusade and its leader, referred to in some of the sources as the Master of Hungary, see Barber, 'The Crusade of the Shepherds in 1251', pp. 1–23; *The Seventh Crusade*, trans. by Jackson, pp. 179–93.

would often first read the papal bull announcing the crusade out loud, thus justifying the coming expedition as well as legitimizing their own preaching.[14] The
pope's authority was important for both the 'true' crusaders and the 'true' crusade preachers. Those crusade preachers who did not have papal authorization
for preaching could be considered 'false' preachers. They might try to justify
their unauthorized preaching, as the leaders of the Shepherds' Crusade appear
to have done. According to the chronicler Primat, the leaders of the shepherds
claimed that they had been instructed directly by God to preach the crusade,
and thus there was no need for the papal authorization.[15]

The pope's authority could also be used in the crusade model sermons to
convince the local administration of churches to support those clerics who
wanted to participate in the expeditions. In his crusade sermon delivered during the preparations for the Seventh Crusade in 1248, during the feast of the
Conversion of St Paul, Eudes de Châteauroux explained that it was the decision
of the lord pope to give the revenues of the churches 'for up to three years' to the
clerics who wished to go on the pilgrimage, that is, on the Seventh Crusade.[16]
The local administration of the churches might well be unenthusiastic about
losing three years' income, but they could not oppose the direct demands of
the pope.

However urgent the appeal to join the crusade movement, the idea remains
that the *crucesignandi* should not be pressured, forced, or ordered by anyone,
neither the preachers nor the pope, to take the cross. Crusading should remain
optional. No one could be compelled to make the crusade vow, for according to
canon law all vows, including the crusade vow, should be made voluntarily. To
force someone to take the cross would be against the principles of crusade ideology.[17] Philippe le Chancelier underlined this in his crusade sermon, explaining that both the crusaders themselves and those supporting the campaigns
should make their commitment voluntarily. The cross should not be taken out

---

[14] *CPI*, p. 30.

[15] Primat, *Chronique de Primat traduite par Jean du Vignau*, ed. by Bouquet, pp. 8–10,
esp. p. 8: 'lesquelz l'en nommoit les mestres des pastours, qui distrent que il avoient pris l'office
de preeschier la croiz du propre commandement de Nostre Seigneur'. The chronicle of Primat,
which was written in Latin, has survived only in Jean du Vignau's French version.

[16] Eudes de Châteauroux, 'Sermo in conversione sancti Pauli et exhortatio ad assumendam
crucem', *CPI*, p. 136: 'sic dominus papa vult quod proventus ecclesiarum sequantur clericos in
hac peregrinatione usque ad tres annos'.

[17] Riley-Smith, *The Crusades, Christianity, and Islam*, p. 36; Jotischky, *Crusading and the
Crusader States*, p. 16.

of fear of people with more authority or in a moment of danger, not in fear of the sea nor out of zeal for revenge or for reasons of blood vengeance. There should be no necessity other than that of the will, created in one's heart and mind. The crusaders or the supporters of the movement had to have a sincere desire, a will to take part in the enterprise.[18]

Roger of Salisbury also emphasized this in his crusade sermon. The free will of the crusaders and of those doing penitence for their sins needed to be respected. There was freedom of judgement involved in becoming a crusader or a penitent, a disciple in the school of Christ. Everyone needed to make this decision by themselves and for themselves. Christ had given the Christians an example, a path which they should take, and told them that 'if any man will come after me, let him deny himself'. This meant, according to Roger, that the Lord had wished that there would be a desire to follow Christ, 'a state of free will' that would be observed by his followers, in this case the crusaders and other penitents. Christ had not ordered or forced people to be his disciples, but had required that they had a will to follow him and deny themselves.[19] When one sacrificed oneself, as the crusaders did in imitation of Christ when they took the cross, it could only happen voluntarily through their own free decision.

In his *De predicatione sancte crucis* Humbert de Romans also underlined that becoming a crusader was a voluntary act. He wanted preachers to make clear in their crusade sermons that Christ had taken up his cross voluntarily. This ought to be an example for the prospective crusaders. Humbert also used a similar biblical passage from Luke, with which he, like Roger, emphasized Christ's choice of words: Christ had said that if anyone *wanted* to follow him, they needed to deny themselves. Humbert further pointed out in his manual the difference between serving earthly lords or Muhammad and serv-

---

[18] Philippe le Chancelier, 'Sermo de eodem, de gaudio quod rex et principes assumpserunt crucem', Avranches, MS 132, fol. 251va: '*Quos ferrum non tetigit*: per ferrum necessitas quecumque significatur, quandoque infirmitas, que competit aliquos intrare religionem, sumere crucem: hos ferrum tangit; quandoque timor superioris vel timor in mari vel in periculo nonne compulit: hos ferrum tangit, non est hic; quandoque zelus ultionis et vindictam sanguinis: hos ferrum tangit, sed non ita est hic. Immo vere possunt dicere illud Ps. [liii, 8]: *Voluntarie sacrificabo tibi. Nazareos quidem Domini non tangit* ferrum neque *novacula*, quia nichil necessitate faciunt set voluntate'. Transcribed by Maier and Bériou. Philippe built his sermon on the biblical passage from Joshua, where an altar was built for the Lord on Mount Hebal. The altar was made of unhewn stones, which 'iron had not touched'. The phrase 'ferrum non tetigit' used in the passage derives from there. See Jos. 8. 31.

[19] Roger of Salisbury, '*Ascendente* Ihesu *in naviculam*', *PCHL*, p. 230: 'Hunc ergo sequamur sicut ipse docet: *Si quis vult post me venire, abneget semetipsum.* Per hoc quod dicit vult notat voluntatem remanendi esse in libertate arbitrii'. Mt. 16. 24.

ing Christ. Secular lords could demand compulsory service from their vassals, and Muhammad had forced people to serve him, but Christ did not want this kind of service. God wanted Christians to fight for him voluntarily. Finally, Humbert pointed out the practical side of the requirement of volunteering in crusade ideology — those who fought voluntarily were more useful in battle than those who were compelled to fight.[20]

Vassals of the Lord

A crusader's path began by making a crusade vow and by taking the cross. Both the making and the keeping of the crusade vow had considerable relevance for the crusade preachers. The making of the vow meant that the *crucesignandi* bound themselves with an oath to do service for God, either by going on a crusade, by sending a substitute, or by making a financial payment. However, we do not have much detailed information about the crusade vows. Historians know of only a few recorded cases of individual vows.[21]

The crusade model sermons in general offer little information about the crusade vows or vow-making. Jacques de Vitry states in his crusade sermon that many Christians had acquired an indulgence for themselves, because these people had taken the cross 'out of devotion with a contrite heart, binding themselves by a solemn vow to the Lord'.[22] This statement is one of the few instances in the crusade model sermons when the vow or the vowing is specifically mentioned. Jacques's use of the term 'solemn vow' may indicate that he was informed of the separation made by some canonists between the simple vow and the solemn vow. The latter was more explicit, more conclusive, and made steadfastly and out loud, binding both parties involved, God and the crusader, more firmly to the agreement and hence bringing the indulgence, the promised reward, to the crusader.[23]

---

[20] Humbert de Romans, *De predicatione sancte crucis*, cap. ix, Quare nullus ad hoc cogitur. Lk. 9. 23. *PCHL*, p. 206.

[21] There is, for example, a recorded vowing of a certain notary from Marseilles, named Hugoni de Fonte, who in 1290 pledged to join 'the next, upcoming general *passagium* to the Holy Land' or to pay a financial subsidy. Gottlob, *Kreuzablass und Almosenablass*, pp. 308–09; Housley, *Fighting for the Cross*, pp. 48–49.

[22] Jacques de Vitry, 'Item sermo ad crucesignatos vel -signandos', *CPI*, p. 116. See also Humbert de Romans's brief references to the crusade vow in his manual. Humbert de Romans, *De predicatione sancte crucis*, esp. cap. vi, Quare crux ponitur in humero dextro.

[23] Brundage, *Medieval Canon Law and the Crusader*, pp. 64–65.

However, most of the crusade preachers do not discuss the crusade vow in their sermons. In fact, Guibert de Tournai, who followed Jacques's model sermon closely in his own sermon, seems to have avoided the term 'vow' deliberately. Guibert used the same words and examples as Jacques did in his sermon but changed the wording in some of the key phrases of the passage. He preferred to speak only of the crusaders' 'preparations' for leaving.[24] The preachers' reluctance to make comments on this issue may result from the private nature of the vow. The vow was made voluntarily for personal reasons. It could be made silently and alone, or it could be announced out loud in the company of priests, bishops, or other witnesses. This was something the crusade preachers could not really get heavily involved in. The vow was ultimately between God and the crusader, both of whom knew what was vowed and why. The individuality of each vow made it difficult for the authors of the crusade model sermons to give guidance on the subject. Instead, the preachers focused on the act of service to God.

The parallel between crusading as a performance of one's duties and the military service of vassals has caught the eye of many modern scholars.[25] The theme of vassalage has been examined mainly from the viewpoint of how it was used to inspire crusading — explaining how the knights were persuaded to take the cross with the application of the feudal theme. The focus has been on the ways by which crusade preachers attempted to enlist new crusaders. However, the feudal theme provided more than just inspiration for new crusaders or those considering becoming a crusader. Crusade preachers also utilized the theme of vassalage to guide the crusaders in their conduct.

In the secular sources of the crusading period, in vernacular songs and poems, the relationship between God and crusaders was often depicted in the form of feudal relations. The love of God was associated with the 'love' between vassals and lords.[26] Initially, the papacy seems to have been reluctant to use this association with feudal relations in crusade propaganda, because it oversimplified matters.[27] From the beginning of crusading God was portrayed as

[24] Guibert de Tournai, 'Ad crucesignatos et crucesignandos sermo primus', *CPI*, p. 188: 'quia veri crucesignati, qui vere contriti et confessi ad servitium Dei accinguntur et in ipso moriuntur'.

[25] See, for example, Riley-Smith, 'Crusading as an Act of Love', pp. 190–91; *PCHL*, p. 105; Smith, *Crusading in the Age of Joinville*, pp. 82–87.

[26] Smith, *Crusading in the Age of Joinville*, pp. 83–86. In the Middle Ages the bond between vassals and lords was strong. The term 'vassal' was synonymous with 'ami'. Bloch, *Feudal Society*, p. 231; Riley-Smith, 'Crusading as an Act of Love', p. 190. The term 'fideles' was also applied when referring to vassals. Reynolds, *Fiefs and Vassals*, p. 20.

[27] Smith, *Crusading in the Age of Joinville*, p. 83; Riley-Smith, 'Crusading as an Act of Love', p. 181.

a lord who had lost his inheritance and needed the assistance of his faithful, but specific feudal allusions were avoided. During the early thirteenth century, after Pope Innocent III's willingness to exploit the popular notion more straightforwardly, the idea of vassalage was incorporated into the propaganda of the Roman Church. When Innocent III proclaimed a crusade in 1213, he demanded that Christians help their brothers in the East who were persecuted by the Saracens. In the encyclical *Quia maior* the pope focused his attention on the love of God and the nature of the relationship between the soldiers of Christ and their Lord. For the first time, Innocent portrayed God as a celestial king and the crusaders as his vassals.[28]

There were some fundamental ideological problems with the comparison of relations between crusaders and God and between vassals and their lords. Firstly, God could not be regarded as obliged by law to perform certain duties as feudal kings were. Vassalage was a bilateral contract with mutual responsibilities for vassals and lords. In return for homage and allegiance the vassals received protection, rewards, wages, or other benefits from their liege lords. Lords were supposed to perform certain duties and take care of their vassals under the obligations of feudal law.[29] God, however, was omnipotent and above law. God could not be impelled or influenced by regulations to perform. Secondly, the crusaders could not be considered as obliged to take part in crusades under duress. This would have undermined the notion of free will.[30] Crusaders made the decision to go on crusade out of love for God. They were expressing their devotion, not implementing an action which they were liable for by regulations of feudal law.

Jacques de Vitry and Guibert de Tournai used the feudal theme explicitly in their crusade sermons. Both underlined the reciprocal obligations of vassals and lords. The great compensation which awaited the vassals was emphasized: God offered his vassals the heavenly kingdom in return for their 'light' military

[28] Innocentius III, *Quia maior*, in *PL*, CCXVI, cols 817D–818A: 'Si enim rex aliquis temporalis a suis hostibus ejiceretur de regno, nisi vassalli ejus pro eo non solum res exponerent, sed personas, nonne cum regnum recuperaret amissum, eos velut infideles damnaret, et excogitaret in eos inexcogitata tormenta, quibus perderet male malos? Sic Rex regum, Dominus Jesus Christus, qui corpus et animam et caetera vobis contulit bona, de ingratitudinis vitio et infidelitatis crimine vos damnabit, si ei quasi ejecto de regno, quod pretio sui sanguinis comparavit, neglexeritis subvenire'.

[29] Reynolds, *Fiefs and Vassals*, pp. 17–43. For the feudal laws of vassalage in the kingdom of Jerusalem, see, for example, Jean d'Ibelin, *Le Livre des Assises*, cap. 127–217, ed. by Edbury, pp. 309–563.

[30] See above, pp. 95–96.

service.[31] Jacques maintained that the crusaders should act like 'faithful vassals' and 'liegemen'. The vassals should hurry to help their lord, to fight as his soldiers against his enemies, as well as help themselves by taking part in the crusades.[32]

Jacques was quite careful in the wording of his sermon. He explained that the crusaders were expected to serve the 'highest emperor' as loyal subjects.[33] The crusaders' obligation was to defend 'the patrimony' of their lord, that is, God. This obligation was, however, a moral one. Jacques stressed that the crusaders were not 'bound by feudal law' to take action. God summoned Christians to battle and everyone should participate 'willingly', because of the great rewards offered.[34] Guibert de Tournai followed Jacques's example closely in his crusade sermon. He too compared the crusaders to vassals. According to Guibert, God wanted to test his friends and find out who his faithful vassals were. Guibert also wanted to make clear that crusaders were not forced to act in compliance with feudal regulations. He pointed out that the crusaders should defend their lord, but that they were not obliged to do so under feudal law.[35] The crusade preachers thus utilized the theme of vassalage in their sermons, but in their references to feudal customs took caution to avoid any suggestion of mandatory crusading.

The *Vie de Saint Louis*, the account of Louis IX's life by the chronicler and crusader Jean de Joinville, gives confirmation of the view that the taking of the

---

[31] Guibert de Tournai, 'Ad crucesignatos et crucesignandos sermo primus', *CPI*, p. 188: 'modo Dominus de regno suo optimum facit forum, dum crucesignatis exponit pro peregrinatione modici temporis regnum celorum'; Jacques de Vitry, 'Item sermo ad crucesignatos vel -signandos', *CPI*, p. 126. Both Jacques de Vitry and Guibert de Tournai also paralleled crusading practices and feudal customs. Jacques de Vitry, 'Item sermo ad crucesignatos vel -signandos', *CPI*, p. 126: 'Consuetudo quidem est nobilium et potentium quod per cirothecam vel aliam rem vilis pretii vasallos suos investiunt de feodis pretiosis, sicut Dominus per crucem ex modico filo vel panno vasallos suos investit de celesti regno'. Guibert de Tournai, 'Ad crucesignatos et crucesignandos sermo primus', *CPI*, p. 188.

[32] Jacques de Vitry, 'Item sermo ad crucesignatos vel -signandos', *CPI*, p. 126.

[33] Jacques de Vitry, 'Sermo ad crucesignatos vel -signandos', *CPI*, p. 98: 'Dominus quidem affligitur in patrimonii sui amissione et vult amicos probare et experiri si fideles eius vasalli estis'.

[34] Jacques de Vitry, 'Sermo ad crucesignatos vel -signandos', *CPI*, pp. 98–99: 'Qui enim a domino ligio tenent feodum, si desit illi dum inpugnatur et hereditas sua illi aufertur, merito feodo privatur. Vos autem corpus et animam et quicquid habetis a summo imperatore tenetis, qui vos hodie citari facit, ut ei in prelio succuratis, et licet iure feodi non teneremini'.

[35] Guibert de Tournai, 'Ad crucesignatos et crucesignandos sermo primus', *CPI*, p. 186: 'et licet iure feodi non teneremini'.

cross was deeply connected to feudal and kin relations. Jean describes how he himself took the cross together with other feudal lords, following the king like a true vassal, after which he and his cousin travelled together to the expedition.[36] However, the *Vie de Saint Louis* also gives the impression that the higher nobility at least believed that their participation was voluntary. Jean took the cross during the Seventh Crusade in 1245–54 but refused to take part in the Eighth Crusade in 1267–70, despite being pressured by both of his feudal lords, the King of France, Louis IX, and the King of Navarre, Thibaud V.[37] Jean did not want to take part in another crusade, which he regarded as ill-advised, and, ironically, pleaded not to go on grounds of feudal obligations. According to Jean, after the Seventh Crusade the agents of Louis IX and Thibaud V had oppressed 'his people', the dependents of the house of Joinville and perhaps more broadly the people of Champagne, so greatly that he could not leave them behind. Jean maintained that if he took the cross a second time, these people would suffer even more: moreover, if he should happen to die on the expedition, his dependents would suffer too. Jean had to remain at home to protect his impoverished people.[38] Thus Jean utilized the mechanisms of the feudal system as an argument against going on crusade, refusing to obey the demands of his feudal lords so that he could look after his dependents.

---

[36] Jean de Joinville was born *c.* 1224 and was the seneschal of the county of Champagne. He participated in the Seventh Crusade and wrote the famous work the *Vie de Saint Louis* in 1309. This work was written to prove the sanctity of Louis IX, and it includes a lengthy account of the Seventh Crusade. Jean died in 1317. For a critical edition, see Jean de Joinville, *Vie de Saint Louis*, ed. by Monfrin, which is used in the current study. For a recent English translation, see *Joinville and Villehardouin, Chronicles of the Crusades*, trans. by Smith. Jean de Joinville is another fine example of the important role that lineage and family traditions played in motivating the nobility to take part in crusades: Jean decided to become a crusader after a long line of crusaders from the Joinville family. Jean's great-great-grandfather, Geoffrey III de Joinville, participated in the Second Crusade; Geoffrey IV de Joinville died during the Third Crusade; Geoffrey V de Joinville participated in the Fourth Crusade; Jean's father, Simon de Joinville, participated in the Fifth Crusade, while he himself participated in the Seventh Crusade. See the epitaph for Geoffrey III de Joinville composed by Jean de Joinville in 1311, *Joinville and Villehardouin, Chronicles of the Crusades*, trans. by Smith, pp. 346–48.

[37] Jean de Joinville was the seneschal of Champagne and thus the vassal of the Count of Champagne, King Thibaud. In 1252, Jean also became the vassal of Louis IX, as the King of France was so pleased with his service during the Seventh Crusade that he granted Jean an annual income. *Joinville and Villehardouin, Chronicles of the Crusades*, trans. by Smith, p. 366 n. 5.

[38] Jean de Joinville, *Vie de Saint Louis*, ed. by Monfrin, p. 364.

Charlemagne and the Question of Trust

Medieval vassalage was a display of loyalty and service. The crusaders needed to prove their allegiance and serve God, for this was a test of their loyalty. Both Jacques de Vitry and Guibert de Tournai following him explained, in their sermons, why why God tested his friends. The Lord could have saved the Holy Land himself, if he had wanted to do this, but he preferred to give them a chance to acquire eternal reward. God had lost his patrimony so he could find out who his faithful vassals and true friends were.[39] This Bernadine explication rested on the idea of God's mercifulness: God pretended to be in a vulnerable position, in need of help, so sinners could serve him and gain salvation.[40]

One common failing of the knights and nobles, according to medieval ecclesiastical writers and some of the authors of the crusade sermons of this study, was their tendency to quarrel constantly amongst themselves and their inability to hold to truces. Loyalties shifted, knights served different feudal lords, and vassals fought against each other, all at the expense of the Holy Land. Many felt that the rivalry between Philip II Augustus and Richard I had ruined the Third Crusade.[41] One knight might do homage to several different lords, which also created difficulties. In time of crisis, if those lords fought against each other, whom should the vassal serve?[42] The theme of service to God made it clear where the knights should place their loyalties. The vassals of God ought to serve first and foremost their celestial lord and put aside their feuds and earthly ambitions.

---

[39] Jacques de Vitry, 'Sermo ad crucesignatos vel -signandos', *CPI*, p. 96: 'Sicut autem lapidem ponderosum solent proicere ad probandas vires, ita Dominus per civitatem illam probat qui fortes sint animo et qui pusillanimes et qui sint amici eius'. See also Jacques de Vitry, 'Item sermo ad crucesignatos vel signandos', *CPI*, pp. 117–18. Guibert de Tournai argued in his sermon, following Jacques's example, that God wanted to give his friends the opportunity to suffer on his behalf. God's true friends could distinguish themselves and gain the great rewards offered. Guibert de Tournai, 'Ad crucesignatos et crucesignandos sermo primus', *CPI*, p. 186: 'Affligitur Dominus in sui patrimonii amissione et vult amicos suos probare, si sunt fideles vasalli eius. Qui enim a domino ligio tenet feodum, si desit ei dum impugnatur et hereditas sua illi aufertur, merito feodo privatur'. See also Eudes de Châteauroux, 'Sermo in conversione sancti Pauli et exhortatio ad assumendam crucem', *CPI*, p. 136.

[40] Bernard of Clairvaux, *Epistolae*, in *PL*, CLXXXII, cols 565–67. See also Tamminen, 'The Test of Friendship', p. 224.

[41] Jacques de Vitry, *Historia orientalis*, CI, ed. by Donnadieu, p. 456; Guibert de Tournai, *Collectio de scandalis ecclesiae*, ed. by Stroick, p. 39.

[42] Bloch, *Feudal Society*, p. 213; Reynolds, *Fiefs and Vassals*, pp. 21–22.

In his crusade sermon, Eudes de Châteauroux reminded the audience, some of whom were probably preparing for the Seventh Crusade, that in the service of Christ the crusaders should not serve others. Eudes's sermon was preached during the feast of the Conversion of St Paul, possibly in 1248, just prior to the crusade.[43] Eudes emphasized different aspects of conversion in the sermon. He explained how the crusaders served God and what it meant to be in Christ's service. Eudes pointed out that when people 'converted' to some king, they naturally abandoned another king who was hostile. To validate his viewpoint, he also quoted Matthew, 'no man can serve two masters: for either he will hate the one and love the other or sustain the one and despise the other'.[44]

As the legate of the coming crusade, Eudes wanted to prepare the partici-pants of the expedition for the difficulties lying ahead and the hardships of the approaching departure. In the service of Christ, the crusaders should give up everything else. They should make a full conversion, leave everything behind, and do service for their new lord. All this should happen because the crusad-ers loved God more than anything else.[45] The crusaders should depart without worries and leave their wives and children behind, for they were now serving God. The crusaders could not serve earthly masters, their beloved, their desires, their riches, or other lords, because as vassals of God they could serve only their celestial lord.

With the theme of vassalage the crusade preachers could explain the mili-tary dimension of crusading and demand from the Christians true service to God. The soldierly features of the ideal crusaders and their faithfulness to their lord could be asserted. With this theme the crusade preachers could also explain the pain of separation, which many crusaders found difficult to cope with. The theme of vassalage further allowed the preachers to address problems of disu-nity and the divisions of loyalty which afflicted crusade armies. The preachers could dismantle the semi-independent units of the army, the small groups of liegemen following their own lords or different and rival political groups such as those from the Italian maritime cities, and attempt to create a more cohesive group, an army bound by an oath of vassalage to one common lord, to God.

---

[43] See Appendix V.

[44] Eudes de Châteauroux, 'Sermo in conversione sancti Pauli et exhortation ad assumendam crucem', *CPI*, p. 130: 'Sicut quando aliqui convertunt se ad aliquem regem, eo ipso regem alium inimicantem illi derelinquunt, unde Matheo vi: *Nemo potest duobus dominis servire: Aut enim unum odio habebit et alterum diliget aut unum sustinebit et alterum contempnet*'. Mt. 6. 24.

[45] Eudes de Châteauroux, 'Sermo in conversione sancti Pauli et exhortation ad assumendam crucem', *CPI*, p. 130.

In his sermon for the crusaders and pilgrims Jacques de Vitry gives practical advice on how to avoid internal conflicts within the crusade host. He urged people to choose their travelling companions wisely and instructed them not to engage in litigation when harmed by the host or by fellow participants, for it was better to suffer small losses than to harm one's soul in legal disputes.[46] The 'true' crusaders should thus focus on serving their celestial lord and refrain from all altercations between other participants in the crusades. To avoid the quarrelling of the great lords during the expeditions and to maintain continual aid for the Holy Land, Pope Gregory IX suggested (in 1238) that it might be more fruitful for the Holy Land if the princes did not go there all at the same time, but rather on different, successive occasions.[47]

Medieval vassalage was an agreement founded on trust, which worked in two diverging ways: a liege lord had to be able to trust that his vassals would obey him and serve him accordingly, while vassals needed to be able to rely on their lord to give righteous decisions and to provide for them. The crusade preachers emphasized these two aspects of trust in their sermons. The crusaders as vassals of God had to be trustworthy and defend the patrimony of their liege

---

[46] Jacques de Vitry, 'Ad peregrinos. Thema sumpta ex Zacharias ultimo', *JVSP*, p. 98: 'Pari modo a litibus et contentionibus necesse est ut abstineant peregrini. Melius enim modicum dampnum ab hospite vel socio sustinere quam litigando animam suam ledere'. Jacques had been astounded at the constant conflicts and legal disputes between the different Christian groups of the East when he arrived there. The Christian groups of the Holy Land and the various groups inside the army of the Fifth Crusade all appeared to have their own vested interests, their own policies, and their own rules. Jacques de Vitry, *Epistola*, II, ed. by Huygens, pp. 85–85; *JVSP*, p. 86.

[47] Pope Gregory IX made this suggestion during a conflict between Richard of Cornwall and Henry III, caused by Richard's determination to go crusading and Henry's reluctance to let him leave. The pope tried to balance the two opposing views by giving the king a mandate not to allow the *crucesignatus* Richard to leave for the Barons' Crusade because 'the good of the kingdom' necessitated this. Gregory IX advised the Earl of Cornwall to put himself in the service of the king instead of leaving for the Holy Land. The pope explained that it would be better for the Holy Land if the lords went separately on crusades. Richard, therefore, ought to wait until Henry was ready to let him leave and not try to depart in the same general passage with Thibaud de Champagne and the French crusaders. However, Gregory also decreed that if Richard was determined to go, the crusading subsidies needed to be given to him when he arrived at his destination. Gregorius IX, *Reg.*, no. 4267, no. 4268, in *Les Registres de Gregoire IX*, ed. by Auvray, II, 973–75: 'Preterea, et si comes ipse deberet in presenti transire, multipliciter tamen fore dinoscitur fructuosum, ut executionem voti sui ac baronum qui secum in Terram Sanctam sunt parati procedere, in tempus proroget oportunum; presertim cum ejusdem Terre negotium utilius dirigatur et melius, si a magnatibus secundum diversa tempora subventio sibi successiva proveniat, quam quod ab ipsis illuc in uno et eodem passagio procedatur'. See also *Calendar of Entries in the Papal Register*, ed. by Bliss, XIX, 169.

lord faithfully. Their lord God, who was always just, would then take care of his own and reward the vassals generously for their services.

In his crusade sermon, Jacques de Vitry explained how the crusaders should trust their lord, taking their example from Charlemagne. Charlemagne was a contemporary model of an ideal lord, used as an example for the crusaders already during the First Crusade.[48] Medieval Christians were accustomed to hearing tales about Charlemagne. He appeared frequently in the *chansons de geste*. Many of the stories dealt specifically with issues related to feudal relations.[49] In the sermon, Jacques told a story in which Charlemagne tested the obedience of his three sons, Gobaudus, Ludovicus, and Loerins. Each son had to open his mouth in front of everyone and take a piece of apple from Charlemagne, which Gobaudus refused to do as he was not willing to suffer such shame. Ludovicus instead took the apple and replied, 'as you wish; treat me as you would treat your servant', after which Charlemagne decided to give him the kingdom of Francia. Loerins also accepted the apple and got the duchy of Lotharingia as a reward. When Gobaudus realized that he had erred and wanted to take a piece of the apple, Charlemagne told him that he had acted too late and would not get any apple or any land. Gobaudus's disobedience had cost him his inheritance and the respect of everyone.[50]

Jacques's exemplum made clear what was at stake in crusading and how the business of the cross should be conducted. Christians should rise to the challenge and take the cross, as God tested Christians to see who were loyal to him, so that he could distinguish them, just as Charlemagne tested his sons; those who refused to comply would be disinherited, as was Gobaudus. The 'anti'-crusaders would lose their place in paradise and go to hell. Because they would not act as faithful vassals, their fief would rightly be taken from them. Although the taking of the cross might seem precarious, just as the taking of the apple in

---

[48] In Robert the Monk's version of the Clermont sermon, King Charles the Great is referred to as an 'inspiration', whose deeds and achievements the crusaders could follow. Robert the Monk, *Historia Iherosolimitana*, in *RHC Occ.*, III, 728: 'Moveant vos et incitent animos vestros ad virilitatem gesta praedecessorum vestrorum, probitas et magnitudo Karoli Magni regis, et Ludovici filii ejus aliorumque regum bestrorum, qui regna paganorum destruxerunt et in eis fines sanctae, Ecclesiae dilataverunt'. Stuckey, 'Charlemagne', pp. 70–77. See also Curta and Stuckey, 'Charlemagne in Medieval East Central Europe'.

[49] Charlemagne was also linked to the crusading theme in the *chansons de geste*, making him a kind of proto-crusader. Stuckey, 'Charlemagne', pp. 19–20, 28, 50, 69, 73; Trotter, *Medieval French Literature and the Crusades*, pp. 25–26.

[50] Jacques de Vitry, 'Item sermo ad crucesignatos vel -signandos', *CPI*, p. 124: 'Cui ille: Sicut placet vobis; de me tamquam de servo vestro facite'.

front of everyone might seem embarrassing, the crusaders should act like true vassals and trust in their lord, for they would be rewarded abundantly as were the faithful sons of Charlemagne.

Jacques encouraged the crusaders to blindly trust in and obey their lord, which was important not only in the opening stages of the crusader's journey, in the taking of the cross, but also during the actual expedition. The crusaders needed to express their trust while serving their lord. This important component of the agreement was at times overlooked by the crusaders, according to contemporary ecclesiastical commentators. In the failed crusade expeditions, the soldiers of Christ were described as having put their trust in their numbers, in their fighting skills, and in the decisions of earthly lords, failing to trust completely the celestial lord whom they were serving. This was an indication of a lack of allegiance that would result in the disfavour of the lord and in the failure of the crusade.[51]

In his crusade sermon against the Mongols, Eudes de Châteauroux mentioned the knights as a particular group of people who had shown that they trusted in Christ. Eudes took a positive standpoint on the matter of trust, possibly because his audience was composed of *milites*, and asked who, in his day, confessed that Christ was their lord better and more expressly than the knights.[52] Eudes used positive encouragement when persuading his audience of knights to take the cross. The argument also urged those who had already taken the cross to continue to put their trust in God. By confessing that Christ was their lord the vassals showed their respect for God and accepted that they ought to fight on his behalf. This way the crusaders fulfilled the requirements of 'good vassalage', and God would fulfil the requirements of 'good lordship' by rewarding his servants. As Humbert de Romans pointed out, the celestial lord had also demonstrated his goodness, for he had already suffered on behalf of his servants.[53]

Humbert used the theme of vassalage and the example of Charlemagne in his *De predicatione sancte crucis*, recommending the king and his adventures in Spain as a source of inspiration for the promotion of crusades. When composing

---

[51] See, for example, Jacques de Vitry, *Historia orientalis*, XCVI, ed. by Donnadieu, p. 434.

[52] Eudes de Châteauroux, 'Sermo de invitatione ad crucem', *CPI*, p. 146: 'Et qui hodie melius et expressius confitentur Christum esse suum dominum quam milites?'

[53] Humbert de Romans, 'De predicatione crucis in genere quocumque', *CPI*, pp. 218–20: 'Si ergo homines propter fidelitatem servandam domino terreno, a quo non habent nisi temporalia et pro quo frequenter multa mala sustinent et a quo modicam vel nullam remunerationem expectant, sic pugnant viriliter, quanto magis debent hoc pro Domino celesti facere, a quo habent corpus et animam et qui tot pro eis passus est et tam gloriose remunerat pugnantes pro se!'

their crusade sermons the preachers should, according to Humbert, utilize the *Gesta Karoli Magni in Hispania* of Pseudo-Turpin and show how Charlemagne had piously fought for God and in return gained divine assistance.[54]

Humbert's manual also depicted Roland as an example of a true vassal. Roland had served Charlemagne faithfully and fought for God in an ideal manner. Before the Battle of Roncevaux, Roland received the Eucharist, confessed all his sins, and prayed to God. In the manual Humbert included a lengthy quotation from the prayer from *Gesta Karoli Magni in Hispania*, where Roland explained that he had fought for Christ, to exalt his name, and 'endured countless blows and wounds' and 'suffered abuse and ridicule', 'fatigue, cold, hunger, thirst' for Christ's sake. Roland committed his soul to God and wished that God would send his archangels to guide those who had died in the hands of Saracens directly to heaven.[55]

Famous crusaders were often compared to Roland in the crusade chronicles of the period.[56] Humbert utilized this popular notion in his preaching manual and portrayed the heroic vassal of Charlemagne as a model that the crusaders could emulate. Humbert also provided the crusade preachers with the model of a 'bad vassal' from *Gesta Karoli Magni in Hispania*. The treacherous Ganelon had betrayed the Franks, which resulted in Roland's death. Again, Humbert quotes a lengthy passage, where the 'good vassal' Roland is celebrated: Charlemagne calls him, among other things, 'the honour of the French', 'the destroyer of Saracens', 'a wall to the clergy', 'a staff to the orphans', 'food for widows', and 'refreshment for the poor'. Roland is depicted as having ascended to heaven, where he is now in the company of angels and saints, praised with the martyrs. Humbert also mentions the fate of the 'bad vassal'. Ganelon suffers a traitor's death. The Judas-

---

[54] Humbert summarized parts of the *Gesta Karoli Magni in Hispania* in his manual, in two separate chapters, mentioning Charlemagne's dream where St James had requested him to free the saint's church so that Christian pilgrims could visit there. Humbert de Romans, *De predicatione sancte crucis*, cap. xxxvi, De gestis Karoli magni in hispania. For the Pseudo-Turpin, see Trotter, *Medieval French Literature and the Crusades*, pp. 23–24. For the chronicle, see *Die Chronik von Karl dem Grossen und Roland*, ed. by Klein. See also *PCHL*, pp. 214–15.

[55] Humbert de Romans, *De predicatione sancte crucis*, cap. xxxvi.

[56] See, for example, the *Gesta Tancredi* of Raoul de Caen, where some of the leaders of the First Crusade were compared to Roland and Oliver. Raoul de Caen, *Gesta Tancredi*, trans. by Bachrach and Bachrach, p. 53; Trotter, *Medieval French Literature and the Crusades*, pp. 21–22. Eudes de Châteauroux also made a reference to Roland's death in his crusade sermon that was delivered for the feast of the Holy Relics, possibly in 1251 in the Holy Land. Eudes de Châteauroux, 'Sermo in festo sanctarum reliquiarum', *UEE*, ii, 764: 'sicut memoria mortis Rotholandi non tangit cor eius qui de eo cantat, sed tangit aliquando corda eorum qui audiunt'.

like character is torn apart by four horses as punishment for betraying both his earthly and heavenly lords, Charlemagne and God.[57]

The crusade preachers could use this popular story of Pseudo-Turpin in their sermons to convince the Christians of the need to serve God as true vassals. The crusaders could be compared to Roland and considered to possess the same celebrated qualities as he possessed. The story also implied that the 'true' crusaders, who served their lord and died on their journey, would die as martyrs and ascend directly to heaven, as Roland did. The 'anti'-crusaders, who did not serve their lord, on the other hand, could be thought of as traitors, and they would suffer the punishment for refusing to do service for their lord.

The Imitatio Christi

The Christocentric features, rooted deep in crusade ideology, made Christ the most important character of the crusade sermons, the person most frequently referred to, whose teachings are repeated in all the sermons. This also made Christ the most important role model for the crusaders. Likeness to a role model could be achieved through imitation. The *imitatio Christi*, a concept that can be traced to early Christian times, was a widespread phenomenon in thirteenth-century society and an important ideal in crusade ideology.[58] The imitation or the following of Christ has had different meanings and emphasis at different times. The concept is primarily founded on passages from the Gospels of Matthew and Luke, and the so-called 'Pauline imitation texts'. The patristic writers of Antiquity, who dealt with various doctrinal issues such as the two natures of Christ and the Holy Trinity in an effort to achieve consistency of faith in a world full of different Christian branches and beliefs, had different concerns with the concept than the later medieval theologians.[59]

---

[57] Humbert de Romans, *De predicatione sancte crucis*, cap. xxxvij, De visione Turpini episcopi super animas in bello defunctorum.

[58] Constable, *Three Studies in Medieval Religious and Social Thought*, pp. 145–46; Purkis, *Crusading Spirituality*, pp. 22–29; Smith, *Crusading in the Age of Joinville*, pp. 103–05; Housley, *Contesting the Crusades*, p. 57.

[59] For St Paul's views on the imitation of Christ, see 1 Cor. 4. 16; Eph. 5. 1; 1 Thes. 1. 6. See also Sanders, 'Imitating Paul'; Belleville, '"Imitate Me, Just as I Imitate Christ"'; Plummer, *Paul's Understanding of the Church's Mission*, pp. 81–105. For the passages in the Gospels, see, for example, Mt. 11. 29 and 16. 24; Lk. 9. 23. For the concept of imitation of Christ in the New Testament, see Tinsley, *The Imitation of God in Christ*; Betz, *Nachfolge und Nachahmung Jesu Christi*; Constable, *Three Studies in Medieval Religious and Social Thought*, pp. 146–49. On the medieval term *imitatio*, see esp. Ghellinck, 'Imitari, Imitatio'.

In the early Middle Ages, the *imitatio Christi* focused on the divinity of Christ. The imitation was linked to the deification of man. This was a way for men to attain divine features, to become again the image of God. The early monks followed the example of the martyrs and Christ by attempting to achieve a life of perfection. In the early Middle Ages, Christ was often regarded as a mediator between man and God.[60] During the Carolingian period, Christ was described as a leader in war, the cross was his battle standard, and soldiers could imitate Christ by following him to war.[61] Christ was also identified as a divine lord or a king. Emperor Charles II was called the *salvator mundi*, whom God had elevated as a king in imitation of the true king Christ. The *imitatio* was applied in the sanctification of kingship, and the ruler could be regarded, like Christ, as a mediator between men and God.[62]

In the high and late Middle Ages, the focus in the concept of the *imitatio Christi* shifted, with new emphasis being given to the humanity of Christ and to the human body of Christ. In essence these were two different types of imitation — the imitation of Christ's divinity and the imitation of his humanity — which can be understood as imitations concentrating on either his being or his doing, on the spirit or on the matter.[63] The papacy of the high Middle Ages utilized both of these types by describing the pope as a *pauper* following the human steps of Christ, as a vicar following Christ's priestly role, and as a ruler replacing Christ on the royal earthly throne.[64]

Recently, some modern scholars have taken a critical approach to the utilization of the theme of *imitatio Christi* in the crusading context. William Purkis has argued that by the time the Second Crusade was in the making the importance of the concept of *imitatio Christi* was diminishing. According to Purkis, Bernard of Clairvaux and Pope Eugenius III avoided the theme in the promotion of the Second Crusade. Purkis has described the Cistercian view of *imitatio Christi* in crusade spirituality as an 'elite perception', in contrast to 'popular perceptions' of the period, such as those expressed by Peter the Venerable or Eudes de Deuil. With this dichotomy between the elite and the popular perceptions, Purkis has

[60] Constable, *Three Studies in Medieval Religious and Social Thought*, pp. 150–59.

[61] Haendler, *Epochen karolingischer Theologie*, pp. 86–89, 120–22; Constable, *Three Studies in Medieval Religious and Social Thought*, p. 159 n. 96.

[62] Kantorowicz, *The King's Two Bodies*, pp. 87–88.

[63] Constable, *Three Studies in Medieval Religious and Social Thought*, p. 169; Kantorowicz, *The King's Two Bodies*, p. 89.

[64] Maccarrone, *Vicarius Christi*; Constable, *Three Studies in Medieval Religious and Social Thought*, p. 161; Kantorowicz, *The King's Two Bodies*, pp. 89–90.

explained the use of the concept of *imitatio Christi* and the lack of utilization of the theme in the crusade propaganda of the Second Crusade.[65] Purkis has also pointed out that during the period 1150–87 crusade preachers did not utilize the ideas of Christo-mimesis at all in their crusade propaganda.[66]

Purkis's thesis that there was a lack of utilization of the concept of *imitatio Christi* in certain periods during the twelfth century, in large measure a consequence of Cistercian influence on crusade ideology, is certainly interesting; however, a dichotomy between elite and popular perceptions is problematic. It is difficult to argue that Peter the Venerable was a popular thinker and not a member of the twelfth-century elite. As a period when crusade preachers did not utilize the theme of imitation of Christ, 1150–87 is a rather unrepresentative sample, as this falls between two large-scale crusades, the Second and the Third, and there are only limited sources from those years available for studying the propaganda of the crusade preachers. The model sermons of the thirteenth century offer a different point of view.

The biblical quotation from Matthew, 'If any man will come after me, let him deny himself, and take up his cross, and follow me', was repeated with different emphasis in many of the crusade sermons of this study. This passage was used in crusade sermons from the beginning of crusading. Pope Urban II is reported to have cited it in Clermont in 1095.[67] The following and taking up

---

[65] Purkis, 'Elite and Popular Perceptions of *Imitatio Christi*'.

[66] Purkis, *Crusading Spirituality*, pp. 85–98, 114–15. Purkis has argued that Cistercian influence was the reason for the replacement of the *imitatio Christi* as the most important in the crusade ideology by other motifs. Susanna Throop has also taken a critical approach to the use of the theme of *imitatio Christi* in the crusading context. Throop has studied the concept of vengeance in crusade ideology and explored carefully the use of such terms as 'aemulatio' and 'zelus' in different crusade related sources. She has drawn attention to the slight difference in meaning between the terms 'emulation' and 'imitation' and has accordingly contributed to our understanding of notions of revenge in crusade ideology. In a recent article, Throop has argued that the *imitatio Christi* was a 'limited strain of crusading rhetoric'. It appears to me that she has misinterpreted Purkis's studies in her article, or made an excessively broad generalization from Purkis's conclusions. Throop, 'Zeal, Anger and Vengeance', p. 198. For notions of vengeance in crusade ideology and the use of the terms 'aemulatio' and 'zelus', see Throop, *Crusading as an Act of Vengeance*, esp. pp. 165–66.

[67] Mt. 16. 24. See *Anonymi Gesta Francorum et aliorum Hierosolymitanorum*, ed. by Hagenmeyer, p. 101. Philippe le Chancelier, '*Dicit Dominus ad Moysen*', Avranches, MS 132, fol. 273rb; Federico Visconti, 'Quando idem dominus predicavit crucem litteraliter clero pisano de mandato domini Pape', *SVP*, p. 544; Roger of Salisbury, '*Ascendente* Ihesu *in naviculam*', *PCHL*, p. 230; 'Brevis ordinacio de predicacione', *QBSS*, p. 20; Humbert de Romans, *De predicatione sancte crucis*, cap. vi, Quare crux ponitur in humero dextro; see also cap. iv, cap. xxvii.

of the cross could be interpreted in various ways in the context of the crusades. Christians who had become crusaders had taken up the cross, and they were now in the service of Christ, signed with his cross, but this could also mean that those who had taken up the cross wanted to follow Christ, that they had become his disciples, or that they sought a closer relationship with him or a better understanding of him and his sufferings.[68]

The crusade preachers instructed the crusaders to deny themselves as they followed Christ and participated in the campaigns.[69] This meant that the crusaders needed to be willing to suffer for Christ, but it also suggested that the crusaders should be ready for a radical change in their lives and renouncement of the past. Roger of Salisbury regarded the self-denial of the followers of Christ to mean a wholehearted spiritual conversion. The crusaders or the penitents who boarded the ship of Christ were his disciples and ought to have contempt for worldly goods. Those who had taken the cross had decided to abandon the world.[70]

This spiritual conversion of the crusaders meant that they renounced everything and transformed themselves in imitation of Christ. Eudes de Châteauroux urged the crusaders to follow Christ, just as St Paul had converted himself from a sinner to a devout follower of Christ. Paul, of course, had formerly been Saul of Tarsus, a persecutor of Christians. Paul left behind his people and country, gave up his nobility, his wealth, his honours, his mastership, and his future as a husband or a father, deciding to become a virgin, all this because of his burning

---

Eudes de Châteauroux quoted the similar passages from 1 John and Luke in his crusade sermons: 'Whoever claims to remain in Christ must himself walk just as he walked' (1 John 2. 6) in 'Sermo in conversione sancti Pauli, et exhortatio ad assumendam crucem', *CPI*, p. 139; and 'If any man will come after me, let him deny himself, and take up his cross daily, and follow me' (Lk. 9. 23) in two of his sermons: 'Sermo de cruce et de invitatione ad crucem', *CPI*, p. 164, and 'Sermo ad invitandum ad crucem', *CPI*, p. 170. Guibert de Tournai also quoted the passage from Luke in his sermon 'Ad crucesignatos et crucesignandos sermo primus', *CPI*, p. 180.

[68] *CPI*, p. 60.

[69] Philippe le Chancelier, '*Dicit Dominus ad Moysen*', Avranches, MS 132, fol. 273rb; Federico Visconti, 'Quando idem dominus predicavit crucem litteraliter clero pisano de mandato domini Pape', *SVP*, p. 544; Roger of Salisbury, '*Ascendente* Ihesu *in naviculam*', *PCHL*, p. 230; Eudes de Châteauroux, 'Sermo de cruce et de invitatione ad crucem', *CPI*, p. 164, and 'Sermo ad invitandum ad crucem', *CPI*, p. 170; Guibert de Tournai, 'Ad crucesignatos et crucesignandos sermo primus', *CPI*, p. 180.

[70] Roger of Salisbury, '*Ascendente* Ihesu *in naviculam*', *PCHL*, pp. 227, 230. See also Federico Visconti, 'Quando idem Dominus predicavit crucem litteraliter clero pisano de mandato domini Pape', *SVP*, pp. 544–45.

love for Christ.[71] Eudes wanted his audience of current and potential crusaders to do the same by following Christ. They should not just love God, but should 'be set on fire and burn with his love', and this fire and burning devotion would lead to a total renunciation of all else.[72]

According to the crusade preachers the imitation of Christ implied that those who had taken the cross needed to lay aside their ordinary lives, forget about their personal ambitions, abandon loved ones, and leave behind all their possessions, homes, and fatherlands,[73] as well as relinquish old habits and refuse to take care of their individual needs; in short, the crusaders were told to renounce themselves and become more like Christ. The preachers viewed it as perfectly possible that in ideal cases the crusaders could achieve a remarkable likeness to Christ. For the Franciscan preacher Guibert de Tournai this was not just a question of emulating Christ, but of 'conforming' to Christ. Guibert believed that true righteousness could appear in the crusaders, those who exercised the service of Christ in all aspects, 'with their hearts, mouths, and works'.[74] The crusaders might spiritually conform to Christ through their sufferings, imitation, and contemplation of Christ's sufferings. They could actively seek the love of Christ by expressing their own devotion through crusading. Their love, self-denial, and sacrifice were akin to the love of Christ.[75]

Burning Love

The love for God and Christ as the initial motivating force was promoted by many of the authors of the crusade model sermons. In fact, this appears as one

[71] Eudes de Châteauroux, 'Sermo in conversione sancti Pauli et exhortatio ad assumendam crucem', *CPI*, pp. 128–39.

[72] Eudes de Châteauroux, 'Sermo in conversione sancti Pauli et exhortatio ad assumendam crucem', *CPI*, p. 134: 'Sic ergo, ut dictum est, debemus non tantummodo diligere Deum, immo amore eius ardere et inflammari. Si enim eum diligeremus, tunc omnia delinqueremus corde nichil diligendo nisi propter ipsum vel in ipso, et si arderemus eius amore, tunc etiam omnino omnia abdicaremus sicut Paulus'.

[73] Jacques de Vitry, 'Sermo ad crucesignatos vel -signandos', *CPI*, p. 98; Eudes de Châteauroux, 'Sermo in conversione sancti Pauli et exhortatio ad assumendam crucem', *CPI*, p. 132; Guibert de Tournai, 'Ad crucesignatos et crucesignandos sermo tertius', *CPI*, p. 202.

[74] Guibert de Tournai, 'Ad crucesignatos et crucesignandos sermo tertius', *CPI*, pp. 204–05: 'Crux etiam signum iustitie. Iustitia enim est, ut conformemur Christo [...]. Sed verum signum iustitie apparet in crucesignatis, qui corde, ore et opere se exercent in servitio Dei: corde per devotionem, ore per gratiarum actionem, corpore et opere per laboris satisfactionem'.

[75] *CPI*, p. 60.

of the most consistent themes used by the authors.[76] Eudes de Châteauroux utilized the theme heavily in several of his sermons preached during the preparations for the Seventh Crusade. In the *Sermo in conversione sancti Pauli et exhortatio ad assumendam crucem*, he elaborated on the different aspects of love, making a distinction between illicit and licit love. Eudes explained that lustful love was love of things that were loved for selfish reasons, but natural love was love of things that were loved for the sake of God. He maintained that the reform and conversion of people from sinners to 'true' crusaders would happen only through love.[77]

In another crusade sermon, which appears also to have been preached during the preparations for the Seventh Crusade in 1248, Eudes demonstrated how the love between God and crusaders was a passionate kind of love. Eudes used an image of a deer in heat to describe the crusaders' burning love for God. Just as the deer leaves the woods to find a mate during the mating season, so the crusaders undertook their journey.[78] In a crusade sermon preached during the feast of St George, Eudes also described the love of the warrior-saint that the crusaders could imitate.[79] In this sermon he made a distinction between good and bad horses — the love of St George and the maliciousness of the devil. The Christians needed to choose the right horse, the good one, because this horse was strong and its strength emerged from love and charity. Eudes argued that *'love is strong as death, nothing is stronger than a mind that has love'* and that there was 'nothing more courageous than love'.[80] Therefore, the crusaders ought to be motivated by love of God and their hearts should be filled with charity.

---

[76] *CPI*, pp. 57–58.

[77] Eudes de Châteauroux, 'Sermo in conversione sancti Pauli et exhortatio ad assumendam crucem', *CPI*, p. 130: 'Et loquimur de amore libidinoso qui illicitus est, non de amore naturali qui licitus est. Qui quomodo licitus sit, magna questio est eo quod videtur esse quedam fruitio nature. Sic ergo hec conversio fit per amorem. Et ex quo convertit se quis ad Dominum per amorem, mundum et ea que in mundo sunt derelinquit, ut non amet ea'.

[78] Eudes de Châteauroux, 'Sermo de invitatione ad crucem', *CPI*, p. 152: 'sic et hodie benedicit Dominus illos, qui pro amore eius velut cervi spirituales lustra dimittunt propria, id est terram, in qua nati fuerunt et nutriti. Cervi enim tempore amoris propria cubilia et silvas sibi domesticas dimittunt, flumina transeunt et ad loca ignota se transferunt. Sic hiis temporibus amore Dei ardentes patriam derelinquunt et non tantum flumina transire immo maria festinant et adire barbaras regiones'.

[79] Eudes de Châteauroux, 'De sancto Georgio', *UEE*, ii, 703–05.

[80] Eudes de Châteauroux, 'De sancto Georgio', *UEE*, ii, 703. 'Equs iste fortis est. [...] *Fortis est ut mors dilectio, nichil fortius animo habente caritatem.* [...] Nichil enim audacius caritate'. Eudes quotes Cant. 8. 6.

Their actions should be made with the intention to do good, guided by the example of St George. If love and charity were the things that motivated the crusaders, they would be strong and invincible.

Guibert de Tournai utilized the same biblical passage as Eudes in his crusade sermon but drew a more drastic conclusion from it. Guibert explained that the cross was a similar sign that friends gave each other to remember one another and their friendship while they were apart. He argued that '*love is as strong as death*' and encouraged the crusaders to put the sign of the cross in their hearts, 'through the affection of love', and on their arm through the effect of their actions. Finally, Guibert suggested that if the crusaders truly loved Christ, they would be ready to die for his sake.[81] In Guibert's view, crusading love should have no limits, but those who genuinely loved Christ would sacrifice themselves if need be, for their love was stronger than any other desire they might have, stronger than their zest for life or fear of death. With this argument the Franciscan preacher prepared the crusaders for self-sacrifice and the death that might await them on their journey.

Eudes also made clear in his crusade sermon that Christians should not profess 'the love of a mercenary', who did not love unless he was loved in return. Eudes utilized a biblical quotation to make his point: 'the Lord says: *Love your enemies. If you love them that love you, what reward shall you have? Do not even the publicans do this?*'[82] Eudes used an Old French word *espavein* in the passage of the sermon, referring to a disease in a horse or a swelling in the leg of a horse that causes lameness.[83] This appears to be an allegory of a vice of some

---

[81] Guibert de Tournai, 'Ad crucesignatos et crucesignandos sermo primus', *CPI*, p. 184: 'Est etiam crux signum rememorativum sicut signum quod datur amicis in perpetuandis amicitiis, ut viso signo fiat amici absentis rememoratio. Hoc enim signum nobis relinquit Dominus ad Patrem per crucem recessurus, Can. viii: Pone me ut signaculum super cor tuum, ut signaculum super brachium tuum, quia fortis est ut mors dilectio. Ponamus ergo crucem Christi super cor, hoc est in corde per affectum amoris, et super brachium per effectum operis. Et si vere Christum diligis, pro Christo mori paratus eris'. Humbert de Romans also included this biblical quotation in his manual. Humbert de Romans, *De predicatione sancte crucis*, cap. xxvii: '*quia fortis est ut mors dilectio*'.

[82] Eudes de Châteauroux, 'De sancto Georgio', *UEE*, ii, 704: 'Sunt alii equi habentes vicium quod dicitur espavein, qui non possunt ire, quousque sint calefacti. Hic est amor mercennarius, qui non amat nisi ametur, cum Dominus dicat Mt. v: *Diligite inimicos vestros. Si enim diligitis eos qui vos diligunt, quam mercerdem habebitis, nam et publicani hoc faciunt*'. Mt. 5. 44, 46. Here Eudes may be reflecting the suspicions which the Parisian theologians had about the mercenary. Mercenaries were regarded as morally dubious by many of the Paris reformers, and their profession was often criticized. Russell, *The Just War in the Middle Ages*, pp. 242–43.

[83] In Medieval Latin this condition of the horse is referred to with the word 'spavenus', and in the Middle English 'spavein'. Lewis, *Middle English Dictionary*, p. 378.

Christians who seemed lame in that they were unable to ride for God no matter how much they were inspired. These Christians did not love God as they should. They were waiting to be rewarded before they acted. 'True' crusaders would take the cross out of love, not because they were paid or obliged to do so — their love was unconditional.

On the other hand, Christ could also be described as having already rewarded Christians. Many crusade preachers argued that God and Christ had already proved their love for Christians many times. The love of God had been demonstrated, particularly when he gave his only son to be crucified for the sake of Christians. The crusaders and those intending to go on crusade should pay back this love by offering their services to God. Jacques de Vitry maintained that Christians were, in fact, 'forced' to love Christ, because he had died for them.[84] Guibert de Tournai regarded Christ's sacrifice on the cross as an 'inexpressible' demonstration of his love.[85] The preachers also asserted that those crusaders who would do service for God and Christ would be the objects of even greater love. The crusaders would be handsomely rewarded by God for their friendship, who was 'a true friend' and would help the crusaders when no other friend would be able to help them anymore.[86]

In his crusade sermon, Humbert de Romans listed six reasons why people should take the cross against the Saracens. Four of these reasons were clearly connected to the theme of love. Humbert maintained that the cross ought to be taken out of 'zeal for the divine honour' and 'zeal for the Christian law'. This zeal and fervour for God's honour or for the Christian doctrine were born out of love for God and Christ. The third and fourth reasons for taking the cross were even more distinctly linked to the theme of love. According to Humbert, the crusaders should be motivated by 'brotherly love' and 'devotion to the Holy Land'.[87] These four reasons derived from different aspects of the Christian con-

---

[84] Jacques de Vitry, 'Item sermo ad crucesignatos vel -signandos', CPI, p. 110.

[85] Guibert de Tournai, 'Ad crucesignatos et crucesignandos sermo tertius', CPI, p. 200: 'Sicut enim Christus in cruce per dilectionem inexpressibilem, quam ad nos habuit, per quinque canales corporis quinque fluvios sanguinis patefecit sufficiens diluvium ad lotionem totius mundi, ita et nunc per viscera misericordie sue se totum crucesignatis diluendis exponit'.

[86] Jacques de Vitry, 'Sermo ad crucesignatos vel -signandos', CPI, p. 98: 'Non igitur deesse debetis vero amico, qui vobis non defuit, sed se ipsum pro vobis morti tradidit, qui vobis in necessitate succurreret quando alii amici vestri succurrere non valebant'.

[87] Humbert de Romans, 'In predicatione crucis contra Sarracenos', CPI, p. 228: 'Notandum quod ad sumendum crucem contra Sarracenos sunt sex que debent movere: primum est zelus honoris divini, secundum est zelus Christiane legis, tertium est fraterna caritas, quartum est devotio ad Terram Sanctam, quintum est exempla precedentium, sextum conditio belli'.

cept of love: during the Middle Ages the word *zelus*, zeal, was associated with love and in particular with passionate love.[88] True Christians burned for the love of God and wanted to honour him; they had a burning desire to follow God's commandments and defend the law of God.

Many crusade preachers refer in their model sermons to the 'zeal for God' that the crusaders should possess. Eudes de Châteauroux explained in one of his sermons that the love of God of the *crucesignandi* would, in fact, grow in the crusaders' hearts, so that it would turn into zeal.[89] This was thus a higher expression of the love of God, a deeper and a more passionate emotion. The Israelites had had the same kind of zeal for God: for example, the Maccabees had great zeal, as mentioned in many of the model sermons.[90] The Israelites, however, lacked true knowledge of God, as they crucified Christ, but they could be considered freed from blame for this, because they were motivated by zeal for God.[91] Humbert de Romans pointed out in his crusade sermon that even the infidels and the heretics had demonstrated great zeal for their perverted faith or false beliefs; how much more should the Christians burn with their zeal for God, when their faith was the true one.[92]

Susanna Throop has linked the use of the term *zelus* in the crusading context to the theme of crusading vengeance. She has shown that the zeal of the crusaders was associated with righteous anger; hatred could be expressed through zeal, which would not make this emotion a vice, unlike vicious anger.[93]

Humbert also listed the example of the previous crusaders and the situation of the war as reasons for crusading. See also Humbert's further explanation of these reasons in his crusade manual, Humbert de Romans, *De predicatione sancte crucis*, particularly cap. x, De zelo diuini amoris qui mouere debet ad crucis assumptionem, cap. xiij, De fraterna charitate que mouere debet ad crucis assumptionem, cap. xiiij, De deuotione habenda ad terram sanctam, cap. xv, De conditione belli in saracenos, cap. xvi, De exemplis antiquorum que inducunt ad bellum contra saracenos, cap. xx, De zelo christiane legis ad idem.

[88] Throop, *Crusading as an Act of Vengeance*, pp. 150–60.

[89] Eudes de Châteauroux, 'Sermo in conversione sancti Pauli et exhortatio ad assumendam crucem', *CPI*, p. 130: 'Et quando crescit amor Dei, ut zelus fiat, vel quando convertitur amor in zelum'.

[90] See above, pp. 59–66.

[91] Throop, *Crusading as an Act of Vengeance*, pp. 152–53.

[92] Humbert de Romans, 'De predicatione crucis in genere quocumque', *CPI*, p. 218: 'Item infideles pro sua fide, immo pro infidelitate, ita zelant quod se tradunt igni et mortibus acerbis pro ea, ut patet in hereticis. Ita etiam zelant quod semper impugnant alios pro sua fide dilatanda, ut patet in Sarracenis'.

[93] Throop, *Crusading as an Act of Vengeance*, pp. 158–67. Susanna Throop has argued that

In their crusade sermons the crusade preachers portrayed zeal for God as an expression of passionate love, which the crusaders ought to have for God. This flaming love, the burning zeal of the crusaders, could be compared with the zeal demonstrated by the Maccabaean heroes who had fought wars for God during biblical times.[94] The preachers were, however, cautious in the matter of vengeance. There are only a few, incidental, direct references to the theme of revenge in the thirteenth-century crusade sermons.[95] Even though the preachers usually avoided specific allusions to vengeance and to the destruction of enemies, aspects of anger and retribution were discussed in their model sermons.[96]

During the Second Crusade, Pedro Pitões, the Bishop of Oporto, reportedly guided the crusaders to 'take vengeance upon' the enemies of the Roman Church, explaining that the crusaders should take part in a 'just war with the zeal of justice, not with the gall of anger'. In his crusade sermon, the Bishop of Oporto quoted St Jerome and maintained that there could be 'no cruelty' where piety for God was expressed.[97] Many crusade preachers of the thirteenth century appear to have agreed with these views put forward during the Second Crusade. The zeal for God was an acceptable form of passionate emotion, a burning desire to fight for God. This zeal as a motivating force prevented the crusaders from committing the sin of wrath as they felt feelings of anger when they fought against their enemies. The zealous emotion of righteous anger might lead to the killing of enemies, or to ostensible cruelties. However, those crusaders who had zeal for God had pure intentions, and their acts of violence

zeal in itself was always 'good', even if some of the acts deriving from that zeal might not be.

[94] Jacques de Vitry, 'Sermo ad crucesignatos vel -signandos', *CPI*, p. 94; Eudes de Châteauroux, 'Sermo in conversione sancti Pauli et exhortatio ad assumendam crucem', *CPI*, p. 140; Humbert de Romans, 'De predicatione crucis in genere quocumque', *CPI*, p. 218.

[95] Eudes de Châteauroux, 'Sermo de rebellione Sarracenorum Lucherie in Apulia', *CR*, p. 379. Eudes de Châteauroux, 'Sermo contra hereticos de Albigensibus partibus', Arras, MS 876, fol. 89vb; Jacques de Vitry, 'Sermo ad crucesignatos vel -signandos', *CPI*, p. 92.

[96] One exception is in Eudes de Châteauroux's sermon against the Lucera Muslims. Eudes de Châteauroux, 'Sermo de rebellione Sarracenorum Lucherie in Apulia', *CR*, p. 379: '*Et quicquid illis facere cogitaveram vobis faciam*, o Christiani. O Christe, vox sanguinis filiorum tuorum, id est Christianorum, quem fuderunt impii Sarraceni et patres eorum et ad hoc adhuc parati sunt et etiam introducere Sarracenos transmarinos, excitet te ad vindicationem et move non tam terram sed et celum et expelle eos et destrue'. Num. 33. 56.

[97] 'De expugnatione Lyxbonensi', ed. and trans. by David, pp. 78–81: 'Clamat, certe clamat! "Vindictam facite in nationibus, increpationes in populis". [...] "Non est vero crudelitas pro Deo pietas." Zelo iusticie, non felle ire, iustum bellum committite'. Ps. 149. 7. Hieronymus, *Epistolae*, 'ad Riparium', in *PL*, xxii, col. 908. See also Throop, *Crusading as an Act of Vengeance*, p. 147.

would be similar to the acts of justice witnessed in the Old Testament. The zeal and love for God gave the crusaders a just motive for taking the cross; their intentions were righteous even if their actions were ultimately unsuccessful or had unwanted consequences.

Jacques de Vitry, Eudes de Châteauroux, and Humbert de Romans all utilized the term 'zeal' in their crusade models when referring to the Maccabean leader Mattathias, whose zeal for God the crusaders could imitate.[98] With his own hands Mattathias killed a Hellenistic Jew who intended to worship an idol in the Temple.[99] This Old Testament zeal was righteous anger and could result in acts of righteous violence. Jacques de Vitry also linked the crusading zeal to another figure from the Old Testament, Phineas. Jacques asked a rhetorical question in his sermon: Where was 'the zeal and the dagger of Phineas' now?[100] Phineas, a grandson of Aaron, was a high priest of the Israelites, like Mattathias, who also killed with his own hands. Phineas stabbed and killed a man and a woman by running a spear through the couple as they were having sexual intercourse. After the killings, God said to Moses that Phineas was moved with God's own zeal against the Israelites and had, by acting violently, removed the Lord's wrath from them.[101]

These biblical figures utilized in the crusade sermons were religious men who were full of pious fury and zeal for God, and killed defending God's law. Their anger was justified by God himself. These violent actions were in fact outbursts of God's anger. Mattathias and Phineas were acting according to God's wishes; they were signalling the wrath of God. The crusaders, who had the same kind of zeal for God, could also be considered as pious, religious men, who as instruments of God's will were bringing God's vengeance upon their enemies. The crusaders would fulfil God's commandments in the spirit of love with the zeal for God which they possessed.

The crusade preachers of the thirteenth century also linked zeal for God to the crusaders' readiness for self-denial, to their willingness to leave everything behind. The zeal of the crusaders was connected to the self-sacrifice that

[98] Jacques de Vitry, 'Sermo ad crucesignatos vel -signandos', *CPI*, p. 94; Eudes de Châteauroux, 'Sermo in conversione sancti Pauli et exhortatio ad assumendam crucem', *CPI*, p. 140; Humbert de Romans, *De predicatione sancte crucis*, cap. xii, De zelo christiane legis ad idem, invitatio xiiij.

[99] I Mcc. 2. 22–27.

[100] Jacques de Vitry, 'Sermo ad crucesignatos vel -signandos', *CPI*, p. 94: 'ubi zelus et pugio Phinees'.

[101] Num. 25. 7–12.

the *crucesignati* ought to be prepared to go through during their journey. The 'true' crusaders, who had 'zeal for the law', would expose themselves willingly to death.[102] Their crusading zeal, an amalgam of passionate love and righteous anger, was so great that they no longer cared about other things, other persons, or their own conventional existence. The ordinary life of those burning with the zeal for God would become 'tedious' for them. The crusaders who burned with the zeal for God would hate their former life of sin, just as St Paul had hated his.[103]

The Limits of Crusading Charity

Jonathan Riley-Smith has noted, in his classic study of crusading as an act of love, that the crusaders did not show any love for their enemies. According to Riley-Smith, in crusade propaganda the references to love were always one-dimensional: love was depicted purely in terms of fraternal love for Christians, love and charity were shown merely to friends, and the love of enemies was not part of the message. This, it has been suggested, was because the medieval audience could not comprehend the concept of loving an enemy.[104] However, the concept of 'crusading love' may be broader than this interpretation suggests.[105]

In their sermons Eudes de Châteauroux and Federico Visconti attempted to explain the nature of crusading love. Both men used the four-dimensional explanation of God's love: Eudes connected this explication to the good horse, while

---

[102] Eudes de Châteauroux, 'Sermo in conversione sancti Pauli et exhortatio ad assumendam crucem', *CPI*, pp. 132, 140: '*Exclamavit Mathatias voce magna in civitate dicens: Omnis qui zelum legis habet statuens testamentum exeat post me.* Quare dicit: *Statuens testamentum*, quod est morientium, nisi ad innuendum quod exire post ipsum erat ad mortem currere et se morti exponere?' I Mcc. 2. 27; Humbert de Romans, 'De predicatione crucis in genere quocumque', *CPI*, p. 218.

[103] Eudes de Châteauroux, 'Sermo in conversione sancti Pauli et exhortatio ad assumendam crucem', *CPI*, p. 130: 'Sic ergo hec conversio fit per amorem. Et ex quo convertit se quis ad Dominum per amorem, mundum et ea que in mundo sunt derelinquit, ut non amet ea. Et quando crescit amor Dei, ut zelus fiat, vel quando convertitur amor in zelum, tunc derelictio in tedium, ut etiam ipsum mundum sustinere non possit, immo eum a se omnino abicit. Sic in beato Paulo factum est, qui conversus est ad Deum per amorem. Sed amor iste conversus in ardorem et zelum mutavit dilectionem in odium, ut omnia que sunt mundi a se abiceret'.

[104] Riley-Smith, 'Crusading as an Act of Love', pp. 184–85; Cole, d'Avray, and Riley-Smith, 'Application of Theology to Current Affairs', p. 235.

[105] Tamminen, 'The Test of Friendship', p. 227.

Federico used the more conventional interpretation of the cross of Christ and its four parts.[106] These explanations were based on biblical descriptions of the love of Christ and the dimensions of the heavenly city of Jerusalem.[107] The great crusade ideologist of the twelfth century, Bernard of Clairvaux, also made use of the four-dimensional explanation in his treatise *De consideratione ad Eugenium papam*, which included a crusading apology.[108] In the treatise, Bernard maintained that God was 'the length, the breadth, the height and the depth'. The breadth of God was charity without boundaries, God loved all things created, and his love extended even beyond his enemies.[109] Bernard guided Eugenius III to 'love patiently and with perseverance', so as to achieve the length, and 'extend your love as far as the enemies', so as to gain the breadth.[110] According to Bernard, one should view the majesty of God with astonishment, try to imitate and understand the four divine traits, and fear the abyss of God's judgements. Charity required fervour, and eternity called for perseverance and durability.[111]

Both Eudes de Châteauroux and Federico Visconti used the same explanation in their crusade sermons. Eudes's 'good horse' walked on four feet. He connected some of the divine attributes mentioned by Bernard to these feet: the astonishment of the majesty of God, the fear of the abyss of the judgements of

---

[106] Federico Visconti, 'Quando idem dominus predicavit crucem litteraliter clero pisano de mandato domini Pape', *SVP*, pp. 548–49.

[107] Paul explained the dimensions in the Epistle for the Ephesians; see Eph. 3. 18–19.

[108] Bernard of Clairvaux had been deeply involved in the making of the Second Crusade, in 1146–47. After the failure of the expedition in 1149, he wrote the treatise to counsel Pope Eugenius III, in which he explained at length the defeat and touched upon a number of other things. See Bernard of Clairvaux, *De consideratione ad Eugenium papam*, ed. by Leclercq and Rochais.

[109] Bernard of Clairvaux, *De consideratione ad Eugenium papam*, lib. V, XIII, cap. 27–28, ed. by Leclercq and Rochais, pp. 489–91: 'Quid est Deus? Longitudo, latitudo, sublimitas et profundum. [...] Nam hoc monitum habemus ab ipso auriga et primo currus huius exhibitore, ut studeamus comprehendere cum omnibus sanctis quae sit longitudo, latitudo, sublimitas et profundum. [...] Est et latitudo. Et ipsa quid? Caritas. [...] Deus aeternitas est, Deus caritas est: longitudo sine protensione, latitudo sine distensione. In utroque partier locales quidem excedit temporalesque angustias, sed libertate naturae, non enormitate subtantiae'.

[110] Bernard of Clairvaux, *De consideratione ad Eugenium papam*, lib. V, XIII, cap. 30, ed. by Leclercq and Rochais, p. 492: 'Ama igitur perseveranter et longanimiter, et habes longitudinem; dilata amorem tuum usque ad inimicos, et latitudinem tenes'.

[111] Bernard of Clairvaux, *De consideratione ad Eugenium papam*, lib. V, XIII, cap. 31, ed. by Leclercq and Rochais, p. 492: 'Aut, si mavis quattuor aeque tuis divinis quattuor respondere, facis hoc, si stupes, si paves, si ferves, si sustines: stupenda plane sublimitas maiestatis; pavenda abyssus iudiciorum. Fervorem exigit caritas, aeternitas perseverantiam sustinendi'.

God, the fervour, and the perseverance. Eudes concluded that with these traits, these four feet, it was possible 'to comprehend with all the saints, what is the length, the breadth, the height, and the depth'. However, he pointed out that if one of these feet falters, the horse was worth nothing.[112]

Federico Visconti's crusade sermon, delivered in 1260 to an audience of ecclesiastics, placed special emphasis on the themes of love and charity. Federico explained the love of God with the four dimensions of the cross, which pointed to love and charity, to perseverance, to obedience to the will of the Father, and to the secret judgements of God.[113] Federico saw the sufferings of Christ on the cross as an expression of the immense love of God, which the Christians ought to try to imitate.[114]

In the epistle for the Ephesians, St Paul explained that Christ demonstrated his love and charity, which surpassed all knowledge, on the cross. Federico cited this Pauline explication in his sermon, stating that the Christians 'may be able to comprehend, with all the saints, what is the length, the breadth, the height, and the depth of the cross'.[115] The Archbishop of Pisa went through these different dimensions one by one in his sermon. The breadth signified love and charity; this love was exceedingly broad, ranging all the way to the enemies.[116] Federico quoted the famous passage from the Gospel of Matthew, 'Love your

---

[112] Eudes de Châteauroux, 'De sancto Georgio', *UEE*, II, 705: 'Bonus equs caritas. Hic equs quasi quatuor pedibus ambulat: stupore maiestatis eius quem diligit; pavore abyssi iudiciorum Dei; fervore et perseverencia, ut possit comprehendere cum omnibus sanctis que sit longitude, latitude, sublimitas et profundum. Si alter istorum pedum deficiat, nichil valet equs iste'.

[113] Federico Visconti, 'Quando idem dominus predicavit crucem litteraliter clero pisano de mandato domini Pape', *SVP*, pp. 548–49. Federico presented different explanations for the dimensions: these could also point to the different peoples, who lived at different times; or the four woods of the cross may mean the people in four parts of the world who are called to worship God; or they may be interpreted to mean the four different woods, the palm tree, cypress, olive tree, and cedar, with different significance given to each tree.

[114] Federico Visconti, 'Quando idem Dominus predicavit crucem litteraliter clero pisano de mandato domini Pape', *SVP*, p. 546. 1 Pet. 2. 21. He also encouraged his audience to be obedient like Christ, who had proven his obedience to God on the cross. Federico Visconti, 'Quando idem Dominus predicavit crucem litteraliter clero pisano de mandato domini Pape', *SVP*, p. 549: 'non que super terram; sic et ipse voluntatem Patris pretulit, inquiens: *Verumtamen non sicut ego volo, sed sicut tu vis*'. Mt. 26. 39.

[115] Eph. 3. 18–19. Federico Visconti, 'Quando idem dominus predicavit crucem litteraliter clero pisano de mandato domini Pape', *SVP*, p. 545: '*Ut possitis comprehendere cum omnibus sanctis, que sit longitudo, latitudo, sublimitas et profundum, crucis scilicet*'.

[116] Federico Visconti, 'Quando idem dominus predicavit crucem litteraliter clero pisano de mandato domini Pape', *SVP*, p. 548.

enemies', as Eudes de Châteauroux also did.[117] According to Federico, Christ himself had left the Christians an example of the breadth of Christian charity as he prayed for his enemies on the cross.[118] Federico urged his audience of ecclesiastics to show charity, to 'offer the olive tree, through the works of mercy', so as to help the brethren in need, and to 'offer the palm tree of victory', so as to overcome both the visible and the invisible enemies.[119]

Eudes de Châteauroux and Federico Visconti both regarded the biblical quotation of loving the enemy suitable for a crusade sermon. The quotation could be used in different kinds of sermons, for those intended for either ecclesiastical or lay audiences.[120] This appears not to have been an obscure theme, incomprehensible for a medieval audience, but rather a more complex scheme of things linked to the concept of crusading charity, to the definitions of *or* nature attributed to God, and to ideas of Christo-mimesis in crusade ideology.

By emulating Christ's love the crusaders were imitating one of his divine features. The extent of Christ's love was infinite, almost inconceivable for human beings. Through contemplation, imitation, and by practicing asceticism and expressing compassion, Christians could try to comprehend this love. However, the most important thing for all was to love Christ. Only those who truly loved Christ could know the love of Christ. This was one of the main points of St Paul's Epistle for the Ephesians. And even those Christians who loved Christ could hardly understand the extent of his love.

Christians could emulate Christ's divinity by imitating his love and by expressing their own love to God, particularly by doing charitable works. Charity was regarded during the Middle Ages as a virtue that might include various acts and which might have various recipients.[121] Thomas Aquinas held

---

[117] Eudes de Châteauroux, 'De sancto Georgio', *UEE*, ii, 704.

[118] Federico Visconti, 'Quando idem dominus predicavit crucem litteraliter clero pisano de mandato domini Pape', *SVP*, p. 548: 'Latitudo in operibus caritatis, cuius *mandatum latum* est *nimis*, idest valde, quia etiam extenditur usque ad inimicos, Domino dicente: *diligite inimicos vestros*, sicut ipse Christus, expansis in cruce manibus, pro inimicis oravit, inquiens: *Pater, dimitte illis: non enim sciunt quid faciunt*'. Mt. 5. 44.

[119] Federico Visconti, 'Quando idem dominus predicavit crucem litteraliter clero pisano de mandato domini Pape', *SVP*, pp. 550–51: 'Offeramus olivam per opera misericordie, ut cum videamus fratres nostros necessitatem habentes, non claudamus viscera nostra ab eis [...]. Offeramus etiam palmam victorie, ut hostes visibiles et invisibiles superemus'.

[120] Eudes de Châteauroux's crusade sermon appears to have been preached to an audience of crusaders of the Seventh Crusade, among whom were most likely both lay and ecclesiastical members. See Appendix V.

[121] The term *caritas* had broad meaning during the Middle Ages: it could be used to refer to

the opinion that charity was a special form of love, a chief virtue, through which
all Christians could express their love for God. For Thomas, loving the enemy
was also possible, even if those enemies had to be killed, for evildoers could be
punished, even killed, and they still could be loved out of charity.[122]

Philippe le Chancelier explained what charity meant to the ecclesiastics
supporting the crusade movement in his crusade sermon. Philippe focused
on the good works that the scholars might devote themselves to on the home
front and through which they could give their assistance to the crusade fought
elsewhere. He presented different intercessory tools available for his audience
of scholars. Praying, fasting, and works of mercy were all ways by which the
clergy could participate in the movement and give long-distance aid. Philippe
encouraged the ecclesiastics to perform works of charity, because piety and love
must appear in actions, 'piety in compassion for the wicked and love in con-
gratulating the good'.[123] The clergy could imitate the love of Christ and then
express their love for God by supporting the crusades by intercessory means.
They ought to do good works and be generous with their charity, which benefited the movement. The clergy's input in charitable works might include both
spiritual and financial contributions.[124]

---

the love of God. From this love of God derived also other affectionate feelings, those directed
towards friends, neighbours, and strangers. Love and charity could have many expressions:
communal harmony, friendship between individuals, alms-giving, caring for the sick or offering food and a place to stay for travellers, praying for one's fellow men, etc. For discussions on
charity see, for example, Henderson, *Piety and Charity in Late Medieval Florence*; Brodman,
Charity & Religion in Medieval Europe. The imitation of the divinity of Christ could mean different things to different people. The ecclesiastical reform of the eleventh and twelfth centuries
rested largely on the ideals of the *imitatio Christi*. Both the secular and the regular clergy were
to imitate the divine features of Christ, while searching for spiritual perfection in the seclusion
of the monasteries or in the world outside. Lawrence, *Medieval Monasticism*; Purkis, *Crusading
Spirituality*, p. 27.

[122] Thomas Aquinas, 'Quaestiones disputatae de virtutibus', q. 2 a. 8 ad 10: 'quod licite
potest ille ad quem ex officio pertinet, malefactores punire, vel etiam occidere, eos ex caritate
diligendo' (*Opera Omnia*, ed. by Frette, XIV, 255).

[123] Philippe le Chancelier, 'Sermo de eodem, de gaudio quod rex et principes assumpserunt
crucem', Avranches, MS 132, fol. 252ra: 'in exemplo ut in operibus appareat affectus pietatis vel
caritatis; pietatis quantum ad compassionem malorum, caritatis quantum ad congratulationem
bonorum'. Transcribed by Maier and Bériou.

[124] Philippe le Chancelier combated the vices of the clergy and gave thanks in his sermon
for the reconciliation achieved between the clergy and the knights. The French clergy was reluctant to give financial support for the Albigensian Crusade. The problem, in Philippe's view,
was partly caused by the immorality of the clergy. Philippe le Chancelier, 'Sermo de eodem,

Roger of Salisbury also urged the crusaders, and penitents in general, to follow Christ's example as he 'taught the practice of mercy against avarice', and
to be merciful as God was merciful.[125] In the crusade sermons this example of
Christ's love, which all Christians should imitate, was mainly used in relation
to God, Christ, or Christians. For the crusaders love and charity usually meant
service to God, fighting against God's enemies on behalf of God and Christ, and
for the benefit of all Christians. Thus the crusaders most commonly expressed
their love for Christ and God, or for all Christians, near or far. However, there
was also a form of crusading charity that could be expressed to the enemies in
imitation of Christ's limitless, absolute love for all things.

In his anniversary sermon for Robert d'Artois and the other nobles who
had died at the Battle of Mansurah during the Seventh Crusade, Eudes de
Châteauroux made an interesting point about the charitable nature of crusading.[126] Eudes claimed that Robert and the other crusaders had fought with the
pure intention of rescuing 'the impious Saracens from an infidel death as well
as an infernal death'.[127] This appears to be a reference to the crusaders' attempts
to convert the Muslims to Christianity. At the beginning of the thirteenth
century, increasing attention was paid to the conversion of infidels. Jacques de
Vitry linked crusading and conversion together in one of his letters, viewing the
crusades as a way to bring the Muslims under Christian rule. Under Christian
authority the Muslims could be 'easily converted' with missionary work.[128]

de gaudio quod rex et principes assumpserunt crucem', Avranches, MS 132, fols 251[ra]–252[vb];
Philippe le Chancelier, 'Sermo in die veneris infra octabas Assumptionis beate Virginis',
Avranches, MS 132, fol. 244[rb]. See also Federico Visconti, 'Quando idem dominus predicavit
[crucem] respondendo nuntiis Tartarorum in clero pisano', *SVP*, p. 554.

[125] Roger of Salisbury, '*Ascendente* Ihesu *in naviculam*', *PCHL*, p. 230: 'Qui contra avari-
tiam docuit misericordiam dicens: *Estote misericordes sicut pater vester misericors est*'. Lk. 6. 36.

[126] Eudes de Châteauroux delivered two sermons during the Seventh Crusade, possibly in
1251, or 1252–53, in Acre, for the remembrance of Robert d'Artois and other nobles who died
in 1250. The two sermons, with the addition of Eudes's memorial sermon for Innocent IV, have
been carefully studied by Cole, d'Avray, and Riley-Smith, 'Application of Theology to Current
Affairs'. See also Tamminen, 'The Test of Friendship', pp. 225–28.

[127] Eudes de Châteauroux, 'Sermo in anniversario Roberti comitis Attrabatensis et aliorum nobilium qui interfecti fuerant a Sarracenis apud Mansuram in Egipto', *PCHL*, p. 236: 'Illi
etiam nobiles ad hoc intendentes ut impios Sarracenos a morte infidelitatis et a morte etiam
inferni eruerent pugnabant et eos reducerent ad salutem, sicut pastor nititur eruere oves suas de
ore leonis vel lupi'.

[128] Jacques de Vitry, *Epistola*, II, ed. by Huygens, p. 97: 'de Sarracenis, si sanam doctrinam
audirent, facile, ut credo, ad dominum converterentur'. Oliver von Paderborn held similar beliefs

These were acts of Christian charity as expressed to their infidel enemies. The crusade preachers did not promote coercive conversion of the Muslims, which would have been against the policy of the Roman Church. The Muslims had to convert of their own volition, like all non-Christians. Crusaders were helping Christian missionaries in their work by creating the conditions suitable for conversion. At the same time, the crusaders were helping their enemies. By accepting the Christian faith, the infidel enemies could save their souls. In a sermon given to the Templars, Jacques de Vitry explained how the Christians in many instances showed 'harsh benevolence' towards their enemies.[129]

There was also another aspect to this charitable work that Humbert de Romans brought forth in his writings. Humbert did not have high hopes for conversion of the Muslims. In the *De predicatione sancte crucis*, he suspected that the Saracens could not be converted and would not be of any use to the Christians, since the Bible made no mention of them.[130] However, according to Humbert, crusading was quite legitimate and just, because the crusaders waged a war 'out of friendship with Christ', whereas those who waged unjust wars were motivated by their devotion to the world.[131] In another work, the *Opus tripar-*

and also justified crusading by the attempts to convert the Muslims. Oliver von Paderborn, *Epistola salutaris regi Babilonis conscripta*, ed. by Hoogeweg, pp. 299–300.

[129] Jacques de Vitry, 'Item sermo ad fratres ordinis militaris', Troyes, MS 228, fol. 134[va]: 'Nam et ipsa exteriora bella sine benevolentia non geruntur, multa enim agenda sunt cum inimicis, quadam benigna asperitate plectendis'. This sermon has been edited in *Analecta Novissima*, ed. by Pitra, p. 419. It has been pointed out that this reference to the showing of a benevolent attitude towards the Muslim enemies is not intended for common crusaders, but rather aimed at the members of the military orders. Cole, d'Avray, and Riley-Smith, 'Application of Theology to Current Affairs', p. 235. However, Jacques de Vitry also regarded the actions taken against the Muslims by the lay people living in Acre as too extreme. The Catholic Christians of Acre did not allow their Saracen servants to convert to Christianity. According to Jacques, the people of Acre did not wish for the conversion of Muslims because this would have prevented the all-out exploitation of them. Also, on two separate occasions Jacques saved captive Muslim children from the hands of crusaders during the Fifth Crusade, personally buying their freedom. It seems Jacques was concerned about the treatment of Muslim enemies. The lack of benevolence towards the enemy on the part of common crusaders or Eastern Christians generated bitter criticism from him. Oliver von Paderborn, *Historia Damiatina*, ed. by Hoogeweg, pp. 167, 229; Jacques de Vitry, *Epistola*, VI, ed. by Huygens, pp. 127–28.

[130] Humbert de Romans, *De predicatione sancte crucis*, cap. viij: 'De conuersione vero saracenorum nulla scriptura loquitur. nec nos iuuat eorum vita in aliquo, sed potius multos infirmos scandalisant'.

[131] Humbert de Romans, *De predicatione sancte crucis*, cap. ii, secunda invitatio: 'Movet multos ad bella mundi amicitia seculi, moveat vos ad istud amicitia Cristi'; *PCHL*, p. 204.

titum, Humbert further explained that it was not against Christian religion to shed the blood of infidels. Some of the Saracens might be converted 'indirectly' by crusading, and it was not wrong to send them to hell. When the crusaders killed Saracens, they did them a favour, for it was better that the infidels 'die more speedily than slowly because of their sins, which would increase as long as they lived'.[132] As Eudes de Châteauroux pointed out in his sermon, the crusaders laboured in an effort to ease their enemies' afterlife.

Hence crusading and killing were represented as acts of mercy, which may appear rather distasteful justifications to the modern observer, just as expressions of love may seem hypocritical; nonetheless, for medieval crusade preachers these acts constituted Christian charity for their enemies in practice. There were boundaries for the crusaders' love, and there were limits to crusading charity. In crusade propaganda the infidel enemies were not represented as friends of Christians, nor were Christians urged to love the Saracens as neighbours, quite understandably since this would not have motivated Christians to go on crusades. The crusade preachers instead made use of the Christian concept of charity, explaining to their audiences that the Muslims should also have a chance to enjoy the charitable work of Christians. Enemies should be converted, either saved from hell or relieved from the tortures of hell as much as possible by death at the hands of the crusaders.[133]

The Humble Crusader

Crusade preachers emphasized in their sermons that during their journey the soldiers of Christ should try to act like Christ. This 'open imitation' of Christ's humanity made considerable moral demands on the crusaders. If they were supposed to act like Christ, to achieve likeness to his human features, how should they behave? How should the 'true' crusaders conduct themselves on the expeditions, when they attempted to follow in the footsteps of Jesus? The concepts of emulating the love of Christ or the sufferings of Christ have been noticed by a number of modern scholars.[134] However, other aspects of the *imitatio Christi*

---

[132] Humbert de Romans, *Opusculum tripartitum*, ch. XVI, ed. by Brown, p. 196: 'Nihilominus tamen divina providentia bene agitur cum eis, quia melius est eis cito mori, quam tarde propter peccata, quae, quamdiu vivunt, plus adaugent'. Humbert de Romans presented his treatise, the *Opus tripartitum*, at the Second Council of Lyons in 1274. For further information on the *Opus tripartitum*, see Brett, *Humbert of Romans*, pp. 176–94; Throop, *Criticism of the Crusade*, pp. 147–213.

[133] Tamminen, 'The Test of Friendship', pp. 225–28.

[134] See, for example, Smith, Crusading in the Age of Joinville, pp. 103–08; *CPI*, pp. 60–61;

have drawn less attention, and few studies have dealt specifically with crusade ideology and the imitation of Christ.[135]

In his *Epistola de imitatione Christi*, the famous scholastic theologian of the thirteenth century Bonaventure, the seventh minister general of the Franciscan Order, praised five qualities of Christ which should be imitated: deep humility, extreme poverty, perfect love, immense patience, and admirable obedience.[136] During the thirteenth century the *imitatio Christi* developed into a comprehensive emulation of Christ, his life, his example, his moral behaviour, and even his appearance. The theologians promoted the ideal of imitation of Christ's humanity, although their ultimate interest was the divinity of Christ and the exaltation of man closer to God.[137]

The crusade preachers described various different aspects of the human life of Christ in their sermons, including many of the features mentioned by Bonaventure, which appear in one form or another. The focus was not just on the teachings and the examples or the sufferings of the adult Christ. There were important aspects in the early life of Christ that should also be considered and imitated. Guibert de Tournai used an image of the child Jesus 'lying in a manger' to guide the crusaders to an appropriate outlook on their journey. Guibert explained what the manger signified: Christ suffered tribulations from the beginning to the end of his human life. The baby Jesus was 'not adorned with silk but wrapped in rags'. From the moment of his birth he was 'exposed to the cold of winter'. This humble birth exemplified, according to Guibert, the poverty of Christ, while the manger reflected 'the baseness' of it.[138]

Baby Jesus gave the crusaders an example of humility and poverty which they could imitate. Guibert continues in his sermon to compare different sides of Christ's human life and the life of the crusaders. He created a dichotomy between these lives, which the crusaders should dissolve so that they could achieve likeness to Christ and become 'true' crusaders. Guibert enumerated a long list of inconsistencies: Christ in a manger, you in a palace; Christ in

Housley, *Fighting for the Cross*, p. 25.

[135] Purkis, *Crusading Spirituality*, pp. 3–4.

[136] Bonaventura, *Epistola de imitatione Christi*, p. 499: 'consideremus, per quam viam ipse ambulavit; et si diligenter consideremus vitam Christi, qui *est speculum sine macula*, inveniemus, quod ipse primo ambulavit per viam *profundae humilitatis*. — Secundo, per viam *extremae paupertatis*. — Tertio, per viam *perfectae caritatis*. — Quarto, per viam *immensae patientiae*. — Quinto, per viam *admirabilis obedientiae*'.

[137] Constable, *Three Studies in Medieval Religious and Social Thought*, pp. 235–37.

[138] Guibert de Tournai, 'Ad crucesignatos et crucesignandos sermo tertius', *CPI*, pp. 204–05.

worthless clothes, you in silk and ornaments; Christ on a donkey, you on horses with rich trappings; Christ on the cross, you in baths.[139] These contrasts made by Guibert appear as examples for the wealthier, knightly crusaders, as the poorer participants did not reside in palaces or dress themselves in silk, nor could excessive bathing be considered a vice of theirs. However, in all probability Guibert's message made its mark with both rich and poor crusaders. He seems also to have exaggerated deliberately so as to make his point forcibly: the humble Christ had not cared for earthly riches.

Guibert battled against the luxurious lifestyle of the wealthy Christians in his crusade model sermons. When taking the cross and becoming crusaders, Christians should renounce the luxury goods to which they were accustomed in their everyday lives. The crusaders should leave their 'ivory beds' behind, so imitating the humility of Christ. They should not set such store by honour, or invest so much in their clothing, and they should avoid vanity.[140] Many of Guibert's contradictions focused on clothes: Christ was naked on the cross, his bare hands and feet were pierced with nails, yet the Christians changed their clothing and owned wardrobes, they wore gloves and rings on their hands, and on their feet they had shoes, which were 'crescent shaped' or 'curved, laced, and perforated'.[141]

Guibert de Tournai was clearly annoyed with the way the Christians behaved and dressed. He pointed out that Christ's behaviour had been totally different: Christ wore a crown of thorns, whereas the Christians wear hairpins, hats, ribbons, and garlands; Christ ran towards the iron nails, whereas the Christians run after cloves.[142] The true values of the crusader, his piety and his penitence,

[139] Guibert de Tournai, 'Ad crucesignatos et crucesignandos sermo tertius', *CPI*, pp. 204–05: 'Christus in presepio, tu in palatio; Christus in vilibus pannis, tu in sericis et ornamentis; Christus in asino, tu in equis et phaleris; Christus in cruce, tu in balneis'. Guibert de Tournai may have drawn the unflattering reference to the baths of the crusaders from a similar statement made by Jacques de Vitry in *Historia orientalis*. Jacques described the Latins living in the crusader states as useless men who were more accustomed to baths than battles.

[140] See also Jacques de Vitry's sermon for the members of the military orders. Jacques de Vitry, 'Sermo ad fratres militaris insignitos charactere militiae Christi', Troyes, MS 228, fol. 132[vb].

[141] Guibert de Tournai, 'Ad crucesignatos et crucesignandos sermo tertius', *CPI*, pp. 204–05: 'Christus in sepulcro, tu in lectis eburneis et superstitiosis; Christus nudus in cruce, tu in mutatoriis que pendent in perticis; Christus confixus manus, tu in manicis consuticiis et cyrothecis et anulis; Christus confixus pedes, tu in calceis rostratis, laqueatis, lunulatis, perforatis'.

[142] Guibert de Tournai, 'Ad crucesignatos et crucesignandos sermo tertius', *CPI*, pp. 204–05: 'Christus in corona spinea, tu in discriminalibus mitris, vittis et collitergiis et sertis; [...] Christus cucurrit ad clavos ferreos, tu ad gariophilos'.

should be visible also in his outward appearance. This was not merely an internal source of motivation or an inward mindset; the crusader's open imitation of the humility of Christ should reverberate to the exterior.

From the beginning of crusading, crusade ideology emphasized the humility and poverty of Christ. The first crusaders were regarded as men and women who had adopted voluntary poverty and self-imposed exile as they set out on the crusade. They had chosen to become poor; they had no desire for earthly riches, but wanted to abandon everything, to leave their homes and travel to foreign lands in imitation of Christ and the apostles.[143] Pope Gregory VIII also referred to this in his bull *Audita tremendi*, which proclaimed the Third Crusade in 1187. The pope explained that Christians ought not to go crusading to gain glory or money, but they ought to leave their riches behind, as they would leave them behind in the end — when they died — to heirs they did not know.[144]

The ideological bases for the voluntary poverty and exile of the crusaders derived from two, partly overlapping ideals: the *imitatio Christi* and the *vita apostolica*. The imitation of Christ's human features included imitation of his humility and poverty, while the apostolic way of life meant the return to the ways of the primitive Church, to simplicity, poverty, renunciation, and evangelical work.[145] Roger of Salisbury referred to the modesty of the apostles and to the 'nudity' of Christ in his crusade sermon, stating that some Christians renounced material things altogether, 'so that naked they follow the naked Christ, just as his apostles and other religious people did'.[146] In Roger's reference the concepts of *imitatio Christi* and *vita apostolica* were conjoined — the crusaders could follow the example of the humble Christ and go throughout the world in a state of voluntary poverty as the apostles did.

The ideal crusaders emulating Christ's poverty could be regarded as the 'holy poor' walking through the Holy Land, literally in the footsteps of Christ

---

[143] Purkis, *Crusading Spirituality*, pp. 21–24.

[144] Gregorius VIII, *Audita tremendi*, in *PL*, CCII, cols 1541–42: 'et nolite ad lucrum vel gloriam temporalem attendere, sed voluntatem Dei, qui pro fratribus animas in seipso docuit esse ponendas, et ei vestras commendate divitias, quas, sive volentes, sive nolentes, nescitis tandem quibus haeredibus sitis relicturi'. See also the portrayal of ideal crusaders by Peter de Blois, the crusade propagandist of the Third Crusade, as *pauperes Christi*. Markowski, 'Peter of Blois and the Conception of the Third Crusade', pp. 266–67.

[145] Purkis, *Crusading Spirituality*, pp. 56, 180. For the *vita apostolica*, see, for example, McDonnel, *The Beguines and Beghards*, pp. 141–53.

[146] Roger of Salisbury, '*Ascendente* Ihesu *in naviculam*', *PCHL*, p. 230: 'Quod faciunt quidam per rerum abdicationem; unde Christum nudum nudi sequantur sicut fecerunt apostoli et alii religiosi'. For this literary topos, see also d'Avray, *The Preaching of the Friars*, p. 44.

or the Christians of the early Church. This imitation of the poverty of Christ and the apostles did not necessarily mean that all crusaders had to be materially poor. This would have effectively prevented successful crusading, for the expeditions were expensive enterprises and the knights needed their costly armour, weapons, and horses with them as they served Christ. Rather it meant that the crusaders embraced poverty and expressed their humility by being spiritually humble.[147] It also meant that the 'true' crusaders would abandon all luxuries and would refrain from unnecessary expressions of grandeur — their humility lay in their lack of pretension.

The nobles and the knights were the main targets of these demands for outer humility. Knights who were about to engage in battle usually wanted to make an impressive entrance onto the field, displaying their noble origins by their coats of arms emblazoned on their shields, their surcoats, and their banners.[148] In the First Council of Lyons in 1245, crusaders were also urged to show moderation in both eating and style of dressing.[149] Guibert de Tournai's focus on the outer imitation of Christ — on the modest appearance of the crusaders — may also reflect his background, as he belonged to the Franciscan Order. Voluntary poverty was central to the Franciscan way of life. However, other crusade preachers also touched upon the issue, and modesty was required not only from the crusading nobles, but also from the common people, from the crusading pilgrims, from the members of the military orders, and from the ecclesiastics participating in the movement.[150]

The crusade preachers tried to correct the sins of the crusaders with examples from the life of Christ. They instructed the participants to imitate the example of Christ rather than be deluded by the devil. The devil drove people to many kinds of sins, but by following in the footsteps of Christ they could avoid these

---

[147] Tyerman, 'Who Went on Crusades to the Holy Land?', p. 26.

[148] See, for example, Jean de Joinville's report of the landing of the Count of Jaffa on the shores of Damietta during the Seventh Crusade in 1249, where the count's magnificent arrival and his shields of gold are described in detail. Jean de Joinville, *Vie de Saint Louis*, ed. by Monfrin, pp. 76–78: 'Ce fu celi qui plus noblement ariva, car sa galie ariva toute peinte dedens mer et dehors a escussiaus de ses armes, les queles armes sont d'or a une croiz de gueules patee. Il avoit bien .CCC. nageurs en sa galie, et a chascun de ses naguers avoit une targe de ses armes, et a chascune targe avoit un pennoncel de ses armes batu a or'.

[149] *COD, Super cruciata*, p. 274: 'Et si quando in peccatum lapsi fuerint, per veram poenitentiam mox resurgant, gerentes humilitatem cordis et corporis, et tam in victu quam in vestitu mediocritatem servants'.

[150] Jacques de Vitry, 'Sermo ad fratres militaris insignitos charactere militiae Christi', Troyes, MS 228, fol. 132vb.

evil inclinations. Roger of Salisbury urged the crusaders and penitents to fol-low the advice of Christ as he taught 'abstinence against gluttony by going into the desert and fasting for forty days and forty nights'.[151] Roger also exhorted his audience to imitate Christ, as he 'taught humility against arrogance by saying, *learn from me*'.[152] The pride and arrogance of the crusaders were denounced in several sermons, and the humility of Christ was stressed as a counterpoint. The preachers also pointed out that the crusaders were not supposed to boast or seek their own glory, for their glory was in the cross of Christ.[153]

While the crusade preachers often focused on the humanity of Christ, the divinity of Christ could also be emphasized. Philippe le Chancelier utilized both sides of Christ in his sermons, thus guiding Christians to penitence and explain-ing crusading to his audience. In his crusade sermon preached at Saint-Victor in Paris in 1226, Philippe reminded the nobles, the rich, and the educated mem-bers of society that Christ chose to be poor and weak. Philippe referred to the divine Christ as noble, rich, and powerful, but underlined his human traits, his poverty and humility on earth, which the Christians should imitate.

> The boasts of the educated and learned, the rich, powerful, and noble, are in vain. For though Christ is wise, or rather wisdom itself, and rich and powerful and noble, and in this respect they resemble him, yet he does not recognize them because he did not give this as a sign, but on our behalf became poor, weak, and ignoble, and came in simplicity, and recognizes these. Poverty is his sign.[154]

---

[151] Roger of Salisbury, '*Ascendente* Ihesu *in naviculam*', *PCHL*, p. 230: 'qui contra gulam docuit abstinentiam exiens in desertum ubi xl diebus ieiunavit et xl noctibus'.

[152] Roger of Salisbury, '*Ascendente* Ihesu *in naviculam*', *PCHL*, p. 230: 'Qui etiam contra superbiam docuit humilitatem dicens *Discite a me*, etc.'. Mt. 11. 29. Philippe le Chancelier used similar argumentation in his sermon *Dicit Dominus ad Moysen*: 'Hec omnia sanavit Christus in cruce: superbiam per humilitatem quam exibuit et etiam in capiti inclinatione significavit, Ioh xix; cupiditatem per caritatem quam exibuit in manuum extensione et larga sanguinis effusione; luxuriam per dolorem et angustias quas passus est in toto corpore'. Philippe le Chancelier, '*Dicit Dominus ad Moysen*', Avranches, MS 132, fol. 272va. Transcribed by Maier and Bériou.

[153] Jacques de Vitry, 'Item sermo ad crucesignatos vel -signandos', *CPI*, p. 112; Philippe le Chancelier, 'Sermo in die veneris infra octabas Assumptionis beate Virginis', Avranches, MS 132, fol. 243vb; Federico Visconti, 'Quando idem dominus predicavit crucem litteraliter clero pisano de mandato domini Pape', *SVP*, p. 545; Eudes de Châteauroux, 'Sermo in festo sanctarum reliquiarum', *UEE*, II, 744. Gal. 6. 14.

[154] Philippe le Chancelier, 'Sermo in die veneris infra octabas Assumptionis beate Virginis', Avranches, MS 132, fol. 244ra: 'Frustra gloriantur literati et scientes, divites et potentes et nobiles. Licet enim Christus sapiens sit, immo ipsa sapientia, dives et potens et nobilis et in hoc sint similes ei, non tamen hos cognoscit quia non hoc dedit pro signis, sed factus est pro nobis

Philippe emphasized the poverty, the infirmity, and the modesty of Christ in his sermon. The son of a carpenter did not choose philosophers as his followers, but the uneducated.[155] There were probably Paris-educated members of the clergy amongst the audience of Philippe when he delivered his crusade sermon at Saint-Victor, as was the case with his three other crusade sermons.[156] The demands for modesty and simplicity, and the stress on the lack of education of Christ's followers, the *idiotae* who were chosen by him rather than the intellectuals, were intended to convince the *scolares* and *doctores* of the audience to accept their learnedness without pretension and imitate the humbleness of Christ.[157]

In Philippe le Chancelier's crusade sermon, all the different participants in the Albigensian Crusade were invited to imitate Christ and by so doing to give their support to the crusade movement. First of all, Louis VIII is described as imitating Christ by going on the crusade; indeed Philippe's sermon made a comparison between Louis VIII and Christ. According to Philippe, Louis imitated Christ when he aspired to receive a kingdom from the Albigensians. In imitation of the celestial king, Louis would claim a realm in 'a far country', in Languedoc, just as Christ claimed the heavenly kingdom himself when he ascended to heaven.[158] With the reference to the divine 'kingship' of Christ and Louis's ability to emulate this, Philippe justified and rationalized the appropriation of land in the south of France by the Capetian dynasty. Christ as the son of God had the right to govern the realm of heaven, and Louis VIII,

---

pauper, infirmus et ignobilis et in simplicitate venit, et hos cognoscit. Paupertas eius signum est'. Transcribed by Maier and Bériou.

[155] Philippe le Chancelier, 'Sermo in die veneris infra octabas Assumptionis beate Virginis', Avranches, MS 132, fol. 244ra.

[156] See Appendix II.

[157] Philippe also cited a convenient passage from St Paul to strengthen his point: 'there are not many wise by means of the flesh, nor many powerful, nor many noble, but God has chosen the foolish things of the world that he may confound the strong'. Philippe le Chancelier, 'Sermo in die veneris infra octabas Assumptionis beate Virginis', Avranches, MS 132, fol. 244ra: 'Simplicitas eius signum est, unde non elegit philosophos sed idiotas, ut i Ad Cor. i: *Videte vocationem vestram, fratres, quia non multi sapientes per carnem, non multi potentes, non multi nobiles, sed que stulta sunt mundi elegit Deus ut confundat fortia* etc'. 1 Cor. 1. 26–27. Transcribed by Maier and Bériou.

[158] Philippe le Chancelier, 'Sermo in die veneris infra octabas Assumptionis beate Virginis', Avranches, MS 132, fol. 243vb: '*Homo* iste nobilis Christus, qui *abiit* scilicet in die Ascensionis *in regionem longinquam*, scilicet in celum, *accipere sibi regnum*, scilicet diadema regni celestis [...]. *In regionem longinquam* scilicet contra Albigenses, *accipere sibi regnum*, nam et ille partes pertinent ad eius regnum'. For biblical passages see Lk. 19. 12. Transcribed by Maier and Bériou.

by imitating Christ and battling against heresy, had the right to govern the southern realm.

The crusaders following Louis VIII on the crusade were doing service for Christ and imitating his example of humility and simplicity. Those Christians who had not chosen to participate in the expedition in person should, in Philippe's opinion, also participate in the movement from a distance. At home, too, the imitation of Christ was essential. The supporters of the crusade movement should follow Christ's example of poverty and infirmity. God would recognize those who chose his path, renounced their sins, and adopted the simple life of Christ. The demands that the nobles and the rich assume a simpler life and that scholars humbly accept their sophistication were primarily directed to these particular groups, but the arguments must have also appealed to the townspeople and to the common or low-ranking members of society. The weak and the humble things were picked out by God, not the wise or the powerful. The crusaders and the supporters of the crusade movement, whatever position they held in Christian society, needed to imitate the humility of Christ, which God favoured above all else. Poverty, infirmity, and austerity were qualities by which God recognized his own. The 'true' crusaders and 'true' supporters of the movement did not search for their own glory, but they could imitate and witness the glory of Christ on the cross.

Bearing the Stigmata and Suffering with Christ

The imitation of the sufferings of Christ was as old a notion as the *imitatio Chisti*. In fact, the imitation of Christ's humility would almost certainly involve some kind of suffering.[159] However, during the thirteenth century new emphasis was given to the body of Christ, which had an influence on the imitation of the *Passio Christi*. The sufferings of Christ and the marks of these sufferings in his body, the wounds of Christ, became a major concern for thirteenth-century theologians.[160] In the crusade model sermons the concept of literally emulating the bodily sufferings of Christ was put forward. The preachers encouraged the crusaders to carry the stigmata of Christ on their own bodies.

There were similar references made about the stigmata already during the First Crusade. Raymond d'Aguilers reported in his history that crusaders who had been captives and died at the hands of the enemy were found to be

---

[159] Tinsley, *The Imitation of God in Christ*, p. 116; Constable, *Three Studies in Medieval Religious and Social Thought*, p. 146 n. 7.

[160] Constable, *Three Studies in Medieval Religious and Social Thought*, pp. 194–95, 200–205.

marked with the cross on their right shoulders.[161] Both Fulcher de Chartres
and Guibert de Nogent also told how crusaders who had drowned during the
First Crusade had been marked with crosses on their shoulders.[162] Ekkehard
von Aura spoke of the crosses of some of the participants that were 'divinely
imprinted' upon their foreheads or other parts of their bodies.[163] The crusader's
stigmata was usually the cross itself, which in the crusade accounts is most commonly reported to have been imprinted on the crusader's shoulder.[164]

In the crusade model sermons of the thirteenth century the theme of stigmata was further developed. Guibert de Tournai urged the crusaders to bear
the stigmata of Christ on their bodies, and 'while offering inside the sacrifice of
whole burnt offering', they could have Christ's 'skin on the outside'.[165] The stigmata would be a visible, outer expression of the inner devotion to Christ — a
proof of the pious desire of the crusaders to take part in the sufferings of Christ.
Guibert encouraged 'open imitation' of Christ, his works, and his sufferings in

---

[161] Raymond d'Aguilers, *Historia Francorum qui ceperunt Iherusalem*, ch. xiv, in *RHC Occ.*,
III, 272: 'sex vel septem de nostris pauperibus a paganis capti et interfecti sunt: hi autem omnes
defuncti cruces in dextris habuerunt humeris'. Housley, *Fighting for the Cross*, pp. 51–52.

[162] Fulcher de Chartres, *Historia Hierosolymitana*, lib. I, cap. VIII, ed. by Hagenmeyer,
pp. 169–70: 'nam cum corpora iam mortua qui circumstabant pro posse collegissent, repertae
sunt in carnibus quorundam super spatulas scilicet cruces insignitae. nam quod in pannis suis
vivi gestaverant, competebat, Domino volente, in ipsis servitio suo sic praeoccupatis idem signum victoriosum sub pignore fidei permanere'. Guibert de Nogent, *Gesta Dei per Francos*, vii,
cap. 32, in *RHC Occ.*, IV, 250–51. Constable, *Crusaders and Crusading in the Twelfth Century*,
pp. 67–68. Humbert de Romans included a short reference to the episode in his preaching manual. Humbert de Romans, *De predicatione sancte crucis*, cap. xxxix.

[163] Ekkehard von Aura, *Hierosolymita*, ch. x, in *RHC Occ.*, V, 19: 'Nonnulli etiam crucis
signaculum sibimet in frontibus vel vestibus seu in quolibet corporis loco divinitus impressum ostendebant, ipsoque se stigmate ad eamdem Domini militiam praescriptos credebant'.
Constable, *Crusaders and Crusading in the Twelfth Century*, p. 67. Bernold von Konstanz
stated that Urban II made all the participants who had vowed to go on the journey to the Holy
Land mark themselves with the cross on their clothes, but for some there appeared the sign of
the cross in their flesh. Bernold von Konstanz, *Chronicon*, ed. by Pertz, MGH, SS, 5, p. 464:
'Omnes quoque qui ad hoc iter se devoverunt, signo crucis se ipsos in vestibus notare fecit, quod
etiam signum quibusdam in ipsa carne notatum apparuit'. Purkis, *Crusading Spirituality*, p. 35;
Tamminen, 'The Crusader's Stigmata'.

[164] Purkis, *Crusading Spirituality*, p. 35; Tamminen, 'The Crusader's Stigmata'.

[165] Guibert de Tournai, 'Ad crucesignatos et crucesignandos sermo primus', *CPI*, pp. 184–87:
'Hanc crucem Christi in corde habeas et eius stigmata in corpore tuo feras, ut intus offerens vic-
timam holocausti etiam foris habeas pellem eius. *Debet* enim *qui se dicit* per internam dilectionem *in Christo manere* per apertam operum et passionum eius imitationem *sicut* ille *ambulavit
et ipse ambulare*'. I John 2. 6.

the sermon. If the crusaders truly loved Christ as they ought to, if their motivations for crusading were correct, they should be ready to follow Christ's example, relive his life, and repeat his actions.

Guibert explained in his sermon that the crusader's cross was a sign that had different kinds of features, even talismanic qualities. The cross was a sign that kept away enemies, guarded the crusaders, edified their neighbours, and delighted Christ.[166] Guibert was not suggesting that all the crusaders should have the wounds of Christ inflicted on them. Rather, he viewed the crusader's cross as a sign, like the stigmata, that the crusader could wear on his body like the wounds of Christ and in doing so resemble Christ and express his compassion. The crusader's cross was a new type of stigma, a sign which marked the crusaders, branding them as loyal followers of Christ.

Philippe le Chancelier also referred twice to the stigmata in his crusade sermons. In the *Sermo de eodem, de gaudio quod rex et principes assumpserunt crucem*, preached against the Albigensian heretics at Candlemas in 1226, Philippe explained the *imitatio Christi* with the concept of the stigmata. He used the different elements of the feast of the Purification and the details of the biblical story as a background from which he drew lessons and moral examples. Philippe described to an audience of ecclesiastics the virtues of the different persons associated with the feast. Using the biblical figure of Simeon, Philippe urged the audience to be patient.[167] He interpreted Simeon to mean 'the sorrow of hearing' and viewed him as an embodiment of patience.[168] According to Philippe patience meant enduring afflictions of two kinds, 'the troubles of the soul and the tribulations of the body'. Philippe cited St Paul, saying 'I bear the stigmata of our Lord Jesus Christ constantly in my body', and explained that those supporting the crusade movement from the home front should not cease in imitating Christ, but always strive for perfection. Although the different kinds of sufferings belonged to the imitation of Christ, they were easy to bear, for Christ's yoke was sweet and his burden light.[169]

---

[166] Guibert de Tournai, 'Ad crucesignatos et crucesignandos sermo primus', *CPI*, pp. 184–85.

[167] Simeon was 'a just and devout' man, who encountered Mary, Joseph, and the child Jesus at the Temple during the purification in Jerusalem and prophesied to Mary. Lk. 2. 22–39.

[168] Philippe follows Jerome's interpretation of the meaning of the name Simeon. 'Symeon audiens uel audivit tristitiam': Hieronymus, *Liber interpretationis*, ed. by de Lagarde, p. 141.

[169] Philippe le Chancelier, 'Sermo de eodem, de gaudio quod rex et principes assumpserunt crucem', Avranches, MS 132, fol. 252[va]: 'Designantur hic brachiis portabat puerum, quia paciencia duplex, quasi duo brachia, paciencia, scilicet molestiarum anime et tribulationum corporis, unde, ad Gal. vi: *Stigmata Domini nostri Ihesu Christi* iugiter *porto in corpore meo*; hic portabat puerum in ulnis nec multum eo honerabatur, quia paciencia ex amore quicquid pertinet ad imi-

Philippe's sermon *Dicit Dominus ad Moysen*, preached originally to Louis VIII and his crusading army at Bourges in 1226, is also filled with different images of Christ's passion, his wounds, his bruised body, and his sufferings on the cross.[170] The sermon has been edited considerably. Today, in its extant version, it appears mainly as a model sermon for the feast of the Exaltation of the Cross or the Invention of the Cross. There are, however, hints to the original circumstances when the sermon was first preached to an audience of crusaders. The passage in which Philippe describes the cross as a sign of victory, 'a banner of the Lord' that is raised in the camp of the Lord, may point to an army of crusaders camped at Bourges. Philippe views the sign of the cross as the war banner of God and again cites Paul's epistle to the Galatians, '*stigmata Domini* etc'.[171]

Philippe le Chancelier used the images of the stigmata in much the same way in his different kinds of crusade sermons. The images of the wounds of Christ could be utilized in sermons directed to both the crusaders and to the supporters of the crusade movement. The stigmata were a sign which marked out the crusaders and the supporters as the members of the camp of Christ and distinguished them from the rest of the Christians. This image also had a clear allusion to the crusaders' explicit readiness to suffer for Christ. There were similar themes used in the crusade sermons, such as the references to the letter *thau* or the scarlet of Rahab. These biblical allusions were used in several of the sermons to explain what the sign of the cross meant and how it separated the crusaders from the rest of the Christians and from their enemies, but these lacked the connotations of self-sacrifice and suffering of the stigmata.

Both Guibert de Tournai and Philippe le Chancelier wanted to present crusading in terms of taking part in the *Passio Christi* and used the images of the stigmata to underline the crusaders', the penitents', and the supporters' willingness to suffer pain. The patient enduring of tribulations in imitation of Christ was demanded by both Guibert and Philippe. The service of God required perseverance, but it was sweet and rewarding.[172] The Dominican preacher

tacionem Christi sibi inponit et facile portat et hylariter, quod dicitur Mt. xi: *Iugum meum suave et honus meum leve*'. Mt. 11. 30; Gal. 6. 17. Transcribed by Maier and Bériou.

[170] Philippe le Chancelier, '*Dicit Dominus ad Moysen*', Avranches, MS 132, fols 272rb–273vb. For the dating of the sermon, see Appendix II.

[171] Philippe le Chancelier, '*Dicit Dominus ad Moysen*', Avranches, MS 132, fol. 273rb. Gal. 6. 17.

[172] Philippe le Chancelier, 'Sermo de eodem, de gaudio quod rex et principes assumpserunt crucem', Avranches, MS 132, fol. 252va; Guibert de Tournai, 'Ad crucesignatos et crucesignandos sermo tertius', *CPI*, 206: 'quia mittitur a Deo ros dulcedinis et gratia consolationis celestis in cor crucesignati, quod non est per impatientiam fractum sed celitus confortatum'.

Humbert de Romans did not use the term 'stigmata' or refer to the wounds of Christ in his crusade model sermons, but utilized the theme in his manual intended for crusade preachers. In the *De predicatione sancte crucis*, Humbert made it clear that the Christians ought to bear the stigmata of Christ in their hearts and mouths through faith and confession, and in their bodies through their willingness to suffer for Christ.[173]

Not all crusade preachers, however, appeared to be comfortable with using the term 'stigmata'. Jacques de Vitry may have avoided the potentially dangerous term deliberately. Jacques had had a close companionship with a stigmatized saintly person, Marie d'Oignies, the spiritual mother of the Beguines.[174] He wrote a hagiographic account of Marie, the *Vita Mariae Oigniacensis*, in which he described the wounds found on Marie's body after her death. According to Jacques, Marie offered her whole body to the Lord, tortured and sacrificed herself daily in imitation of Christ. She inflicted the wounds of Christ upon herself in a state of ecstasy.[175] Jacques deeply admired Marie's extraordinary piety, but warned people not to try to achieve all that she had achieved. According to Jacques, they could try to imitate Marie's virtues, but they could not imitate the deeds of her virtues, because she had achieved them by the privilege of grace, 'a personal privilege'. Jacques explained that though people should try to 'bear the stigmata of the Lord Jesus Christ in their body', they should not impoverish their bodies too much: vices should be repressed, but people should not be compelled to take extreme measures.[176]

---

[173] Humbert de Romans, *De predicatione sancte crucis*, cap. iv: 'Siquidem portavit in humeris suis crucem nostrum id est peccatis nostris debitam in hac via. Johan xix. Et baiulans sibi crucem exiuit in eum qui dicitur caluarie locum. Justum est ergo ut nos crucem suam in humeris nostris propter ipsum portemus. non solum habentes eam in corde per fidem. vel in ore per confessionem. sed et in corpore per penatum sustinentiam. Exemplo Pauli qui dicit ad Galla. Ultimo. Stigmata passionis Domini nostri Ihesu Christi in corpore meo porto'.

[174] The so-called Beguines or *mulieres religiosae* were uncloistered religious women. The Beguine movement was born at the end of the twelfth and the beginning of the thirteenth century in northern Europe, in Brabant, and particularly in the diocese of Liège. Jacques de Vitry was one of the first influential supporters of the movement. Marie d'Oignies was a saintly woman, a mystic who had visions. She has been regarded as a sort of prototype of a Beguine. Miller, 'What's in a Name?'; Vauchez, 'Prosélytisme et action antihérétique'. For more information about the Beguines, see, for example, McDonnel, *The Beguines and Beghards*.

[175] Jacques de Vitry, *Vita Maria Oigniacensi*, I, cap. ii, (22), *AASS*, v, 552A; Constable, *Three Studies in Medieval Religious and Social Thought*, pp. 216–17.

[176] Jacques de Vitry, *Vita Maria Oigniacensi*, I, cap. i, (12), *AASS*, v, 550C. See also Bynum, *Holy Feast and Holy Fast*, pp. 84–85.

Giles Constable has noted the caution in the way Jacques de Vitry refers to the stigmata of St Francis in his sermon given to the Franciscans after the demise of the founder of the order.[177] Jacques also used an exemplum *De homine illo qui seipsum cruci affixit* in a sermon preached in 1229, in which he described how 'a simple layman', devout but oblivious, was deceived by an evil spirit in disguise. The spirit convinced the man that he should suffer for Christ as Christ had suffered for him, and that he should crucify himself on a cross on a hilltop — which the foolish man proceeded to do. Luckily, he was found by shepherds, and his stigmata were cured after a few days.[178] The message of Jacques's exemplum is clear: it would be foolish for people to try to imitate Christ's sufferings on the cross literally. Indeed, this was the devil's way to misguide simple Christians. People ought to use common sense, and be reasonable and moderate in their approach to the imitation of Christ. Radical asceticism and mortification of the flesh were not meant for all.[179]

Jacques de Vitry appears more cautious with the theme of suffering than Guibert de Tournai, Philippe le Chancelier, or Humbert de Romans. Nonetheless, Jacques also utilized the theme of *Passio Christi* in his crusade sermons. Jacques explained to the crusaders that they imitated the sufferings of Christ as they took the cross and became crusaders, but he made it clear that the crusaders' agony was infinitely lighter than Christ's. According to Jacques, God signed Christ first, so others could follow him, but Christ's signing was exceptional, for Christ was 'attached with iron nails' through his flesh to the cross, whereas 'a soft thread is attached' on the crusaders' cloaks.[180]

---

[177] Constable, *Three Studies in Medieval Religious and Social Thought*, p. 219.

[178] *Die Exempla*, ed. by Greven, pp. 31–32: 'Audivi de quodam simplici layco valde fervente et sine sciencia zelum nimium habente: [...] maligno spiritu in specie angeli lucis ipsum arguente et ammonente quod talia pro Christo pati deberet qualia Christus passus est pro ipso, ipse fecit fabricari quatuor clavos acutissimos et duo ligna pro cruce facienda [...]. Et cum crucem sibi aptasset, tenens malleum in manu duos pedes clavis cruci affixit [...]. Cumque aliquantulum ibi pependisset et iam mortis articulus immineret, deprehensus est a pastoribus, qui clamantem et renitentem deposuerunt et ad domum suam semivivum reduxerunt'. See also Constable, *Three Studies in Medieval Religious and Social Thought*, p. 216.

[179] See also Jacques de Vitry's sermon for the knights of the military orders, where he warns against immoderate fasting: Jacques de Vitry, 'Sermo ad fratres militaris insignitos charactere militiae Christi', Troyes, MS 228, fol. 132[vb].

[180] Jacques de Vitry, 'Sermo ad crucesignatos vel -signandos', *CPI*, p. 86: 'Patet igitur quod signum Dei vivi habet Christus, ut signet milites suos; qui etiam prior cruce signari voluit, ut alios precederet cum vexillo crucis. Hunc enim *Deus Pater signavit*, cuius carni crux clavis ferreis affixa est, que molli filo affigitur palliis vestris'. John 6. 27. Guibert de Tournai followed closely

The crusaders were required by the preachers to bear their stigmata or wear their signs openly. Those who had been signed and were in the service of Christ should always wear the crusader's cross on their outer garments so others could observe it. This was important for several reasons. Firstly, those signed with the cross were a conspicuous example to others, and their piety might encourage others to follow them.[181] Secondly, the cross should be put on display, because of its protective and comforting qualities, and because 'the infernal dogs were very afraid' when they saw it.[182] Thirdly, the cross should be worn openly because God immediately recognized those wearing his sign of victory.[183] The 'true' crusaders would thus take the cross publicly and wear it openly, attracting attention with their clothing. Their appearance would be symbolic: the crusaders wore white clothes with red crosses, 'the passion of Christ in a pure heart', as Guibert de Tournai put it.[184]

All of the crusade preachers examined in this volume use the theme of suffering in their sermons. This appears to have been significant subject matter from both motivational and didactic standpoints: the tribulations of Christ were used to convince people to become crusaders; since Christ had suffered

this passage of Jacques de Vitry in his own sermon. Guibert de Tournai, 'Ad crucesignatos et crucesignandos sermo primus', *CPI*, p. 178: 'Hoc enim signum habuit Christus ut signet milites suos, qui prior signari voluit, ut alios precedere cum vexillo crucis. *Hunc Pater signavit Deus*, cuius carni crux affixa fuit, que modo molli filo affigitur vestris vestibus'. In a Sunday sermon, Jacques also encouraged his audience to bear the stigmata of Christ on their body, that is, to be part of the army of Christ and to take up the cross by imitating Christ's sufferings. Jacques de Vitry, 'Eadem dominica thema sumptum de Epistola Philip. 2', p. 316: '*Stigmata Jesu in corpore meo porto*, id est, signa militiae eius, quae me probat militem eius esse. Stigma enim dicitur nota, vel punctum aliquo ferro impressum. Stigmata igitur illius portamus: dum notas poenarum eius passiones, scilicet, et tribulationes ad eius imitationem in nobis suscipimus. Tollamus ergo crucem nostram per sanguinis effusionem, per carnis macerationem, per proximi compassionem'.

[181] Philippe le Chancelier, '*Dicit Dominus ad Moysen*', Avranches, MS 132, fol. 273rb; Jacques de Vitry, 'Item sermo ad crucesignatos vel -signandos', *CPI*, p. 120.

[182] Guibert de Tournai, 'Ad crucesignatos et crucesignandos sermo primus', *CPI*, p. 184: 'Sic crucis signum non est abscondendum sed aperte portandum et accipiendum contra canes infernales, qui multum timent baculum, quo gravissime verberati sunt et veri fideles consolati'.

[183] Jacques de Vitry, 'Sermo ad crucesignatos vel -signandos', *CPI*, p. 88: 'Magnum honorem reputantes, si eisdem vestibus induantur, quibus rex eorum est indutus, et si eodem caractere insignantur. Non reputantes vere Christi milites qui aliquid panicellum, quod vulgari Gallico "pannuncel" appellatur; de armis eius non habent'. Guibert de Tournai, 'Ad crucesignatos et crucesignandos sermo primus', *CPI*, p. 186.

[184] Guibert de Tournai, 'Ad crucesignatos et crucesignandos sermo primus', *CPI*, p. 182: 'ad litteram scilicet crux rubea in albo panno, Christi scilicet passio in corde mundo'.

for them, they should suffer for him. The theme was also utilized to explain the experience of crusading: the journey was difficult and full of agony. The crusaders ought to prepare themselves for these difficulties. The value of suffering was explained in the sermons in various ways.

Firstly, there was the conventional Christian view that there were merits to be gained in the chastisement of the flesh. Bodily sufferings guided Christians to a better life, away from sin, and reduced the possible pains awaiting them in purgatory or in hell. Jacques de Vitry, for example, viewed the sufferings or the illnesses of the body as guards against sins. These could be regarded as gifts from God. Physical pain might remove vices and purify the soul.[185] For this reason, Roger of Salisbury, Philippe le Chancelier, and Federico Visconti all used their model sermons to urge the crusaders, the penitents, and the supporters of the movement to suffer: Christians should chastise their bodies and bring them into subjection.[186]

In the sermon *Dicit Dominus ad Moysen*, Philippe le Chancelier also argued that the crusaders had made a 'good deal' when they took the cross.[187] He expounded the benefits of imitating Christ and the merits of 'taking up the cross'. If a lesser person took the cross, he was immediately raised up in status to a higher position. The amount of suffering for Christ stored up a corresponding amount of merit for the afterlife. According to Philippe, 'all good persons' had their own crosses to bear, 'but in accordance with the difference in their merits'. Some encountered minor complications in life, some suffered the theft of their possessions, some suffered 'insults', and still others suffered 'verbal and physical abuse', which meant that they raised up their crosses 'more highly' than

[185] Jacques de Vitry expresses these views in his sermons for the lepers and the infirm. See also Guibert de Tournai's sermons in Bériou and Touati, *Voluntate Dei leprosus*, esp. pp. 101–04. See also Pincikowski, *Bodies of Pain*, pp. 15–16.

[186] Roger of Salisbury, '*Ascendente* Ihesu *in naviculam*', PCHL, p. 230; Philippe le Chancelier, 'Sermo de eodem, quomodo apparuit potentia Dei', Avranches, MS 13, fol. 250ʳᵃ; Federico Visconti, 'Quando idem dominus predicavit crucem litteraliter clero pisano de mandato domini Pape', *SVP*, p. 546. The preachers cited Peter in the passage. 1 Pet. 2. 21.

[187] Philippe le Chancelier, '*Dicit Dominus ad Moysen*', Avranches, MS 132, fol. 273ʳᵃ: 'Maxime autem festum Inventionis et Exaltationis celebrant qui crucesignantur, et de hoc gaudent videntes bonum mercatum'. Transcribed by Maier and Bériou. Jacques de Vitry makes a similar argument about the good bargain in his crusade sermon. Jacques has a humorous tone in his passage. He states that the deal was so good for the crusaders that it was as if 'God was drunk' when he made it. 'Dominus velut ebrius modo facit bonum forum et quasi pro nichilo dat regnum suum. Regno quidem Dei nichil vilius cum emitur, nichil carius cum possidetur': Jacques de Vitry, 'Item sermo ad crucesignatos vel -signandos', *CPI*, p. 118. See also Guibert de Tournai, 'Ad crucesignatos et crucesignandos sermo primus', *CPI*, p. 188.

those who suffered less.[188] There were differences in the way people expressed their commitment to and love of God, differences in the amount of suffering they were willing to endure for Christ, and different causes for their self-denial. Those who were truly penitent, who suffered the most tribulations voluntarily and imitated the *Passio Christi* to the fullest, would receive the greatest merits.

Many Christians would say that they followed Christ, but the crusaders suffering for him truly followed him. This was God's way to find out who was truly willing to follow him, and who was following him only in word and not in deed.[189] According to Philippe le Chancelier, God recognized 'those hanging with him on the cross, or standing by the cross, that is, those who are either on the cross of passion or compassion'.[190] God would know and identify those who were suffering with him, as the good thief had suffered next to Christ on the cross. He would recognize those who stood by Christ when he was crucified, as the Virgin Mary and John did, that is, all those who were truly penitent and humble, who would suffer for Christ and assist him, as the crusaders and the supporters of the movement did.

In the *Brevis ordinacio*, the theme of suffering, the crucifixion, and the wounds of Christ were used extensively to explain the theology of salvation and the reasons behind crusading. The author of the manual encouraged the crusaders to emulate Christ's sufferings, for 'on the cross our whole life' was described by the Lord and every action of Christ ought to be taken as an instruction.[191] The Passion of Christ is on display in the manual: the nails and the pierced hands and feet are described and their allegorical meaning discussed; the position of Christ on the cross, his attitude, and his gaze are interpreted in different ways and connected to the love of God and to the salvation of all sinners.[192]

---

[188] Philippe le Chancelier, '*Dicit Dominus ad Moysen*', Avranches, MS 132, fol. 273ra: 'Patitur quis rerum suarum rapinam, exaltat crucem, patitur contumelias, exaltat crucem magis, patitur verba et iniurias corporales, magis exaltat'. Transcribed by Maier and Bériou.

[189] Jacques de Vitry, 'Sermo ad crucesignatos vel -signandos', *CPI*, p. 96; Eudes de Châteauroux, 'Sermo in conversione sancti Pauli et exhortation ad assumendam crucem', *CPI*, p. 138; Guibert de Tournai, 'Ad crucesignatos et crucesignandos sermo primus', *CPI*, pp. 184–86.

[190] Philippe le Chancelier, 'Sermo in die veneris infra octabas Assumptionis beate Virginis', Avranches, MS 132, fols 243vb–244ra: 'Dominus cognoscit secum pendentes in cruce vel cruci assistentes, hoc est illos qui sunt vel in cruce passionis vel compassionis'. Transcribed by Maier and Bériou.

[191] 'Brevis ordinacio de predicacione', *QBSS*, pp. 11–14, esp. p. 13: 'Dominus in cruce describit nobis totam vitam nostram, ut imitemur eum, quia omnis Christi accio nostra est instruccio'.

[192] 'Brevis ordinacio de predicacione', *QBSS*, pp. 11–14.

In the crusade sermons the ultimate imitation of Christ was crusading martyrdom. This was the highest sacrifice, a genuine act of love that resembled the
sacrifice of Christ on the cross. This was the furthest demonstration of the *imitatio Christi*.[193] In such a martyrdom the different dimensions of crusading —
the military, the devotional, and the penitential aspects — were conjoined. The
crusader could imitate Christ's sacrifice and fight in a war for Christ's sake. He
could prove his love, do repentance for his sins, honour God, and die on behalf
of Christ and for the sake of others.[194] The reward in heaven would compensate
for all the sufferings of the crusader on earth — those who laboured for Christ's
sake on crusades could rest in heaven.[195]

The sufferings of the crusaders could also have unexpected, positive consequences. In one of his crusade sermons, Eudes de Châteauroux explained why
God had allowed Robert d'Artois and other crusaders to perish in the Battle of
Mansurah during the Seventh Crusade. Eudes pointed out that the self-sacrifice
of Robert and the others had benefited those who survived the battles. The survivors were left in an extremely difficult situation, either as captives of the enemy,
like Louis IX and many others, or as refugees who had escaped to Damietta, as
Eudes himself was, or as troops left behind to defend the captured city. The surviving crusaders had no hope of defeating the enemy, of holding Damietta, or of
rescuing the captive king from the enemy. However, the self-sacrifice of Robert
d'Artois and those who died at Mansurah had its effect on subsequent events.
According to Eudes, the death of the crusaders was a powerful intercession. The
crusaders' self-sacrifice had such an effect that it led to the Mamluk coup, which
resulted to the killing of the sultan while Louis IX was still a captive. This led to the
king's quick release, which occurred in time to prevent the crusading army from
disintegrating. The refugees in Damietta were planning to escape and to return
to Europe while the king was away, but as he returned, the army stayed intact.[196]

---

[193] Guibert de Tournai, 'Ad crucesignatos et crucesignandos sermo primus', *CPI*, pp. 184–87.
See also Tamminen, 'Who Deserves the Crown of Martyrdom?'.

[194] *CPI*, p. 60.

[195] Jacques de Vitry, 'Item sermo ad crucesignatos vel -signandos', *CPI*, p. 116; Jacques de
Vitry, 'Ad peregrinos, thema sumpta ex epistola ad Galathas iii', *JVSP*, p. 93. Guibert de Tournai
also underlined that the crusader's cross was a key to paradise. Guibert de Tournai, 'Ad crucesignatos et crucesignandos sermo tertius', *CPI*, p. 208. See also Humbert de Romans, *De predicatione sancte crucis*, cap. xix, inuitatio 22.

[196] Eudes de Châteauroux, 'Sermo in anniversario Roberti comitis Attrabatensis et aliorum
nobilium qui interfecti fuerunt a Sarracenis apud Mansuram in Egipto', *PCHL*, p. 239: 'Hoc
etiam permisit Dominus fieri ut intercedente morte istorum residui a mortis periculo eriperen-
tur quod apparuit in admirabili liberatione regis et suorum. [...] Sed hoc mirabile quod Sarraceni

Eudes de Châteauroux found a clever way of explaining the crusading failure to the disheartened participants of the expedition in his sermon. In this explanation he managed to include, as the sixth reason given in the sermon for the disaster, a further reason for the sufferings of the crusaders. Men could not know the intentions of God, but they could trust that his decisions were just and that they should suffer for him, for these sufferings would bring fruit. All the miraculous things that happened after the disaster of Mansurah had taken place because the crusaders had been willing to suffer and die. The sufferings of crusaders were not futile, just as the sufferings of Christ had not been.[197]

The different features of the *imitatio Christi* provided behavioural models for the crusade preachers. The 'true' crusaders were counselled to adopt humility and voluntary poverty, following the example of the humble Christ. The ideal crusaders were told to deny themselves, to abandon their old life and start a new one by emulating the example of Christ and the apostles. The 'true' crusaders should try to love Christ, God, and other Christians, as Christ had loved them. They should also be ready to suffer as Christ had suffered for them. With the theme of suffering for Christ, the ideal crusaders could be persuaded to embrace the hardships of their journey, to search for suffering, to imitate the passion of Christ, to prove their love, and to earn the great rewards.

The Treasury of Christ's Passion

The crusaders who, truly contrite and confessed, prepare themselves for the service of God, are thought to be true martyrs, provided that they die in the service of Christ, freed from venial and also mortal sins, from all penitence imposed upon them, absolved from the punishment for sins in this world, the punishment of purgatory in the other, secured from the torments of hell, crowned with the glory and honour in eternal blessedness.[198]

regem et omnes alios pugnatores habentes in manibus suis interfecerunt soldanum dominum suum qui eis post captionem regis magna donativa tribuerat regem et suos liberaverunt maxime cum Christiani Damiatham non possent aliquatenus retinere cum illi pauci qui ibi erant fugere proponerent, et fugissent nisi rex tam cito liberatus fuisset'. See also Cole, d'Avray, and Riley-Smith, 'Application of Theology to Current Affairs', p. 237.

[197] Eudes de Châteauroux, 'Sermo in anniversario Roberti comitis Attrabatensis et aliorum nobilium qui interfecti fuerunt a Sarracenis apud Mansuram in Egipto', *PCHL*, pp. 236–39. See also Eudes de Châteauroux, 'Sermo de eodem anniversario', *PCHL*, pp. 240–43; Eudes de Châteauroux, 'Sermo in festo sanctarum reliquiarum', *UEE*, ii, 763–67.

[198] Jacques de Vitry, 'Item sermo ad crucesignatos vel -signandos', *CPI*, pp. 112–13: 'Unde

In his crusade model sermon Jacques de Vitry neatly summarizes the benefits of crusading. The crusader's main reward, the so-called crusade indulgence, mentioned as one of the gains, was the most sought-after recompense for those who had taken the cross.[199] In the crusade sermons this indulgence is often discussed in a vague but inspiring manner. The intention of the preachers was to promote the crusades and acclaim the different advantages the movement presented. The crusade indulgence had particular value as a propagandistic tool because of its motivating force, and it was utilized widely in the sermons.

The preachers portray the crusade indulgence as a special compensation for all the trials of the crusader. It is described as a generous reward gained for relatively little effort. Even people who wore a hairshirt and fasted for sixty years did not usually manage to obtain this reward.[200] The indulgence, amongst other things, is presented in the sermons as a key to paradise, as a heavenly treasure, as a cleanser of all sins, and as a sign of God's special friendship.[201] Considering the significance of the indulgence to the crusade movement, the references to the subject and the utilization of the term appear cursory and unspecific. The authors of the sermons rarely go into details in their discussions of the indulgence.

The different crusades often had different requirements and different terms of indulgence for the participants. During the Albigensian Crusade in 1226, some of the crusaders regarded their crusade vows as fulfilled after forty days of service for King Louis VIII, a minimum requirement of feudal service.[202] A Holy Land crusade, on the other hand, took approximately three years, and the Holy Land crusaders often vowed not to go home until they had visited Jerusalem, which could extend the journey further.[203] To go into details in the

et crucesignati qui vere contriti et confessi ad Dei servitium accinguntur, dum in Christi servitio moriuntur, vere martires reputantur, liberati a peccatis venialibus simul et mortalibus, ab omni penitentia sibi iniuncta, absoluti a pena peccatorum in hoc seculo, a pena purgatorii in alio, securi a tormentis gehenne, gloria et honore coronandi in eterna beatitudine'.

[199] *CPI*, p. 64.

[200] Jacques de Vitry, 'Item sermo ad crucesignatos vel -signandos', *CPI*, p. 120.

[201] Jacques de Vitry, 'Sermo ad crucesignatos vel -signandos', *CPI*, p. 96; Guibert de Tournai, 'Ad crucesignatos et crucesignandos sermo tertius', *CPI*, p. 208; Humbert de Romans, 'De predicatione crucis in genere quocumque', *CPI*, p. 220.

[202] Strayer, *The Albigensian Crusades*, pp. 70, 133.

[203] Giles Constable has noticed that in the charters three years appears as a standard period of time that the crusaders were considered likely to be away on their journey, though five, seven, and even ten years are also mentioned. Constable, *Crusaders and Crusading in the Twelfth Century*, p. 110.

terms of the indulgence in the model sermons would limit the use of the models, so it was more convenient to leave these specific requirements unstated.

During the thirteenth century crusade preachers usually had papal bulls with them, which gave them authority to preach the crusade, to sign people with the cross, and to collect money for the expeditions. These bulls were visible signs which distinguished the authorized crusade preachers from imposters, those pretending to preach a crusade and collecting the money for themselves. The papal bulls contained detailed information about the crusade that was promoted. The specific circumstances, the requirements, the terms of the indulgence, and the different privileges which could be gained were described in the bulls and were often read aloud by the preachers.[204]

The theology of the indulgence was still obscure during the thirteenth century. The crusade indulgence, which basically meant the plenary indulgence, was a remission of temporal punishment due for mortal sin. During the Middle Ages sins could be roughly divided into three categories: original sin, *peccatum originale*, mortal sin, *peccatum mortale*, and venial sin, *peccatum veniale*. Original sin was inherited by all Christians, traceable to Adam and Eve, the fall of man, and the loss of paradise. This sin could not be atoned for by any human measures. Mortal sin was believed to be such a serious offence that it killed the soul and separated it from God. The venial sins were not such grave offences. These lesser sins would result in only partial separation from God and did not lead to eternal death. Satisfaction for venial sins could be made by confessing them to a confessor and performing acts of penance or simply by doing good works and expressing repentance for the sins.[205]

Medieval theologians made a distinction between two consequences of mortal sin: guilt, *culpa*, and the penalty, *pena*. The guilt of mortal sin condemned the sinners to eternal death, that is, to hell, but if the sinners repented, confessed their sins, and asked for God's forgiveness, they would be condemned only to temporal death, which meant separation of the soul from the body until the Last Judgement. The confessor who heard the sinner's confession could, through the sacrament of penance, absolve the penitent from the guilt of sin. However, divine justice still required a penalty for the sinner, which meant that the penitent must complete acts of penance imposed upon him by the confessor before he could achieve full atonement.[206]

---

[204] Maier, *Preaching the Crusades*, pp. 80, 105–06, 118–19; *CPI*, p. 30.

[205] Shaffern, *The Penitents' Treasury*, p. 94.

[206] Shaffern, *The Penitents' Treasury*, p. 95.

Penance and the punishment for sin posed a puzzling question for medieval theologians, as the penance enjoined upon the penitent was not the same thing as the temporal punishment that was owed for the sin. The confessor could not know how much temporal punishment divine justice demanded for the penitent. Thus a theological distinction was made between the remission of imposed penance for the sin and the remission of the temporal punishment owed for the sin.[207]

The theological explanation for the validity and effectiveness of the indulgence was based upon the doctrine of the treasury of merit. According to this theory indulgences were grants that were bestowed from the infinite treasury of merit which Christ, the martyrs, and the saints had gained for the Church through their sufferings and good works. This treasury gave the Church, and the pope in particular, power to grant indulgences, remissions of the punishment owed for sins. According to Humbert de Romans, this treasury, the treasury of Christ's passion, was fully completed on the cross.[208]

Virtue of Contrition

Of the crusade model sermons, the two cardinal-bishops of Tusculum, Jacques de Vitry and Eudes de Châteauroux, discuss the qualities of the indulgence most extensively. Eudes focused his attention in the *Sermo de rebellione Sarracenorum Lucherie* on the penitential nature of crusading. He connected the indulgence to the number seven, which he took from the Bible passage used in the sermon, and compared the seven qualities of the indulgence to the seven violations of

---

[207] Brundage, *Medieval Canon Law and the Crusader*, p. 146.

[208] Humbert de Romans, 'De predicatione crucis in genere quocumque', *CPI*, p. 216: 'in signum quod larga indulgentia, que datur eis, tota assumitur de thesauro passionis Christi in cruce complete'. Although these ideas, the distinction between penance and punishment and the theory of the treasury of merit, were not fully developed until the mid-thirteenth century, similar notions appear to have had a bearing already during the late eleventh century in the creation of the *Reconquista* and the First Crusade. Modern scholars have usually underlined the differences between the 'indulgence' granted by Urban II and the crusade indulgence of the thirteenth century. The development of the theology of the treasury of merit had great impact on the concept of the crusade indulgence. However, Robert Shaffern has recently argued that the similarities between the grants of Urban II and the later popes of the twelfth and the thirteenth centuries are 'more striking than the differences'. Shaffern, *The Penitents' Treasury*, pp. 44–51, 79–84; Brundage, *Medieval Canon Law and the Crusader*, pp. 145–47. See also Shaffern, 'Images, Jurisdiction, and the Treasury of Merit'. See also the three-part work of Catholic historian Paulus, *Geschichte des Ablasses im Mittelalter*.

the Saracens. The symbolic number from the Old Testament embodied the seven benefits of crusading and, by contrast, in Eudes's interpretation, the seven ways that the Lucera Muslims offended and persecuted innocent Christians.[209]

In his sermon Eudes gives a rather long description of the crusade indulgence. He explains carefully that those who had taken the cross against the Lucera Muslims were 'absolved from the vow of abstinence, from pilgrimages which they had bound themselves by a vow to perform, from pilgrimages imposed upon them, and from the punishment owed to them on account of mortal sins'.[210] Eudes seems to have wanted to make clear that the crusade indulgence was fully available to the crusaders, even though they were participating not in a Holy Land crusade, but in a crusade against the Muslims in Italy. According to Matthew Paris there was disbelief, at least in England, in the crusade against the Hohenstaufen and the indulgence promised to the crusaders. It seemed incredible that by serving God in the fight against the Hohenstaufen and the Lucera Muslims a crusader could obtain the same reward as by serving God in the fight against the infidels in the Holy Land.[211] Eudes assured his audience that the indulgence was truly the same, and if the participants had vowed to do something else, for instance, if their initial vow was to go on a pilgrimage or to fight the Muslims beyond the sea, they had no need to worry about that, for by papal mandate their vows could be commuted, and they could instead fight the infidels in Apulia.[212]

According to Eudes, crusading against the Lucera Muslims was extremely beneficial: it absolved the participant from the punishment of all sins, and in one stroke freed people from all sorts of commitments, vows which they might have pledged or penances which they were obliged to do. Other crusade preachers agreed with this view, describing the crusade indulgence as profitable for the participants in multiple ways and promising full remission of sins.[213] In one of

---

[209] Eudes de Châteauroux, 'Sermo de rebellione Sarracenorum Lucherie', *CR*, p. 380. See also Humbert de Romans's description of the seven graces given by the Church to the crusaders. Humbert de Romans, *De predicatione sancte crucis*, cap. xvij, De gracijs ecclesie datis ad idem.

[210] Eudes de Châteauroux, 'Sermo de rebellione Sarracenorum Lucherie', *CR*, p. 380: 'absolvebant enim assumentes crucem contra predictos Sarracenos a voto abstinentie, a peregrinationibus quibus proficiendis se voto obligaverunt, a peregrinationibus sibi iniunctis, et a pena sibi debita pro peccatis mortalibus sibi per contritionem dimissis'.

[211] Matthew Paris, *Chronica majora*, ed. by Luard, p. 521; *CR*, p. 349.

[212] Eudes de Châteauroux, 'Sermo de rebellione Sarracenorum Lucherie', *CR*, p. 380.

[213] Guibert de Tournai, 'Ad crucesignatos et crucesignandos sermo primus', *CPI*, pp. 186, 188; Humbert de Romans, 'De predicatione crucis in genere quocumque', *CPI*, p. 220.

his crusade sermons, Jacques de Vitry declared that by crusading the *crucesignati* earned remission from both *a pena et a culpa*. Robert Shaffern has noted this in his excellent study of medieval indulgences and argued that this view differed from the official teachings of the Church, as well as from the view Jacques himself professed in his other sermon for the crusaders.[214] However, in my opinion there is no great incongruity between the two sermons of Jacques de Vitry.

In the *Sermo ad crucesignatos vel -signandos*, Jacques compared God to a feudal lord and tried to promote the crusades with the theme of vassalage to God. The conclusion to Jacques's excursion into feudal relations was that the crusaders would earn 'the remission of all sins, with regard to penalty and guilt, and moreover eternal life' by serving the highest emperor, that is, God.[215] Shaffern has interpreted Jacques's passage to be strictly about indulgences — a direct reference to the crusade indulgence. However, Jacques does not use the term 'indulgence' at all in this section of the sermon. The passage is a customarily vague discussion of crusading benefits, most likely deliberately presented in an unspecific manner.

Jacques de Vitry was a trained theologian, who must have known about the distinction made between guilt and penalty by the canonists and theologians of the thirteenth century.[216] According to the official teachings of the Church, penances and indulgences would cancel penalty, but only a valid confession could nullify guilt. Indulgence for both *a pena et a culpa* was against the doctrine. However, in this section of the sermon Jacques appears to be referring to the entire benefits of 'true' crusading. He does not say that the crusade indulgence would free the crusaders from both guilt and penalty or give eternal life, but that true crusading from beginning to end would.

Many crusade preachers promoted the crusades as a way of earning full remission of all sins. These broad promises of rewards and indulgences *a pena et a culpa* presented by the crusade preachers of the thirteenth century had an effect on the development of the concept of the indulgence, and the remarks

---

[214] Shaffern, *The Penitents' Treasury*, pp. 147–48.

[215] Jacques de Vitry, 'Sermo ad crucesignatos vel -signandos', *CPI*, p. 98: 'Tanta et talia stipendia offert vobis quod sponte currere deberetis, remissionem cunctorum scilicet peccatorum quantum ad penam et culpam et insuper vitam eternam'.

[216] See, for example, Jacques's down-to-earth explanation of how the sins of humans could be absolved — how the sin dies in contrition, how it is carried outside the house in confession, and how it is buried in satisfaction — in the sermon *ad conjugates*, Gasnault, 'Jacques de Vitry', esp. p. 55: 'La contrition change la peine temporelle de la géhenne en peine du purgatoire, la confession en peine temporelle, la satisfaction adequate l'annule. Par la contrition le péché meurt, par la confession il est porté hors de la maison, par la satisfaction il est enseveli'.

were repeated by the preachers of the fourteenth century. Nevertheless, as Robert Shaffern has noted, this did not mean detachment from the tradition of the indulgence or a break from the official doctrines of the Church, but rather development of the terminology.[217] During the thirteenth century the indulgences were still subordinate to the sacrament of penance.[218]

The dual purpose of the crusade model sermon may have had an effect on the terminology used in the sermons. The model sermons were often written for the crusaders and for those intending to become crusaders. Those who had already taken the cross could be guided in their task and the sermons used to instruct them, for example, on how they should behave to gain the crusade indulgence. However, those who were still considering whether they should take the cross or not needed to be persuaded by the sermons, in which case it was important to explain the indulgence as simply and as attractively as possible — as a great pardon for all sins.

Humbert de Romans also explained in detail the 'graces' received by the crusaders for their services and the consequences of mortal sin, in his *De predicatione sancte crucis*. Humbert believed that the crusade preachers needed to know what it was that they offered for the crusaders in their sermons and how the rewards of crusading could be gained. The preachers needed fully to understand the difficult concepts involved so that they could explain crusading consistently to their audiences, refute the opinions of the 'anti'-crusaders, and respond to opposition with counterarguments. Humbert maintained that the 'first grace' which the crusaders received was the plenary indulgence, which freed people not only from the penalty suffered in hell, but also of purgatory.[219]

Humbert described at length in *De predicatione sancte crucis* the Catholic doctrine which held that mortal sin condemned man to eternal penalty, but through repentance the guilt was removed and the penalty mercifully commuted into a temporal one.[220] Humbert also emphasized in several parts of the manual the requirement for genuine contrition, where the crusaders needed to

---

[217] Shaffern, *The Penitents' Treasury*, pp. 150–59.

[218] Purcell, *Papal Crusading Policy*, p. 37.

[219] According to Humbert, the graces given by the Church were the plenary indulgence, relaxation of penalties, the commutation of vows, absolution from excommunication, protection of the Church, relaxation of many different burdens (such as taxation or paying of debts), and for the ecclesiastics dispensations from obligations. Humbert de Romans, *De predicatione sancte crucis*, cap. xvij. See also *PCHL*, p. 209.

[220] Humbert de Romans, *De predicatione sancte crucis*, cap. xxv, Multi retrahuntur a cruce propter defectum fidei.

confess their sins to priests after taking the cross with 'true contrition of heart'. This was the only way of gaining the indulgence. The crusader's 'true contrition' meant also that they had a 'firm intention' to avoid sin in the future and to serve only God.[221]

In the English crusade manual, the *Brevis ordinacio de predicacione sancte crucis*, the sacrament of penance is discussed at length. First, the author sets out to affirm the effectiveness of the crusade indulgence. The pope will remit the crusader's penalty for sins. The burden of sins, like a heavy weight of stones, will be lifted and the crusader freed from the penalty for sins by serving God.[222] Later, the author explains thoroughly how the sacrament of penance works. Confession, devotion, and contrition were required from the penitent. The sufferings of the crusader were part of the penitential act; however, to earn salvation one had to do more. The sufferings would lead to tears of contrition. These tears, 'the true compunction of heart', would purify the crusader's soul, convert him, and bring him salvation.[223]

The crusade preachers of the thirteenth century did not mean to deceive their audiences with broad promises of full pardon for their sins. Many of the authors of the model sermons took careful notice of the spiritual and confessional state of the crusaders. The requirement for the crusaders to have confessed all their sins as they began their journey was compulsory, and it was repeated in several of the crusade sermons. In fact, this demand appears to have had great importance in the creation of the 'true' crusader. Guibert de Tournai, who followed Jacques de Vitry's description of the benefits of crusading closely, maintained in his model sermon that 'true crusaders' were those who prepared for the service, who were 'truly contrite', 'having confessed their sins'.[224] These two requirements had to be met in order for the crusaders to fulfil the conditions of 'true' crusading and earn the crusade indulgence.

---

[221] Humbert de Romans, *De predicatione sancte crucis*, cap. ii, vi, xxv, xliiij.

[222] 'Brevis ordinacio de predicacione', *QBSS*, pp. 8–9: 'Si aliquis esset oneratus pluribus lapidibus, et quidam acciperet ab eo unum lapidem et alius alium et tercius tercium et sic deinceps, ipse totaliter exoneraretur, similiter cruce signatus deoneratur a pena peccatorum per dominum papam et universalem ecclesiam'.

[223] 'Brevis ordinacio de predicacione', *QBSS*, pp. 13–14.

[224] Guibert de Tournai, 'Ad crucesignatos et crucesignandos sermo primus', *CPI*, p. 188: 'quia veri crucesignati, qui vere contriti et confessi ad servitium Dei accinguntur et in ipso moriuntur, veri martires reputantur, liberati a peccatis mortalibus et venalibus et ab omni penitentia sibi iniuncta, absoluti et a pena peccatorum in hoc seculo et a pena purgatorii in alio, a tormentis gehenne securi gloria eterna per hoc signum investientur'.

Eudes de Châteauroux also made it clear, while explaining the different aspects of the indulgence in the *Sermo de rebellione Sarracenorum Lucherie*, how important true contrition was for the crusaders. After announcing that the crusaders would receive full remission of sins, Eudes went on to explain quickly the nature of mortal sin and the complexity pertaining to its forgiveness. Eudes's discussion of mortal sin and its punishment and forgiveness reflects the ongoing theological discourse. According to Eudes, 'perpetual punishment is owed to mortal sin, but it is commuted into temporal punishment through the virtue of contrition'.[225] This meant that people who had committed serious sins, mortal sins, were condemned to suffer eternal penalty, but the severe punishment could be transformed into transitory penalty if they truly repented their sins and confessed them to a priest. The crusade indulgence would give the crusaders absolution, so the punishment for mortal sin of the crusaders would be alleviated, but this would only happen 'through their contrition'.[226]

Perseverance from the Beginning to the End

The crusaders were obliged to complete their journey and fulfil their pilgrimage in the manner they had vowed to do in order to gain the crusade indulgence. The participants in the crusades should not return too early, leave the task unfinished, or disregard their vows. Jacques de Vitry demanded perseverance from the crusaders, in his sermon for the pilgrims.[227] Humbert de Romans also stressed in his crusade sermon that the crusading pilgrimage required persistence. Levity, adversity, or any other reason should not prevent the crusader from fulfilling his pilgrimage.[228] This requirement of tenacious resolution appears as a significant feature in the creation of a 'true' crusader. Many of the crusade preachers refer to this virtue in their model sermons.[229]

---

[225] Eudes de Châteauroux, 'Sermo de rebellione Sarracenorum Lucherie', *CR*, p. 380: 'Peccato enim mortali debetur pena perpetua sed virtute contritionis in penam transitoriam commutatur'.

[226] Eudes de Châteauroux, 'Sermo de rebellione Sarracenorum Lucherie', *CR*, p. 380: 'a pena sibi debita pro peccatis mortalibus sibi per contritionem dimissis'.

[227] Jacques de Vitry, 'Ad peregrinos. Thema sumpta ex Zacharias ultimo', *JVSP*, p. 97; Jacques de Vitry, 'Item sermo ad crucesignatos vel -signandos', *CPI*, p. 114.

[228] Humbert de Romans, 'Ad peregrinos crucesignatos', *CPI*, pp. 212–14: 'Item perseveranter, ut nec levitate nec adversitate nec aliis causis retrahantur ab incepto quousque compleverint'.

[229] Philippe le Chancelier, 'Sermo in die veneris infra octabas Assumptionis beate Virginis',

There were two sides to the virtue of perseverance in the crusading context: a practical one and an ideological one. In the first place, the crusade preachers tried to convince the *crucesignati* to stay true to their commitment: the preachers urged the Christians to make the crusade vow and then demanded that they keep it. The influence of the 'anti'-crusaders was taken into account, and attempts were made to diminish it.[230] The preachers advised the crusaders to bear in mind that they had taken the cross for penitential reasons, thus trying to free themselves from their sins. Jacques de Vitry condemned those crusaders, 'the miserable ones' who had many years ago taken the cross but had decided to conceal it or hide the cross, thus breaking their crusade vows. These *crucesignati* mocked God with their empty promises.[231]

Humbert de Romans warned crusade preachers using his manual that there were some crusaders who wavered in their commitment. According to Humbert some of the *crucesignati* were reluctant to fulfil their vows. These crusaders performed their duties and served God in a feeble manner. Their conviction and commitment was weak. They could be slow to act, or they could appear unhappy. These 'untrue', unhappy crusaders would be useless in warfare. The crusade preachers thus needed to urge the crusaders to follow the example of the Maccabees, to '*behave manfully in the law*', to fulfil their vows with conviction. The preachers had explained to those signed with the cross why the sign was worn on the right shoulder: this led to the right side of God and was equivalent to a good state of penitence, and the right hand was naturally stronger than the left.[232]

The papacy of the thirteenth century reacted in varying ways to the reluctance shown by some of the *crucesignati* to go on the expeditions. In some instances, the royal crusader's decision not to go was condoned, and the situations which prevented crusading were accepted, in which case the king could be freed from his oath or his vow commuted. In some instances the decision was condemned, in some the pope appeared indifferent or too busy with other ven-

---

Avranches, MS 132, fol. 244vb; Federico Visconti, 'Quando idem dominus predicavit crucem litteraliter clero pisano de mandato domini Pape', *SVP*, p. 548; Eudes de Châteauroux, 'De sancto Georgio', *UEE*, ii, p. 705; Jacques de Vitry, 'Ad peregrinos. Thema sumpta ex Zacharias ultimo', *JVSP*, p. 97; Humbert de Romans, 'Ad peregrinos crucesignatos', *CPI*, p. 212.

[230] See below, pp. 206–12.

[231] Jacques de Vitry, 'Ad peregrinos. Thema sumpta ex Zacharias ultimo', *JVSP*, p. 97: 'Quam miseri qui crucem deponunt vel abscondunt, sicut multi qui iam a multis annis crucem acceperunt et votum frangentes ipsam absconderunt'.

[232] Humbert de Romans, *De predicatione sancte crucis*, cap.vi. 1 Mcc. 2. 64.

tures to become too heavily involved, and in some instances the papal decisions themselves may have in part ruined the royal plans to go crusading.[233]

The papacy was not, however, toothless in the fight against the crusading renegades and perjurers. Even the higher nobility could be pressured to stay true to their crusade vows by means of ecclesiastical censure. The crusaders who did not keep their vows ran the risk of being excommunicated. In fact, the *crucesignati* who did not leave for the expedition at the appointed time — those whose departure was delayed or whose departure was premature — would face automatic excommunication, interdict, or suspension. Those crusaders who did not redeem their vows or did not redeem the vows with the settled sum were also excommunicated.[234] The 'false' crusaders were reproached and condemned, but it was difficult to force the laggards to join the armies.[235] Crusaders who failed to leave when they should have were absolved if they took part in the next general *passagium*, while those who failed to redeem their vows accordingly were absolved when they paid the full amount of their vow redemption.[236]

Just as in the initial stages of becoming a crusader it was important for the preachers to emphasize that the cross should not be taken too lightly and that those who backed out after taking the cross were the worst kinds of perjurers,

---

[233] Purcell, *Papal Crusading Policy*, pp. 89–90, 110–13. The commutation of the crusade vows from one crusade to another created difficulties and at times diverted aid originally intended for the Holy Land to some other direction by papal approval or instigation. See, for example, Lower, *The Barons' Crusade*. Henry III's multiple vow commutations finally prevented him from going on crusade at all, as the circumstances in England became unfavourable in 1262. Weiler, *Henry III of England and the Staufen Empire*, pp. 140, 150–52. For Henry's intentions and his crusade vows, see Forey, 'The Crusading Vows of the English King Henry III'.

[234] The heirs of a crusader who had died could also be excommunicated and disinherited if they refused to make satisfaction for the unfulfilled vow of the deceased. X, 5.40.20, *Corpus Iuris Canonici*; Brundage, *Medieval Canon Law and the Crusader*, pp. 129–30; Purcell, *Papal Crusading Policy*, pp. 175–76. Although excommunication has been described as an occupational hazard for medieval rulers, this was not a situation in which one wanted to find oneself. The struggle between the papacy and the Hohenstaufen during the reigns of Gregory IX and Frederick II culminated in the issue of the emperor's crusade vow and his unwillingness to fulfil it. Frederick II was 'a serial *crucesignatus*', using Tyerman's apt term, taking the crusade vow for the first time in 1215, and again in 1220, 1223, and for the last time in 1225. After a decade of taking the crusade vows, Frederick finally went on the Sixth Crusade in 1228–29. By then, the papacy had run out of patience with him and excommunicated the emperor. Tyerman, *God's War*, p. 740; Abulafia, *Frederick II*, p. 167.

[235] Riley-Smith, *The Crusades: A History*, p. 16.

[236] Purcell, *Papal Crusading Policy*, p. 176.

so too was it important to stress in the sermons that those who were already participating in the journey had to stay with the army for the period of time which was needed or the period for which they had vowed to stay.[237] The crusades often lasted several years, and deserters who left the expeditions prematurely created serious problems for the crusade armies. The legate of the Fifth Crusade, for example, excommunicated all those who left the ranks of the army too soon.[238]

In his letters from the Egyptian crusade, Jacques de Vitry harshly condemned those crusaders who deserted the troops, calling them 'cowards' who made all kinds of false excuses. These 'untrue' crusaders did not fulfil their vows. Their desertion also pre-empted any plans to take action against the Saracens before fresh troops arrived.[239] Humbert de Romans also warned that many crusaders would become weary and discouraged during their journey and would want to return home. In the *De predicatione sancte crucis* he urged the crusaders to find comfort in each other, to help one another, and to stay firm and constant in their commitment.[240] This was the practical side of the virtue of perseverance. The crusade preachers underlined the need for the crusaders to maintain their resolve in order to avoid the problems that might be created by desertion.

The need for the crusaders to remain steadfast was thus important for the crusade armies as a whole, not least to the potential success of the crusade expeditions. At the same time, this requirement was important for the individual crusader him- or herself and for his or her chances of salvation. In his sermon for the pilgrims Jacques de Vitry emphasized that the crusaders and pilgrims needed to stay true to their vows and not withdraw from their avowed intentions by putting down the cross prematurely, so contaminating their penitential journey and their own regeneration and spiritual sanctification.[241] Roger of Salisbury also condemned those who reverted to the life of sin. In his crusade

---

[237] See above, p. 144.

[238] *JVSP*, pp. 84–85.

[239] Jacques de Vitry, *Epistola*, IV, ed. by Huygens, pp. 101–02: 'multi pusillanimes et inconstantes ab exercitu domini inexpleto voto recedentes multa et varia falsa locuntur, in excusatione sue ignavie solatium querentes. [...] multis autem peregrinis a nobis recedentibus et repatriantibus nichil magni aggredi ausi sumus'.

[240] Humbert de Romans, *De predicatione sancte crucis*, cap. xliiij, De his que sunt necessaria his bonis peregrinis crucesignatis.

[241] Jacques de Vitry, 'Ad peregrinos. Thema sumpta ex Zacharias ultimo', *JVSP*, p. 97: 'Qui enim prius confessi sunt et professi ut hanc peregrinationem facerent dum de bono quod inceperunt penitent sanctificationem suam contaminant'.

sermon, Roger reminds his audience that Christ had refused to come down from the cross, and that the penitent crusaders should also remain steadfast, 'for he who comes down from the cross of penitence is like a dog returning to his vomit'.[242] This was the ideological side to the crusader's perseverance — the crusaders needed to complete their journey and fulfil their votive obligations for their own sake.

These demands made by the crusade preachers appear to have been taken very seriously by some of the crusaders, and less seriously by others. The chronicler Primat, who incorporated into his work a description of the second crusade of Louis IX, the Eighth Crusade, condemned the leaders of the army who left the crusade too soon. They decided to return home in 1270, after Louis IX died in Tunisia. The French nobles did not attempt to travel to the Holy Land and visit Jerusalem, which they had vowed to do, according to Primat. The chronicler also described the agreement made between Louis's brother Charles of Anjou and the enemy as deeply unpopular among 'the common knights', who wished to attack the Saracens and not leave the crusade unfinished.[243] The leaders of the crusade did not show perseverance, as their pilgrimage was left uncompleted and their vows unfulfilled.[244]

Prince Edward of England, however, who also took part in the Eighth Crusade, wanted to stay true to his crusade vow and continue the expedition despite the death of Louis IX. Edward arrived late in Tunisia, as did Charles of Anjou, but he wanted nonetheless to attack the Muslim forces there. Charles forbade him to engage the enemy in combat. In spite of the decision of the French nobles

---

[242] Roger of Salisbury, '*Ascendente* Ihesu *in naviculam*', *PCHL*, p. 230: 'Caveat ergo qui sic crucem ascendit, ne descendat, intelligens quod cum de Christo diceretur, *Descendat nunc de cruce*, noluit descendere. Qui enim de cruce penitentiali descendit quasi canis ad vomitum redit'. Mark 15. 32. Roger utilized the image from Proverbs of a dog returning to his own vomit, which was often used during the Middle Ages as an image of heretics or sinners who lapsed into their former sin. Pr. 26. 11. See also Ferreiro, 'Simon Magus, Dogs, and Simon Peter', esp. pp. 60–61.

[243] Primat, *Chronique de Primat traduite par Jean du Vignau*, ed. by Bouquet, pp. 80–84. See also Lower, 'Louis IX, Charles of Anjou, and the Tunis Crusade of 1270', p. 182; Smith, *Crusading in the Age of Joinville*, p. 110.

[244] Primat, *Chronique de Primat traduite par Jean du Vignau*, ed. by Bouquet, p. 82: 'il ne povoient avenir affin de leur pelerinage à leur veu acomplir [...]. Mais ce ne povoient il faire se il ne passoient à nage en Iherusalem, et se il n'estoient passez en la Terre sainte pour visiter le lieu de la resurrection Nostre Seigneur et les sainz liex où il habita, se il eussent povoir, et que il destruisissent la gent Sarrazine à tout leur povoir qui avoit prise et occupée la Terre de promission; et tel estoit le propos de leur veu'.

not to continue the crusade and the pressure King Henry III put upon his son to return to England, Edward wanted to continue his journey. According to the chronicler of Saint Albans Abbey, Edward claimed that he would keep his oath no matter what and go to Acre in the company of his 'palfrey custodian Sowino' alone, if he had to.[245] In the end a small group of French and English crusaders accompanied Edward to the Holy Land: the crusade accomplished little, but the prince fulfilled his vow and gained, without dispute, the crusade indulgence.[246]

While we do not know what Charles of Anjou or the rest of the French nobles had vowed to do, we do know that a common contemporary view of the French nobles of the Eighth Crusade was that they had turned out to be 'untrue' crusaders, whereas Edward was considered to have behaved like a 'true' one. According to the Florentine chronicler Giovanni Villani, many accused Charles of Anjou of making the treaty with the Muslims out of avarice, for in accordance with the peace treaty Charles received tribute from the King of Tunisia. This way he did not have to share the booty which would have been gained by conquering the Kingdom of Tunisia with the other crusaders or with the Church and he could keep it all for himself.[247] Salimbene di Adam also noted that after the arrival of Edward and his troops, there was a formidable force of pilgrims in Tunisia that might have recovered the Holy Land and conquered the entire Saracen territory, but because of the sins of the crusaders, far from attacking the enemy, the army disintegrated, and the whole expedition was quite futile.[248]

---

[245] Rishanger, *Chronica et Annales*, ed. by Riley, p. 68: "'Quamvis omnes commilitones et patriotae mei me deseruerint, ego tamen, cum Sowino, custode palefridi mei" — sic enim vocabatur curator equi sui, "intrabo Tholomaidam" — id est, Accon, vel Acram, — "et pactum juramenti servabo, usque ad corporis et animae divisionem."'

[246] Rishanger, *Chronica et Annales*, ed. by Riley, p. 68. See also Tyerman, *England and the Crusades*, pp. 131–32.

[247] Villani, *Chronica*, ed. by Moutier, p. 204: 'Altri dierono colpa al re Carlo, che'l fece per avarizia, per avere innanzi per la detta pace sempre a tributario il re di Tunisi in sua spezialità; che se'l regno di Tunisi fosse conquistato per lo stuolo de' cristiani, era poi a parte del re di Francia, e di quello d'Inghilterra, e di quello di Navarra, e di quello di Cicilia, e della Chiesa di Roma, e di più altri signori ch'erano al conquisto'.

[248] Both Giovanni Villani and Salimbene di Adam do also acknowledge the desperate state of the crusade army: the deaths of Louis IX, his son Jean Tristan, the papal legate, and many others, as well as the vacancy at the Holy See, all contributed to the disintegration of the army. Villani, *Chronica*, ed. by Moutier, p. 204; Salimbene di Adam, *Cronica Fratris*, ed.by Bernini, II, 173–74.

The medieval sources also agree that by the decision of God, divine venge-ance was brought on Charles and the French crusaders as they left Tunisia: on the way back home the crusade army was caught in a storm. Most of Charles's ships were wrecked, countless men drowned, and the treasure that he had received from the King of Tunisia was lost.[249] To contemporaries, these crusad-ers did not deserve the rewards gained by crusading and were rightly punished by God, because they did not complete their journey or fulfil their vows.[250] The shame of abandoning the crusade too early and the public disgrace which would follow could also persuade crusaders who had left prematurely to go on another crusade to vindicate their honour. This had occurred in 1098, when Étienne de Blois, who had set out on the First Crusade but left for home in 1098 during the prolonged siege of Antioch, returned to the Holy Land for a second time to make amends and regained the reputation of a 'true' crusader by dying at Ramlah in 1102.[251]

There was one further aspect to the ideological side of the virtue of the cru-sader's perseverance that some of the preachers attempted to explain. Of the authors of the model sermons, Jacques de Vitry laboured hardest to get this point across to his audience. Jacques argued in his sermon for the pilgrims that many crusaders tried to save themselves from their sins when they left for their journey, but later returned to sin and consequently ruined all that they had achieved by going on the journey in the first place. Their pilgrimage was use-less if they did not show perseverance.[252] Jacques also calculated the different benefits of crusading in his sermon for the crusaders and observed that one particular good thing that came from crusading was that the people hurried to confession after taking the cross and afterwards struggled hard 'to abstain from sins' so that they would not lose the great reward which they had earned for themselves.[253]

---

[249] Rishanger, *Chronica et Annales*, ed. by Riley, pp. 66–68; Villani, *Chronica*, ed. by Moutier, p. 204.

[250] Part of the blame for the disaster of the Eighth Crusade also fell on the usual suspects, the clergy, who were described as hypocrites in the customary fashion. Throop, 'Criticism of Papal Crusade Policy', esp. p. 409.

[251] Tyerman, *England and the Crusades*, pp. 24–25.

[252] Jacques de Vitry, 'Ad peregrinos. Thema sumpta ex Zacharias ultimo', *JVSP*, p. 97: 'Quod etiam potest de quibusdam peregrinis et crucesignatis qui se a peccatis servant sed redeundo ad vomitum peregrinationem suam fedant. Sicut enim ungula cadente inutilis est equus, ita peregri-natio sine finali perseverantia inutilis redditur'. Compare the similar passage of Roger of Salisbury quoted above, p. 155. Roger of Salisbury, '*Ascendente* Ihesu *in naviculam*, et cetera', *PCHL*, p. 230.

[253] Jacques de Vitry, 'Item sermo ad crucesignatos vel -signandos', *CPI*, p. 122: 'Quintum

By these comments Jacques wanted to clarify certain aspects of the crusade indulgence that might seem ambiguous to his audiences of pilgrims and crusaders. These features of the crusade indulgence had great importance ideologically and theologically, but they are often overlooked by modern scholars. The indulgence freed the crusaders from the punishment of mortal sin which the crusaders had committed before taking the cross and which they had subsequently confessed and repented. The 'true' crusaders would, immediately after the present life, gain the indulgence and follow the signpost of Christ to eternal blessedness.[254] This, of course, meant that the main reward of the crusaders, the plenary indulgence, was received only after death. For some crusaders this might mean many more years of life during which those who had returned home from a crusade after completing it needed to abstain from sinning so as not to lose their reward in heaven. The crusade indulgence did not free the crusaders from any future sins.

The 'true' crusaders, who had taken the cross with a contrite heart and confessed all their sins, could expect to be rewarded as they persevered until the end, thus fulfilling their crusade vows, but who then firmly kept to the spiritual, penitential path which they had chosen for themselves. This lifelong need for perseverance is one of the reasons why the preachers promoted the crusades as a comprehensive conversion. The crusaders needed to reform themselves fully so as to avoid punishment for subsequent sins made after the crusade campaign was over.

This was ideologically an important point, otherwise some crusaders might think that they could do as they wished after they had first served God. Some might believe that they could commit all sorts of crimes and would not get punished for them, because they had earlier obtained the crusade indulgence. Some of the criminals who were forced to become crusaders had the opinion that after they had taken the cross they could continue to commit crimes and their felonies had no consequences, as they had been signed with the cross. The crusader's privilege was thought to have given them immunity.[255]

autem et precipuum bonum est quod, postquam cruce signati sunt, ne tantum premium laboris sui ammitant, ad confessionem currunt et de cetero a peccatis abstinere student ne tantum bonum perdant'.

[254] Jacques de Vitry, 'Item sermo ad crucesignatos vel -signandos', *CPI*, p. 114: 'quia statim et quasi inmediate veri crucesignati obtenta indulgentia et servata post terminum vite presentis eterne beatitudinis titulum consequuntur'.

[255] Pope Innocent IV reacted against these abuses during the preparations for the Seventh Crusade, demanding that Eudes de Châteauroux, as the legate of the crusade, be careful not to

All crusaders who fulfilled their crusade vows would gain the indulgence, but only the 'true' crusaders would benefit from the indulgence immediately after dying. It was possible that crusaders who had sinned after the crusade would have to do satisfaction for their sins and could suffer in purgatory before entering heaven, or, theoretically, even end up in hell, despite having completed their crusade honourably. These aspects of the crusade indulgence are not accentuated in the crusade model sermons, because they were rather uninspiring and did not serve propagandistic purposes, but in the spirit of the pastoral reform movement they also needed to be subtly communicated to the crusaders.

Some modern scholars have regarded Louis IX as 'the ideal crusader' or 'one of the best incarnations' of this concept, because of the many different qualities the French king possessed.[256] Louis proved himself a true penitent: he prepared piously for the Seventh Crusade, purified himself and his realm before leaving, and expressed his devotion and penitence on several occasions during the journey. However, perhaps most importantly, Louis IX may be considered one of the best representatives of the 'ideal' crusader because of his actions after the Seventh Crusade. Louis appears to have accepted the crusade preachers' insistence on comprehensive conversion. The French king did not return to his old ways when he returned home from his first crusade, but continued the life of penance. According to Louis's biographers, the king renounced luxuries and was moderate in his eating habits after the crusade. He dedicated his life to many different acts of penance, of which the Eighth Crusade may be conceived as the final expression.[257]

Louis IX was not the only crusader to have adopted a new life after a crusading expedition. Some crusaders joined religious orders and became monks after fulfilling their crusade vows. In particular, the military orders attracted veteran crusaders whose campaigns had ended. Others stayed in the Holy Land, with-

---

let those who had been signed with the cross believe that they could commit all sorts of crimes without fear of prosecution because of their privileged status. Innocentius IV, *Reg.*, no. 2230, in *Les Registres d'Innocent IV*, ed. by Berger: 'regis Francie illustris fuit propositum coram nobis quod nonnulli crucesignati regni sui, cum deberent ab excessibus abstinere propter libertatem eis indultam, furta, homicidia, raptus mulierum, et alia perpetrant detestanda. Nolentes igitur ut aliqui crucesignati occasione libertatis eis indulte presumant ad talia extendere manus suas, mandamus quatinus crucesignatos eosdem in hujusmodi criminibus non defendas'. Purcell, *Papal Crusading Policy*, p. 167.

[256] Le Goff, *Saint Louis*, p. 778: 'Si l'on se réfère au concept de "croisé idéal", Saint Louis a été, aux yeux de ses contemporains, de la postérité et des historiens modernes l'une des meilleures incarnations de ce personnage imaginaire'. See also Le Goff, 'Saint Louis, croisé idéal?'.

[257] Le Goff, *Saint Louis*, p. 778.

out joining any religious orders, and continued to fight against the enemies of God.[258] These 'ex-crusaders' wanted to carry on in the service of God and tried to secure the reward which they had gained — the crusade indulgence — by entering a cloister, where God and Christ were served and strict religious rules followed, so as to avoid sinning; or found other ways of expressing their continuous devotion and repentance.

Partial Indulgences

There were many kinds of indulgences, which both the active participants, the crusaders who took part in the expeditions, and the more passive participants, those supporting the movement from the home front, could gain for themselves. Humbert de Romans repeatedly mentions the benefits of crusading, using a plural form 'indulgences' in his sermons. According to Humbert, God had opened the gates of heaven and granted an abundance of indulgences from his treasuries.[259] This abundance of indulgences was born out of the development of the crusade movement and the many different ways the crusades could be supported during the thirteenth century. The papacy was prepared to grant partial indulgences for those who took part, in one way or another, in the business of the cross. Eudes de Châteauroux, for example, was instructed by Pope Innocent IV to grant a partial indulgence, a remission of forty days, for those giving donations to the confraternity of the *crucesignati* of Châteaudun.[260] This

---

[258] For crusaders who joined the military orders, see, for example, Schenk, *Templar Families*, p. 230. Olivier de Termes may be considered an example of a crusader who devoted his life to the service of Christ after participating in an expedition. Olivier participated in the Seventh Crusade. This appears to have been imposed upon him as a penance for his former heresy. Olivier was the son of Raymond III de Termes, who held the lordship of the castle of Termes near Carcassonne, lost in 1210 to the army of the Albigensian crusaders. Olivier supported the Cathar resistance during the Albigensian crusades in 1209–29. He also participated in the revolts of the 1240s, for which he was excommunicated by the Church. Olivier was reconciled with the French Crown and joined Louis IX's first crusade in 1248. After the Seventh Crusade he was involved in various battles in the East. Olivier also took part in Louis IX's second crusade to Tunisia in 1270 and served as the commander of the French garrison at Acre from 1273 until his death in 1274. Smith, *Crusading in the Age of Joinville*, pp. 152–70.

[259] Humbert de Romans, 'De predicatione crucis in genere quocumque', *CPI*, pp. 216, 220: 'de thesauris suis profert largissima dona indulgentiarum ad elargiendum istis militaturis'; 'Porro tempore crucis predicante cataracte celi aperte sunt in habundantia indulgentiarum, sancta mater ecclesia manus suas aperit et palmas suas extendit ad pauperes'.

[260] Innocentius IV, *Reg.*, no. 2644, in *Les Registres d'Innocent IV*, ed. by Berger; Purcell,

confraternity had been established to gather funds for the Seventh Crusade, which could be used for hiring ships, acquiring war materials, and aiding poor crusaders so that they could take part in the expedition.[261]

Eudes was also allowed by Innocent IV to grant partial indulgences for all those hearing his crusade sermons, up to one hundred days of remission.[262] As a legate of the Seventh Crusade, Eudes was in charge of the propaganda campaign for the expedition. The pope's grant of partial indulgences for all attending the crusade sermons must have helped his preaching. Jacques de Vitry also mentions this reward in his crusade model sermon. According to Jacques, those who heard crusade sermons were granted twenty or forty days of remission of penance, for which they would be very grateful when they suffered in purgatory.[263] During the thirteenth century, not only those who heard the crusade preaching gained indulgences, but also those who gave the sermons. The crusade preachers themselves earned partial or plenary indulgences for their labours, as did those collecting the crusade taxes, donations, and vow redemptions.[264]

Interestingly, the *crucesignati* also appear to have been interested in gaining partial or additional indulgences, even though they were rewarded the plenary indulgence for their services. Eudes de Châteauroux ordered the crusaders of the Seventh Crusade to participate in processions that were held in Damietta to hasten and ensure the safe arrival of Alphonse de Poitiers and the second detachment of the crusade army in Egypt in 1249. Those crusaders who attended these processions and a sermon preached by Eudes were granted a pardon for their sins by the legate, that is, an extra crusade indulgence.[265]

Maureen Purcell has suggested that by the mid-thirteenth century — especially during the reign of Innocent IV — the doctrine of the treasury of merit had not yet been fully developed and that the plenary indulgence might have been viewed as effecting only 'a quasi-plenary remission of sins', which would

Papal Crusading Policy, p. 62.

[261] Tyerman, *God's War*, pp. 775–76.

[262] Innocentius IV, *Reg.*, no. 4663, in *Les Registres d'Innocent IV*, ed. by Berger; Purcell, *Papal Crusading Policy*, pp. 62–63.

[263] Jacques de Vitry, 'Item sermo ad crucesignatos vel -signandos', *CPI*, p. 120: 'Secundum bonum quod venientibus ad sermonem viginti vel quadraginta dies aliquando de penitentia relaxantur, quod multum proderit eis maxime post mortem in purgatorio, quando pro unius hore relaxatione, si possibile esset, magnum thesaurum dedisse voluissent'.

[264] Purcell, *Papal Crusading Policy*, pp. 60–62.

[265] Jean de Joinville, *Vie de Saint Louis*, ed. by Monfrin, p. 88: 'La fu le roy et les riches homes de l'ost, aus quiex le legat donna grant pardon'. Purcell, *Papal Crusading Policy*, p. 26.

explain the crusaders' determination to seek further indulgences.[266] However, there may be another simpler explanation. The crusaders' desire to earn additional indulgences may simply arise from the basic qualities of the indulgence and from the mechanisms involved in gaining the remission of sins. Theoretically, after the confession and the taking of the cross, the crusader should sin no more, for these future sins would not belong to those confessed and could not be forgiven without the sacrament of penance.

In his preaching manual Humbert de Romans explained how the crusaders should act on their journey. The crusaders should 'abstain from all sin' during the voyage. If, because of 'human frailty', they would nonetheless sin, the crusaders ought to do 'penance swiftly'. The sins ought to be confessed and satisfied by the crusaders immediately. Humbert utilized a biblical example in the manual to make his point. When the Israelites went to war against their enemies, they had to be pure, both spiritually and bodily. If there was a man amongst the Jews who was 'defiled in a dream by night', he had to go out of the camp, wash himself with water, and return only after the sun had set. Humbert concluded that if this had been important for the Jews, how much more so for the Christians fighting for Christ? He also argued that the crusaders ought to be 'zealous in punishing evil' which had been done by the crusaders during the journey.[267]

The crusaders should thus confess sins committed after becoming *crucesignati* to a confessor while they were participating in a crusade. Guilt for these new sins could then be absolved and satisfaction made. The penalty could be included in the plenary indulgence granted to them while still in the service of Christ, but the penalty owed for the new sins might also require further works of penance from the crusader, as, for example, was the case during the diverted Fourth Crusade.[268] Pope Innocent III tried to steer the crusaders back to their original purpose during the expedition, but he needed to address several problems first. He had previously excommunicated the Venetians, who failed

---

[266] Purcell, *Papal Crusading Policy*, p. 26.

[267] Humbert de Romans, *De predicatione sancte crucis*, cap. xliiij. Dt. 23. 10–11. Humbert's list of things that the crusaders ought to take care of or take into account included fourteen points. Eight of these dealt with issues that the crusaders should observe before the actual journey. Six points dealt with issues that the crusaders ought to observe during the expeditions. The list included confession of sins, true contrition, good counsel, asking advice from the wise, restitution of goods, reconciliation with enemies, making a will, disposal of house and goods, being constant during the expedition, taking comfort in companions, giving aid, abstaining from sin, doing penance quickly, zealously punishing evil, and fighting bravely against the enemy. See also *PCHL*, p. 216.

[268] See above, pp. 57–59.

to express any regret about the diversion, but absolved the barons, who had displayed due remorse. The barons could not, however, make any expedition without the assistance of their excommunicated colleagues, as the Venetians were in charge of the transportation for the crusade army, and the barons had already paid dearly to obtain passage from them.[269] Innocent III, fearing the crusade might collapse altogether, explained the situation astutely to the barons. The pope personified his sentence of excommunication to the Venetian doge, expounding that the doge was excommunicated like 'paterfamilias', but the crusaders were 'like his family, excused while they were in the ships'. The excommunication of the doge, and the rest of the Venetians, did not affect the barons and the Frankish crusaders during the voyage if the crusaders travelled with 'sorrow of heart'. Thus the Franks were able to communicate with the excommunicated Venetians, whose company they could not in any case avoid on the ships, but they should hope for their repentance.[270]

In other words, the Frankish crusaders could continue their expedition, but they needed to acknowledge that their travelling companions were not absolved, and as soon as the ships reached their destination, if the Venetians were still unremorseful, the Franks should abandon their company. This was not a trivial matter, but one about which the barons had also expressed their concern. How could the crusade be continued with excommunicated partners?[271] The pope made it clear that the Franks and the Venetians should separate after disembarkation, for continuing the crusade with the anathematized might jeopardize the whole campaign. The participants of the Fourth Crusade had

---

[269] Innocentius III, *Regestorum sive epistolarum*, CII, in *PL*, CCXV, cols 107–10.

[270] Innocentius III, *Regestorum sive epistolarum*, CII, in *PL*, CCXV, col. 108: 'Licet ergo dux Venetorum dominus navium, tanquam paterfamilias domus, in excommunicatione persistat, vos tamen, tanquam ipsius familia, dum in navibus ejus fueritis, ipsius excommunicatio non continget, et excusabiles eritis apud Deum, si, in excommunicatorum navibus existentes, cum dolore cordis sub spe poenitentiae excommunicatis ipsis communicaveritis, in quibus communionem eorum nequiveritis evitare'.

[271] The Frankish barons wished to keep the excommunication of the Venetians a secret known only to them and asked the pope not to make the bull of anathema public. In fact, the leader of the crusade, Marquis Boniface de Montferrat, had decided to temporarily suppress the bull sent to him and to the crusaders at Zara in 1203. The barons argued that the concealment of information was done out of fear that the crusade could not be continued: the army would dissolve, souls and bodies would be in peril, and the Holy Land would be desolate if the bull was made public. Andrea has argued that these arguments were a pretext and that the sole reason behind the concealment was the attempt to hide harmful information so that the plan to attack Constantinople would not be hindered. Andrea, *Contemporary Sources for the Fourth Crusade*, pp. 57–58.

to show signs of genuine repentance after attacking Christians and make satisfaction for their sins, even though they were still on the crusade and had been
granted the plenary indulgence.

The Frankish barons felt that communication with the excommunicated
Venetians might impede their salvation and their chances of gaining the plenary indulgence. Pope Innocent III had to repeatedly assure the barons that
they should not worry about the effects of this communication. Innocent
reminded the Frankish crusaders of one of the privileges granted to the *crucesignati*: according to canon law, the crusader could pass through the lands
of heretics or excommunicated persons, have contact with them if need be,
and purchase necessities from them.[272] Innocent also gave the barons further
absolution, another indulgence for surety: if the crusaders had to communicate
with the Venetians, they would nonetheless be 'safe from the stain of sin by our
indulgence'.[273]

Considering that many participants in the crusades were deeply preoccu-
pied with the consequences of mortal sin, for which they attempted to make
restitution and find absolution by joining in the expeditions, it seems plausible
that they might have had feelings of guilt and sinfulness even though they were
crucesignati and had been promised the crusade indulgence for their previous
sins.[274] The crusaders could search for absolution for new sins committed during the crusade. Their sins were regarded as harmful to the expeditions. This
belief was asserted both by the crusade preachers in their model sermons and
by the clergy participating in the crusades. The crusading clergy encouraged the
crusaders to take part in processions, fasts, and other penitential acts so that
they could purify themselves during the crusades. Sinning should be avoided
on the campaigns, and measures should be taken to cleanse those crusaders

---

[272] Innocentius III, *Regestorum sive epistolarum*, CCIX, in *PL*, CCXV, col. 236: 'cum sit
etiam cautum in jure, quod, si quisquam per terram haereticorum aut quorumlibet excommunicatorum transierit, communicare in emendis et recipiendis necessariis possit eis'. Innocent III's
ruling and the case against the Venetians was also incorporated by Gregory IX into the Decretals,
X. 5.39.34, *Corpus Iuris Canonici*.

[273] Innocentius III, *Regestorum sive epistolarum*, CCIX, in *PL*, CCXV, p. 236: 'Unde, si
propter urgentem necessitatem oporteat communicare te Venetis, in quibus sine gravi scandalo,
et grandi dispendio illos non poteris evitare, de indulgentia nostra secures, labem peccati propter hoc nullatenus pertimescas'.

[274] The preoccupation with mortal sin was one of the major reasons for the initial com-
mitment of many crusaders. Jean de Joinville tells a revealing story in his history about how
Louis IX personally explained to him the effects of deadly sin. Jean de Joinville, *Vie de Saint
Louis*, ed. by Monfrin, pp. 13–14.

who had sinned.[275] The crusaders were guided to seek further indulgences by the clergy. Humbert de Romans admitted in his manual *De predicatione sancte crucis* that although the crusaders were freed from all penances owed for sin when they took the cross, having confessed their sins and left for the expeditions, 'men should not be without some penance, for the sake of the doubt of uncertainty'.[276] It was better for people to fear divine justice and be cautious in their actions than to believe that all wrongdoing had been forgiven.

Virtually all crusading difficulties, among them illness, starvation, natural disasters such as flooding rivers, storms, and earthquakes, deaths of crusaders, loss of territory, and defeats in battle, as well as failures of entire campaigns, were linked to the sins of Christians and to the sins of the crusaders.[277] This was more than a mere topos for many of the crusaders. Louis IX, for example, took the crusading defeat at Mansurah in 1250 and his own imprisonment to heart. Louis was not prepared to return home after his release but continued the journey from Egypt to the Holy Land. There he devoted himself to intense penance. Louis IX personally took part in the construction of the fortifications 'to gain pardon' for himself. On one of these occasions, the king carried with his own hands the corpses of Christians killed recently to their place of burial. According to Jean de Joinville, Louis took his penance very seriously: he did not close his nostrils to avoid the putrid smell, unlike the others carrying the bodies.[278]

These actions of the crusaders of the Fourth and the Seventh Crusades give us an insight into the question of why the *crucesignati* also wanted partial

---

[275] See below, pp. 183, 282.

[276] Humbert de Romans, *De predicatione sancte crucis*, cap. xvij: 'quamvis non debeant homines esse sine aliqua penitentia propter dubium incertitudinis'.

[277] Siberry, *Criticism of Crusading*, pp. 84–86, 89–90; Hanska, *Strategies of Sanity and Survival*, pp. 116–26.

[278] Jean de Joinville, *Vie de Saint Louis*, ed. by Monfrin, p. 256, p. 288: 'Le roy meismes y vis je mainte foiz porter la hote aus fossés pour avoir le pardon. [...] et il meismes son cors portoit les cors pourris et touz puans pour mettre en terre es fosses, que ja ne se estoupast, et les autres se estoupoient'. Jean de Joinville's intention was to represent Louis IX in a saintly light in his history, which these passages also indicate. Louis IX has been described as 'a changed man' after the crusading failure of 1250. Louis spent many years in the Holy Land demonstrating his willingness to do penance, repairing and building new fortifications out of his own funds, and neglecting his realm in Europe in the process. The king was determined to be true to his crusade vow and leave the Holy Land in a better state than it was before the Seventh Crusade began. Folda, *Crusader Art in the Holy Land*, pp. 244–45; Jordan, *Louis IX and the Challenge of the Crusade*, pp. 127–30.

indulgences on top of the plenary indulgence promised to them. The crusaders were freed from previous sins, but the sinful acts that were committed during the preparations for the expedition, which might take several years before the actual departure, or those committed during the voyage, needed to be confessed, repented, and satisfaction made for. Louis IX had gained the crusade indulgence with his expedition to Egypt, but he actively sought opportunities to earn further, partial indulgences, because he felt responsible for the unsuccessful outcome of the crusade and wished to be absolved from subsequent sins committed after those confessed when taking the cross.

Help for the Dead

Some crusade preachers went as far as describing the crusade indulgence as effective for the deceased as well. The indulgence was presented as extending all the way to purgatory and benefiting people other than the crusaders. Jacques de Vitry claimed in his crusade model sermon that if the crusader had the intention of helping his parents, 'whether living or dead', he could do so by taking the cross. The implication was that if the parents were still alive, the crusader could earn merit for them and assist them in this life by crusading. However, if the parents of the crusader had already died and presumably suffered punishment in purgatory, the crusader's good deeds would not go unnoticed in the afterlife. The crusader could bring his dead parents relief or even salvation by doing service for Christ.[279]

Eudes de Châteauroux agreed with this view in his crusade model sermon. Eudes also insisted in the *Sermo de invitatione ad crucem* that the crusader could help his loved ones suffering in purgatory, if this was the reason for taking part in the pilgrimage. Crusading was profitable in many ways, for the crusader could pay back the Lord's sacrifice on the cross, aid his own deceased relatives or beloved, and gain eternal life all at the same time, just by taking up the cross.[280] The crusade preachers wanted to give additional reasons for Christians

---

[279] Jacques de Vitry, 'Item sermo ad crucesignatos vel -signandos', *CPI*, p. 112: 'Sed et parentibus defunctis qui bona sua illis reliquerunt, si hac intentione ut eis subveniant crucem accipiunt, multum eis succurrere possunt. [...] Unde nullo modo dubitetis quod non solum vobis ad remissionem peccatorum et eterne vite premium valet hec peregrinatio sed etiam uxoribus, filiis, parentibus, tam vivis quam defunctis, multum proderit quidquid boni feceritis in hac via pro ipsis'.

[280] Eudes de Châteauroux, 'Sermo de invitatione ad crucem', *CPI*, p. 164: 'Letitia etiam debet ei inesse, quod pro modulo suo vicem rependit Domino, quod etiam caros suos qui sunt in purgatorio iuvare potest, si crucem et hanc peregrinationem assumpserit pro eis, et quod per crucem acquirit sibi vitam eternam'.

to participate in the crusade movement by appealing to their feelings of devotion to close relatives and loved ones. This way the impediment posed by the crusaders' love for wives, children, or parents could be turned into an encouragement to take the cross and used for the benefit of the crusade movement.

The proposition that the crusade indulgence could help the dead suffering in purgatory was, however, a disputed matter, and not all the crusade propagandists shared Jacques de Vitry and Eudes de Châteauroux's perception. Caesarius von Heisterbach, a fellow crusade preacher of Jacques and Eudes during the Albigensian Crusade, harshly condemned such views. Caesarius accused preachers who promoted this idea of not thinking about what they preached. These preachers wanted only to persuade as many as they could to take the cross. They were trying to free people from purgatory and even from hell, according to the irritated Cistercian monk.[281]

The great theologians of the thirteenth century debated whether it was possible to give pardons for the dead. Bonaventure, Albertus Magnus, and Thomas Aquinas all expressed their opinions on the matter. Bonaventure took a critical view: the dead could be assisted in purgatory, but the Church or the pope did not have authority over the dead. Bonaventure had the opinion that the indulgence could be given only after the sacrament of penance, which did not exist in purgatory. For him the aid that the living could provide for the dead was a powerful suffrage, not an indulgence. Albertus Magnus and Thomas Aquinas took a less critical view, accepting that indulgences could be given to the dead in purgatory and that the Church's authority extended over the dead as well. Albertus noted that the dead suffering in purgatory benefited greatly from the indulgences granted by the Church, but those in hell did not profit at all from them.[282]

During the papacy of Innocent IV a first pontifical definition of purgatory was made. Innocent tried to find an agreement with the Greek Orthodox

---

[281] Caesarius von Heisterbach, 'Homilia de eadem', ed. by Coppenstein, p. 46: 'non attendunt, quid predicent, quid proponant: dummodo multos capiant. Tales sunt hodie quidam predicatores crucis, qui signari volentibus, quotquot vel quas animas requirunt, de purgatorio vel, quod maioris vesanie est, de inferno repromittunt'. Shaffern, *The Penitents' Treasury*, p. 161. For Caesarius von Heisterbach's views on purgatory, see Le Goff, *The Birth of Purgatory*, pp. 300–303.

[282] Shaffern, *The Penitents' Treasury*, pp. 163–66. Albertus Magnus, *Commentarii in IV Sententiarum*, ed. by Borgnet, Lib. 4, XX, xviii, 855A: 'videtur sine praejudicio dicendum, quod existentibus in inferno nihil prosunt indulgentiae: sed existentibus in purgatorio prosunt multum. Et causa hujus est, quia insusceptibiles sunt boni, sicut et daemones qui sunt in inferno'.

Church on spiritual matters and attempted to establish a union between the churches.[283] Eudes de Châteauroux, while still on the Seventh Crusade, returning from the Holy Land and stopping in Cyprus in 1254, received a letter from the pope in which purgatory was given definition and which he as the legate of the pope was to present to the Greek Orthodox Church of Cyprus. In the letter, the pope maintained that those suffering in purgatory could be helped by the suffrages of the Church.[284]

The comments of Eudes in his crusade sermon were thus in accordance with the official views of the Church and had papal backing at the time. Jacques de Vitry, on the other hand, appears to have acted as a precursor in the matter when he made his comments on purgatory in the 1230s. Jacques was careful with his wording in the crusade sermon, perhaps anticipating opposition such as that displayed by Caesarius von Heisterbach. Jacques does not say that the dead would receive an indulgence in purgatory, and never once mentions hell, but concludes that the dead in purgatory would profit 'greatly' from the crusading of others. Jacques also uses the same rationale that Innocent IV later used, arguing that if the deceased could be helped with prayers and alms by the living, why not by crusading? What greater charity could there be than to go crusading on behalf of the dead, leave loved ones behind and risk everything for the sake of those in purgatory?[285] However, as both Jacques and Eudes underlined in their sermons, the intentions of the crusader had to be explicit. In order to help dead relatives or loved ones in purgatory, the crusaders needed to make clear that this was their purpose from the beginning. The intentions of the crusaders had to be clear and pure.

---

[283] During the thirteenth century there were several negotiations held in an attempt to accomplish a union between the Roman and the Greek churches. In the negotiations with the Greeks, the papacy wanted to end the schism and to substantiate the position of Roman Church over the other patriarchates. Byzantine emperors in exile, for their part, were keen to use the negotiations for a union of churches as a political weapon. The negotiations functioned like bribery or diplomacy for them. The idea was to avoid costly warfare and to exert political pressure when necessary. Nicol, 'Crusades and the Unity of Christendom', esp. p. 173.

[284] Le Goff, *The Birth of Purgatory*, pp. 283–84. Innocent IV agreed with the views of Albertus Magnus and Thomas Aquinas that the Church had jurisdiction in purgatory. The pope specifically defended papal indulgences for the dead in his commentary on the Decretals, referring to the different good works, prayers, almsgiving, and fasting, by which the living could help the dead. Innocent IV stated in the gloss *Quod autem* that those who were commanded by the Church to make a pilgrimage on behalf of the dead could earn an indulgence which was also valid in purgatory. Shaffern, *The Penitents' Treasury*, pp. 166–68.

[285] Jacques de Vitry, 'Item sermo ad crucesignatos vel -signandos', *CPI*, p. 112.

Crusading Martyrdom

There has been wide scholarly interest in the crusader's martyrdom in the last few decades. The main focus has been on the First Crusade and the so-called *précroisade* period, the undefined period of time during the eleventh century before the First Crusade, when similar notions of Christian *militia* were expressed, such as those made by Pope Gregory VII in 1074, or similar Christian wars declared, such as the wars of the *Reconquista*.[286] The discussion has mainly dealt with the question of whether Pope Urban II initially promised the crown of martyrdom in 1095 to those who might die during the crusade, or whether the popular belief in martyrdom developed during the actual expedition.[287]

Many crusade preachers of the thirteenth century discuss martyrs and martyrdom in their model sermons. Philippe le Chancelier praised the ordeals of the martyrs in one of his sermons. According to Philippe, there were different ways the Christians could express their piety, penitence, and love of God. These different ways varied in difficulty, some being more arduous than others, and they differed in the glory and merit gained: 'the chaste were surpassed by the virgins, the penitent by those who embraced a more profound religious commitment, and the martyrs had the greatest cross of all'.[288]

Philippe's model is heavily reworked; however, this passage may initially belong in the crusading context as it discusses Louis VIII's decision to take the cross. Louis's merit is underlined, because he was the first to take the cross against the Albigensians. In the following passage Philippe also linked the sacrifices which the Christians were willing to make to the imitation of the Passion

[286] Flori, 'Ideology and Motivations in the First Crusade', esp. pp. 15–16.

[287] Flori, 'Ideology and Motivations in the First Crusade', pp. 22–23, 33, n. 28. Riley-Smith, 'Death on the First Crusade'. See also Cowdrey, 'Pope Gregory VII and Martyrdom'; Morris, 'Martyrs on the Field of Battle', esp. p. 93. For the later period, see, for example, Smith, 'Martyrdom and Crusading in the Thirteenth Century', esp. p. 189; Tamminen, 'Who Deserves the Crown of Martyrdom?', p. 295.

[288] Philippe le Chancelier, '*Dicit Dominus ad Moysen*', Avranches, MS 132, fol. 273ra: 'Quantum ad meritum: omnes enim boni crucem suam habent sed secundum differentiam meritorum, verbi gratia casti sed maxime virgines, penitentes simpliciter sed maiorem religionem intrantes, maximam martires'. Transcribed by Maier and Bériou. Martyrs ranked high in the heavenly hierarchy. According to medieval belief, after the Virgin Mary, archangels, and angels came John the Baptist, the apostles, and the evangelists, followed by the Christian martyrs. Martyrs therefore held a higher rank than the confessors, the virgins, the widows, the innocents, or the penitents. Cowdrey, 'Martyrdom and the First Crusade', esp. pp. 46–47; Tamminen, 'Who Deserves the Crown of Martyrdom?', pp. 293–94.

of Christ.[289] Philippe may have incorporated these references to martyrs into the original sermon preached to crusaders and the king at Bourges in 1226, which encouraged the crusaders in their task, applauded their willingness to sacrifice themselves, and implied that if they died on the crusade they would earn the greatest merit, which only the martyrs gained.

Jacques de Vitry also mentioned the reward of martyrdom in his long list of crusading benefits. He regarded it as possible that the crusaders would be considered martyrs if they died in the service of Christ. In the sermon passage, Jacques discussed both the crusade indulgence and martyrdom and brought forward some requirements for the *crucesignati*: the crusaders must have made full confessions and they had to be penitent, sincere, and contrite.[290] These conditions were not a new invention, but rather conventional remarks that point to the general terms of the agreement made by the crusaders as they took the cross — to gain the crusade indulgence the crusaders had to confess their sins and have a contrite heart.[291]

However, the traditional conditions which Jacques mentions in the sermon were important in the creation of the 'true' crusader, and in that sense they were important requirements for crusading martyrdom as well. Caroline Smith has correctly noted that Jacques did not offer definite martyrdom for crusaders in his sermon, but reputed martyrdom.[292] Jacques held out the possibility of martyrdom to the crusaders, promising that those who died during the expeditions would be 'thought to be true martyrs', but he did not promise that all dead crusaders would become martyrs.[293] Jacques seems to follow papal example in this passage of the sermon. In 1213, when Innocent III proclaimed the Fifth Crusade in the encyclical *Quia maior*, he praised previous crusading efforts and argued that even though the Holy Land had not been recovered, many had already benefited from the journeys, for in their attempts to liberate the land many had attained a crown of glory 'as if they had gone through the agony of martyrdom'.[294] Both Jacques de Vitry and Innocent III avoided explicit

---

[289] Philippe le Chancelier, '*Dicit Dominus ad Moysen*', Avranches, MS 132, fol. 273^(ra–rb).

[290] Jacques de Vitry, 'Item sermo ad crucesignatos vel -signandos', *CPI*, p. 112.

[291] Tamminen, 'Who Deserves the Crown of Martyrdom?', p. 297.

[292] Smith, *Crusading in the Age of Joinville*, p. 140.

[293] Jacques de Vitry, 'Item sermo ad crucesignatos vel -signandos', *CPI*, p. 112.

[294] Innocentius III, *Quia maior*, 407, in *PL*, CCXVI, col. 817C: 'O quanta jam provenit utilitas ex hac causa! quam multi conversi ad poenitentiam pro liberatione terrae sanctae mancipaverunt se obsequio crucifixi, et quasi per agonem martyrii coronam gloriae sunt adepti'.

promises and referred to the crusader's martyrdom with terms such 'as if' and 'thought to be'.

Guibert de Tournai utilized Jacques de Vitry's passage in his own crusade sermon and changed the wording slightly, but nonetheless maintained the same traditional conditions, stating that the 'true crusaders' could be 'considered true martyrs' if they died in the service of Christ.[295] Guibert thus linked crusading martyrdom firmly to true crusading. It seems that, according to Guibert, only the true crusaders could gain the reputation of a martyr. In another passage of his sermon, Guibert was even more straightforward. Here he did not use any evasions inherited from Jacques but said plainly that the 'devout crusaders' were made 'true martyrs' and they would fly to heaven from earth.[296] Again, there is a specific requirement made by Guibert, the obligation to be devout. Not all crusaders, but the pious ones, would have the chance to become martyrs.

Crusade preachers utilized the popular belief in crusading martyrs. The brief or cautious references in the model sermons of Jacques de Vitry and Guibert de Tournai were meant to affirm the popular belief. Humbert de Romans also made repeated references to martyrs and martyrdom in his *De predicatione sancte crucis*. At the end of the manual, he advised crusade preachers to make use of the legends of famous saints who had suffered martyrdom or whose legends were connected to the sign of the cross or to the crucifixion of Christ. The crusaders ought to emulate the piety of Saints Peter and Andrew, who were themselves crucified. The crusade preachers could build up crusading enthusiasm with the examples of Christian martyrs, to encourage the crusaders to stay firm in their devotion to Christ, and to prepare them for possible death.[297] Finally, Humbert

---

[295] Guibert de Tournai, 'Ad crucesignatos et crucesignandos sermo primus', *CPI*, p. 188: 'quia veri crucesignati, qui vere contriti et confessi ad servitium Dei accinguntur et in ipso moriuntur, veri martires reputantur, liberati a peccatis mortalibus et venalibus et ab omni penitentia sibi iniuncta, absoluti et a pena peccatorum in hoc seculo et a pena purgatorii in alio, a tormentis gehenne securi gloria eterna per hoc signum investientur'.

[296] Guibert de Tournai, 'Ad crucesignatos et crucesignandos sermo primus', *CPI*, p. 180: 'Crux autem citissime facit crucesignatos devotos, immo martires veros, pro causa Christi de terra ad celum evolare'.

[297] Humbert de Romans, *De predicatione sancte crucis*, xliij, De diuersis legendis sanctorum; for references to martyrdom in the manual see also, cap. xvi, De exemplis antiquorum que inducunt ad bellum contra saracenos; cap. xxiij, Contra nimiam affectionem erga suos que ad idem facit. With the stories of Charlemagne and Roland, and the vision of Turpin, Humbert further suggested that the crusaders could expect martyrdom if they fought for God. See cap. xxxvi, De gestis Karoli magni in Hispania; cap. xxxvij, De visione Turpini episcopi super animas in bello defunctorum.

concluded that the crusaders could expect to be rewarded for their service and for suffering for Christ's sake, as the martyrs had been rewarded.[298]

Martyrdom of St George

Eudes de Châteauroux also used the theme of martyrdom in several of his sermons from the Seventh Crusade. The three sermons for the feast of St George appear to have been preached by the legate of the crusade at different stages of the expedition: during the recruitment campaign, during the journey, and during 'a midway crisis' after a crushing defeat in battle. The sermons give us invaluable information on how the crusaders were guided through the different phases of a *passagium*. Eudes utilized the theme of martyrdom in diverse ways in these sermons and linked the martyrdom of the warrior-saint to the trials of the crusaders.[299]

St George was a celebrated figure in medieval chivalry. The warrior-saint was promoted by the Church as an exemplar of militant knightly piety that the warriors of the West should emulate.[300] The various legends of St George depict him as a Christian soldier, 'a valiant knight', and in some accounts, 'a pilgrim' who suffered torture and eventually martyrdom for the Christian faith. In the legends the saint is mentioned as buried at Lydda in the Holy Land.[301] These associations of St George made him an ideal model not only for Christian knights, but for crusaders as well. His willingness to fight against oppression and to witness the Christian faith by martyrdom and the location of his tomb made him a well-suited example for the crusaders fighting on behalf of God and labouring for the recovery of the Holy Land.

St George was also an active participant in crusades. During the First Crusade the saint was believed to have made, together with fellow warrior-saints Mercurius and Demetrius, a successful intervention from the heavens. During the prolonged siege of Antioch in 1098, when the crusade army was in dire straits, there appeared from the mountains troops of Christ on white horses, bearing white standards, whose leaders were the saints George, Mercurius, and

[298] Humbert de Romans, *De predicatione sancte crucis*, cap. xlv.

[299] See above, p. 28, also below, Appendix V.

[300] MacGregor, 'The Ministry of Gerold d'Avranches', p. 229. Initially, the veneration of St George was more common among the Eastern Christians, where his legend had its origins, but after the First Crusade the popularity of the warrior-saint grew in the West.

[301] Matzke, 'Contributions to the History of the Legend of Saint George'; Jacopo da Varazze, *Legenda Aurea*, LVI, ed. by Maggioni, p. 391.

Demetrius. The warrior-saints made their intercession, 'which no one should doubt, for many men saw it', and Antioch was captured.[302]

The heavenly help from the saints proved that the crusaders fought a just war against the Saracens. Christ and his warriors fought alongside the crusaders, so that the will of God might be implemented.[303] Humbert de Romans mentioned St Luke in his crusade preaching manual, who appeared after the capture of Antioch during the First Crusade. According to Humbert, St Luke told a man from Tripoli that God was assembling a heavenly army of apostles and martyrs who would assist in the fight against the Turks.[304]

In the first sermon for the feast of St George, Eudes de Châteauroux built up crusading enthusiasm with passages from II Maccabees and with exemplars provided by the saint. He connected the heavenly aid given to the Maccabees, which was mentioned in the Bible, to the heavenly aid which St George had given to the crusaders. Eudes quoted the Bible, where Judas Maccabaeus and his men saw 'a horseman going before them to Jerusalem' who was clothed in white and had golden armour and a spear.[305] This was an allusion to the appearances

---

[302] *Anonymi Gesta Francorum et aliorum Hierosolymitanorum*, ed. by Hagenmeyer, pp. 374–76: 'Exibant quoque de montaneis innumerabiles exercitus, habentes equos albos, quorum vexilla omnia erant alba. Videntes itaque nostri hunc exercitum, ignorabant penitus, quid hoc esset et qui essent, donec cognoverunt esse adiutorium Christi, cuius ductores fuerunt sancti, Georgius, Mercurius et Demetrius. Haec verba credenda sunt, quia plures ex nostris viderunt'. See also Holdsworth, 'An "Airier Aristocracy"'.

[303] After the First Crusade, St George became a patron and a protector of the crusaders. The warrior-saint was frequently mentioned in the crusade chronicles, and his portraits decorated the numerous churches and monuments in the Latin East. Gerstel, 'Art and Identity in the Medieval Morea'; Deschamps, 'Combats de cavalerie et épisodes des Croisades'. In 1263 in Frankish Morea, St George made an appearance similar to that in Antioch almost two centuries earlier. This time, according to the *Chronicle of Morea*, the saint participated in the fight against the schismatic Greeks. 'Some of those who took part in that battle saw and testified that they saw a knight mounted on a white charger, carrying a naked sword and always leading the way wherever the Franks were. And they said and affirmed that it was St. George and that he guided the Franks and gave them courage to fight': *Crusaders as Conquerors*, trans. by Lurier, p. 211.

[304] Humbert de Romans, *De predicatione sancte crucis*, cap. xxvi: 'In historia legitur quod capta Anthiochia beatus Lucas apparuit cuidam Furiano in Tripoli dicens quod veniebat de Anthiochia, ubi Dominus congregauerat celi militiam et apostolos et martires ad pugnandum cum nostris contra Turcos'.

[305] Eudes de Châteauroux, 'De sancto Georgio', *UEE*, II, 700. II Mcc. 11. 8–9. Humbert de Romans quoted the same biblical passage in one of his formal invitations in the preaching manual. Humbert de Romans, *De predicatione sancte crucis*, cap. iij, invitatio xv.

made by St George during the crusades. By his use of the quotation Eudes suggested that the warrior-saint would assist the crusaders of the Seventh Crusade, guide them by his example, and defend them with his prayers.[306]

In the first sermon, Eudes attempted to inspire people to take the cross, but also to encourage those who had already done so in their task, and to give them advice about the coming journey. Eudes used St George as a model by which he could instruct the crusaders to achieve an appropriate frame of mind. As a skilled preacher, he had no difficulties in moving from the spiritual sphere of biblical quotations to an earthly theme of horses. The theme of horses must have been particularly pertinent to medieval knights, and the lengthy utilization of this theme suggests that they were the main audience of the sermon. Eudes mentions Alexander the Great and his horse 'Bucephalus', as well as Gaius Caesar, the king of the Scythians, King Nichomedes, and their horses. The horses of these ancient figures did not allow anyone but their masters to ride them, or died with their master, or protected the corpse of their master by kicking and biting their enemies.[307]

Eudes connected the character of St George to the theme of love and charity by using the horses as his example. The equestrian saint was a representation of God's love. St George carried horsemen as their horses carried them. The Christians needed, however, to be careful, for there were also bad horses available to them. These horses were the evil horses that the devil rode. Eudes listed

---

[306] Eudes de Châteauroux, 'De sancto Georgio', *UEE*, ii, 700–701: 'Et quia in consimilibus casibus legitur beatus Georgius promtus esse et paratus ad ferenda auxilia christianis, immo ostenditur quomodo factus sit in exemplum desiderantibus ire ad Dominum, et quomodo adhuc nos sua oratione defendit'.

[307] Eudes de Châteauroux, 'De sancto Georgio', *UEE*, ii, 704: 'Equs Alexandri Bucefala post ipsum numquam alium vehere dignatus est. Sic caritas sanctam indignacionem generat, ut dedignetur homo diligere aliud nisi Deum aut propter Deum. Simile legitur de equo Gaii Cesaris. Equs regis Scitarum interfectorem Domini sui calcibus et morsibus laceravit. Equs Nichomedis regis regum cum domino suo intravit'. In his excellent study on Eudes de Châteauroux, Alexis Charansonnet states that he was unable to find a source which Eudes may have used in these passages. Charansonnet points to the general knowledge and use of the classical heroes in sermon exemplas and the mentioning of the Scythians in the Bible. *UEE*, i.1, 122 n. 103. However, Eudes must have used a medieval bestiary as a source for his passages. In the famous *Aberdeen Bestiary*, for example, there is a very similar account of horses: 'Alexandri magni equus, Bucefala dictus, [...] cum ab equario suo alias etiam molliter sedetur accepto regio stratu neminem unquam preter dominum vehere dignatus est. [...] Equus Gaii Cesaris nullum preter Cesarem dorso recepit. Regem Scitarum singulari certamine interemptum, cum adversarius victor spoliare vellet, ab equo eius calcibus morsuque est laceratus. Nichomede rege interfecto equus eius inedia vitam expulit'. Aberdeen University Library, MS 22, fol. 22ʳ.

several sins in the sermon. He revealed the many faults of the bad mounts: some horses were ill in different ways; some had farcy, with which they infected others, that is, 'the love of luxuries'; some had caught another disease, 'the love of gluttony', that is, 'the excessive love for oneself'.[308] Eudes tried to guide the knights to humility and adaptability, to sound judgement over rashness. The legate attempted to convince current and prospective crusaders to give up their sins, particularly the capital sin of pride. The noble knights should not take too much pleasure in their lordship and should not be extravagant.[309]

Eudes's second sermon for the feast of St George, delivered for an audience of travelling crusaders in 1249 in Cyprus, continued on the path of the first sermon. The themes were much the same, drawing images from classical figures such as Julius Caesar and using contemporary, allegorical descriptions of the canals of Flanders, or combining biblical quotations with philosophical arguments made by Augustine. Eudes first explained that just as in ancient times the senate of Rome conquered lands with its army, so too the Lord conquered lands with his army, whose captains were the apostles and whose soldiers were the martyrs, 'who by faith conquered kingdoms, served justice, won undertakings'.[310] These soldiers were men like the proto-martyrs St Stephen and St George. Eudes made clear to his knightly and noble audience that St George was also a knight of noble birth. He was a good soldier of Christ who laboured for him 'all the way to death'.[311]

---

[308] Eudes de Châteauroux, 'De sancto Georgio', *UEE*, ii, 705: 'Alii habent equos farcinosos qui inficiunt alios. Hic est amor luxuriosus. Alii habent umbraciles: amor gule, nimius amor sui'. These were the sins of the nobility and the higher clergy, the upper class, with whom the sins of luxury and gluttony were usually associated during the Middle Ages. Le Goff, *L'Imaginaire médiéval*, pp. 253–54.

[309] Eudes de Châteauroux, 'De sancto Georgio', *UEE*, ii, 703–05, esp. p. 704: 'Equs plenus super ossibus et rigidus est superbia, et frequenter cadit et precipitat se et sessorem, sicut factum est in diabolo, cuius superbia flecti non potest ad bonum vel ad concordiam vel ad pacem. Leo gestus habet superbie, quia collum habet inflexibile. Hec est pertinacia, que frequenter provenit ex amore excellencie et dominii'.

[310] Eudes de Châteauroux, 'De sancto Georgio sermo', *UEE*, ii, 738: 'Sicut enim antiquitus senates romanus miliciam habebat quam ad diversas regions mittebat et per quam eas sibi subiciebat, sic Dominus milites suos habet qui sibi subiecerunt regna, et imperia subiugauerunt. Cuius milicie capitanei fuerunt apostoli; martires vero fuerunt milites christiani *qui per fidem vicerunt regna, operati sunt iusticiam, adepti sunt repromissiones*'. Hebr. 11. 33.

[311] Eudes de Châteauroux, 'De sancto Georgio sermo', *UEE*, ii, 738: 'Ipse enim laboravit usque ad mortem sicut bonus miles Christi Ihesu'. The reference to the 'good soldier of Christ' is from Paul's second epistle to Timothy. ii Tim. 2. 3.

In the sermon Eudes maintained that in the warrior-saint 'the spirit of the martyrs is doubled', as the spirit was doubled in Eliseus.[312] St George had first fought against the enemies of Christ while he was still living, through which he gained martyrdom, and afterwards continued to fight against the enemies from the heavens and had not ceased to fight them yet.[313] By this statement, Eudes wanted to reassure the crusaders that St George would accompany them in the forthcoming war against the Saracens and join them on the battlefield.[314]

Eudes also focused on the model provided by St George for the crusaders. The overall emphasis of the second sermon was on the leadership of George and on the divine assistance which the saint was willing to give during the crusade.[315] Both sermons for the feast of St George, preached before the crusaders arrived at their destination, elaborated on how the *crucesignati* should behave during the campaign. The legate appears to have believed that there were still many sins which had not been given up by the crusaders after the taking of the cross. The crusaders of the Seventh Crusade needed to clean up their act so that the expedition might succeed and the crusaders could gain absolution.

Eudes advised the participants of the crusade to fight for a great kingdom, a kingdom which was in themselves. This meant that the crusaders, who fought for God and tried to free Christians and Christian holy places, should also try to free themselves from sin. They should lay aside 'evil desires', 'perverse thoughts', 'evil words and evil works'.[316] In the sermon, Eudes addressed the sins of greed and pride in particular. He connected the sin of avarice to the ditches of the county of Flanders. This suggests that among the audience, in the church at Cyprus where the sermon seems to have been given, were men who were familiar with the difficulties in Flanders at the time. This might have included the

---

[312] According to the biblical story, after Eliseus was buried another man was buried in the same grave and as this corpse touched Eliseus's bones, the man came to life and stood up in the grave. IV Reg. 13. 14, 20–21.

[313] Eudes de Châteauroux, 'De sancto Georgio sermo', *UEE*, II, 738: 'Sic in beato Georgio dupplicatus est spiritus martirum, quia et dum viveret expugnavit inimicos fidei christiane, et adhuc licet mortuus eos expugnare non cessat'.

[314] Eudes de Châteauroux, 'De sancto Georgio sermo', *UEE*, II, 738–39.

[315] Eudes de Châteauroux, 'De sancto Georgio sermo', *UEE*, II, 737–41.

[316] Eudes de Châteauroux, 'De sancto Georgio sermo', *UEE*, II, 740: 'Similiter ex multitudine habitantium apparet magnitudo huius regni. Hec sunt mala desideria, perverse cogitaciones, mala verba et mala opera. Et ista pugnant contra nos nec permittunt quod homo seipsum sibi subiciat, et sic Deo'.

new Count of Flanders, Guillaume de Dampierre, who had taken the cross for the Seventh Crusade, and King Louis IX, as well as other nobles and knights who had knowledge of the problematic situation.

Before leaving for the crusade in 1246, Louis IX had acted as an arbitrator, with Eudes, in negotiations that were intended to resolve the struggle over the lordship of Flanders and Hainaut. This was a difficult conflict between the children of Marguerite, the Countess of Flanders, from her two marriages, and between the families of Avesnes and Dampierre. The situation was further complicated by the fact that Flanders was part of both the Kingdom of France and the Holy Roman Empire.[317] Contemporary Flanders was thus a place where the feudal schemes of the nobles were plotted and where knights were engaged in bitter disputes with each other, and where the nobles' and knights' greed was clearly observed by others.

Eudes stated in the sermon that the realm of oneself was even more difficult to capture than Flanders, and its ditches could not be filled with greed, for 'an avaricious man shall not be satisfied with money'.[318] This kingdom was surrounded by the deep waters of Charybdis and Scylla, which were the various sins of *luxuria*, and it had the highest towers of pride, which had to fall.[319] People built walls around this kingdom, that is, excuses for their sins, which the

---

[317] Marguerite had first married Bouchard d'Avesnes, the bailiff of Hainaut, from which marriage she had two sons. This marriage was, however, annulled already in 1216 in Rome, because Bouchard wanted to pursue an ecclesiastical career. Marguerite then married Guillaume de Dampierre and had three sons from this marriage. Both the Avesnes and the Dampierre family claimed the lordship of Flanders and Hainault as inheritance. Louis IX was called in to intervene in the dispute several times. The county of Flanders belonged to the Kingdom of France and the duchy of Flanders to the Holy Roman Empire. In 1246, it was decided that Hainaut was to be given to the Avesnes and Flanders to the Dampierre. Marguerite's son from the second marriage would inherit the title of Count of Flanders, and thus Guillaume de Dampierre became the count. Le Goff, *Saint Louis*, pp. 252–55.

[318] Eudes de Châteauroux, 'De sancto Georgio sermo', *UEE*, II, 740: 'Hoc regnum difficilius est ad capiendum ut terra Flandrie. Hec sunt fossata avaricie que repleri non possunt, Ecclesiastes v: *Avarus non implebitur pecunia*'. Ecl. 5. 9. After the failure of the expedition in Egypt, Eudes preached another crusade sermon in the Holy Land, where he once again reminded his audience, with the use of the same biblical passage, that 'an avaricious man shall not be satisfied with money, and he who loves riches shall reap no fruit from them'. Eudes de Châteauroux, 'Sermo in festo sanctarum reliquiarum', *UEE*, II, 764. '*Auarus non implebitur pecunia, et qui amat diuitias fructum non capiet ex eis*'.

[319] Eudes de Châteauroux, 'De sancto Georgio sermo', *UEE*, II, 740: 'Hoc regnum aqua profundissima circumdatur, Caripdi et Scilla, id est diversis generibus luxuriarum. [...] Hoc regnum habet turres altissimas superbie'. See also Isa. 30. 15.

preachers attempted to bring down with their words.[320] These examples drawn from recent political conflict enabled the legate to guide the noble members of the army — who were on their way to Damietta, but who could easily recollect the struggles at home — to renounce their sins. Eudes linked the political difficulties to the sins of avarice and pride, and urged the nobles now, as knights of God, to give up all such sins, to abandon old ways and make the journey in a pure spiritual state. They were fighting for a much larger kingdom than Flanders or Egypt, a kingdom which was within them.

The crusade preachers combated these sins of the knights and the nobles and tried to make them better crusaders, 'true' crusaders. The sin of pride, which had certain subcategories in the Middle Ages, such as *vana gloria* and *arrogantia*, was repeatedly condemned by the preachers. Federico Visconti, Jacques de Vitry, Philippe le Chancelier, Eudes de Châteauroux, and Humbert de Romans all drew attention to the sin of pride. All five preachers cited the same relevant biblical passage, which Federico utilized twice, in both of his crusade sermons: 'Far be it from me to boast save in the cross of our Lord Jesus Christ'.[321] Jacques de Vitry explained that the crusaders should not take pride 'in the power of their honour', they should not brag on account of their 'noble descent', nor should they boast because of their beauty, strength, speed, or oratorical skills.[322] The noble crusaders should express humility and restrict their appetite for glory. Their noble origins did not make them 'true' crusaders.[323]

---

[320] Eudes de Châteauroux, 'De sancto Georgio sermo', *UEE*, II, 741.

[321] Jacques de Vitry, 'Item sermo ad crucesignatos vel -signandos', *CPI*, p. 112: 'Michi absit gloriari nisi in cruce Domini Nostri Ihesu Christi'; Philippe le Chancelier, 'Sermo in die veneris infra octabas Assumptionis beate Virginis', Avranches, MS 132, fol. 243vb; Federico Visconti, 'Quando idem dominus predicavit crucem litteraliter clero pisano de mandato domini Pape', *SVP*, p. 545; Federico Visconti, 'Quando idem dominus predicavit [crucem] respondendo nuntiis Tartarorum in clero pisano', *SVP*, p. 553; Eudes de Châteauroux, 'Sermo in festo sanctarum reliquiarum', *UEE*, II, 744; Humbert de Romans, *De predicatione sancte crucis*, cap. ii, xxvij: 'sicut fit heu a multis hodie qui vel ex superbia. vel ex avaricia. vel vana gloria contra alios preliantur. non sic in isto exercitu sed pugnatur pro summa iusticia scilicet iusticia fidei'. Gal. 6. 14.

[322] Jacques de Vitry, 'Item sermo ad crucesignatos vel -signandos', *CPI*, p. 112: 'Quidam gloriantur in potentia honoris, alii in nobilitate generis, alii in pulcritudine carnis, alii in viribus corporis, alii in velocitate currendi, alii in peritia loquendi'.

[323] Jacques also fought against the pride of the knights in his sermons for the members of the military orders, explaining that nobility was only in the mind, a virtue, nothing else. Jacques reminded the Templars that even if the knights had wisdom, grace, and beauty, the sin of pride could deface them all. Jacques de Vitry, 'Sermo ad fratres militaris insignitos charactere militiae Christi', Troyes, MS 228, fols 131vb: 'Nobilitas animi sola est atque unica virtus. [...] Si tibi gratia, si sapientia, formaque detur, inquinat omnia sola superbia, si dominetur'.

In the *De sancto Georgio* sermon, Eudes de Châteauroux made it clear that the crusaders needed to follow closely the example of the warrior-saint, emulating him in spirit, deed, and appearance. The crusaders should imitate the saint as closely as possible. They ought to be clothed in white, as a sign of their innocence and as a symbol of their good works, as St George was clothed, and as the angels who appeared after the resurrection of the Lord were clothed.[324] The golden armour of St George signified patience and his lance the prayers with which the crusaders were defended. The crusaders should find the qualities of the saint in themselves. By imitating the virtues of St George the crusaders could become more like him; by emulating his appearance they might see themselves in his image: they would be like heavenly warriors in battle, unrecognizable to their enemies, and the emulation might well bring celestial aid from the saint against both 'temporal and spiritual enemies'.[325]

In the third sermon for St George, which appears to have been preached in Damietta in 1250, a few weeks after the defeat of Fariskur and when Louis IX was the captive of the enemy, Eudes tried to convince his audience that they should rely on the warrior-saint. Eudes's sermon seems to have been preached for the refugees of the army, who like the legate himself had escaped captivity, and to the other Christians who had stayed behind in Damietta.[326] In the sermon, Eudes attempted to fortify those wavering in their faith. He quoted a passage from the book of Judges, where the Israelites asked God who would lead them against the Canaanites after the death of Joshua, to which God answered Judas, meaning the tribe of Judah.[327] The crusaders were in a similar situation, without their leader. Eudes acknowledged the dangerous circumstances but was

---

[324] Eudes de Châteauroux, 'De sancto Georgio', *UEE*, II, 705: 'Sic et nos debemus indui albis. Quidam nigris induntur per omnia male operantes. Alii uariis, bona malis intermiscentes'.

[325] Eudes de Châteauroux, 'De sancto Georgio', *UEE*, II, 705: 'Simulacio vero hominem depingit et facit quasi personas larvatas que cognosci non possunt. [...] Rogemus ergo Dominum ur per intercessionem beati Georgii defendat nos ab hostibus spiritualibus et temporalibus'.

[326] For the dating of the sermon, see Appendix V.

[327] Eudes de Châteauroux, 'Sermo de sancto Georgio', *UEE*, II, 747: '*Quis ascendet ante nos contra Chananeum et erit dux belli? Dixitque Dominus: Iudas ascendet*'. Jud. 1. 1–2. See also Eudes's anniversary sermon for Robert d'Artois, where he associated the French people to the Isarelites. Eudes de Châteauroux, 'Sermo in anniversario Roberti comitis Attrabatensis et aliorum nobilium qui interfecti fuerunt a Sarracenis apud Mansuram in Egipto', *PCHL*, p. 235: 'Gallici qui consueverunt primi esse ad debellandum inimicos fidei Christiani secundum quod de tribu Iuda legitur in principio Iudicum, *Post mortem Iosue consuluerunt filii Israel Dominum dicentes: "Quis ascendet ante nos contra Chananeum et erit dux belli?" Dixitque Dominus: "Iudas ascendet"*'.

consistent in his argumentation and assured his audience once again that St George would help them: the saint would now lead them in the war against the Saracens as the king was away.[328]

Another sermon of Eudes from the Seventh Crusade, possibly given a few years later, reveals that there were some Christians who questioned the Christian faith after the disasters of Mansurah and Fariskur. According to Eudes, some Christians apostatized, while others blasphemed God.[329] Eudes's third St George sermon suggests an immediate reaction from the legate and an intention to strengthen the faith of those who were in disbelief or falling into despair. St George could be trusted, and God had not deserted the faithful. Eudes used the same quotation that he had used in the *Sermo de invitatione ad crucem*, in which Moses hoped that God would show the way, and another passage from Exodus, in which God promised to send an angel to accompany the Israelites on their journey. According to Eudes, this meant that God, seeing their current circumstances, had sent them St George, who was a good leader, especially in wars.[330]

Some of the audience in Damietta may have questioned why God had not helped the Christians already during the crusade, or why St George had not fought with them earlier, as promised by the legate in his two other sermons. There may have been crusaders who had heard one or both of these sermons during the voyage. The dire situation in the spring of 1250 did not allow Eudes to deal with these questions at length at that time. In his later sermons from the Seventh Crusade he did use his extraordinary powers as a preacher to explain the disaster in various ways. The fleeing crusaders, the wounded and the sick crowding Damietta, and the absence of the captured king would most certainly have resulted in a chaotic situation inside the city. Eudes's sermon is short and reflects the urgency of his attempts to restore faith, but he does use some of the themes which he later utilized in discussing the disaster.

In the later sermons from the crusade, the theme of the sins of the Christians, *peccatis exigentibus hominum*, was applied. The sins of men had been an obsta-

---

[328] Eudes de Châteauroux, 'Sermo de sancto Georgio', *UEE*, ii, 747: 'Sic Dominus facto ostendit et respondet populo christiano. Ac si quereret populus christianus: quis ascendet ante nos contra Sarracenos?, respondet Dominus: beatus Georgius'. Jud. 1. 1.

[329] Eudes de Châteauroux, 'Sermo in eodem anniversario', *PCHL*, p. 242: 'Multi debiles in fide qui audito hoc casu, apostataverunt; alii Deum blasfemaverunt qui hoc permisit fieri'.

[330] Eudes de Châteauroux, 'Sermo de sancto Georgio', *UEE*, ii, 747: 'Non recedam de loco isto nisi Tu precedas nos, et Dominus respondet ei: *Ecce Ego mittam angelum meum qui precedet te et custodiat in uia et introducat ad locum quem preparaui tibi*. Sic necesse habet populus christianus habere bonum capitaneum, maxime in bellis. Et Dominus dedit eis beatum Georgium contra Chananeum'. Ex. 33. 15, 23. 20.

cle on the crusaders' path to victory. Eudes used this conventional explanation for a crusading defeat in many of his sermons, and also as an explanation for other calamitous events such as natural disasters.[331] The Seventh Crusade had failed because of the sins of all Christians; therefore all had to renounce their sins. Robert d'Artois and those who sacrificed themselves at Mansurah had not been guilty of the failure, and their sins were not a reason for the defeat. In fact, Robert and the others were killed on account of the sins of others, just as many of the Israelites killed in the Old Testament and Christ were killed.[332] The crusading survivors, on the other hand, had not been as pure as those who had died. They had sins on their conscience. One of the reasons behind the defeat, according to Eudes, was that it would strike the sinners with fear of God and make them repent of their sins.[333]

In the sermon preached for the refugees and the crusaders in Damietta during the feast of St George in 1250, the legate had no wish to further dishearten those who were already demoralized. He avoided direct accusations of sinning but maintained that the surviving crusaders now needed to make a full confession of all their sins with a contrite heart and place their trust in God. This way they might still win. Eudes used St Jerome's interpretation of what Judas meant to clarify his message. According to Jerome, Judas could be interpreted as 'the trusting or the glorifying' one.[334] From this Eudes concluded that if the crusaders wished to be victorious, they should truly confess their sins and praise God. St George had given the crusaders an example which they could follow as he had confessed and glorified the name of Christ by becoming a martyr. The crusaders ought to fight manfully against their enemies. This way they would earn an eternal crown as a reward for their labours.[335]

[331] Hanska, *Strategies of Sanity and Survival*, pp. 116–28, 180–82.

[332] Eudes de Châteauroux, 'Sermo in eodem anniversario', *PCHL*, p. 242: 'Sed sicut in veteri testamento propter peccata que non commiserant mactabantur, sic et isti mactanti sunt, sic etiam et Christus'.

[333] Eudes de Châteauroux, 'Sermo in anniversario Roberti comitis Attrabatensis et aliorum nobilium qui interfecti fuerunt a Sarracenis apud Mansuram in Egipto', *PCHL*, p. 237.

[334] Eudes de Châteauroux, 'Sermo de sancto Georgio', *UEE*, ii, 748: 'Ad ascendendum contra istum Chananeum dedit nobis Dominus ducem Iudam, qui interpretatur confitens vel glorificans, id est beatum Georgium qui pro confessione nominis Ihesu Christi et ut Christiani in se glorificarent, martir effectus est'. Hieronymus, *Liber interpretationis*, ed. by de Lagarde, p. 136: 'Iudas confitens vel glorificans'.

[335] Eudes de Châteauroux, 'Sermo de sancto Georgio', *UEE*, ii, 748–49: 'Et nos si uolumus habere uictoriam de inimicis nostris, habeamus nobiscum Iudam, id est ueram confessionem peccati et laudis. [...] Manus quibus pugnat confessio sunt cordis contricio et satisfactio.

Eudes made versatile use of the theme of martyrdom in his three sermons for the feast of St George: He argued that it was the knights' task to fight against injustice and God's enemies in this world, for which they would earn due honour and glory, perhaps martyrdom. He also insisted that St George's martyrdom still benefited the crusaders, who could count on the saint's aid while they were fighting the infidels. However, Eudes was also reluctant to make any specific promises or explicitly state that the crusaders who died on their journey would become martyrs. The authors of the crusade model sermons discussed crusading martyrdom in a guarded and careful manner.

The Kin of God

Eudes de Châteauroux also delivered two other sermons that discussed crusading martyrdom, during the Seventh Crusade. These sermons were composed after the defeat which the crusade army suffered in Egypt, for the remembrance of Robert d'Artois and other nobles who had died at Mansurah in 1250.[336] In the first sermon, Eudes gave six different reasons why God permitted the 'ungodly' Saracens to persecute Christians and why Louis IX's crusade had ended in failure. Eudes asked Christians to consider why the king's brother, Robert d'Artois, and the other noble men, 'such great friends of God', were allowed to be killed.[337] His explanation rested partly on the theme of the sins of Christians, but the legate also found other ways of handling the defeat, linking crusading martyrdom, the friendship with God, and Christian charity.[338]

Eudes's fourth and fifth reasons for the defeat were linked to the theme of crusading martyrdom. First, Eudes stated that by dying for God the nobles

---

Pugnemus ergo uiriliter auxilio huius Iude ut uictoriam adepti, coronam aeternam consequi mereamur prestante Domino nostro Ihesu Christo'.

[336] The two sermons, with the addition of Eudes's memorial sermon for Innocent IV, have been studied carefully by Cole, d'Avray, and Riley-Smith, 'Application of Theology to Current Affairs'.

[337] Eudes de Châteauroux, 'Sermo in anniversario Roberti comitis Attrabatensis et aliorum nobilium qui interfecti fuerant a Sarracenis apud Mansuram in Egipto', *PCHL*, p. 236: 'Quo modo ergo sustinuit quod servi empticii immo quod peius est servi diaboli pleni omni spurcitia tam nobiles viros tam strenuos amicos Dei et propugnatores totius populi Christiani interfecerunt?'

[338] Eudes de Châteauroux, 'Sermo in anniversario Roberti comitis Attrabatensis et aliorum nobilium qui interfecti fuerant a Sarracenis apud Mansuram in Egipto', *PCHL*, p. 237: 'Ideo enim Dominus hoc permisit fieri ut ostenderet populo Christiano quam graviter eum offenderant et quam gravia peccata commiserant contra eum [...]. Sic intelligere poterunt Christiani quod nisi peccata eorum fuissent, nunquam iste casus mirabilis emersisset'.

were cleansed from all sins. He viewed the crusaders' death as an act of 'perfect and final cleansing' that was made with their own blood. If there were some sins that the crusaders had committed out of 'human frailty' and that had to be cleansed, the Lord could reap these with 'the sickle of martyrdom'. The crusaders could thus follow the example of Christ, who had *entered the holy place through his own blood*, and enter heaven through their own blood.[339] The sermon is theologically contemplative and cautious. Eudes ponders questions of forgiveness and punishment for sins and comes to the conclusion that if the penalty for sin is paid by punishment and 'no punishment is greater than the pain of violent death', then by paying the punishment of death, that is, 'voluntarily suffering death for Christ', the dead crusaders 'are liberated from every other punishment'.[340]

These considerations of Eudes give further support to the conclusions made in the preceding chapters discussing the crusade indulgence. Eudes does not claim outright that Robert d'Artois and the other nobles had gained the plenary indulgence and a direct path to paradise but takes into account that they might have committed sins that still needed to be cleansed. He concludes that by dying for Christ, Robert and the others must have made adequate satisfaction for all their sins and suggests that God had perhaps made them martyrs. Eudes continues this line of thought in his next explanation for the disaster.

According to the legate, God allowed Robert and the other nobles to be killed because he 'wanted to show to them and to everybody else how much he treasured them'.[341] Eudes argued that God loved the dead noblemen above all others, since he granted that they should suffer for him. As a sign of love,

---

[339] Eudes de Châteauroux, 'Sermo in anniversario Roberti comitis Attrabatensis et aliorum nobilium qui interfecti fuerant a Sarracenis apud Mansuram in Egipto', *PCHL*, p. 238: 'Quarta ratione hoc permisit Dominus ut aliquid in sepedictis nobilibus purgandum erat quod ex humana fragilitate contraxissent, illud falce martirii resecaret ut, *sicut in sanguine proprio intravit in sancta*, sic et ipsi in suo sanguine intrarent. Perfecta autem purgatio et ultima fiebat in sanguine in veteri testamento'. Heb. 9. 12.

[340] Eudes de Châteauroux, 'Sermo in anniversario Roberti comitis Attrabatensis et aliorum nobilium qui interfecti fuerant a Sarracenis apud Mansuram in Egipto', *PCHL*, p. 238: 'Si enim pena solvitur pena et nulla pena maior pena mortis violente, constat quod solvendo penam mortis, scilicet, voluntarie pro Christo patiendo mortem, ab omni alia pena liberati sunt'.

[341] Eudes de Châteauroux, 'Sermo in anniversario Roberti comitis Attrabatensis et aliorum nobilium qui interfecti fuerant a Sarracenis apud Mansuram in Egipto', *PCHL*, p. 238: 'Quinta etiam ratio fuit quare Dominus hoc permisit ut ostenderet et eis et omnibus aliis quantum eos diligebat. [...] Sic Dominus in hoc facto ostendit quod dictos nobiles pre aliis diligebat dando eis ut pro eo mortis supplicium sustinerent'.

God let Robert and the others sacrifice themselves and drink from his own cup: 'For they drank of the chalice of the Lord and have become God's friends'.[342] In Eudes's vision, the crusaders' imitation of Christ was made complete in their demise. The dead crusaders had achieved a remarkable likeness with Christ. Robert and the other nobles were 'clothed in the same purple' with Christ and shared his cup, drank his wine, and wore his cloak.[343]

Eudes also used biblical examples in the sermon to explain martyrdom and God's goodness. He applied again the example of Eliseus, as he did in the sermon preached for the crusaders during the feast of St George in 1249. Eudes's audience was probably composed of much the same people — the nobles and other crusaders who had survived the Egyptian expedition — and he may have suspected that the audience wanted resolution to the suggestions made about martyrdom in Cyprus after the defeat in Egypt. By using the same example of Elias and Eliseus, Eudes maintained that there 'are different kinds of martyrdom', which was rather vague and imprecise, but provides yet another suggestion that deceased crusaders could be considered martyrs.[344]

Neither of the Old Testament prophets mentioned in the sermon were traditional martyrs: Eliseus did not die violently at the hands of persecutors but from illness, and his father Elias, strictly speaking, did not die at all but ascended to heaven in 'a whirlwind'.[345] The prophets were nonetheless good examples of remarkable ways of entering heaven or working miracles after death: Elias and his fiery chariot to heaven and Eliseus's double spirit — waking people from

[342] Eudes de Châteauroux, 'Sermo in anniversario Roberti comitis Attrabatensis et aliorum nobilium qui interfecti fuerant a Sarracenis apud Mansuram in Egipto', *PCHL*, p. 239: 'Ipsi enim calicem Domini biberunt et amici Dei facti sunt'.

[343] Eudes de Châteauroux, 'Sermo in anniversario Roberti comitis Attrabatensis et aliorum nobilium qui interfecti fuerant a Sarracenis apud Mansuram in Egipto', *PCHL*, pp. 181, 239.

[344] Eudes de Châteauroux, 'Sermo in anniversario Roberti comitis Attrabatensis et aliorum nobilium qui interfecti fuerant a Sarracenis apud Mansuram in Egipto', *PCHL*, p. 239: 'Dimisit enim eis pallium suum ut Helyas Eliseo, pallium scilicet, martirii cuius est multiplex usus; sicut usus pallii multiplex est, sic diversa sunt genera martiriorum'. IV Reg. 2. 8–15. Eudes appears to have favoured this biblical theme when discussing martyrdom in his sermons. In the sermon for the feast of Thomas Becket, possibly preached in 1247, Eudes also utilized the story of Eliseus and Elias. The sermon explores the martyrdom of Thomas in relation to the 'martyrdom' of Eliseus. The upcoming crusade of Louis IX is also briefly discussed in the sermon. Eudes de Châteauroux, 'Sancti Thome martyris', *UEE*, II, 714–20. The modern English names for Eliseus and Elias are 'Elisha' and 'Elijah'.

[345] IV Reg. 2. 11. The manner of Eliseus's death was not important for Eudes, but the incidents which occurred afterwards were.

death after dying — were in Eudes's interpretation different expressions of martyrdom and convenient biblical examples when discussing the unconventional, possible martyrdom of the crusaders.

Elias's cloak, taken by Eliseus after his father's ascension, was also an example of God's goodness and grace and Christ's redeeming powers. Another biblical example taken from Ruth provided Eudes with a further way of explaining this point. The widowed Ruth had asked Boaz to spread his cloak over her, which meant that she asked Boaz to marry her. This way Boaz, a near kinsman of Ruth, could save her from poverty.[346] In an analogous way God had spread his cloak over the dead crusaders at Mansurah. Boaz decided to marry Ruth and redeem her, which was an allegory for Christ's decision to redeem the dead crusaders, his close friends and near kinsman. This example illustrated Eudes's point about God's benevolence and explained the just decision behind the crusading disaster.

Eudes connected the crusaders' death, the self-sacrifice which they made, strongly to crusading martyrdom, making several references to martyrs and using multiple images of martyrdom. He ended his sermon on a careful and important note. Eudes asked God to show forgiveness to all those among the great multitude of dead who had died at Mansurah, who perhaps were not in the state of devotion that they ought to have been in at the moment of death. The legate appealed to the Lord and asked that those crusaders who were slain, but who had feared suffering so that they had not accepted death, would be given indulgence and would be led to everlasting rest.[347]

In another sermon for the same anniversary — possibly delivered for a different audience, and possibly at a different time, perhaps 1252, the following year — Eudes deliberated further on the matter, arriving at the conclusion that people should not mourn for those who died at Mansurah, but rather mourn for themselves, 'who have been unworthy to suffer as they suffered'.[348]

---

[346] Eudes de Châteauroux, 'Sermo in anniversario Roberti comitis Attrabatensis et aliorum nobilium qui interfecti fuerant a Sarracenis apud Mansuram in Egipto', *PCHL*, p. 239. Ruth 3. 9.

[347] Eudes de Châteauroux, 'Sermo in anniversario Roberti comitis Attrabatensis et aliorum nobilium qui interfecti fuerant a Sarracenis apud Mansuram in Egipto', *PCHL*, p. 239: 'Plangamus ergo peccata nostra et rogemus ut si in tanta multitudine interfectorum fuerunt aliqui qui timore passionis prepediti fortassis non ea devotione qua debuerunt, mortem susceperunt, ut Dominus eis indulgeat et ad requiem sempiternam eos perducat'.

[348] Eudes de Châteauroux, 'Sermo in eodem anniversario', *PCHL*, p. 243: 'Plangamus ergo non nobiles antedictos, sed nos ipsos qui non digni fuimus talia sustinere qualia ipsi sustinuerunt'. This sermon may have been preached to an audience composed of ecclesiastics in Acre, which would explain the heavy use of scriptural exegesis and even more cautious handling

Crusading martyrdom is intertwined with the theme of the sins of Christians and the *imitatio Christi* in Eudes's fusion of crusade ideas. In the sermon, the crusaders who survived the Seventh Crusade are described as of less value than those who died. The crusaders who escaped death were unable and unworthy not only of defeating the infidels, but also of gaining God's ultimate reward, crusading martyrdom.[349] The crusaders who survived had not succeeded in imitating Christ's sacrifice on the cross, unlike Robert d'Artois and the other nobles, who had died. Eudes did not want to criticize Robert, who in other contemporary sources was often considered to be guilty for bringing disaster upon the crusade army through his own carelessness.[350] Eudes had close relations to the French royal family, and he chose to turn this argument around: the purest of the crusaders were those who had died, while the others were unworthy of such a great reward from God. The sins of the crusaders, of those who had escaped death, had partly caused the defeat and prevented them from gaining martyrdom.

Eudes also ended this second sermon with the same important appeal that he had made in the first: that God would show indulgence to deceased crusaders, if there was 'anything in them' that still needed to be cleansed, so that they would have eternal rest and that those who had survived could have a share in their glory.[351] These appeals made to God on behalf of the dead belong to the tradition of the sermons *de mortuis*. The funeral or memorial sermons had several functions during the thirteenth century, and one of these was to offer help for those who had died. By praying the living could aid the dead suffering in purgatory.[352] However, these appeals also had significance with regard to

---

of the theologically difficult question concerning the crusading martyrdom. Cole, d'Avray, and Riley-Smith, 'Application of Theology to Current Affairs', p. 231.

[349] Smith, 'Martyrdom and Crusading in the Thirteenth Century', p. 189.

[350] Matthew Paris blamed Robert d'Artois for ruining the expedition. 'Cujus ruinae causa comes Atrabatensis Robertus, infelix et superbus, fuisse perhibetur'; 'Numerus interfectorum in exercitu Francorum per superbiam comitis Atrabatensis R[oberti]': Matthew Paris, *Historia Anglorum*, ed. by Madden, pp. 84, 102. Salimbene di Adam agreed that Robert had many faults and that the crusade failed because of the sins of the French. Salimbene di Adam, *Cronica Fratris*, ed. by Bernini, p. 463: 'Postea vero, peccatis Francorum exigentibus, interfectus est frater regis maior post regem Robertus nomine. Sed et ipse multum culpabilis fuit, quia credebat omnes Saracenos involvere et subito uno ictu occidere'.

[351] Eudes de Châteauroux, 'Sermo in eodem anniversario', *PCHL*, p. 243: 'Et si aliud purgandum sit in eis, rogemus ergo Dominum ut ipsis indulgeat et ipsos ad requiem eternam perducat et nos faciat participes glorie eorum'.

[352] Cole, d'Avray, and Riley-Smith, 'Application of Theology to Current Affairs', pp. 231–33.

crusader martyrdom. To achieve this ultimate reward, crusaders needed to be pure and without sin, and their state of devotion at the time of death needed to be considered.

In a sermon intended for the brothers of the military orders, Jacques de Vitry also tried to guide the Christian knights to a mental state suitable for dying. Jacques explained meticulously how the knights should proceed to battle. First, he quotes the book of Deuteronomy: 'When you are fighting against your enemies, restrain yourself from every evil thing'.[353] Then he explained what these evil things might be: 'a soldier of Christ must keep away from pride and glorification and boasting and vanity, from wrath and envy, from sloth and torpor, from avarice and carnal pleasure, and from every other evil thing'.[354] These were improper emotions and impure desires for Christian soldiers fighting for God, and more importantly, they created the wrong state of mind for those who might receive the crown of martyrdom.

There was one major dilemma when trying to determine whether crusaders who had died in battle had suffered martyrdom. The crusaders had fought for God and they had been killed by the enemy, but it was extremely difficult to deduce afterwards the state of devotion of those who had been killed. There was no way of knowing the spiritual state of mind of a crusader who died in the heat of battle. The crusader could have been poorly prepared. He may have been furious or terrified. He may have had many regrets or sins on his conscience that he had not confessed or repented, or he may have given his life unwillingly.[355]

These considerations caused some ambiguity in the concept of crusading martyrdom during the thirteenth century, which is illustrated also in a letter sent to France by Louis IX from the Seventh Crusade in 1250. Caroline Smith has examined the letter and noticed the cautiousness with which Robert d'Artois's death is discussed. Instead of claiming outright that Robert was a crusading martyr, the letter expresses a humble wish: 'for certain, we believe and hope him [Robert], crowned a martyr, to have flown to the heavenly home-

---

[353] Jacques de Vitry, 'Sermo ad fratres militaris insignitos charactere militiae Christi', Troyes, MS 228, fol. 131vb: 'Quando fueris adversus hostes tuos in pugnam, custodies te ab omni re mala'. Dt. 23. 9.

[354] Jacques de Vitry, 'Sermo ad fratres militaris insignitos charactere militiae Christi', Troyes, MS 228, fol. 131vb: 'a superbia et elatione et iactantia et vanitate, ab ira et emulatione, a desidia et torpore, ab avaricia et carnali voluptate, et ab omni alia re mala Christi miles se debet conservare'.

[355] Tamminen, 'Who Deserves the Crown of Martyrdom?', p. 301.

land and to rejoice there perpetually with the holy martyrs'.[356] In another passage of the letter, where the deaths of captive crusaders are discussed, the tone is different. There are no hopes or requests but a clear statement that these crusaders had 'legitimately received their crowns of martyrdom reddened with blood'.[357]

Smith has suggested that Eudes de Châteauroux may have had a hand in writing the letter, which may be the case.[358] What is more certain is that Eudes's preaching must have influenced the views of Louis IX and the rest of the crusaders on crusading martyrdom. The many sermons preached by the legate during the build up to the crusade or during the actual expedition referred to the possibility of martyrdom, but there was always a certain amount of circumspection that was clearly expressed in the sermons. Twice in his sermons Eudes referred to the spiritual state of devotion that the martyrs ought to have as they died. In the memorial sermons for Robert d'Artois, he asked God quite specifically to forgive those crusaders whose state of devotion had not been what it should have at the moment of death.[359]

Voluntary Martyrdom without Suicidal Tendencies

No other preacher discusses the question of martyrdom in a crusade sermon to the extent that Eudes de Châteauroux does. However, Jacques de Vitry's sermon addressed to the brothers of the military orders also deals with martyrdom. This sermon, though not meant for ordinary crusaders, gives us an additional viewpoint on the matter and is thus given a brief but in-depth examination here. Jacques's sermon appears originally to have been intended solely for the Templars, and there is internal evidence that the sermon was first preached

---

[356] Smith, 'Martyrdom and Crusading in the Thirteenth Century', p. 190; 'Epistola sacnti Ludovici Regis de captione et liberation sua', *Historiae Francorum Scriptores*, ed. by Duchesne, p. 429: 'Quoniam pro certo credimus et speramus eum, coronam martyrii, ad coelestem evolasse patriam, et ibi cum SS. martyribus perenniter congaudere'.

[357] Smith, 'Martyrdom and Crusading in the Thirteenth Century', p. 190; 'Epistola sacnti Ludovici Regis de captione et liberation sua', *Historiae Francorum Scriptores*, ed. by Duchesne, p. 431: 'Caeteri vero, tanquam Athletae fortissimi, in fide radicari, et in firmo proposito constantissime persistentes, minis vel flagellis hostium superari nullatenus potuerunt: sed certantes legitime, coronas martyrii receperunt sanguine rubritas'.

[358] Smith, 'Martyrdom and Crusading in the Thirteenth Century', p. 190.

[359] Eudes de Châteauroux, 'Sermo in anniversario Roberti comitis Attrabatensis et aliorum nobilium qui interfecti fuerant a Sarracenis apud Mansuram in Egipto', *PCHL*, p. 239; Eudes de Châteauroux, 'Sermo in eodem anniversario', *PCHL*, p. 243.

to the Knights of the Temple in the Kingdom of Jerusalem, probably during Jacques's office as the Bishop of Acre.[360] The sermon was later edited, and the rubrics make it a sermon intended for all the military orders, but the focus of the sermon is clearly on the Templars.

Jacques deals at length with questions related to crusading martyrdom in the sermon. He uses characteristically lively examples to convey his messages. The knights of the Temple were not common crusaders: like other members of military orders, they were both knights and monks, religious soldiers guided by monastic rules. However, the instructions given in the sermon were applicable for the most part to all crusaders, for any soldier of Christ had to follow these in order to gain the crown of martyrdom. In fact, in one exemplum Jacques makes a lay crusader's or a 'pilgrim's' pious sentiment towards martyrdom a model for the brothers of the Temple to follow.[361]

According to Jacques, a French knight had been captured by the enemy together with some brothers of the order. The Saracens wanted to kill all the Templars, whom they hated, but all the secular knights captured were to be spared and imprisoned. The French knight had the appearance of a Templar, bald and bearded, and was suspected to be a member of the order. When first asked if he was a Templar, the knight answered truthfully that he was not, but when asked again by the sceptical enemy, the man changed his mind. Burning with the zeal of faith, the secular knight answered that 'in God's name, I am a Templar', and hence he too was killed alongside with the brother knights. This 'new Templar migrated to the Lord and was happily crowned with martyrdom', according to Jacques.[362]

---

[360] One occasion when the sermon may have been delivered was during Jacques's preaching tour in Palestine in 1217. In a letter sent to his friends in the West, Jacques explains how he arrived at Chastel Blanc, the town of the Templars, on his journey, where he preached the word of God to the knights for several days. Jacques de Vitry, *Epistola*, II, ed. by Huygens, p. 93: 'Inde vero venimus ad opidum quoddam Templariorum, quod dicitur Castrum Album. Fratres autem milicie Templi, postquam ibi per dies aliquot verbum dei predicavi'.

[361] This secular knight is described in the sermon as 'a knight and a pilgrim' who had come overseas from the Kingdom of France. The setting of the story suggests that the French knight in question was a crusader. Jacques used both the terms 'peregrini' and 'crucesignati' when he referred to the crusaders in his writings. In this instance, the 'secular knights' who had been captured would appear to be crusaders who had engaged in battle against the enemy alongside the Templars, rather than ordinary pilgrims. However, one cannot be entirely sure which Jacques is referring to. Jacques de Vitry, 'Sermo ad fratres militaris insignitos charactere militiae Christi', Troyes, MS 228, fols 132vb–133ra.

[362] Jacques de Vitry, 'Sermo ad fratres militaris insignitos charactere militiae Christi',

Étienne de Bourbon expressed similar kinds of ideas about crusading martyrdom in a grisly crusading exemplum. According to Étienne, in the history of Antioch there was a story where a Christian knight, a captive of the enemy army, was ordered by the Saracens to tell the crusaders besieging the city that they could not conquer Antioch. The knight, however, decided not to follow the instructions and praised the crusaders' efforts from the city walls. The Saracens then decapitated the knight. As they were about to catapult his head over the walls it started to laugh. The joyful, dead crusader had gained salvation.[363]

Jacques's and Étienne's stories reveal some important aspects of crusading martyrdom. Like crusading itself, crusading martyrdom was of a voluntary nature. The martyrs chose to die for God of their own accord rather than renounce his name. This was briefly noted also by Eudes de Châteauroux in his anniversary sermon for Robert d'Artois.[364] At the same time, although the decision to die for God had to be made voluntarily, the crusaders should not be too 'active' in this matter. The martyrs-to-be should not specifically try to die, but if confronted with a situation where martyrdom could be anticipated, they should not hesitate to seize the moment.

Jacques de Vitry explained the complexities surrounding the voluntariness of becoming a martyr and the need to avoid excessive enthusiasm for gaining the crown in his sermon for the Templars. He used an amusing example of a knight who had fasted too much. The Templar had become physically weak. In

---

Troyes, MS 228, fols 132vb–133ra: 'In nomine domini sim templarius. [...] novus templarius ad dominum migravit, martyrio feliciter coronatus'.

[363] Étienne de Bourbon, 'Quod passio et crux letificant, maxime in morte', ed. by Lecoy de La Marche, p. 91: 'In historia Antiochiensi dicitur quod, cum Sarraceni cepissent quemdam militem, rogabant ut murum ascenderet turris in qua servabatur et clamaret quod Franci inutiliter laborarent obsidendo urbem; quam viriliter obsiderent. Cujus caput crucesignati cum amputassent Sarraceni et cum machina Christianis projecissent, in signum adquisiti gaudii, inter manus eorum ridebat'. This exemplum is likely based on the story told by Pierre Tudebode. Pierre tells in his history that a knight called Rainald Porchet suffered martyrdom in very similar circumstances during the First Crusade. See, for example, MacGregor, 'The First Crusade in Late Medieval *Exempla*', esp. pp. 34–35. Étienne also noted in the exemplum the difference between the dead crusaders and the dead Saracens lying in the battlefield: the crusaders were found smiling, while the Saracen faces had horrible expressions. Étienne de Bourbon, 'Quod passio et crux letificant, maxime in morte', ed. by Lecoy de La Marche, p. 91: 'Item audivi a quodam quod, cum fuisset in campo ubi multa corpora prostrata jacebant crucesignatorum et Sarracenorum, crucesignati eciam mortui videbantur ridere; Sarraceni autem horribiles risus et vultus habebant'.

[364] Eudes de Châteauroux, 'Sermo in anniversario Roberti comitis Attrabatensis et aliorum nobilium qui interfecti fuerant a Sarracenis apud Mansuram in Egipto', *PCHL*, p. 238.

a battle, he fell off his horse at the first strike. This 'lord of bread and water' was rescued, but immediately after remounting he fell out of the saddle again after another blow, all because of his 'immoderate fasting'.[365] The Templar's excessive fasting and the consequential inability to fight made his intentions suspicious. Was this Templar trying to defeat the enemies of God or was he trying to gain a crown of martyrdom for himself?

This kind of behaviour was inappropriate, for the Christians could not expect to overcome the enemy if every soldier of Christ was aspiring to become a martyr without being able to contribute in any way to the fight against the enemy. This was also blatantly against the teachings of the Church and canon law: soldiers who yearned to die were dangerously close to committing the sin of suicide. Christians engaged in the violence of war should not act recklessly or disregard their own safety.[366] Suicide was a capital sin, and those who tried to get themselves killed in a combat against the enemies of God could be considered guilty of it. These Christian soldiers could not be regarded as martyrs, for martyrs had pure intentions and they were supposed to be without sin, in a pure spiritual state as they died.[367]

In his sermon for the Templars, Jacques admonished the Christian soldiers not to test God and put themselves in a vulnerable situation. They should follow reason when they advanced to battle.[368] Here it seems that Jacques did not practice what he preached, considering his own actions during the Fifth Crusade and the situation he, the legate, and the patriarch placed themselves in.[369] In

[365] Jacques de Vitry, 'Sermo ad fratres militaris insignitos charactere militiae Christi', Troyes, MS 228, fol. 133vb; Jacques de Vitry, 'Sermo XXXVII', ed. by Pitra, p. 412: 'Unde audivimus de quodam valde religioso, sed non secundum scientiam, quod in Sarracenorum conflictu, primo ictu lanceae de equo suo cecidit, quem quidam frater eius cum magno personae suae periculo relevavit. [...] Dixit ei frater eius, miles scilicet qui eum iam bis levaverat et a morte liberaverat, increpans eum de immoderatis ieiuniis: Domine panis et aquae, caveatis de caetero vobis, quia si iterum cecideritis, nunquam per me relevabimini'.

[366] Brundage, 'Voluntary Martyrs and Canon Law', pp. 159–60.

[367] Murray, Suicide in the Middle Ages; see also the discussion on Augustine's views on martyrdom and suicide, ii, 104–10.

[368] Jacques de Vitry, 'Sermo ad fratres militaris insignitos charactere militiae Christi', Troyes, MS 228, fol. 132vb: 'Non enim deum temptare debetis, sed facere quod in vobis est, praevia ratione, et tunc secure pro Christo mortem potestis suscipere'.

[369] In a letter sent to Pope Honorius III, Jacques de Vitry complained that he had personally failed to reach the standards of crusading martyrdom. Jacques had advanced with the papal legate Pelagius and the Patriarch of Jerusalem, Raoul de Mérencourt, beyond the safety of the crusade host and close to the enemy lines. The three men exposed themselves to danger as they

the sermon, he nonetheless stressed that martyrdom should not be deliberately sought. There was a fine line between showing permissible desire for martyrdom and being too eager to die. The desire for martyrdom was linked to the imitation of Christ's sufferings. Longing to die was regarded a saintly feature, a demonstration of one's piety and devotion to God. In the canonization processes of the thirteenth century the desire for martyrdom was often mentioned. St Francis in particular was believed to have shown this desire, for which he received the reward of the stigmata.[370] In the context of the crusades, the imitation of the Passion of Christ could eventually lead a crusader to self-sacrifice and death.

In the crusade preaching manual the *Brevis ordinacio de predicacione sancte crucis*, the theme of crusading martyrdom is heavily utilized. The manual mentions by name several crusading heroes who had won martyrdom. The author tells a story of two brothers from Flanders, Gaufridus and Eustachius, or Godfrey and Eustace, who went on a journey to the Holy Land. Godfrey was physically in a weak condition and could not take part in a coming battle. He asked his brother to wait for him for fifteen days so he could regain his health. Eustace, however, would not wait. 'As a true soldier of Christ' he was anxious 'to dissolve and be with Christ'. The following day, Eustace went to battle and died, which made him a crusading martyr.[371]

The names in the story, Godfrey and Eustace, are an interesting choice by the author. The two brothers would presumably remind the medieval audience of another pair of brothers who had the very same names and came from the same region, Godfrey of Bouillon and Eustace III of Boulogne, the famous participants of the First Crusade. The author likely was aware that Eustace of Boulogne had not died on the crusade, but had returned home.[372] Hence, the

had no arms or shields, Jacques wearing only his cape and surplice and bearing the Holy Cross, but they were deprived of martyrdom. Jacques lamented that 'it did not please the Lord' to summon him 'unworthy and miserable' to the company of God's martyrs, but he was 'reserved to bear labour and grief'. Jacques de Vitry, *Epistola*, VI, ed. by Huygens, p. 130: 'Ego vero die illa absque armis cum cappa et suppellicio cum domno legato et patriarcha, qui sanctam crucem ferebat, exieram et non placuit domino cum suis martyribus indignum et miserum me vocare, sed adhuc voluit me ad laborem et dolorem reservare'.

[370] Gaposchkin, *The Making of Saint Louis*, pp. 169–75. See also Smith, 'Martyrdom and Crusading in the Thirteenth Century', p. 193.

[371] 'Brevis ordinacio de predicacione', *QBSS*, p. 20: 'Respondit autem Eustachius tanquam verus miles Christi cupiensque *dissolvi et esse cum Christo*'. Phil. 1. 23.

[372] For Eustace of Boulogne, see, for example, Tanner, 'In His Brothers' Shadow'. See also MacGregor, 'The First Crusade in Late Medieval *Exempla*', p. 33.

manual was not explicitly referring to these more renowned crusaders. The use of these names may have caused some confusion among the medieval audience. Some modern scholars at least have been misled by the author.[373] However, the author may have wanted to evoke positive memories by utilizing the names of famous crusaders. Godfrey and Eustace from Flanders would give the story credibility and would bring to mind the crusading success of Godfrey of Bouillon and his brothers.

The theme of crusading martyrdom is then continued in the manual with the story of Jacques d'Avesnes. Jacques took part in the Third Crusade and died in 1191. He was a famous crusader, whom Jacques de Vitry also regarded a crusading martyr and whose heroic deeds were remembered by numerous medieval chroniclers, poets, and preachers.[374] The author of the manual depicts Jacques d'Avesnes as an ideal crusader who is committed to his vow. According to the *Brevis ordinacio de predicacione sancte crucis*, Jacques's companions advised him to withdraw from a battle that had killed many crusaders. However, Jacques replied that he would go to fight the Saracens 'voluntarily', and no one should try to stop him. Jacques was then killed by the Saracens, and he won the crown of martyrdom.[375]

In both of these stories the author of the crusading manual underlined once again the voluntariness of the decision to go into battle and the desire of the crusader to become a martyr. The true soldiers of Christ would not step aside or try to flee when confronted with an overwhelming enemy or with difficult circumstances, which might persuade others to retreat. The true crusaders wished above all to fight for Christ and to die for him. They willingly chose martyrdom. In the *Brevis ordinacio*, crusading martyrdom is clearly promoted. At the end of the manual, further exempla are provided, which all deal with martyrdom and urge Christians to take the cross. The author depicts the dead, heroic crusaders as factual martyrs, not reputed martyrs, and takes a straightforward position on the matter of martyrdom: those crusaders who would die on the expeditions would be true martyrs.[376]

---

[373] *QBSS*, p. ix; *PCHL*, p. 124.

[374] Tamminen, 'Who Deserves the Crown of Martyrdom?', pp. 307–08; Tyerman, *God's War*, p. 459.

[375] 'Brevis ordinacio de predicacione', *QBSS*, p. 20: 'Socii Iacobi de Aventhnes militis dixerunt: Socii nostris omnes moriuntur, recedamus a Saracenis et Iacobus dixit: Iou ireie plus volentiers là u nus home ne me conestreit'.

[376] 'Brevis ordinacio de predicacione', *QBSS*, pp. 20–26, esp. p. 20: 'et ivit in bellum et martyr Dei factus est'.

Fear of Dying and the Manner of Death

The crusaders could thus have a legitimate desire for martyrdom, and they were specifically encouraged to emulate the sufferings of Christ, the deeds of famous crusaders, or the sacrifice of St George. The 'true' crusaders were supposed to be ready to sacrifice themselves and to die for Christ's sake, if that was needed.[377] In the sermon for the Templars, Jacques de Vitry depicted the Order of the Temple as 'a bipartite order', partly based on the 'order of martyrs'. According to Jacques, the Templars were like 'calves' that killed 'themselves for Christ's sake'.[378] In the sermon, Jacques gave instructions on how the knights ought to behave before and during battle. He advised the Templars to purify themselves with vigils, fasts, and prayers during peacetime, so that they would 'be ready to lay down their souls in battle for the Church's defence'.[379] The knights should not be fearful if faced with a situation where the crown of martyrdom could be expected, for 'a just man can defeat many impious' and only the hypocrite has reason to fear. Jacques emphasized that the soldiers of Christ must be wholly purified, so that 'they are always ready to die — not for one day should they dare to live in a state in which they dared not die'.[380]

Jacques made the same point in his sermon for the crusaders and pilgrims, where he underlined that the sins of the crusaders were making their enemies stronger. The crusaders should in fact fear the sins of the Christians more than they feared the Saracens.[381] For this reason the crusaders should avoid sinning and 'always' hurry to make their confessions before battle. After making their confessions, gaining remission of sins, and drawing up their last wills, the crusaders could go securely into battle.[382] However, if these preparations were

---

[377] Guibert de Tournai, 'Ad crucesignatos et crucesignandos sermo primus', *CPI*, p. 182; Eudes de Châteauroux, 'De sancto Georgio sermo', *UEE*, II, 738.

[378] Jacques de Vitry, 'Sermo ad fratres militaris insignitos charactere militiae Christi', Troyes, MS 228, fol. 131ᵛᵃ: 'Hic enim ordo sanctus et venerabilis bipartitus est ex ordine martirum et ex ordine monachorum vel claustralium [...]. ipsi enim vituli sunt semet ipsos pro Christo mactando'.

[379] Jacques de Vitry, 'Sermo ad fratres militaris insignitos charactere militiae Christi', Troyes, MS 228, fol. 131ᵛᵃ.

[380] Jacques de Vitry, 'Sermo ad fratres militaris insignitos charactere militiae Christi', Troyes, MS 228, fol. 131ᵛᵃ⁻ᵛᵇ: 'Valde igitur purificati esse debent et sancti martires milites Christi, ut semper parati sint mori, nec uno die vivere audeant, in statu in quo mori non auderent'.

[381] Jacques de Vitry, 'Ad peregrinos. Thema sumpta ex Zacharias ultimo', *JVSP*, p. 99: 'Magis autem timemus de peccatis christianorum quam de viribus sarracenorum. Peccata enim nostra faciunt eos potentes'.

[382] Jacques de Vitry, 'Ad peregrinos. Thema sumpta ex Zacharias ultimo', *JVSP*, p. 99: 'Facta

neglected and if the crusader would go into battle 'unprepared' and 'in a state of mortal sin', he could not be sure of gaining 'the crown of victory' or 'the eternal reward' promised to him.[383]

The 'true' crusaders who had purified themselves before battle were ready to kill and be killed. This readiness to die for God separated the 'true' crusaders from the hypocrites. The 'true' crusaders were not afraid. They had taken into account that they might be killed on the crusade and were prepared to perish — they had nothing to fear from death or imprisonment, for they were true servants of God and trusted in him.[384] In the sermon for the Templars, Jacques de Vitry ended his discussion with a positive conclusion: if the Christian soldiers went into battle properly prepared and did not try to get themselves killed, but died all the same, they would be thought of as martyrs, for anyone who died while defending the Church would earn the reputation of a martyr.[385] Again, Jacques avoided using precise terms and did not promise definite martyrdom for the dead Christian soldiers, but reputed martyrdom.

Eudes de Châteauroux also discussed different aspects of fear in relation to martyrdom in his sermons. In the sermon for the feast of Thomas Becket, preached in 1247 when the Seventh Crusade was promoted and while the difficulties between the French barons and the Church were being resolved, Eudes explained how fear should be dealt with.[386] Thomas Becket, a martyr of the Church, had not been afraid of any man, neither the English king nor the

autem confessione et recepto Christi corpore factoque testamento vestro secure potestis ad bellum prodere, certi de corona victorie et eterna remuneratione'.

[383] Jacques de Vitry, 'Ad peregrinos. Thema sumpta ex Zacharias ultimo', *JVSP*, p. 99.

[384] In the disastrous Battle of Hattin in 1187, the leaders of the crusade army had failed to place their trust in God and to control their fears, according to Jacques de Vitry. In his history, the *Historia orientalis*, Jacques explained that the destruction of the crusade army by Saladin's forces was proof of God's wrath. The crusaders of the King of Jerusalem, Guy de Lusignan, had not advanced to battle in a proper state of devotion, but had been proud and full of sin, and because of this, 'the Lord delivered them into the hands of the impious'. The conduct of the leaders of the crusade army, especially King Guy, was further proof of their misplaced trust and impure spiritual state. The leaders 'fled like cowards' and so did the rest of the army 'humiliated by the Lord with fear and timidity'. Jacques de Vitry, *Historia orientalis*, XCVI, ed. by Donnadieu, pp. 434–36: 'In tantum enim formidine et pusillanimitate humiliavit eos Dominus, quod unus ex hostibus versa vice centum persequebatur ex nostris'.

[385] Jacques de Vitry, 'Sermo ad fratres militaris insignitos charactere militiae Christi', Troyes, MS 228, fol. 132ᵛᵇ: 'Quotquot enim ex vobis pro defensione ecclesiae moriuntur, martires reputantur'.

[386] See above, p. 29.

princes. Thomas had not feared for his life but was ready to earn the crown
of martyrdom for God's sake. The saint's example was to be imitated by true
Christians. Eudes did not, however, propose that Christians should be fearless.
Christians should both love and dread God the most, because 'the fear of God
expels sin' and 'he who is without fear cannot act justly'.[387]

In the anniversary sermon for Robert d'Artois, Eudes also explained how
Robert and the other dead crusaders had proved that they feared God as they
ought to. This was demonstrated by Robert's and the others' readiness to leave
their loved ones behind, who were now 'exposed to their enemies', and in their
readiness to expose themselves and those loved ones whom they had taken with
them to the expedition 'to death'. According to Eudes, one reason for the disaster was the fact that God wanted people to know how much Robert and the
other crusaders feared him.[388] This fear made Robert willing to die for Christ's
sake and earn the greatest reward from God. This fear of God also marked
Robert out from the other crusaders who had not died at Mansurah. Being
afraid of God alone made Robert a 'true' crusader, truer than the others who
did not earn martyrdom, who were perhaps more afraid to die than they were
afraid of God. If the crusaders genuinely feared God, they would avoid sinning,
and if they should die in battle, they would be in a pure, sin-free state, in which
case they might be considered martyrs.

There is one further aspect that needs to be considered when examining
crusading martyrdom and 'true' crusading — the way the crusaders died. This
question had considerable significance during the Middle Ages. The crusaders
exposed themselves to many different dangers on their journey. Jacques de Vitry
mentioned in his crusade sermon the 'perils on land, perils on sea, the perils of
thieves, the perils of predators, the perils of battles' which the crusaders had to

---

[387] Eudes de Châteauroux, 'Sancti Thome martyris', *UEE*, ii, 716–17: 'Timor Domini exp-
ellit peccatum. *Nam qui sine timore est non poterit iustificari*'. See also Humbert de Romans's references to fear in the manual *De predicatione sancte crucis*. Humbert pointed out that Christians
ought to fear God's punishment for their sins and for lack of faith. The crusaders could also participate in the battles safely because their consciences were pure. They should fight until the end
for justice. If they should die on their journey, they would be rewarded. Humbert de Romans,
De predicatione sancte crucis, cap. xxv, Multi retrahuntur a cruce propter defectum fidei, cap. xlv,
De his que valent ad bene pugnandum contra saracenos.

[388] Eudes de Châteauroux, 'Sermo in anniversario Roberti comitis Attrabatensis et aliorum nobilium qui interfecti fuerant a Sarracenis apud Mansuram in Egipto', *PCHL*, p. 238: 'Sic
Dominus in isto facto cognoscere fecit predictos nobiles et alios Christianos quod ipsi nobiles
timebant Deum eo quod non pepercerunt filiis suis, uxoribus et aliis caris suis, eos dimittendo et
quasi exponendo inimicis suis si quos habebant. Sed nec etiam sibi pepercerunt et etiam quibusdam caris suis quos secum adduxerant se et eos morti exponendo'.

face out of love for Christ.[389] There were good reasons to list the many and varied dangers in this way and also to emphasize risks other than those encountered in battle, which is only the last pitfall mentioned by Jacques. These perils could all result in death, but not all were considered 'glorious' deaths by contemporaries.

From the beginning of crusading, there appears to have been some uncertainty about the possibility of gaining martyrdom in a non-combat situation.[390] In his crusade sermon, Jacques de Vitry assured the audience that those who went crusading and died on their journey deserved 'the remission of sins and the reward of eternal life' without making any distinction as to the manner of death.[391] Once again, however, this passage of the sermon is very unspecific, and the term 'martyrdom' is not used at this point. Could those crusaders who did not die in battle, but died in accidents, from disease, or from hunger also win the crown of martyrdom?

Bernard of Clairvaux made clear how the knights of Christ should die in his treatise written for the new knighthood in 1128–31. According to Bernard, Christian soldiers could become martyrs if they died in battle for Christ. He maintained that it was 'precious' for the Lord, whether his 'holy ones' died in bed or in battle, but it would surely be 'more precious' for the Lord if they died in battle, for it was 'more glorious'.[392] The author of the *Gesta Francorum* stated that many crusaders suffered martyrdom during the siege of Nicea in 1097 and that 'the poorest' crusaders had died of hunger. 'All of these entered heaven triumphantly wearing the robe of martyrdom', according to the author.[393] This appears a reassuring message, as observed by Colin Morris, meant to convince

---

[389] Jacques de Vitry, 'Item sermo ad crucesignatos vel -signandos', *CPI*, p. 112: 'pro Christi servitio relinquere, periculis in terra, periculis in mare, periculis latronum, periculis predonum, periculis preliorum pro amore Crucifixi se exponere?'.

[390] Morris, 'Martyrs in the Field of Battle', pp. 101–02; Tamminen, 'Who Deserves the Crown of Martyrdom?', pp. 309–12.

[391] Jacques de Vitry, 'Item sermo ad crucesignatos vel -signandos', *CPI*, p. 112: 'Unde nullo modo dubitetis quod non solum vobis ad remissionem peccatorum et eterne vite premium valet hec peregrination'.

[392] Bernard of Clairvaux, *De laude novae militiae*, I. 1–2, ed. by Leclercq and Rochais, p. 215: 'Quam beati moriuntur martyres in proelio! [...] Et quidem sive in lecto, sive in bello quis moritur, pretiosa erit sine dubio in conspectu Domini mors sanctorum eius. Ceterum in bello tanto pretiosior, quanto et gloriosior'.

[393] *Anonymi Gesta Francorum et aliorum Hierosolymitanorum*, ed. by Hagenmeyer, VIII, 9, p. 193: 'et multi ex nostris illic receperunt martyrium et laetantes gaudentesque reddiderunt felices animas Deo, et ex pauperrima gente multi mortui sunt fame pro Christi nomine, qui in caelum triumphantes portaverunt stolam recepti martyrii'.

those who had doubts regarding the martyrdom of crusaders who had not died in battle.[394] Jacques de Vitry also seems to have expressed his reservations about the martyrdom of crusaders who had died of illness during the Fifth Crusade in his letters.[395]

A connection was made between illnesses and sins during the Middle Ages. Some diseases could be regarded as punishments inflicted by God on those who had sinned. Leprosy in particular was associated with sins which had been committed and for which God wanted to penalize those who had caught the disease.[396] This link made it more difficult to view the crusaders who had died from illnesses as martyrs. Martyrs were supposed to be pure, those who had received the greatest reward from God, not people who had been punished for their sins. On the other hand, bodily sufferings and illnesses were also regarded as God's gifts during the Middle Ages. In the crusading context, such sufferings could be thought as proof of God's love and fatal illnesses as ways to personal salvation.[397] However, the disease was something which the persons who became sick did not choose for themselves, but which was chosen for them by God, either as a punishment or as a gift. A disease or hunger was difficult to view in the same light as human oppressors who persecuted innocent victims and made them martyrs.

These matters are considered in Jacques de Vitry's letter from the Fifth Crusade. Jacques explains to Pope Honorius III that it was not pleasing for 'divine providence' that the crusaders could cross the Nile during the winter of 1217–18 'without multiple profit' for their souls. According to Jacques, God cast a sickness into the army, which none of the physicians knew how to cure. This contagious disease appeared to be hurled down by God 'to cleanse us from our sins', or to make the crusaders more worthy of the crown of martyrdom.[398] The divine cleansing was thus sent down from the heavens, according

---

[394] Morris, 'Martyrs on the Field of Battle', p. 101.

[395] Tamminen, 'Who Deserves the Crown of Martyrdom?', pp. 309–12. See also the letter written between August 1218 and September 1219, where Jacques informed Honorius III of the siege of Damietta and discussed the death of his close friend Robert of Courçon. Jacques de Vitry, *Epistola*, V, ed. by Huygens, p. 116.

[396] This association was based on the Bible, see II Par. 26. 19. See also Rawcliffe, *Leprosy in Medieval England*, pp. 48–54; Allen, *The Wages of Sin*.

[397] *JVSP*, pp. 86–87.

[398] Jacques de Vitry, *Epistola*, V, ed. by Huygens, pp. 115–16: 'Non tamen divine placuit providentie illud tempus hiemale, quo morati sumus in sabulo, absque multiplici lucro animarum pertransire: inmisit enim dominus nostris morbum nulla arte medicorum curabilem, morbum contagiosum absque fisicis rationibus magne parti exercitus nostri divinitus immissum vel

to Jacques, because of the iniquities of the crusaders. The crusaders of the Fifth Crusade needed to go through purgation so as to become better soldiers of Christ. This also prepared the crusaders for possible martyrdom. However, it did not make crusaders who had died into martyrs.[399]

These reservations also give one explanation why Louis IX was not canonized as a martyr in 1297, but as a confessor. Louis IX died of dysentery in 1270, during the Eighth Crusade in Tunisia.[400] Many contemporaries, also high-ranking churchmen, regarded Louis as a martyr. Some, however, felt they had to defend their position and take into account the way the king had died. In a letter sent to the papal curia in 1275, the Dominican prior Jean de Châtillon argued that even though 'the sword of the persecutor' did not kill Louis, it was easy to believe that 'he did not lose the palm of martyrdom' as he had suffered much and repeatedly for Christ's sake.[401] Jean de Joinville also actively promoted the canonization of Louis IX in his *Vie de Saint Louis*, similarly viewing the king as a crusading martyr. In the opening chapters of his work, Jean expressed his disappointment at the Church's decision not to declare Louis a martyr.[402] According to Jean, Louis's saintliness and piety, his devotion to God, and particularly the sufferings he was willing to endure through crusading were enough to make him a martyr — for if God died on the cross, the king did the same, as he was signed with the cross when he died in Tunisia.[403]

ad purgationem peccatorum vel ad maiorem promerendam coronam'.

[399] Tamminen, 'Who Deserves the Crown of Martyrdom?', pp. 309–12.

[400] Gaposchkin, 'The Place of the Crusades in the Sanctification of Saint Louis', esp. p. 196.

[401] Chapotin, *Histoire des Dominicains de la Province de France*, p. 649: 'Ex quo facile potest credi quod etsi sanctam ejus animam gladius persecutoris non abstulit, palmam tamen martyrii non amisit'. Gaposchkin, *The Making of Saint Louis*, p. 32 n. 72. The Italian chronicler Giovanni Villani, who took a rather critical view of both crusades of the French king, admitted that even though Louis's expeditions did not have much success, the king had success for his soul in his death. Villani, *Chronica*, ed. by Moutier, p. 201: 'E come il detto re Luis non bene avventurato fosse nelle dette imprese sopra i saracini, ma per la sua anima bene avventuroso morisse'.

[402] Jean de Joinville, *Vie de Saint Louis*, ed. by Monfrin, p. 4: 'Et de ce me semble il que en ne li fist mie assez quant en ne le mist ou nombre des martirs'. There seems to be a slight contradiction later in the history, as Jean proclaims at the end of his work that the Church did great justice for Louis IX, as the king was placed among the confessors. The reasons for this contradiction are obscure. Smith, 'Martyrdom and Crusading in the Thirteenth Century', p. 195 n. 15.

[403] Jean de Joinville, *Vie de Saint Louis*, ed. by Monfrin, p. 4: 'pour les grans peinnes que il souffri ou pelerinage de la croiz par l'espace de .vi. anz que je fu en sa compaignie, et pour ce meismement que il ensuï Nostre Seigneur ou fait de la croiz; car se Diex morut en la croiz, aussi fist il car croisiez estoit il quant il mourut a Thunes'.

The crusaders who died of illness or hunger during the expeditions had one advantage that those who died in battle did not have. Usually, those who died of disease passed away slowly. This enabled the crusaders to die a 'good' death, to acquire the proper spiritual state of devotion as they perished. Jacques de Vitry underlined in the letter from the Fifth Crusade that the crusaders who died of illness died well. The sick crusaders lost their strength gradually. They prayed unceasingly, talked with their companions, and finally closed their eyes as if sleeping and then left their bodies 'for the joys of the citizens of heaven'.[404] The sick crusaders had a chance to praise God, to confess their sins, and to leave in peace, in the company of friends and priests.

These things were also taken into account in the descriptions of Louis IX's death. Eudes de Châteauroux was quickly informed of Louis's demise by Thibaud of Navarre in 1270.[405] At the time Eudes was leading the cardinals as *primus inter pares* and presiding over the conclave in Viterbo during the long *sede vacante* of 1268–71, and it was important to let him know that the French king had perished as the cardinals were trying to find an agreement on who would be the next pope. In the letter Thibaud carefully described how Louis had died in a pious manner. According to Villani's account of the letter, King Louis, although very ill, continued to praise God and prayed constantly, not forgetting to pray for his men, the crusaders, whom he was about to leave behind. As his final words, Louis IX is described as quoting a verse of a Psalm: *'I will enter into your house, I will worship towards your holy temple, and praise your name'.*[406]

The crusaders who had died from illness or hunger during the campaigns were celebrated, and their pious deaths were often given prominence in the

---

[404] Jacques de Vitry, *Epistola*, V, ed. by Huygens, p. 116: 'femoribus enim et tibiis primo ingrescentibus et deinde putrescentibus, carnibus etiam superfluis in ore subcrescentibus, diutius absque dolore magno languentes et paulatim corde deficientes cum suis loquendo et iugiter deum deprecando, more dormientium claudentes oculos et spiritum suum domino commendantes relictis corporibus ad gaudia supernorum civium evolabant'.

[405] Carolus-Barré, 'Un recueil épistolaire composé à Saint-Denis sur la Croisade', esp. p. 558.

[406] Giovanni Villani summarizes the letter in his chronicle: 'lo re di Navarra ch'era presente, al cardinale Tosculano per sue lettere lo scrisse, che nella sua infermità non cessava di lodare Iddio, e spesso dicendo questa orazione: *Fa'a noi, Signore, le cose prosperevoli del mondo avere in odio, e nessuna avversità temere.* Ancora orave per lo popolo il quale avea menato seco, dicendo: *Sii, Signore, del popolo tuo santificatore, e guardino;* e l'altre parole che seguitano alla detta orazione. E alla fine quando venne a morte, levò gli occhi a cielo, e disse: *Introibo in domum tuam, adorabo ad templum sanctum tuum, et confitebor nomini tuo:* e ciò detto morì in Cristo'. Villani, *Chronica*, ed. by Moutier, p. 202. Ps. 5. 8. See the similar account of the final words by Salimbene di Adam, *Cronica Fratris*, ed. by Bernini, p. 173. Thibaud II of Navarre himself died of illness on the way back home from the Eighth Crusade, in Trapani in 1270. Le Goff, *Saint Louis*, p. 301.

medieval accounts. These descriptions indicated how crusaders ought to die if they contracted a fatal illness. The sick crusaders died well, without cursing God or expressing regret at going on the expedition. They had fought for Christ until the end, 'to the blood', as demanded by some of the authors of the crusade sermons, and thus they had lived and died as 'true' crusaders.[407] These crusaders did not leave the crusade prematurely, and they imitated Christ perfectly, emulating his sacrifice on the cross by dying for the sake of others.[408] These 'true' crusaders had also a chance to confess their sins to priests before dying — sins which they might have committed after taking the cross — and thus they would receive the crusade indulgence as they died, and they could enter heaven immediately.

Even though the participants who died from illnesses during the expeditions were clearly 'true' crusaders, they were not necessarily thought to have won the crown of martyrdom, as Louis IX's case demonstrates. Louis IX was regarded as a 'true' crusader by many of his contemporaries. There was widespread popular belief in Louis's martyrdom and pressure from both the Capetian and Angevin royal houses. Charles of Anjou, for example, made a strong appeal on behalf of his brother's martyrdom in the canonization proceedings of 1282. Charles testified that Louis had died as a martyr in Tunisia, and also that his two other brothers, Robert d'Artois and Alphonse de Poitiers, had been martyrs.[409] However, the Church did not declare Louis IX a crusading martyr, even if he was conceived of as an ideal crusader. It appears that the connection between 'true' crusading and crusading martyrdom was not a simple or straightforward matter, as represented by Guibert de Tournai in his crusade sermon, at least not officially.[410]

---

[407] Guibert de Tournai, 'Ad crucesignatos et crucesignandos sermo primus', *CPI*, p. 182; Eudes de Châteauroux, 'De sancto Georgio sermo', *UEE*, ii, 738.

[408] See above, pp. 154, 157.

[409] Charles's intentions were to promote the sanctity of his family in general, when he promoted the canonization of Louis IX. For the fragments of the testimony of Charles of Anjou, see 'Déposition de Charles d'Anjou pour la canonisation de saint Louis', in *Notices et Documents*, ed. by Riant, p. 175: 'sancta illa anima solute est, unde sancta radix sanctos ramos protulit, non solum regem sanctum, sed et comitem Atrebatensem, martirem gloriosum, et comitem Pictavensem, affectu [the fragment ends unfinished]'. Later, Charles returns to the martyrdom of Alphonse in the deposition by stating: 'Comes vero Pictaviensis martir extitit voluntate, cum, mortuo sancto Ludovico, omnes cum rege novo redirent de Tunitio'. See also Gaposchkin, *The Making of Saint Louis*, pp. 30, 36–43. Alphonse de Poitiers died while returning home from the Eighth Crusade in 1271. For more information on Alphonse de Poitiers, see Boutaric, *Saint Louis et Alphonse de Poitiers*. See also Le Goff, *Saint Louis*, pp. 301–05, 329–44.

[410] See above, p. 171. Guibert de Tournai, 'Ad crucesignatos et crucesignandos sermo primus', *CPI*, p. 180.

The Crusader and the World

Mundane Obstacles

In the opinion of the crusade preachers there were various impediments that prevented crusading, most of which were connected in one way or another to the earthly aspirations of Christians. These obstacles needed to be discussed in the crusade model sermons and the preaching manuals. The spiritual values of the crusade movement clashed with the mundane values of the world. The devil lured weak Christians with the temptations of the flesh. These desires and urges prevented people from taking the cross. The crusaders needed to empty their hearts and leave behind their ordinary, worldly lives.

At the end of his crusading manual Humbert de Romans included a list of things that the crusaders ought to do before and during the journey that the preachers could relate to their audiences. Prior to departure the crusader should make a full confession to a confessor with a truly contrite heart. After this he should take care of several practical issues. The crusader ought to make restitution of possession of any goods that did not belong to him. He should also make full reconciliation with all his enemies, since his quarrels could stand in the way of his salvation. Humbert cited the Sermon on the Mount from the Gospel of Matthew, where Christ taught that before one could offer his gift at the altar to God, he needed to make reconciliation with his brother. This was all the more important when someone offered himself to God by participating in a crusade.[1]

---

[1] Humbert de Romans, *De predicatione sancte crucis*, cap. xliiij, De his que sunt necessaria his bonis peregrinis crucesignatis. Mt. 5. 25.

Humbert also included many practicalities in his list, such as making all the necessary arrangements with regards to his worldly possessions, house, and belongings. The crusader was exposing himself to mortal danger, according to Humbert, so he needed to acknowledge that he might not return. The crusader needed to draw up his last will and dispose of his home and goods. This would also ensure that there would be no temptation for the crusader to withdraw from his commitment later.[2]

In his crusade sermon (possibly from the year 1248), Eudes de Châteauroux also urged the crusaders to leave behind all their disputes and worldly affairs.[3] Eudes maintained that the crusaders were 'true Nephtalis', a reference to Jacob's son from the biblical theme utilized in the sermon. The crusaders, like Nephtali, were blessed by God. They had decided to leave their loved ones behind and were like spiritual deer. These crusaders had 'emptied their hearts through true penitence and set down the burden of their sins'. Eudes argued that the crusaders had acted as they ought to when leaving for the expeditions: the 'true Nephtalis' wanted to restore things before they left by making amends for all their past misbehaviour and returning the goods they had stolen from others, so that those they left behind were blessing them rather than cursing them — the participants of the Seventh Crusade had truly enlarged their hearts.[4]

These ideological requirements mentioned in Eudes's model and Humbert's manual meant that in ideal cases, before the crusaders left for the penitential journey, they would try to resolve all their differences with others, settle disputes, and make restitution if needed, so that they would have everyone's blessing when they went and their hearts would be 'empty' of sin, quarrels, or any ill feelings.[5] There is plenty of evidence in the medieval cartularies of

[2] Humbert de Romans, *De predicatione sancte crucis*, cap. xliiij; *PCHL*, p. 216.

[3] Appendix V.

[4] Eudes de Châteauroux, 'Ad invitandum ad accipiendum crucem et ad confortandum crucesignatos', *UEE*, ii, 735: 'Crucesignati vero nostri evacuaverunt corda sua per veram penitentiam et deposuerunt onera peccatorum. Dissolverunt *colligationes impietatis*. Reddiderunt et restituerunt ea que male habuerant vel rapuerant, ut relinquant post se benedictionem et non maledictionem. Isti sunt veri Neptalim et possunt vere dicere: *dilatavit me Dominus*'. For the biblical reference to Nephtali, see Gen. 49. 22.

[5] Pope Alexander III had also referred to this in his crusading bull from the year 1181, the *Cor nostrum*. The pope emphasized that the crusaders ought to take the cross, making a confession with a contrite and humble heart, and if they had committed theft, they ought to restore all the goods and make amends for their deeds. Alexander III, *Cor nostrum*, in *PL*, ccxxi, cols 1294–96, esp. 1296: 'de quibus corde contrito, et humiliato confessionem susceperint, absolutionem facimus delictorum: nisi forte aliena bona rapuerint, vel usuras extorserint, aut

various religious houses across Europe indicating that the crusaders who were about to go on the expeditions wanted to resolve past differences and settle old disputes before departure. The crusaders who were leaving understood that they might never return. Thus, they appear to have wanted to wipe the slate clean for the next generation and remove all the obstacles in the way of their own salvation.[6]

For the higher crusading nobility these requirements could mean many complications. The feudal lords were not only accountable for their own past behaviour and liable to correct their own wrongdoings, they also had to answer for the welfare of their feudal subjects and the wrongdoings in their feudal lands. Before leaving for the Seventh Crusade, Louis IX took measures to leave his kingdom in a better spiritual state. In 1248, the king enhanced his support against the heretics of southern France so that his lands or his subjects would not be infected with heresies and so that the orthodox faith would be defended everywhere, particularly in his own realm. He also took measures against the Jews, condemning their moneylending and giving support to the conversion of Jews. Finally, Louis IX wanted to rectify the misdemeanours of his own government by making reparation for the injustice of which some royal administrators had been found guilty.[7]

The feudal lords who were about to leave for the expeditions appear to have regarded the manner in which they would depart as vitally important. Jean de Joinville wanted to be sure that he gained the benefits of crusading, and hence he laboured to resolve all disputes in his lands. Jean made careful preparations before leaving for the Seventh Crusade, summoning all his subjects and vassals to Joinville and feasting them for several days. During these feasts Jean

---

commiserint furta, quae omnia debent in integrum emendari'.

[6] See, for example, the *Cartulaire de l'abbaye de Saint-Père de Chartres*, ed. by Guérard, pp. 603–04: 'Gaufridus de Bero, cum Jerusalem ire disponeret, timens ne hujus propositi sanctitas alicujus fradulentie macula fedaretur, concessit nobis, cum benivolentia et caritate, quecunque pater suus Gaufridus dederat ecclesie nostre'.

[7] Lower, 'The Burning at Mont-Aimé', esp. p. 105. See also Jordan, *Louis IX and the Challenge of the Crusade*. A few years earlier, Eudes de Châteauroux was also involved in the proceedings of the condemnation of the Talmud in Paris. In 1242–44, Eudes, who was then the chancellor of the University of Paris, played a key role in the proceedings which led to the burning of the Talmud. Eudes also preached a sermon, which Louis IX may have heard, in which the Talmud and the Jewish beliefs were condemned and their conversion to the Catholic faith was promoted, the *Sermo de conversione Iudeorum*. See Behrman, '*Volumina vilissima*'. The French king also made similar preparations as he left for the Eighth Crusade. Le Goff, *Saint Louis*, pp. 291–92.

announced his plans to go on the crusade and asked everyone who might have a claim against him or his vassals to present their cases. If Jean had done them wrong, or if they had suffered some injustice from the vassals of Joinville, each one would have their reconciliation in turn before the feudal lord departed.[8]

Wives and Worldly Friends

The opponents of crusades are often described in the model sermons as 'worldly friends', as those who were only interested in temporal things such as carnal pleasures, and as those who were slack and indifferent to the will of God. These people were envious of others, lazy, and idle.[9] They had not resisted the devil's temptations and could try to prevent others from joining the expeditions. These 'anti'-crusaders are represented in the crusade sermons as the opposites of the 'true' crusaders. The crusaders were signed with the cross, while the 'anti'-crusaders were signed with the mark of the devil;[10] the crusaders imitated Christ, while the 'anti'-crusaders imitated the devil;[11] the crusaders were disciples in the school of Christ, while the 'anti'-crusaders were disciples in the school of the devil.[12] With this extreme contrast between the two, the crusade preachers created an image of true Christians who were faithful to God, and the reverse, the unfaithful who opposed crusading or were reluctant to take the cross or participate in other ways in the movement.

Some crusade preachers counted wives among these 'anti'-crusaders. Jacques de Vitry and Guibert de Tournai warned men not to listen to the advice of their wives. Jacques's sermon give a characteristically lively exemplum of a wife determined to prevent her husband from joining in a crusade. According to Jacques, the wife locked her husband upstairs in their home so he could not go to lis-

---

[8] Jean de Joinville, *Vie de Saint Louis*, ed. by Monfrin, p. 56: "'Seigneurs, je m'en voiz outre mer et je ne scé se je revendré. Or venez avant; se je vous ai de riens mesfait, je le vous desferai l'un par l'autre.'"

[9] Jacques de Vitry, 'Sermo ad crucesignatos vel -signandos', *CPI*, pp. 88, 91.

[10] Guibert de Tournai, 'Ad crucesignatos et crucesignandos sermo secundus', *CPI*, p. 194: 'Signo etiam dyaboli signantur invidentes'.

[11] Jacques de Vitry, 'Item sermo ad crucesignatos vel -signandos', *CPI*, p. 124: 'Alii vero velut lutum ad hunc solem indurantur ut sigilli impressionem non recipiant, et ideo caractere bestie sigillantur, dum diabolum imitantur'.

[12] Roger of Salisbury, '*Ascendente* Ihesu *in naviculam*', *PCHL*, p. 229. Eudes de Châteauroux, 'Sermo ad invitandum ad crucem', *CPI*, p. 172: 'ut per assumptionem crucis signentur et distinguantur servi Dei a servis diaboli'.

ten to crusade preaching and would not be signed with the cross. However, the husband, curious to know what was preached, listened through an open window. Moved by the preacher's words and hearing about the great rewards offered, the man jumped out of the window and, despite the wife's objections, took the cross.[13]

Jacques's exemplum portrays in humorous terms the traditional role given to women in the crusade movement. Women were generally accused of being an impediment to crusading.[14] Reluctant wives prevented their inspired husbands from taking the cross. Jacques's exemplum also provided timid husbands with an appropriate pattern of behaviour: they should boldly disregard their wives' opposition and follow God.[15] In fact, Jacques rejects the controversial right of the spouse to influence any crusading decisions of her husband by stating that the crusaders had not consulted their wives when they went to the devil; why should they take counsel to go to God?[16] Those who had been signed with the cross or were about to do so should also keep their promises and adhere to their good intentions for, according to Jacques, the devil often extinguishes a good proposal through the wife or worldly friends.[17]

Guibert de Tournai followed Jacques's lead in his own crusade sermon and urged 'the notorious sinners' who had not been signed with the cross not to await any recommendations. Why should the sinners expect any advice now, when they had not been advised by their wives when they had sinned? Guibert also included parents in the group of people whose advice the sinners should not listen to when they considered becoming crusaders.[18] This was also a contentious point of view. After the so-called Children's Crusade of 1212 and the *Pastoureaux* or the Shepherds' Crusade of 1251, many clerical observers condemned these incidents, because the parents' and the priests' opinions were not honoured on these occasions: the *pueri* are described in the sources as runaways

---

[13] Jacques de Vitry, 'Item sermo ad crucesignatos vel -signandos', *CPI*, p. 120: 'ipse valde compunctus et a Deo inspiratus, timens uxorem, que ostium clauserat et ne exgrederetur, observabat per fenestram, in turbam exivit et ipse primus ad crucem venit'.

[14] *CPI*, p. 65.

[15] Jacques de Vitry, 'Item sermo ad crucesignatos vel -signandos', *CPI*, p. 120.

[16] Jacques de Vitry, 'Item sermo ad crucesignatos vel -signandos', *CPI*, p. 122: 'Non accipiebatis consilium ab uxoribus eundi ad diabolum; quare expectatis consilium eundi ad Deum?'

[17] Jacques de Vitry, 'Item sermo ad crucesignatos vel -signandos', *CPI*, p. 122: 'diabolus per uxorem vel per seculares amicos bonum propositum frequenter extinguit'.

[18] Guibert de Tournai, 'Ad crucesignatos et crucesignandos sermo secundus', *CPI*, p. 196: 'Non accipiebatis consilium ab uxoribus, a parentibus eundi ad dyabolum?'

who disregarded the advice of the priests and disobeyed their mothers' and fathers' wishes.[19]

In their crusade model sermons Jacques and Guibert wanted to reduce the control of wives over their husbands and parents' control over their children. In 1201, Pope Innocent III had decreed in *Ex multa*, a decretal sent to the Archbishop of Canterbury, that men could take the cross without their wives' prior agreement.[20] This decision was objected to by many. The decree created a confrontation between two different vows, both of which were considered sacred by the Church: the marriage vow and the crusade vow. The canonists took the new decree with some reservations. The commentators appear to have been uncomfortable with the implications the law had on marital relations, morality, chastity, and parity between the husband and the wife.[21] Jacques and Guibert, however, regarded papal decision in this matter as correct. Both saw women as obstacles which had to be surpassed: the wives and the parents were considered as 'anti'-crusaders, who were forestalling or preventing the taking of the cross. Women in particular, in their opinion, were discouraging men from crusading, and hence their influence had to be reduced.

Women's negative impact on crusading is also described in the model sermons in another way. Wives, together with children, are portrayed as the underlying reasons for men staying at home rather than leaving.[22] In one of his crusade model sermons, Eudes de Châteauroux suggested that men did not

---

[19] Bacon, *Opus Majus*, ed. by Bridges, I, 401: 'Forsan vidistis aut audistis pro certo quod pueri de regno Franciae semel occurrebant in infinita multitudine post quendam malignum hominem, ita quod nec a patribus nec matribus nec amicis poterant detineri, et positi sunt in navibus et Saracenis venditi; et non sunt adhuc quatuor et sexaginta anni'; Thomas de Cantimpré, *Bonum Universale de Apibus*, ed. by Colvenerius, pp. 139–40. See also Dickson, *The Children's Crusade*.

[20] Brundage, 'The Crusader's Wife', esp. pp. 434–35; Innocentius III, *Regestorum sive Epistolarum*, CVIII, in *PL*, ccxv, 904–05.

[21] Thomas Aquinas disapproved the law on moral grounds; Thomas feared that this law might lead to the infidelity of the wife. Hostiensis found away to deal with the disparity of the decree by acknowledging that the wife might also take the crusade vow without her husband's consent. Brundage, 'The Crusader's Wife', pp. 437–38; Hostiensis, *Summa aurea*, Lib. III, p. 1132. Hostiensis nonetheless wanted to limit the participation of some women: the wealthy, mature women who could hire warriors could and should participate in the expeditions in person with or without their husbands' consent; young women or those of dubious reputation, however, should not be allowed to go on the expeditions at all.

[22] Jacques de Vitry, 'Sermo ad crucesignatos vel -signandos', *CPI*, p. 98; Eudes de Châteauroux, 'Sermo de invitatione ad crucem', *CPI*, p. 156; Guibert de Tournai, 'Ad crucesignatos et crucesignandos sermo tertius', *CPI*, p. 202.

THE CRUSADER AND THE WORLD

want to take the cross because they were reluctant to depart from their loved ones. Eudes invited his audience to reflect on what makes them happy and what makes them sad. The cardinal argued that men should not love women as much as they do, for women are 'bitterer than death'.[23]

Eudes attempted to explain to the crusaders or intending crusaders that women would not bring pleasure for the men, nor would the children. Eudes maintained in his sermon that the joy of children was often transformed into bitterness and many could lose their children with much pain.[24] In another sermon Eudes acknowledged that crusading was not easy, nor leaving the closest family behind painless. Crusading zeal was 'as arduous as hell' since it might seem that the crusaders did not care for their loved ones when they left their wives and sons behind for the sake of the Lord. But this was only because the crusaders' love for God was rightly superior to all other relations.[25]

The authors of the crusade model sermons did not try to dismiss the tribulations resulting from the separation of the crusaders from their wives or children, but attempted to soothe the path. The preachers appear sensitive to the feelings of the crusaders. Abandoning loved ones was difficult, but the crusaders were reminded of their obligations and of the future rewards: the harder the burden was for the crusader, the greater would also be the merit. In the end, affectionate feelings towards wives or children, which threatened to prevent crusading, could also be turned around and used for the benefit of the crusade preacher. In a passage of Jacques de Vitry's sermon, which Guibert also borrowed in his own, he cleverly emphasized the penitential nature of crusading and pointed out that if the fathers and husbands had perhaps sinned against

[23] Eudes de Châteauroux, 'Sermo de cruce et de invitatione ad crucem', *CPI*, p. 162: 'Et unde credunt repleri letitia et delectatione, replentur amaritudine et tristitia, teste Salomone qui dicit in Ecclesiaste: *Inveni amariorem morte mulierem*. Inter cetera maiorem delectationem reperit vir in muliere quam in vino vel cibo seu divitiis vel honoribus. Si ergo mulierem, que dulcissima reputatur, invenit amariorem morte, qua nichil est amarius, quid ergo de aliis?' Ecl. 7. 27.

[24] Eudes de Châteauroux, 'Sermo de cruce et de invitatione ad crucem', *CPI*, p. 162. With the quotation from Ruth, Eudes reminded his audience of a bitter woman who had lost her husband and both her sons and was made 'empty': 'Et gaudium de liberis sive de multitudine liberorum frequenter in amaritudinem conmutatur, et accidit eis quod legitur Ruth i: Nolite me vocare Noemy, quod est pulchra, sed vocate me Marath, quod est amara, quia amaritudine replevit me Omnipotens; egressa enim sum plena, et vacuam me reduxit Omnipotens. Sic multe liberos suos amittunt non sine magno dolore'. Ruth 1. 20–21.

[25] Eudes de Châteauroux, 'Sermo de invitatione ad crucem', *CPI*, p. 156: 'Dura ut infernus emulatio quia, sicut illi qui in inferno sunt non curant de caris suis, sic hii emulatione Dei accensi de caris suis curare non videntur, uxores et filios propter Dominum dimittentes'.

God by having too much affection for their wives and children, they could now do satisfaction by leaving them.[26]

Humbert de Romans also battled against the 'anti'-crusaders in his manual for crusade preachers. In *De predicatione sancte crucis* he devoted eight chapters to different things that might prevent people from taking the cross and provided arguments with which the 'anti'-crusaders' influence could be countered. Humbert's main method was to make unflattering comparisons with those reluctant to go crusading or those impeding the crusading of others, which the preachers could then use in their own sermons to disgrace the 'anti'-crusaders and refute their opinions. Those who did not take the cross were compared to 'ignoble dogs', or to the Jews who did not want to leave Babylon, as they preferred to stay put instead of going to Jerusalem.[27] Those who did not want to take the cross out of fear of physical pain could be compared to 'palfrey' horses that stayed in the stables to eat rather than going into battle, or to the 'oxen' that were meant to be slaughtered.[28] Those who loved their homelands and families so excessively that they refused to go on crusade could be compared to 'domestic chickens', to 'Flemish cows', or to 'the fish' that turned back once they reached the salty sea and were easily captured by fishermen.[29]

Humbert questioned the masculinity, the faith, and the intelligence of 'worldly friends'. He denounced the counsel they gave to others. Though these 'anti'-crusaders might appear to be friends when they advised people not to go on crusades, in reality they were the devil's *fuscinula*, the three-pronged spear that was used to prevent the salvation of people. In fact, worldly friends were the worst enemies anyone could have.[30] The 'anti'-crusaders' evil words and their bad example made people refuse to take the cross. In one of the formal invitations in the margins of the manual, Humbert reminded his audience how Christ had

---

[26] Jacques de Vitry, 'Ad peregrinos, thema sumpta ex epistola ad Galathas iii', *JVSP*, p. 91: 'Si peccavit nimio affectu ad uxorem ac filios satisfacit dimittendo eos'. Guibert de Tournai, 'Ad crucesignatos et crucesignandos sermo tertius', *CPI*, p. 204: 'Et si peccavit nimio affectu ad uxorem et filios, satisfacit dimittendo eos'.

[27] Humbert de Romans, *De predicatione sancte crucis*, cap. xviij, Contra illaqueationem peccati.

[28] Humbert de Romans, *De predicatione sancte crucis*, cap. xix, Contra nimium timorem pene corporalis.

[29] Humbert de Romans, *De predicatione sancte crucis*, cap. xx, Contra nimium dilectionem patrie que ad idem.

[30] Humbert de Romans, *De predicatione sancte crucis*, cap. xxi, Contra verba hominum mala que faciunt ad idem: 'Isti sunt fuscinule dyaboli cum quibus demones retrahunt homines a salute. isti etsi videantur amici hominis tamen sunt eius pessimi inimici'.

acted when he was rebuked by Peter, who did not want him to suffer and die, and how Christ had acted when he was ridiculed and humiliated before crucifixion. Christ did not listen to Peter's advice, but stayed firm, drove off Satan, and took his cross. Crusade preachers fighting against the influence of worldly friends, Humbert maintains, should use this in their sermons as a behavioural example to the prospective crusaders on how they ought to act when faced with ridicule and humiliation, or when given advice by false friends.[31]

According to Humbert, there were some Christians who did not believe in the theology of salvation or in eternal suffering. These people did not care about the plenary indulgence. These *increduli* were the worst of the 'anti'-crusaders, and thus the crusade preachers needed to fight against them with vigour.[32] The 'unbelievers' were particularly dangerous because they questioned Catholic doctrine. They did not want to take the cross for they did not believe in mortal sin and they did not need the crusade indulgence. These 'anti'-crusaders also called into question the foundations of the crusade movement and consequently challenged the relations between Christ and the crusader. The crusader's imitation of Christ's act of redemption and the attempt to gain the crusade indulgence by serving God were pointless activities if there was no mortal sin or need to earn plenary indulgences.

In his manual for crusade preaching, Humbert also acknowledged the negative impact that wives, children, or parents had on prospective crusaders.[33] He linked excessive affection for loved ones to original sin. Humbert provided a string of biblical quotations which the preachers could use to explain why and how the loved ones had to be abandoned. With the quotations from Matthew and Luke, 'He who loves his father or mother more than me is not worthy of me; he who loves his son or daughter more than me is not worthy of me', and 'If any man comes to me, and does not hate his father and mother, and wife and children, and brothers and sisters, cannot be my disciple', crusade preachers could convince their audiences of the need to leave behind those close to them when they became crusaders. Humbert also suggested that the preachers could use the legend of St Sebastian as an example of parental overprotectiveness. The parents of the martyrs Marcus and Marcellianus had attempted to persuade

[31] Humbert de Romans, *De predicatione sancte crucis*, cap. xxi. Mt. 16. 22–23.

[32] Humbert de Romans, *De predicatione sancte crucis*, cap. xxv, Multi retrahuntur a cruce propter defectum fidei.

[33] Humbert de Romans, *De predicatione sancte crucis*, cap. xxiij, Contra nimiam affectionem erga suos que ad idem facit: 'Quomodo inquiunt possem relinquere matrem meam. uxorem meam. liberos meos et similia'.

their children to renounce the Christian faith and save themselves from death during the reign of Diocletian, but St Sebastian convinced them to stay true to their Christian faith, and both Marcus and Marcellianus won the crown of martyrdom, despite their parents' initial opposition.[34]

The negative example of the 'anti'-crusaders gave added definition to the character of the 'true' *crucesignandi*. Those who were about to take the cross were different from those opposing the movement. They were not lazy or idle or selfish or envious, but they cared for God and for other Christians and they wanted to serve Christ, which is why they intended to take the cross. These 'true' Christians would not succumb to the same sins as the 'anti'-crusaders would. The 'anti'-crusaders' bad example and their bad advice were to be avoided. 'True' *crucesignandi* were determined to stay true to their intentions and would surmount the obstacles placed in their path by the 'anti'-crusaders. Those 'bonds that hold' them back — the spouses, the children, the parents, the siblings, the friends, and their advice and pleas — were to be disregarded once the intending crusaders expressed their commitment and took the cross. The 'true' Christians' love for God was greater than their love of temporal things.[35]

The Sin of Avarice

The authors of the sermons pressed for a comprehensive conversion of the participants of the movement. The demand for complete moral regeneration reflected the ideas of the pastoral reform movement, and for this reason the crusade model sermons have many similarities with other sermons preached by the Parisian moralists. Many specific sins of the participants, such as pride, avarice, and lust, were discussed and combated in the crusade sermons, just as they were combated in the sermons addressed to specific social groups by the reformers. The crusades developed into a more penitentially orientated movement during the thirteenth century, in which the sins of the participants were carefully rooted out by the preachers.

The sin of avarice was regarded as both a crusading obstacle that prevented people from joining the movement and an impediment that hampered 'true' crusading and could prevent those who had decided to take the cross from gaining salvation. According to Roger of Salisbury, in the devil's school, where the 'anti'-crusaders and the sinners studied, 'gluttony, avarice, and pride were

[34] Humbert de Romans, *De predicatione sancte crucis*, cap. xxiij. Mt. 10. 37, Lk. 14. 26.

[35] Jacques de Vitry, 'Ad peregrinos, thema sumpta ex epistola ad Galathas iii', *JVSP*, p. 91; Guibert de Tournai, 'Ad crucesignatos et crucesignandos sermo tertius', *CPI*, p. 202.

taught'.[36] These sins, particularly the sin of avarice, were repeatedly condemned in the crusade sermons. During the period greediness was often associated with social groups that owned properties and had assets and possessions, such as the nobility, the clergy, and bourgeois merchants.[37] Eudes de Châteauroux linked the townspeople closely to the sin of avarice in his crusade sermon against the Mongols.

Eudes criticized heavily the *burgenses* as a group of people. He acknowledged that all the Christian faithful were called upon to take the cross, but he made it quite clear that some were more eager to do so than others. In the sermon, Eudes developed an interesting dichotomy between the nobility and the townspeople. Eudes claims that the burghers 'deny Christ', when they refuse to join the Lord's army. Furthermore, they 'prey' on the inheritance of those who have taken the cross. The nobles, on the other hand, are depicted as ready to join the army in order to glorify and honour God, despite the fact that by doing so they endangered all that they had, including their lives.[38]

This specific denouncement of the townspeople may point to some particular circumstances in which the sermon was first preached. What these circumstances were is quite difficult to trace. The precise dating of the sermon is uncertain. It may have been preached at the beginning of the 1260s, when the Mongols posed a threat to Christendom. Another possible date would be around 1241, in the crisis following the Mongol invasion of eastern Europe.[39]

---

[36] Roger of Salisbury, '*Ascendente* Ihesu *in naviculam*', *PCHL*, p. 229: 'Habuit enim diabolus paucos in scola sua discipulos [...]. Tenuit enim diabolus scolam suam de gula [...]. Tenuit etiam de superbia [...]. Tenuit et de avaritia'.

[37] Le Goff, *L'Imaginaire médiéval*, p. 254; Hanska, '*And the Rich Man also died; and He was buried in Hell'*, p. 68–69.

[38] Eudes de Châteauroux, 'Sermo de invitatione ad crucem', *CPI*, p. 146: 'E contrario Christum negant qui nolunt venire in exercitu suo vel equitatione ut burgenses, immo intendunt ad exheredandum eos qui vadunt'.

[39] Christoph Maier has suggested the possibility of 1241 for the date of the sermon. *CPI*, p. 76. For the Mongol offensive of 1241, see Jackson, 'The Crusade against the Mongols (1241)'. Charansonnet has dated the sermon to 1260, to the second attack of the Mongols. Pope Alexander IV had ordered the cross to be preached against the Mongols in 1260 according to the register of Odo Rigaldus. *The Register of Eudes of Rouen*, trans. by Brown, ed. by O'Sullivan, p. 453; Maier, *Preaching the Crusades*, p. 85; *UEE*, ii, 379–80. For the Mongol invasion of the 1260s, see Jackson, *The Mongols and the West*, pp. 87–134, also the Mongol invasions of 1241–44, pp. 58–86; see also Jackson, 'The Crisis in the Holy Land in 1260'. Antti Ruotsala has also dated this crusade sermon of Eudes to 1241. Ruotsala has examined Eudes's *Sermo in concilio pro negotio tartarorum* and dated this sermon also to the years between 1241 and 1243. Ruotsala, *Europeans and Mongols in the Middle of the Thirteenth Century*, pp. 60–67. Jackson

The sermon may also reflect the complex situation with the Guelphs and Ghibellines in Italy during the thirteenth century. Many of the Italian cities were divided into imperial and papal camps in the struggle between the papacy and the empire. The *burgenses* may implicitly refer to the people of Rome, who in the late 1250s were wavering in their allegiance between the Guelph and the Ghibelline factions, forcing Pope Alexander IV to flee from the city to Viterbo.[40] Eudes, Cardinal of Tusculum and a member of the exiled curia, may be giving vent to his frustration with the disloyal citizens of Rome.[41] The juxtaposition created in the sermon between the nobility and the townspeople is noteworthy, for in other sermons Eudes encouraged and defended the participation of non-noble crusaders.[42]

In the sermon, Eudes wanted to compare and contrast the different social groups. The cardinal highlighted the gallant qualities of the nobles by deriding and mocking the townsfolk. Eudes calls the townspeople *feneratores*, usurers, who tried to profit financially from the sacrifices of others. He also insinuated that the burghers wished to take over authority from the nobles. Eudes assured his audience, however, that supremacy would always remain in the hands of the nobles, whether 'the usurers who devour them wish it or not'.[43] Eudes's use of the term 'usurer' in the sermon was particularly offensive. Usury was the sin of the Jews and a vice usually associated with Christian merchants, which was combated all through the thirteenth century by the churchmen.[44]

---

has dated the *Sermo in concilio pro negotio tartarorum* to the year 1261. Jackson, *The Mongols and the West*, p. 153 n. 12. Charansonnet, on the other hand, has dated this sermon to the beginning of the 1240s, like Ruotsala. *UEE*, I, 79–85.

[40] Runciman, *The Sicilian Vespers*, pp. 38, 51–56.

[41] If the sermon was preached in the early 1240s, the reference would most likely point to the townspeople of Paris, as Eudes de Châteauroux was then the chancellor of the University of Paris.

[42] See below, p. 268.

[43] Eudes de Châteauroux, 'Sermo de invitatione ad crucem', *CPI*, p. 148: 'quia dominium semper remanebit penes nobiles, velint nolint feneratores, qui eos devorarent'.

[44] The merchant's occupation was considered risky, potentially damaging for the merchants themselves and for others, by many contemporaries in thirteenth-century society. In previous centuries the merchant's profession was largely viewed as unpleasing to God. By the end of the twelfth century, through the moral reform initiated in the University of Paris, understanding and a certain amount of assent for the merchant's occupation had developed. Baldwin, *Masters, Princes and Merchants*, I, 261–311; Le Goff, *Marchands et banquiers du Moyen Âge*, pp. 70–98; Bolton, *'Paupertas Christi'*, esp. pp. 98–99. For the views of Guibert de Tournai, Humbert de Romans, and Jacques de Vitry, see Guibert de Tournai, 'Ad cives communiter viventes sermo',

Eudes's sermon seems also to reflect the social dislocation of the time, 'the commercial revolution' of the thirteenth century that resulted from growth of population, the economic boom of the West in both local and international markets, and the development of towns and urban cultures, all of which undermined the old structures of feudal society.[45] The noble and ecclesiastical lords' position at the head of communities was called into question and in some areas replaced by the new elite of rich merchants.[46] The Cardinal of Tusculum, a member of the old elite, wanted to reassure his audience of nobles that no matter what happened the nobility would always remain at the top of the hierarchy.

Eudes's crusade sermon represents the townspeople as reluctant Christians who did not want to join the crusade expeditions. The burghers were indifferent to the goals of the crusade movement and only interested in their own gain. Philippe le Chancelier's crusade sermon, although not nearly as harsh as Eudes's sermon, may also convey some criticism towards the townspeople. In one of his crusade sermons Philippe specifically mentioned the *cives* as a group of people who needed to take care of its obligations. Philippe viewed it as the duty of the townspeople to perform military service for their king, Louis VIII. He reminded the townspeople that they had certain responsibilities towards their lord, taxes and military aid, just as the clergy had duties towards their lord, God, in the form of prayers.[47]

---

transcribed by d'Avray, *The Preaching of the Friars*, pp. 260–71, esp. p. 260: 'Aurum enim et argentum nec bonos nec malos faciunt, sed usus eorum bonus est, abusio mala'; Guibert de Tournai, Troyes, MS 1504, fols 195ra–212rb; Humbert de Romans, 'De Modo prompte cudendi', LXXII–LXXVI, LXXVIII–LXXIX, XCVI, pp. 491–95, p. 504; Jacques de Vitry, 'Sermo ad mercatores et campsores', Paris, BnF, MS lat. 17509, fols 114vb–116vb, 116vb–118vb, 118vb–120rb, 120rb–122rb.

[45] For the development of medieval economics and the roots of the commercial revolution, see Lopez, *The Commercial Revolution of the Middle Ages*.

[46] Wood, *Medieval Economic Thought*, esp. pp. 5–6, 26–36.

[47] Philippe le Chancelier, 'Sermo in die veneris infra octabas Assumptionis beate Virginis', Avranches, MS 132, fol. 244vb. In the sermon, Philippe presumably referred to the townspeople of Paris, who should have been a force in the king's army, which had encountered some difficulties in the crusade against the Albigensians and was at the time besieging Avignon. He pointed out that the townspeople should pay what they were supposed to pay and that it was dangerous to keep the revenues to themselves. Philippe's discussion suggests that he believed the townspeople could do much more for their king and that the burghers were reluctant to finance the crusade. Philippe le Chancelier, 'Sermo in die veneris infra octabas Assumptionis beate Virginis', Avranches, MS 132, fol. 244vb: 'Cives vim suam debent regi suo, solvunt census suos et redditus, unde Lk. ii dicitur: Ibant ut profite*rentur* unusquisque *in sua civitatem*, debent miliciam et exer-

In Roger of Salisbury's crusade sermon advice is given simultaneously to both the crusaders and the bourgeois merchants. Roger utilized a nautical theme in his model sermon. This may have been first preached to an audience of townsfolk, some of whom had already taken the cross and awaited embarkation on a ship.[48] Roger gave moral guidance to his audience and encouraged the Christians to do penitence for their sins. While explaining Judas's 'sale and betrayal of Christ', Roger stated that in 'a moral sense all dishonest dealers who commit perjury in order to increase the value of their merchandise, sell Christ'.[49] Among Roger's audience there may have been English merchants who had also taken the cross or whose ships were about to carry the crusaders from England to the crusade. Roger wanted to direct his audience to proper penitence and at the same time instruct the merchants about the ethics of trade. Mercantile deceitfulness and greediness were vices which had to be renounced by the crusaders, those intending to take the cross, but also by the penitent townspeople who would stay at home.

The merchants were a particularly problematic social group from the viewpoint of the crusade propagandists. The merchants' tendency to seek profit and their willingness to enter into trade relations with the enemy were condemned by many contemporaries. This problem appeared serious enough for Pope Innocent III to include a verdict against the merchants' conduct in the constitutions of the Fourth Lateran Council in 1215. Canon number 71 of the council, called *Ad liberandam*, which dealt with the liberation of the Holy Land and made preparations for the coming expedition, stipulated that 'all the false and impious Christians', who were willing to sell arms, iron, wood, war engines, ships, or galleys, or give advice to the Saracens, would be excommunicated and anathematized, they would lose their possessions, and might be taken as slaves by those who captured them.[50] The maritime cities of the West, most notably the Italian

---

citum et hoc est iusticia que reddit unicuique quod suum est. Censum nostrum reddimus dum precepta Dei implemus, dum horas debitas solvimus'. Transcribed by Maier and Bériou. See also Maier, 'Crisis, Liturgy and the Crusade', p. 653.

[48] *PCHL*, p. 168.

[49] Roger of Salisbury, '*Ascendente* Ihesu *in naviculam*', *PCHL*, p. 228: 'Moraliter autem vendunt Christum omnes falsi negotiatores qui plus honerant merces periurio quam precio'.

[50] *COD, Ad liberandam*, p. 246: 'Excommunicamus praeterea et anathematizamus illos falsos et impios christianos, qui contra ipsum Christum et populum christianum Saracenis arma, ferrum et lignamina deferunt galearum; eos etiam qui galeas eis vendunt vel naves, quique in piraticis Saracenorum navibus curam gubernationis exercent vel in machinis aut quibuslibet aliis aliquod eis impendunt consilium vel auxilium in dispendium Terrae sanctae, ipsarum rerum suarum privatione mulctari, et capientium servos fore censemus'.

city-states — Venice, Genoa, and Pisa — had developed trade relations with the Muslim enemies during the crusading period.[51] The canon of the council specifically mentioned that the sentence — the decision about the embargo and the punishment of transgressors — would have to be repeated publicly in all the maritime cities on every Sunday and each feast day thereafter.[52]

The attitude shown by the Venetian, Genoese, and Pisan merchants during the crusades appears to have left those crusade preachers who participated in the expeditions themselves unconvinced. Jacques de Vitry stated in his history that the people from Italian cities could have been 'formidable' to the enemy, but they would not cease fighting against each other, because of their 'envy and insatiable avarice', and the merchants cared more about their commercial benefits than the business of the cross.[53]

Eudes de Châteauroux's letter to Pope Innocent IV of 1249 also voiced the concerns felt by many in the West of the troubles caused by the rivalries of the Italian republics in the Holy Land.[54] Eudes mentioned that a dangerous state of affairs had recently developed in the East: a skirmish between the Genoese and the Pisans had occurred, and a Genoese consul had been killed in Acre. Eudes also complained in the letter that Louis IX's agents could not persuade the Genoese and the Venetians to put a reasonable fee on the use of their vessels. The French king wanted to rent their galleys to transport parts of the army of the Seventh Crusade from Cyprus, but the Venetians and the Genoese merchants appeared unconcerned if the whole expedition was ruined because their excessive payment demands for transportation were not met.[55]

---

[51] France, *The Crusades and the Expansion of Catholic Christendom*, p. 119.

[52] *COD*, *Ad liberandam*, p. 246: 'Praecipientes ut per omnes urbes maritimas diebus dominicis et festivis huiusmodi sententia innovetur'.

[53] Jacques de Vitry, *Historia orientalis*, LXXIV, ed. by Donnadieu, p. 294: 'valde formidabiles existerent Saracenis, si cessante invidia et insatiabili avaritia, pugnas et immortales discordias inter se non haberent. Quoniam autem frequentius et libentius contra se invicem, quam contra perfidam paganorum gentem preliantur, negotiationibus vero et mercimoniis plusquam Christi preliis implicantur, letificant et securos reddunt inimicos nostros, qui parentes eorum viros pugnaces et strenuos quondam maxime formidabant'.

[54] Eudes de Châteauroux, 'Odonis Episcopi Tusculani ad Innocentium IV. Papam', ed. by d'Achéry, p. 627. The perpetual quarrels between the Italian republics, which hindered the crusading efforts, were condemned by many crusade ideologists. See Jacques de Vitry, *Historia orientalis*, LXXIV, ed. by Donnadieu, p. 294; Dubois, *De recuperatione Terre Sancte*, ed. and trans. by Brandt, p. 78.

[55] Eudes de Châteauroux, 'Odonis Episcopi Tusculani ad Innocentium IV. Papam', ed. by d'Achéry, p. 627: 'cum nuntii Regis venissent in Acon pro conducendis vasis, nulla ratione flect-

Federico Visconti's sermons make particularly interesting source material when viewing the crusade preachers' attitudes towards townspeople or merchants. Federico was a great patriot of the city of Pisa, fighting for the Pisan cause when necessary and extending its rights beyond the city walls.[56] In neither of his crusade sermons, however, does Federico touch upon the controversial issue of trade and commerce with the enemy or refer to the vices of the merchants.[57] In a sermon given during the feast of St Andrew, Federico did nevertheless speak out against the actions of the Pisan merchants, stating that the Pisans used to be better Catholics who did not traffic arms to the Saracens, but now 'all from the least to the greatest' had become greedy for gain and the city had been disgraced.[58]

Federico's two crusade sermons were given to strictly ecclesiastical audiences. The sermons explain crusading, encourage clerical participation, and give out information about the crusades, which the ecclesiastics could pass forward to the laity or use in their own crusade preaching. However, there were no lay members among the audiences of these sermons, and therefore little point

ere potuerunt Januenses et Venetos ad hoc, ut rationale pretium ponere vellent in vasis suis; sed potius videbant ad hoc tendere, ut negotium destrueretur, vel quod eis naulum daretur secundum voluntatem suam'.

[56] See, for example, Federico Visconti's endeavours to restore Pisa's authority over the island of Sardinia, in Christiani, 'L'arcivescovo Federico Visconti, Pisa e la Sardegna'.

[57] The merchants' tendency to seek profit and their willingness to enter into trade relations with the Muslim enemy were condemned by many contemporaries. Magister Thadeus from Naples, who wrote the *Ystoria de desolatione et conculcatione civitatis Acconensis et tocius terre sancte*, gives a fine example in his history of the grudge which some contemporaries held against the merchants. Thadeus accused the merchants of deserting the Christian cause: they persistently provided the enemy with everything they needed, unwilling to enforce a commercial blockade, and so the city of Acre and the Holy Land were lost to the enemy in 1291. According to Thadeus even the Muslims despised the Christian merchants. If the merchants complained about maltreatment and claimed that they would not return anymore, the Muslims simply replied that even if they would tear out an eye from a Christian merchant, he would still come back with his remaining eye. 'Inter quas enormes iniurias, quas ibidem ipsi falsi Christiani recipiunt, cum de aliquibus gravaminibus conquerantur et dicant insuper conquerendo se ad eos cum mercimoniis nunquam de cetero reversuros, hac responsione ipsorum querimoniam Sarraceni confundant: Si erueremus vobis alterum oculorum, ad nos cum reliquo rediretis!': Magister Thadeus, *Ystoria de desolatione*, ed. by Huygens, p. 134.

[58] Federico Visconti, 'Sermo quem idem dominus fecit festo sancti Andree ad populum', *SVP*, p. 939: 'deferendo arma ad Saracenos contra excommunicationis sententiam, quod est toti civitati nostre ignominiosum cum consueverint mercatores Pisani homines catholici reputari per mundum, [...] *a minore usque ad maiorem omnes avaritie student et a propheta usque ad sacerdotes omnes faciunt dolum*'. Jer. 6. 13.

in reprehending the merchants about their conduct. The sermon for the feast of St Andrew was given to the people of Pisa, of whom many were merchants. In the sermon Federico did condemn the various sins of the Pisans: lust, pride, and avarice. This occasion was appropriate to guide the Pisan merchants away from the sin of covetousness, to instruct them to follow the papal ban on the export of arms to the Muslims, and generally to make them better Christians.

Earthly Wealth

There were different kinds of *crucesignati*, whose participation in the crusades was dissimilar in many ways from the start: in the taking of the cross, in the making of preparations, and particularly in the funding of the journey. There were the noble crusaders who became the leaders of the expeditions, and who had to finance their own participation as well as the participation of a number of fighting men. The costs of crusading varied for noble crusaders in accordance with their status. The higher nobility led armies on the campaigns and had to finance the participation of large groups of crusaders. These *crucesignati*, who were of great importance for the movement, were nonetheless a minority on the expeditions.

There were also *crucesignati* who had assumed the cross with the intention of sending a substitute to participate in their place on the actual expeditions, and *crucesignati* who had taken the cross with the intention of redeeming their vows with money afterwards. The majority of the *crucesignati* were a third group of people: fighting men whose participation was partly financed by others, for instance by the crusading nobles, the Church, and non-combatant supporters who stayed at home. In principle, all the crusaders had to make good their own vows themselves, and they were individually responsible for the costs of their journey. However, in practice many crusaders were supported by their superiors, during the thirteenth century.

The financial burdens of an individual crusader were difficult to meet: the knight had to have his servants and his horse, arms, armour, and other equipment. The crusaders' transportation across the sea or along the land route had to be funded, which involved taking into account the cost of living abroad. Lastly, the livelihood of the family left behind had to be taken care of. The exact costs of crusading are difficult to assess. The rank of the crusader, the destination, and the length of the expedition had an effect on the costs. According to the varying estimates of modern scholars, a crusade might cost a crusader anything from two to four times his annual income.[59]

[59] Riley-Smith, *The Crusades: A History*, p. 20; Riley-Smith, 'Early Crusaders to the East

Many of the privileges granted for the crusaders were meant to alleviate these huge expenses of crusading. The crusaders were in desperate need of help to finance their journey. The privilege to sell or mortgage properties and lands, even fiefs, helped crusaders to raise funds, and in addition crusaders had the privilege of exemption from tolls and taxes. Ecclesiastical crusaders had the privilege of enjoying full income while away from their benefice.[60] The most important financial privilege of the crusaders during the thirteenth century was the granting of ecclesiastical subsidies.

At the beginning of the thirteenth century, during the pontificate of Innocent III, a precise and detailed system of crusade taxation was developed. Servants of the Church were to pay taxes from their incomes, which were collected by papal collectors and paid either to those crusading magnates who were raising armies and making preparations for the campaigns, or sent directly to the Holy Land, or given to local crusaders so they could participate in the general passage ahead. These subsidies given by the Church to the crusaders were often heavily criticized by the clergy, but they were a vital element of the crusade movement during the thirteenth century and became a standard way of raising funds for the crusades after the pontificate of Innocent III.[61]

Philippe le Chancelier's crusade sermons preached during the Albigensian Crusade in 1226 deal most specifically with issues related to funding. Three of these sermons were preached to an audience of scholars from the University of Paris before Louis VIII's crusade against the southern heretics was launched. In the first sermon, Philippe mentions that there was a conflict between the clergy and the nobles at the time. This feud had arisen because of the French clergy's reluctance to finance the third crusade of Louis VIII against the Albigensians.[62]

Louis VIII had campaigned against the Albigensian heretics while still a prince, in 1215 and in 1219. After the failure of his second crusade in 1219, it

and the Costs of Crusading', esp. p. 246; Constable, *Crusaders and Crusading in the Twelfth Century*, p. 141.

[60] For the different temporal privileges of the cross, see Brundage, *Medieval Canon Law and the Crusader*, pp. 159–87.

[61] For the first pontifical letter, the *Graves orientalis terrae*, from the year 1199, stipulating a tax of a fortieth of ecclesiastical incomes to be paid, see Innocentius III, *Opera omnia*, in *PL*, ccxiv, cols 829–31. In the Fourth Lateran council in 1215, it was decreed that the members of the Church were to pay a twentieth of the ecclesiastical revenues for three years for the aid of the Holy Land, and the pope and the cardinals would pay a tenth. For the papal taxation policies of the thirteenth century, see Gottlob, *Die päpstlichen Kreuzzugs-steuern des 13. Jahrhunderts*.

[62] Philippe le Chancelier, 'Sermo scolaribus inter Epiphaniam et Purificationem', Avranches, MS 132, fol. 249ra. Maier, 'Crisis, Liturgy and the Crusade', pp. 642–43.

took some convincing from Pope Honorius III and his legate to persuade Louis
to lead yet another crusade against the heretics. The papal legate, Romano
Bonaventura of Sant' Angelo, also had difficulties convincing the French
clergy to support Louis's intended crusade and to provide financial aid for it.[63]
According to Roger of Wendover, the crusade of 1226 was very unpopular in
France, for Count Raymond VII of Toulouse had demonstrated at the council
of Bourges that he was a true Christian and wanted to end all hostilities. Roger
maintained that those who took the cross for Louis's crusade did this out of fear
of the king or to gain the favour of the papal legate.[64]

In his first sermon against the Albigensian heretics, Philippe le Chancelier
reprehended both parties involved in the financial conflict — the nobles and
the clergy — for, according to Philippe, those who ought to be fighting together
against the enemies of Christ were instead divided and in conflict with one
another. This disunity benefited only the common enemy, the heretics. Philippe
complained that the nobles and the clergy argued 'against one another in a dispute over temporal matters'.[65] Philippe reminded his audience of scholars that

[63] Louis VIII took the cross from the legate in January 1226 in Paris with several conditions: The king wanted to decide himself when to leave for the expedition and when to return.
This way he could avert the obligations of a crusader imposed by the papacy. Louis also wanted
the feudal overlordship of all the lands conquered from the heretics and a handsome subsidy
paid from ecclesiastical taxes — first, a twentieth of ecclesiastical revenues for ten years, then,
a tenth of ecclesiastical revenues of the French clergy for a further five years. For some of the
conditions, see *Layettes du trésor des chartes*, ed. by Teulet, no. 1743, cols 69–70: 'cum dominus
noster Ludovicus, rex Francie illustris, ad honorem Dei et ad exhortationem nostram; contra
Albigenses et inimicos fidei signum crucis de manu nostri legati suscepisset, ante receptionem
dixit et protestatus est quod ex ista crucis assumptione et tali voto emisso non vult nec inten-
dit obligari ad morandum in terra Albigesii nisi quantum sibi placuerit, nec ad revertendum
illuc cum inde redierit; et, quando placuerit ei de terra recedere, possit sine scrupulo consci-
entie, quantum ad Deum et Ecclesiam, redire; et heredes suos, si de eo contingeret humani-
tus, non vult, ex hac crucis assumptione et voto, aliquo modo teneri'. Maier, 'Crisis, Liturgy
and the Crusade', pp. 642–43; Rist, *Papacy and Crusading in Europe*, pp. 92–97; Strayer, *The
Albigensian Crusades*, p. 129.

[64] Roger of Wendover, *Flores Historiarum*, ed. by Coxe, IV, 124: 'Ad ejus quoque praedica-
tionem multitudo maxima praelatorum et laicorum crucis signaculum susceperunt, plus metu
regis Francorum vel favore legati, quam zelo justitiae'.

[65] Philippe le Chancelier, 'Sermo scolaribus inter Epiphaniam et Purificationem', Avranches,
MS 132, fol. 249ra: 'Set iste manus sese complodunt, quia magna parata est dissensio inter hos et
illos, nisi Deus avertat, modo incipiunt movere querele inter eos, que hactenus non fuerunt, et
qui solebant unanimiter pugnare contra hostes fidei pro fide: isti quasi manus gestans clipeum,
illi quasi manus gladio pugnans; modo sese collidunt et complodunt et hoc pro temporalibus'. Transcribed by Maier and Bériou.

the clergy ought not to be interested in issues related to mundane wealth: they should not be concerned with material goods, for this was in the interests of the devil and it would spoil the holy business, that is, the crusade against the heretics. The clergy should weep and hurry to the aid of Mother Church, as she was being persecuted by her enemies.[66]

In 1225 the legate Romano Bonaventura of Sant' Angelo and the French clergy held several meetings in Paris, Melun, and Bourges, and in January 1226 an agreement was finally made between the legate and the French bishops over the crusading subsidies.[67] The second and the third of Philippe le Chancelier's crusade sermons for the scholars were preached after this conflict had been resolved.[68] In the sermons, Philippe rejoiced over the agreement and explained why it was important to fight against the Albigensians. He also regarded the sins of Christians as an impediment to crusading success. The lack of spiritual values and the sins of the Christians had caused a severe crisis, which put both the true faith and the recovery of the Holy Land in danger.[69]

In his sermons, Philippe urged the clergy to combat and kill the heretics spiritually.[70] The clergy should have high morals and express piety and love through works of mercy. They should live their lives according to doctrine, for they were an example for the others to follow. The heretical beliefs of the

[66] Philippe le Chancelier, 'Sermo scolaribus inter Epiphaniam et Purificationem', Avranches, MS 132, fols 248va–249ra.

[67] The French clergy and the legate also reached an agreement in Paris in January 1226, before the king officially took the cross. See the copy of the legate's letter to the French clergy — sent by the Archbishop of Rouen to the Bishop of Avranches in February 1226 — where the issues over financial subsidies and the king's decision to take the cross are discussed, the excommunication of Raymond of Toulouse mentioned, and the crusade preaching authorized, in *Thesaurus novus anecdotorum*, ed. by Martène and Durand, cols 931–33; Maier, 'Crisis, Liturgy and the Crusade', pp. 642–43.

[68] The rubrics of the third sermon in the Troyes manuscript, for example, attest that the reconciliation had been achieved. Maier, 'Crisis, Liturgy and the Crusade', pp. 643–45. Roger of Wendover gives an elaborate account of the council held at Bourges in November 1225, siding against the papal legate and his schemes. Roger of Wendover, *Flores Historiarum*, ed. by Coxe, IV, 118–23. Matthew Paris also reports the affairs of the council in detail in his history, retelling much of the information given by Roger, but also giving additional information. Matthew Paris, *Chronica majora*, ed. by Luard, pp. 105–09.

[69] Philippe le Chancelier, 'Sermo scolaribus inter Epiphaniam et Purificationem', Avranches, MS 132, fol. 249rb.

[70] Philippe le Chancelier, 'Sermo de eodem, de gaudio quod rex et principes assumpserunt crucem', Avranches, MS 132, fol. 252ra: 'Inimici autem fidei, qui non credunt, spiritualiter interficiuntur'. Transcribed by Maier and Bériou.

Albigensians could be destroyed with examples of life lived in accordance with true faith. Philippe regarded prayer as one of the most important ways in which the clergy could participate in the movement, whereby they could both shield the crusaders and attack their enemies with the help of angels and saints. The prayers of the clergy should not be cursory or superficial. Both the crusaders and those supporting the movement at home ought to renounce the flesh and abandon all carnal pleasures. Their prayers needed to be made with deep devotion and with the bitterness of contrition. The clergy should prepare their souls for prayer, so they would express the right attitude, piety, and humility.[71]

In the sermon *Quando idem dominus predicavit [crucem] respondendo nuntiis Tartarorum in clero pisano*, Federico Visconti also reminded the Pisan clergy of their task in the movement. The clergy, together with the rest of the congregation, was responsible for the raising of funds for the planned expedition against the Mongols. According to Federico, the clergy were 'the other mountains', who had '*gold, not to store up, but to lay out*, at a time of a crisis'.[72] With these words of Ambrose of Milan, Federico made it clear that the clergy should not be greedy or stingy, but should share their wealth for the benefit of the common cause. The clergy should offer donations so that the fighting men might be sent to defend Christendom. This was their lot in the service of the cross. The clergy paying the crusading taxes should not care about their expenses, but instead worry about the salvation of their souls and take care that the rights of the Church were defended, Christians protected, and the will of God fulfilled.

Humbert de Romans also dealt with different questions related to funding in his *De predicatione sancte crucis*. According to Humbert, some claimed that they were unable to go on crusade expeditions because they did not have sufficient funds. However, these people often pretended to be poorer than they actually were. They did not lack money; they lacked faith. The same people would find funds for worldly things and earthly delights. Humbert gave out biblical examples in his manual that the preachers could use in their crusade sermons while explaining to such people the error of their ways. These hypo-

---

[71] Philippe le Chancelier, 'Sermo de eodem, de gaudio quod rex et principes assumpserunt crucem', Avranches, MS 132, fols 251vb–252rb. Maier, 'Crisis, Liturgy and the Crusade', p. 649.

[72] Federico Visconti, 'Quando idem dominus predicavit [crucem] respondendo nuntiis Tartarorum in clero pisano', *SVP*, p. 554: 'Item alii sunt montes, idest alti divitiis, qui similiter debent exire, ut bona sua distribuant propter defensionem et recuperationem Terre sancte [...]. Et exponimus hoc duobus modis. Primo "Ecclesia" idest ecclesiastici viri, secundo "Ecclesia" idest congregatio fidelium, "aurum habet non ut servet, sed ut eroget", tempore silicet talis necessitatis quo debent esse omnia communia [...] ad mittendum balistarios ultra mare vel militem vel peditem'. For the quotation of Ambrose of Milan, *De officiis ministrorum*, II, 28, in *PL*, XVI, col. 140.

crites were not like David and his people, who gave gold and silver to build a house of the Lord, understanding that all that they had was from God, but they were like the prodigal son, who wasted his inheritance, or like Esau, who sold his birthright. Humbert advised the crusade preachers to encourage people to leave behind their worldly affairs.[73]

Life without Riches

The crusade preachers advised the *crucesignandi* to give up everything and live for Christ.[74] The message of the preachers to abandon earthly wealth was similar to those that appeared in anti-usury preaching and was also expressed by the Paris reformers in many different kinds of treatises written at the beginning of the thirteenth century. The Parisian theologians called for a conversion and a change of ways, an adaptation to a life without riches and without sin, and the voluntary adoption of poverty and an apostolic life that would lead to salvation.[75] The Paris-educated crusade preachers incorporated these ideals into their crusade model sermons. According to the authors of the crusade sermons the *crucesignandi* ought not to concern themselves with questions of material wealth. They should be prepared to sell their property in order to meet the costs of crusading.

Eudes de Châteauroux briefly discussed the voluntary poverty of the crusaders in a sermon he preached during the Seventh Crusade, possibly in 1249, in Egypt after the capture of Damietta. In the sermon, delivered during the feast of the Holy Relics, Eudes reminded his audience of crusaders of their sacrifice, how they had rightly abandoned their loved ones and sold their properties so they could serve Christ.[76] God had rewarded the crusaders because of their sac-

[73] Humbert de Romans, *De predicatione sancte crucis*, cap. xxiiij, Contra impotentiam fictam que idem facit. 1 Par. 29. 2. Lk. 15. 11–14. Gen. 25. 30–33.

[74] Eudes de Châteauroux, 'Sermo in conversione sancti Pauli et exhortatio ad assumendam crucem', *CPI*, p. 134: 'Sic ergo, ut dictum est, debemus non tantummodo diligere Deum, immo amore eius ardere et inflammari. Si enim eum diligeremus, tunc omnia delinqueremus corde nichil diligendo nisi propter ipsum vel in ipso, et si arderemus eius amore, tunc etiam omnino omnia abdicaremus sicut Paulus'. Jacques de Vitry, 'Sermo ad crucesignatos vel -signandos', *CPI*, p. 98; Guibert de Tournai, 'Ad crucesignatos et crucesignandos sermo tertius', *CPI*, p. 202.

[75] Bird, 'Reform or Crusade?', pp. 172–74. For the treatises against usury of the Paris reformers, see, for example, Robert de Courçon, *De usura*, ed. by Lefévre.

[76] Eudes de Châteauroux, 'Sermo in festo sanctarum reliquiarum', *UEE*, II, 745: 'Vos etiam qui cruce assumpta uxores et filios reliquistis, predia uestra amantissima distraxistis, et periculo mortis uos exposuistis, uere iuxta consilium apostoli, uos qui uidebamini esse sapientes facti

rifice, and their enemies had lost an important stronghold in Egypt. Thus, the great expenses of crusading should not hamper anyone in taking the cross, as properties could be sold and estates mortgaged. The expenses were irrelevant for the 'true' crusaders.

Despite these ideals, many crusaders struggled to raise funds for their journey and had to borrow money. The crusaders who were short of funds borrowed money from Jewish or Italian bankers.[77] However, during the thirteenth century, by papal decree there was a ban on interest charged on loans made to the *crucesignati* and a moratorium on debts. This made the bankers unwilling to lend money to the crusaders. There appear to have been deals made between the creditors and the *crucesignati* in which the crusaders swore that they would pay interest in spite of the privilege granted to them, if they could get a loan. This arrangement was also made void by papal decision: even if the crusader made an oath and promised to pay interest to the creditor, he was freed from the oath and interest should not be charged. Christian creditors were threatened with excommunication if they tried to force the crusaders to pay their debts before the moratorium had expired, or charge the crusaders with interest on their loans. If the Jewish creditors did not respect the privileges of the

---

stulti estis ut sitis sapientes'. In another crusade sermon, Eudes made a similar mark and noted that the crusaders had 'used up their belongings' as they took the cross. Eudes de Châteauroux, 'Sermo ad invitandum ad crucem', *CPI*, pp. 170–71.

[77] Christians were forbidden to charge interest on loans during the Middle Ages and moneylending was mainly conducted by Jews. Jewish bankers and the Jewish communities in general were forced to support the crusade movement. Many royal crusaders counted on the financial aid provided by 'their Jews' in the funding of the campaigns; protection money was extorted from the Jews, their possessions were confiscated, and the money that they had earned through moneylending was seized by the crusaders in order to finance the expeditions. The practice of seizing the profits of Jewish moneylending was known as *captio*. The money Jews had gained by giving loans for which they charged interest was considered the wages of sin, for usury was a sin. The confiscation of Jewish goods therefore included an element of retribution. Louis IX, for example, utilized the practice of *captio* while preparing for both of his crusades. For the anti-usury campaigns of Louis IX, see Jordan, *The French Monarchy and the Jews*, pp. 129–46; Lower, 'Louis IX, Charles of Anjou, and the Tunis Crusade of 1270', esp. pp. 186–87. See also Chazan, *Medieval Jewry in Northern France*, pp. 103–47. For medieval attitudes towards usury, see, for example, Wood, *Medieval Economic Thought*, pp. 159–205. For the Jews and the crusades, see, for example, Chazan, *European Jewry and the First Crusade*. In a *reportatio* of a crusade sermon, preached in 1213–17, both the usurers and the princes who defended usury are condemned. These are depicted as 'eels from hell' and 'whales'. 'Habet etiam anguillas inferni, scilicet feneratores [...]. Habet cetos, scilicet principes, qui defendunt usurarios; hii non possunt capi'. Quoted in Bird, 'The Victorines, Peter the Chanter's Circle, and the Crusade', p. 27.

crusaders, all Christians were forbidden by ecclesiastical censure to have any communication with them.[78]

The Parisian theologian and crusading legate Robert of Courçon strongly condemned usury and in his anti-usury tract advised crusaders to go naked and follow the naked Christ rather than borrow money from the Jews or other usurers. The crusaders ought to try to find other ways to finance their journeys. However, Robert also acknowledged the difficulties that the crusaders might have and took into account the fact that they would be excommunicated if they did not fulfil their vows. Hence, if the crusaders could not find any other means to finance their journeys, they could ask the usurers for money, preferably without paying interest to them.[79]

The authors of the crusade sermons do not specifically discuss moneylending or the details of crusading costs in their sermons. Nevertheless, the preachers' message with regards to financial issues is clear and consistent. They take an ideological stance on the subject of finance. In general, crusade preachers considered financial issues of secondary importance. The authors of the model sermons emphasized that those who took the cross would be making a good deal: on one end of the scale the preachers placed *deniers*, *oboles*, and *mailles*, pennies and halfpennies, and on the other end celestial bliss and paradise. The *crucesignandi* had the easy task of deciding which were worth more.[80]

Jean de Joinville appears to have taken the ideals put forward by the crusade preachers seriously. Jean was against the borrowing of money and did

[78] Purcell, *Papal Crusading Policy*, p. 138; Brundage, *Medieval Canon Law and the Crusader*, p. 182. At times, the crusaders' loans created conflict between the creditors and the crusaders, which the papacy tried to control. In the 1230s, the financial privileges of the crusaders caused serious difficulties in the Kingdom of France. Gregory IX tried to balance between the crusaders' privileges and the rights of the Florentine merchants, who had complained to the pope of the difficulties in recovering their dues from the French crusaders. The deals between the merchants and the crusaders, in which the crusaders' privileges had been abandoned, were revoked by the pope. However, Gregory also took measures to force the ecclesiastical crusaders to pay their debts to the merchants, and after a three-year moratorium had expired he demanded that the French crusaders who had not yet paid their debts should do so within four months. Gregorius IX, *Reg.*, no. 2512, no. 2766, no. 3723, no. 3882, no. 4180, no. 4198, no. 4264, in *Les Registres de Gregoire IX*, ed. by Auvray; Brundage, *Medieval Canon Law and the Crusader*, p. 182.

[79] Robert de Courçon, *De usura*, ed. by Lefévre, pp. 39–42, 77–79: 'Ergo peregrini potius nudi proficisci habent sequendo nudum Christum quam ditari ex fenore vel rapina'. Bird, 'Reform or Crusade?', p. 182.

[80] Jacques de Vitry, 'Item sermo ad crucesignatos vel -signandos', *CPI*, pp. 118–19; Guibert de Tournai, 'Ad crucesignatos et crucesignandos sermo tertius', *CPI*, pp. 208–09.

not attempt to confiscate any funds from the Jews. He did not want to take 'a penny' with him for the Seventh Crusade that was not his own. Thus the lord of Joinville decided to mortgage most of his lands before leaving. In the spirit of true repentance and self-denial, Jean raised the funds for the crusade from his own estates, so that when he left on the expedition he no longer held lands worth more than a thousand *livres*.[81]

Redemption of Vows with Money

Those crusaders who had taken the cross but were unable to leave or did not want to leave, and who had legitimate grounds for not going in person on the expeditions, could redeem their vows with money. This was also encouraged by the papacy during the thirteenth century, particularly in the case of non-combatant crusaders, who were considered poorly suited for military campaigns and for fighting against the enemy.[82] With the funds gathered from the vow redemptions, other crusaders could be funded or material costs of crusading covered. The expenses of the crusaders who wanted to redeem their vows differed according to their intentions and their status. The wealthier crusaders had to redeem their vows with more money than the poorer ones.[83]

Jacques de Vitry discussed this dimension of crusading in one of his crusade model sermons, stating that the spouses and the children of the crusaders could also benefit from crusading. These groups, which were traditionally viewed as non-combatants, could also take the cross and become crusaders, as they could redeem their vows after being signed. The women and the children would gain benefits in accordance with their contribution.[84] By this, Jacques meant that these *crucesignati* could gain the crusade indulgence, if this was what they sought after and if they were willing to pay the amount that their status and their wealth obliged them to pay, or the *crucesignati* could, if they so wanted, pay a smaller amount of money and gain only partial indulgences.

In his *De predicatione sancte crucis* Humbert de Romans also acknowledged that in their sermons crusade preachers needed to address questions related to

---

[81] Jean de Joinville, *Vie de Saint Louis*, ed. by Monfrin, p. 56: 'Pour ce que je n'en vouloie porter nulz deniers a tort, je alé lessier a Mez en Lorreinne grant foison de ma terre en gage. Et sachiez que au jour que je parti de nostre païz pour aler en la Terre sainte, je ne tenoie pas mil livrees de terre, car ma dame ma mere vivoit encore'.

[82] See below, pp. 249–50, esp. pp. 230–31.

[83] *CPI*, p. 63.

[84] Jacques de Vitry, 'Item sermo ad crucesignatos vel -signandos', *CPI*, p. 112.

financial contributions made by non-combatants. Crusade preachers were to explain that the movement could be supported in ways other than participating in the expeditions in person. According to Humbert, people could offer their support by giving alms or by praying. He wanted the crusade preachers to make clear that the different ways of supporting the movement were all beneficial, although some of them were more meritorious than others: praying was good, financial support even better, and personal participation in the expeditions was the best way of all to bring help to the Holy Land.[85]

The size of the indulgence was important, and this needed to be emphasized by the crusade preachers, as it would persuade people to give money for the crusade. Humbert also wanted crusade preachers to explain that the financial support which the Christians were willing to give for the Holy Land was more important than the alms that they were prepared to give for other kinds of charity. For example, although offering alms to help the infirm or the leprous was good, it was far more important and more meritorious to send help to the Holy Land with alms. This was spiritual charity, whereas the other kind of charity was corporeal, aiming to help those suffering physically in this world. The charity given for the Holy Land had the purpose of helping the whole of Christendom, and because it defended the faith and aimed to save souls it was spiritual in nature.[86]

Many of the authors of the model sermons do not discuss the vow redemptions at all in their crusade sermons. They may have wanted to avoid these complicated matters because of the crusade preachers' ill repute as promoters of vow redemptions and collectors of crusading funds. The focus on money in the model sermons might have created a credibility gap, which some of the preachers at least appear to have recognized. In the 1274 *Collectio de scandalis ecclesiae*, Guibert de Tournai expressed his suspicions about the advantages that the vow redemptions brought to the movement. Guibert stated that the crusade preachers were abused when they talked about all of the different confusing arrangements, the promised benefits, and the money collections of the day. According to Guibert, it was uncertain whether people would take the cross, but it was certain that the preachers would be insulted.[87] In his *Historia occiden-*

[85] Humbert de Romans, *De predicatione sancte crucis*, cap. iii, De triplici suffragio fiendo terre sancte.

[86] Humbert de Romans, *De predicatione sancte crucis*, cap. iii; *PCHL*, pp. 204–05.

[87] Guibert de Tournai, *Collectio de scandalis ecclesiae*, VI, ed. by Stroick, p. 40: 'Revolutum est hoc scandalum in capita praedicantium, qui si denuo crucis indulgentiam predicarent, certum [non] est, quod proficerent, sed certum est, quod varias contumelias sustinerent'.

talis, Jacques de Vitry gives a cautionary example of what happened to a crusade preacher named Pierre de Roissy, who promoted the Fourth Crusade. Pierre was popular in France until he made the error, 'for the reason of cupidity or some other sinister intent', of embezzling the crusade funds and alms entrusted to him. According to Jacques, Pierre de Roissy lost all his credibility after this, and his authority and influence as a crusade preacher quickly declined.[88]

Humbert de Romans also wanted the crusade preachers to be clear about what they promised. In the second part of his *De predicatione sancte crucis*, where Humbert offers a lot of advice to the crusade preachers and discussed their personal qualities and education, he maintained that a good knowledge of the movement was needed. The preachers should not be overenthusiastic, since then they might promise something that did not materialize. They should show discretion and not offer absolutions or dispensations that were not available, nor should they lie to people or deceive them. Crusade preachers needed to have a good knowledge and understanding of what was offered to the *crucesignati*, how the privileges and indulgences worked, and how these rewards could be gained, so that they would not make mistakes and would not mislead people.[89]

The Rich versus the Poor

The discussions on earthly wealth in the crusade sermons led to some interesting comparisons made between the poor and the rich participants of the movement. The participation of the poor was a disputed matter all through the crusading period. Crusade preachers were often accused of indifferently signing all sorts of people with the cross. In 1213, when Jacques de Vitry was preaching the cross, the crusade preachers had allegedly amassed a great army of non-combatants while preparing for the Fifth Crusade: 'children, old men, women, the lame, the blind, the deaf, and the leprous' had all been made cru-

---

[88] Jacques de Vitry, *Historia Occidentalis*, cap. VIII, ed. by Hinnebusch, p. 101: 'Sed et ipse ex fidelium elemosinis maximam cepit congregare pecuniam, quam pauperibus cruce signatis tam militibus quam aliis proposuerat erogare. Licet autem causa cupiditatis vel aliqua sinistra intentione collectas istas non faceret, occulto tamen dei iudicio ex tunc eius auctoritas et predicatio cepit valde diminui apud homines et, crescent pecunia, timor et reverential decrescebat'.

[89] Humbert de Romans, *De predicatione sancte crucis*, cap. xxviij, De necessarijs predicatoribus crucis; cap. xxix. De sex generibus scientie que sunt necessaria eisdem: 'Item scientia de his que eis committuntur cum officio predicationis ut bene intelligant et sane et virtutem indulgentiarum et priuilegia crucesignatorum et quam potestatem habent in absolutionibus et dispensationibus et similibus, ne per errorem faciant aliquid quod non licet'. See also *PCHL*, p. 213.

saders according to one chronicler.[90] In 1226, when Eudes de Châteauroux and Philippe le Chancelier were preaching the cross, similar accusations were made: the poor and the crippled, as well as an army of women and children, had taken the cross and intended to take part in the Albigensian Crusade.[91]

There is some ambiguity with the term *pauperes* in the context of crusade propaganda and ideology. Christopher Tyerman has argued that when crusade preachers or chroniclers use the term, the meaning of the word 'poor' varies and often it does not point to material wealth at all. Also, the term is used repeatedly in the crusade chronicles to refer to people recently impoverished, not to those belonging to the social group of poor, or the chronicles refer to people whose poverty was relative, for example to poor knights in contrast to noble or wealthy knights.[92]

---

[90] *Traduction des chroniques de Rigord et Guillaume le Breton*, ed. by Guizot, p. 320; Dickson, *The Children's Crusade*, p. 126.

[91] The papal legate Romano Bonaventura decided to dispense the vows of these crusaders. Romano's decision to leave the different groups of non-combatants at home has been interpreted as evidence of the decline of 'the older tradition'. This is the view that the crusade as 'a form of mass-pilgrimage' was no longer valid. Sumption, *The Albigensian Crusade*, p. 216; Rist, *Papacy and Crusading in Europe*, p. 91. Rist has argued that this was proof of the papacy's intentions to 'increasingly' encourage 'crusading as a specialized holy war waged by their [the papacy's] friends and supporters rather than as a mass movement of the Christian faithful'. However, similar attempts had already been made by the papacy of the twelfth century to control the participation of non-combatants in the expeditions. Urban II had placed restrictions on non-combatant involvement. According to Urban the participation of the old and the weak or women travelling by themselves would be 'an impediment rather than assistance' to the cause. Pope Paschal II also wanted to limit the participation of non-combatants and gave exemption from their crusade vows to poor crusaders in 1099, on grounds of their poverty. Robert the Monk, *Historia Iherosolimitana*, in *RHC Occ.*, III, 729: 'Et non praecipimus aut suademus ut senes aut imbecilles et usui armorum minime idonei hoc iter arripiant nec mulieres sine conjugibus suis, aut fratribus, aut legitimis testimoniis, ullatenus incedant. Tales enim magis sunt impedimento quam adjumento, plus oneri quam utilitati'. 'Epistula Paschalis II papae ad archiepiscopos et episcopos et abates Galliae', in *Kreuzzugsbriefe*, ed. by Hagenmeyer, pp. 174–75; Housley, *Fighting for the Cross*, p. 117.

[92] Tyerman, 'Who Went on Crusades to the Holy Land?', pp. 24–25. The concept of 'the poor' can be understood in a broad sense or a strict sense. In medieval society, the group of poor could include farmers, workers, and artisans, who earned small wages but were nonetheless very poor compared to the more wealthy members of society. The group of poor could also be defined more strictly, including only the paupers, who had no income whatever and lived mainly on charity. Hanska, *'And the Rich Man also died; and He was buried in Hell'*, pp. 12–13; Murray, 'Religion among the Poor in Thirteenth-Century France', pp. 291–95. In the context of the crusades 'the poor' is used in a wider sense of the word, since all those who had virtually no

The term *pauperes* is used in the crusade model sermons in many different ways. Guibert de Tournai, for example, compares the crusaders to the poor who can participate in a feast, just as the crusaders can proceed freely to paradise.[93] Humbert de Romans refers to those who have decided to take the cross as 'the poor' to whom the Mother Church has opened and extended her arms.[94] Eudes de Châteauroux used Christian poverty as a counterpoint to Saracen perfidy in his sermon against the Lucera Muslims. Eudes portrayed the Saracens as people obsessed with earthly things: the Lucerans desired mundane wealth and loved carnal pleasures, which they sought after with their dealings, depredations, and theft, whereas the Christians and the crusaders were of a better breed, who followed Christ's teachings, and they would inherit 'the kingdom of God', for blessed were the poor.[95]

Tyerman is thus quite correct in arguing that the term 'poor' should be viewed critically in the crusading context.[96] The term is often used as a literal device. Its purpose and meaning fluctuates in different sermons. The word does not always indicate the needy or the materially poor, but can refer to the Christians or to the crusaders as a whole. The term can be used in this way in the sermons in a positive sense, as the crusaders can be regarded as the *pauperes Christi*. They too suffered for Christ, as the poor or the sick or the weak do. The crusaders were spiritually reformed men. They were the disciples of

---

experience in warfare, no weapons of war, and little or no resources to make the crusade journey were considered to be the poor non-combatants by the medieval commentators who worried that they might use up all the supplies of the crusade army.

[93] Guibert de Tournai, 'Ad crucesignatos et crucesignandos sermo primus', *CPI*, p. 186: 'Sic enim pauperes in conviviis introducuntur cum signis, sicut Templarii libere sine pedagio procedunt, quando eorum vestimentis signum crucis ostendunt, sic vere crucesignati sine repulsa ingrediuntur ianuam paradisy'.

[94] Humbert de Romans, 'De predicatione crucis in genere quocumque', *CPI*, p. 220: 'Porro tempore crucis predicante cataracte celi aperte sunt in habundantia indulgentiarum, sancta mater ecclesia manus suas aperit et palmas suas extendit ad pauperes'.

[95] Eudes de Châteauroux, 'Sermo de rebellione Sarracenorum Lucherie', *CR*, p. 382: 'Dicitur enim quod aspis unam aurem affigit terre, alteram cauda obscurat, ne vocem incantantis audiat, sic dicti Sarraceni terrenis adherentes nolunt audire vocem Christi, qui dicit: *Beati pauperes quoniam vestrum est regnum* Dei, quia amor terrenorum in auribus cordium eorum clamat incessanter quod pauperes miseri sunt et viles et despecti. Dicit Christus: *Qui non abrenuntiat omnibus que possidet non potest meus esse discipulus*. Isti autem semper intenti fuerunt et progenitors divitias divitiis aggregare per mercimonia, per depredations et furta, ex quo apparet quod nolunt esse discipuli Ihesu Christi'. Mt. 5. 3, Lk. 14. 33.

[96] Tyerman, 'Who Went on Crusades to the Holy Land?', pp. 24–25.

Christ, who had renounced their earthly possessions and imitated the *paupertatis Christi*.

However, the authors of the crusade model sermons do also use the term 'poor' to refer to those who actually belonged to the social group of poor. The paupers are not simply dismissed in the sermons as a group that cannot contribute anything to the crusade movement. The most explicit account is provided by Eudes de Châteauroux in his crusade sermon given during the feast of St Paul. Eudes was involved in the promotion of a number of crusades throughout his career, and he may have encountered criticism of signing the poor crusaders himself or witnessed situations where the poor were prevented from taking the cross.[97]

In his crusade sermon for the feast of St Paul, Eudes de Châteauroux first connected the poor to the following of Christ and to the *vita apostolica* by quoting a biblical passage from John in which Peter jumped half naked into the water to reach Christ, whereupon the other disciples followed him in a boat. According to Eudes, the poor, after hearing about the reward they would receive by crusading, also jumped into the water, 'naked and poor'. The paupers were willing to take the heavy load of pilgrimage on their shoulders humbly, as it should be taken, while the rich were content to take advantage of their wealth.[98] The rich did not take on the burden of pilgrimage but alleviated their journey's discomforts with money. This was not the way a pilgrimage or a crusade ought to be made.

Following this, Eudes utilized another biblical story where Jonathan fought against the Philistines. Eudes reminded his audience that when Jonathan and his armour-bearer advanced to fight the Philistines they were mocked by the enemy. In the same way, 'the poor and the unarmed' were now ridiculed by the wise when they wanted to join the crusade armies.[99] These supposedly wise men blamed the poor and the non-combatants for draining all the supplies of the

[97] *CPI*, pp. 65–66.

[98] Eudes de Châteauroux, 'Sermo in conversione sancti Pauli et exhortatio ad assumendam crucem', *CPI*, p. 138: '*Symon autem Petrus, cum audisset quia Dominus est, tunica succinxit se, erat enim nudus, et misit se in mare; alii autem navigio venerunt*. Sic pauperes audientes, *quia Dominus* est quem habebunt in premium, si propter ipsum transierint hoc mare, licet nudi et pauperes, mittunt *se in mare*, id est subeunt onus istius peregrinationis. Divites vero *navigio veniunt* amminiculo divitiarum suarum subvecti'. John 21. 7–8.

[99] Eudes de Châteauroux, 'Sermo in conversione sancti Pauli et exhortatio ad assumendam crucem', *CPI*, p. 140: 'Philistei vero de Ionathan et armigero eius dixerunt: *En Hebrei egrediuntur de cavernis, in quibus absconditi fuerant*. Sic pauperes et inermes accipientes crucem a sapientibus deridentur'. 1 Reg. 14. 11.

crusade armies. But Eudes reminded them how much damage Jonathan was able to do, thus implying that the poor would also do damage to the enemies of the crusaders.[100] This was a clear message to those who criticized the personal participation of the non-combatants in the expeditions. In fact, as Eudes pointed out, the poor could be regarded as truer crusaders than the rich, for the poor went on the journeys in the right spirit, in the state of poverty in which they lived. The rich, on the other hand, were not prepared to follow in the footsteps of Christ, for although 'many want to follow him', they were not willing to go 'along the path which he walked'.[101]

In Eudes's crusade sermon, the participation of the poor develops into an antithesis of the participation of the rich. While defending the personal participation of the poor and the unarmed in the campaigns, Eudes states that the poor who wanted to join the expeditions would condemn to hell the rich who were disinclined to go on crusades.[102] Eudes continues and extends the social debate over poverty common in the *ad status* sermons to the crusade sermons.[103]

---

[100] Eudes de Châteauroux, 'Sermo in conversione sancti Pauli et exhortatio ad assumendam crucem', *CPI*, p. 140: 'Dicunt de eis: Isti vindicabunt forratum. Ionathas tamen et eius armiger fecerunt stragem magnam'. In his crusade sermon Guibert de Tournai also accused 'the wise of the world' of leading the rich away from the sign of the cross with their words and conflicting deeds. These wise people were perhaps the critics of the crusade movement who counselled the rich to invest their money elsewhere. Guibert de Tournai, 'Ad crucesignatos et crucesignandos sermo secundus', *CPI*, p. 194: 'Sapientes enim mundi huic signo et divites detrahunt verbo et contradicunt facto similes truncis veteribus, qui nichil aliud quam fumigare faciunt et accendi non possunt'.

[101] Eudes de Châteauroux, 'Sermo in conversione sancti Pauli et exhortatio ad assumendam crucem', *CPI*, p. 138: 'Multi volunt eum sequi, sed non per viam per quam ipse ambulavit'.

[102] Eudes de Châteauroux, 'Sermo in conversione sancti Pauli et exhortatio ad assumendam crucem', *CPI*, p. 140: 'Sic pauperes crucem accipientes et ad auxilium Domini properantes condempnabunt divites et magnates, qui hoc facere noluerunt'.

[103] During the thirteenth century there was a prolonged debate over issues of poverty and riches. Many of the authors of the crusade model sermons took part in this social debate. The Paris-educated reformers and the members of the mendicant orders were particularly involved. Jacques de Vitry, Guibert de Tournai, and Humbert de Romans commented on the subject in several of their *ad status* sermons. Jacques included two sermons that were specifically intended for the poor in his collection of sermons, 'Ad pauperes et afflictos'; see Troyes, MS 228, fols 141va–144vb. Guibert de Tournai included four sermons for the poor; see Assisi, MS 501, fols 109^v–117^r; Humbert de Romans composed one sermon: see Humbert de Romans, *De eruditione praedicatorum*, LXXXVI, 'Ad pauperes', ed. by de la Bigne, p. 499. Jacques de Vitry urged the poor to be patient, unwavering, and enduring in the test of faith, in the test of affliction. In his first sermon for the poor, Jacques quoted Sapientia from the Bible to explain that though the paupers were 'afflicted in few things', they would be 'rewarded in many'. The patient enduring

The rich failed to serve God, but the poor, despite their poverty, wanted to serve him, and because of their poverty served him in a correct way. Eudes was careful at this point of his sermon to use the term *peregrinatio*, rather than to speak in military terms, using words such as 'expedition' or 'service of Christ'.[104] The poor were entitled to participate in pilgrimages just as the rich were, or the rest of Christian society. The other terms would have carried more direct implications of the military activity of the crusaders, for which the unarmed poor were physically and materially less suited.

In the English crusading manual, the *Brevis ordinacio de predicacione sancte crucis*, the contrast between the rich and the poor was also utilized. In the section of the manual 'on the flesh and its delights', the author employed the imagery of fish and drew moral implications from their behaviour. According to the manual, the large fish were easily caught 'in the net of the devil', while the little fish went right through the net. The large fish were the rich, who fell to the temptations of the devil, but the little fish, who were the poor, would pass through the net and find God, 'the author of salvation'.[105] This comparison highlighted the medieval view that the poor were more likely to find salvation than the rich, who were seduced by the devil with all the delights of the world.

However, this was not just a question of comparing the two social groups in the sermon material. Eudes de Châteauroux also believed that the poor crusaders could contribute to the task at hand. He suggested that the poor noncombatants might lead people who 'held to the Saracens' — perhaps those who supported the Muslims or lived under their rule — away from the enemy, as Jonathan and his armour-bearer had led some of the Hebrews who were with

---

of afflictions would enable the poor to pluck the fruits of tribulations, that is, the eternal joys due to them: '*In paucis vexati in multis bene disponentur*'. Sap. 3. 5. Jacques de Vitry, 'Sermo ad pauperes et afflictos', Troyes, MS 228, fols 141va–143rb, esp. fol. 141va. In the model sermons, intended for the diverse groups of poor, the oppressed and the weak were often defended and their difficulties were sympathized with. The poor were guided to sustain the hardships in this life with dignity and embrace their poverty, for they would be rewarded in the afterlife. In the sermons, the rich were often regarded as the oppressors of the poor, and their future in the afterlife was the opposite to that of the paupers: they would suffer for all their sins in hell. It was also considered harder for the rich to be virtuous than it was for the poor.

[104] Eudes de Châteauroux, 'Sermo in conversione sancti Pauli et exhortatio ad assumendam crucem', *CPI*, p. 139.

[105] 'Brevis ordinacio de predicacione', *QBSS*, p. 17: '*Magni pisces non transeunt per medium rete, sed capti permanent, sic divites non pertranseunt rete diaboli, sed capti remanent in eo. Parvi vero pisces pertranseunt rete et effugiunt ad salutem, sic et pauperes pertranseunt temptaciones diaboli et veniunt ad crucem et sic ad Deum, qui est auctor salutis*'.

the Philistines back to Israel in biblical times.[106] With this comment Eudes may be referring to the diverse groups of Christians living among the Muslims in the East. The papacy of the thirteenth century paid some attention to the different Eastern churches. Innocent III, Honorius III, Gregory IX, and Innocent IV all attempted to extend papal authority over them.[107] The crusade ideologists of the thirteenth century also examined the Eastern-rite Christians, such as the Maronites, the Jacobites, and the Nestorians, and entertained the thought of their possible assistance in the fight against the Muslims.[108] Eudes may be suggesting in his crusade sermon that the presence of the poor among the crusade army could convince the rest of the Christians living with the Muslims, including the Eastern Christians, to abandon the enemy and join the crusaders, as the Hebrews had left the Philistines.

In a crusade sermon against the Albigensians, Eudes also stated that 'the Church, or rather the Lord himself, cries out to his sons' to avenge the wrongs done by the heretics. These sons were both the poor and the rich, and the poor even more so, for according to Eudes, the situation in the conflict against the Albigensians was just like the one where 'someone realizes his rich kinsmen failing him and so turns to his poor relatives'. Eudes underlined in the sermon that 'the Church called the poor to give assistance' in the fight against the heretics. The rich were 'nevertheless' also summoned, and so like good sons the poor and the rich could together fight against the wicked.[109]

---

[106] Eudes de Châteauroux, 'Sermo in conversione sancti Pauli et exhortatio ad assumendam crucem', *CPI*, p. 140: 'Dicitur etiam ibi quod *Hebrei, qui ab heri et nudius tertius cum Philistiim fuerant, ascenderunt cum eis in castris et reversi sunt, ut essent cum Israel.* Hoc fortasse accidet de hiis qui modo favent Sarracenis: quod ab eis recedent'. 1 Reg. 14. 21.

[107] Hamilton, *The Latin Church in the Crusader States*, pp. 332–60.

[108] Jacques de Vitry, *Historia orientalis*, LXXX, ed. by Donnadieu, p. 156. Jacques de Vitry made repeated comments about the valiant character of the Eastern-rite Christians in his history. Jacques de Vitry, *Historia orientalis*, LXXVII, ed. by Donnadieu, p. 149. Jacques also regarded himself as successful in converting the Eastern-rite Christians to Catholicism while on his preaching tour in Palestine. These 'heretics remaining in the eastern regions' would be 'easily converted' through missions, he states in one of his letters. After the conversion, the Eastern Christians could help the crusaders in the fight against the Muslims. Jacques de Vitry, *Epistola*, II, ed. by Huygens, pp. 96–97. In many crusading treatises of the thirteenth and fourteenth centuries, the military potential of Eastern Christian allies was taken into consideration. Bird, 'The *Historia Orientalis* of Jacques de Vitry', pp. 60–61; Leopold, *How to Recover the Holy Land*, pp. 16, 63, 117–19.

[109] Eudes de Châteauroux, 'Sermo contra hereticos de Albigensibus partibus', Arras, MS 876, fol. 89vb: 'Et ecclesia, immo ipse Dominus clamat ad filios suos, ut hanc iniuriam vindicent. Et

Eudes may have preached the sermon against the Albigensians in 1226 at the same time when Philippe le Chancelier preached his first sermon against the heretics, when there was a dispute over money and the French clergy was reluctant to finance the crusade. Or he may have preached the sermon first during the siege of Avignon, when the crusade army of Louis VIII had all sorts of difficulties, including problems with financing the campaign.[110] This would explain the failure of 'the rich relatives', the clergy and the nobles. In the sermon, Eudes promoted the use of intercessory means by which the help of the saints could be sought and the crusaders helped from the home front. The common people and the poor, who had not yet enlisted for the crusade, could participate in the movement by offering their aid with prayers, with alms, or by taking part in the processions. This would explain the emphasis on the participation of 'the poor relatives', who were now also summoned and whose easy 'long-distance support' was discussed by Eudes.

Jacques de Vitry also briefly discussed questions related to poverty and riches in his sermon intended for the pilgrims and crusaders. His approach was practical. Jacques reminded his audience that pilgrims and crusaders should not try to gather up and hoard earthly possessions. On the contrary, the rich ought to share their wealth and distribute their funds among the poor pilgrims, or the wealthy Christians could spend their money in the service of the Lord.[111] With this statement Jacques followed in the footsteps of Pope Urban II. Urban is reported to have encouraged the rich crusaders to aid the poor ones in the Clermont sermon in 1095.[112]

This demand for aid was transmitted from the pilgrimage tradition, in which rich pilgrims were supposed to help the poorer ones during the journeys, to crusade ideology. In the First Council of Lyons in 1245, this was again demanded of the rich and the powerful of the army.[113] Jacques de Vitry's comment may be

---

sicut fit, quando aliquis videt quod consanguinei sui divites ei deficiunt, convertit se ad consanguineos suos pauperes; sic facit Dominus, sic facit ecclesia: invocat pauperes ad auxilium suum contra predictos, convocat etiam nichilominus et divites ut omnes sicut boni filii communiter insurgant adversus malignantes, idest hereticos predictos'. Transcribed by Maier and Bériou.

[110] Maier, 'Crisis, Liturgy and the Crusade', p. 652.

[111] Jacques de Vitry, 'Ad peregrinos. Thema sumpta ex Zacharias ultimo', *JVSP*, p. 96: 'Qui autem divicias et temporales sarcinulas in domo sua congregat non se transmigraturum ostendit, sed qui bona sua pauperibus distribuit vel in Domini servitio expendit vel saltem pauperibus peregrinis et crucesignatis distribuit'.

[112] Robert the Monk, *Historia Iherosolimitana*, in *RHC Occ.*, III, 729: 'Divites in opibus subveniant, et expeditos ad bellum de suis facultatibus secum ducant'.

[113] *COD, Super cruciata*, p. 274: 'Nobiles quidem et potentes exercitus ac omnes divitiis

interpreted to mean the funding of the crusades from the home front or the distribution of funds during the campaigns. In the former case this would mean that the rich who did not personally wish to take part in the campaigns could participate in the movement through vow redemptions, and in the latter case poor crusaders ought to be supported by wealthy crusaders if they had run out of funds, so that they could fulfil their vows and continue the journey.[114]

Pilgrimage Through the Torrent of the World

The crusade movement derived from different Christian traditions, most significantly those of just and holy war and pilgrimage. Pope Urban II envisioned the First Crusade in 1095 as a penitential undertaking, a special pilgrimage that would take the participants on a journey to the Holy Land. During the Middle Ages, the crusade expeditions were often referred to as 'pilgrimages', 'journeys', or 'ways'. The crusaders regarded themselves as pilgrims and were often called pilgrims.[115] Many (though not all) of the authors of the crusade sermons discussed in this book use the words 'pilgrim' and 'pilgrimage' when referring to the crusaders or crusades.[116]

In crusade ideology there existed a concept of two cities — the earthly Jerusalem and the heavenly Jerusalem — to which the crusaders made their way. The Augustinian idea of two cities which were separate but were actually one was revised during the High Middle Ages, particularly by Cistercian writers. This revision created an important ideological link between pilgrim-

---

abundantes piis praelatorum monitis inducantur, ut intuitu crucifixi, pro quo crucis signaculum assumpserunt, ab expensis inutilibus et superfluis, sed ab illis praecipue, quae fiunt in commessationibus et conviviis, abstinentes, eas commutent in personarum illarum subsidium, per quas Dei negotium valeat properari et eis propter hoc iuxta praelatorum ipsorum providentiam peccatorum suorum indulgentia tribuatur'.

[114] *JVSP*, p. 85.

[115] Riley-Smith, *The First Crusade and the Idea of Crusading*, pp. 1, 19–24; Tyerman, *God's War*, pp. 58–89; Tyerman, *Fighting for Christendom*, p. 13.

[116] The preachers usually describe the participants with the term *crucesignati*. They also apply the terms 'expedition', 'passage', 'service', 'journey', and the 'business of faith or the cross' when referring to the crusades, or refer to them as a movement aiming to 'recover', 'liberate', or 'defend' the Holy Land. See, for example, Philippe le Chancelier, 'Sermo scolaribus inter Epiphaniam et Purificationem', Avranches, MS 132, fol. 250ra; Federico Visconti, 'Quando idem dominus predicavit [crucem] respondendo nuntiis Tartarorum in clero pisano', *SVP*, p. 552; Eudes de Châteauroux, 'De sancto Georgio', *UEE*, II, 700–703; *CPI*, p. 52.

age and crusade.[117] According to the idea of two cities, there was the Jerusalem where the historical Israelites had lived, where the great biblical kings David and Solomon had governed, and where Christ had suffered and died. This was the earthly Holy City, the destination of Christian pilgrims. The heavenly Jerusalem was the Holy City where the saints and angels lived, and where all good Christians would one day live as citizens of heaven.[118]

The crusaders travelled towards both of these cities. The crusaders were pilgrims who tried to liberate the Sepulchre of Christ, as well as the earthy Jerusalem and the Holy Land, cleanse the infidel filth there, and protect other Christian pilgrims who wanted to visit or help Christians who lived there. The heavenly Jerusalem was also their goal. The crusaders, like the rest of the Christians, made their pilgrimage in the world with the ultimate objective of living in the heavenly city. They were penitent pilgrims trying to cast off all their sins and so clear their way to the celestial Jerusalem. Their crusade was a spiritual, internal journey to the heavenly city. These ideas were influential in the crusade ideal from its beginnings.[119]

Jacques de Vitry and Eudes de Châteauroux both referred to the heavenly city in their crusade sermons. Jacques explained the significance of the sign of the cross to the crusaders and made it clear that no one could reach the celestial Jerusalem without the cross.[120] Eudes laid out the dimensions of the heavenly city in two of his crusade sermons, in the sermon for the Conversion of St Paul and the sermon for the feast of St George. Eudes connected these dimensions to the themes of love and charity in crusade ideology.[121] For both Jacques and Eudes, the Roman Church was the Church Militant, *ecclesia militans*, a church on a pilgrimage, and its active members were the crusader pilgrims struggling in the world, fighting against the devil and earthly sins. The Church itself had to travel 'through the torrent of this world' to the celestial kingdom.[122]

---

[117] See, for example, Morris, *Sepulchre of Christ and the Medieval West*, p. 276.

[118] Schein, *Gateway to the Heavenly City*, pp. 1–5.

[119] Riley-Smith, *The First Crusade and the Idea of Crusading*, p. 119.

[120] Jacques de Vitry, 'Item sermo ad crucesignatos vel -signandos', *CPI*, p. 106: 'ita et vos sine cruce mare huius seculi non potestis transire nec ad supernam Ierusalem pervenire'.

[121] Eudes de Châteauroux, 'Sermo in conversione sancti Pauli et exhortatio ad assumendam crucem', *CPI*, p. 134; Eudes de Châteauroux, 'De sancto Georgio', *UEE*, ii, 705. Apc. 21. 16.

[122] Jacques de Vitry, 'Item sermo ad crucesignatos vel -signandos', *CPI*, p. 106: 'sic ecclesia in ligno crucis torrentem hius mundi pertransiens transfertur in regnum celorum'. For the Church Militant, see Morris, *Sepulchre of Christ and the Medieval West*, p. 276.

Recently, there has been some scholarly debate about the significance of the pilgrimage theme in the crusade ideology of the thirteenth century. In his study on the crusade model sermons, Christoph Maier noticed that the crusaders were more often called *crucesignati* than pilgrims. In the model sermons studied by Maier, only Humbert de Romans and Guibert de Tournai used the term 'pilgrim', Guibert only once.[123] Caroline Smith has interpreted Maier's analysis of the sermon material to mean that 'the crusading realities' of the thirteenth century had made an impact on the sermons and that there was a shift away from 'the use of the idea of pilgrimage to describe the nature of crusades'.[124] It is true that in the model sermons examined by Maier use of the terms 'pilgrim' and 'pilgrimage' is less frequent than that of the terms 'signed with the cross' or 'service', but the term 'pilgrimage' is nevertheless used at least once in seven of the seventeen sermons, as Maier points out.[125]

Caroline Smith has viewed the striking lack of reference to pilgrimage and pilgrims in the sermons of Jacques de Vitry as evidence of the mental shift in crusade ideology.[126] However, by including other crusade model sermons from the thirteenth century in our source material, and by studying more closely the different writings of Jacques de Vitry, we can explore the use of these terms and the association between crusade and pilgrimage in the sermons more widely and gain a better perspective on them. In particular, the feast day sermons for St George of Eudes de Châteauroux, the crusade manual of Humbert de Romans, and the two sermons by Jacques de Vitry intended for the pilgrims as well as the crusaders present further information and give new insight into the matter.

The fact that crusades were more often directed to places other than Jerusalem, such as Egypt or Tunisia, has been represented as a reason why there was less use of the theme of pilgrimage in the crusade model sermons of the thirteenth century.[127] However, both Jacques de Vitry and Eudes de Châteauroux were comfortable using this theme in their crusade sermons that were intended for the crusaders on their way to Egypt.[128] Even though both the Fifth and the

---

[123] *CPI*, pp. 52–53.

[124] Smith, *Crusading in the Age of Joinville*, p. 77.

[125] *CPI*, p. 52.

[126] Smith, *Crusading in the Age of Joinville*, p. 77.

[127] Smith, *Crusading in the Age of Joinville*, pp. 77–78.

[128] Jacques de Vitry, 'Ad peregrinos, thema sumpta ex epistola ad Galathas iii', *JVSP*, pp. 89–94; Jacques de Vitry, 'Ad peregrinos. Thema sumpta ex Zacharias ultimo', *JVSP*, pp. 95–102; Jacques de Vitry, 'Item sermo ad crucesignatos vel -signandos', *CPI*, p. 112; Eudes

Seventh Crusades were directed to Damietta, this did not make the expeditions any less pilgrimages for which the earthly and the heavenly Jerusalem gave motivation and inspiration to the participants. After all, the recovery of the Holy Land was the ultimate goal of both crusades. Norman Housley has shown that although many of the 'later crusades', from the thirteenth to the sixteenth century, were directed to other areas — places like Alexandria or Varna — the recovery of Jerusalem was regarded as the ultimate goal of the expeditions and references to the Holy City were made in the crusade propaganda throughout the later period.[129]

Crusades had already been launched in various directions during the twelfth century. The *Reconquista* was closely linked to the Holy Land crusade at an early stage, and during the Second Crusade an expedition was made to Lisbon. After the capture of the city and several others in Portugal, many of the crusaders travelled to the Holy Land, which was the main destination of the Second Crusade. The so-called 'Wendish Crusade', or 'Slavic Crusade' which was directed against the Wends in 1147 in north-eastern Europe, was also considered a part of the Second Crusade.[130] During the Third Crusade in 1189–92, Richard I attacked Cyprus and conquered the island from the Greeks.[131] All along, despite the variety of destinations and enemies, and the lack of places holy to the Christians in the target areas, the crusaders could be regarded as and were referred to as 'pilgrims'.[132] It is also worth noting the findings of Christopher Tyerman: his study of over three hundred sources connected to the crusades, charters and records of lawsuits from France, the Low Countries, and England written in 1096–1270, revealed that the most commonly used noun to refer to a crusade was *peregrinatio*.[133]

Five out of eight of the authors of the crusade model sermons and manuals examined in this study — Jacques de Vitry, Eudes de Châteauroux, Guibert de Tournai, Humbert de Romans, and the author of the *Brevis ordinacio* — uti-

---

de Châteauroux, 'De sancto Georgio', *UEE*, II, 700–705; Eudes de Châteauroux, 'Sermo in conversione sancti Pauli et exhortatio ad assumendam crucem', *CPI*, p. 136.

[129] Housley, *The Later Crusades*, pp. 46–48.

[130] Tyerman, *God's War*, pp. 305–08.

[131] 'Itinerarium Peregrinorum et Gesta Regis Ricardi', ed. by Stubbs, pp. 184–95.

[132] Tyerman, *The Invention of the Crusades*, p. 20.

[133] Tyerman, *The Invention of the Crusades*, pp. 50–51. Tyerman has concluded that the sources often use verbs of motion when referring to the crusades. The nouns used to refer to the crusade are *peregrinatio* (used sixty-six times), *iter* (fifty-five times), *via* (twenty-two times), *expeditio* (thirteen times), and *profectio* (once).

lize the theme of pilgrimage in one way or another in their models. Philippe le Chancelier does not use either of the terms 'pilgrim' or 'pilgrimage' in his crusade sermons against the Albigensians, nor do Federico Visconti or Roger of Salisbury in their crusade sermons. Eudes de Châteauroux used the theme of pilgrimage in his sermons delivered for the crusaders of the Seventh Crusade, but he did not use the theme in his crusade sermons preached against the Albigensians or the Lucera Muslims.

One might draw the conclusion that the crusade preachers were reluctant to view the crusades against the Christian heretics as pilgrimages, and hence declined to use such terms as 'pilgrim' or 'pilgrimage' in this context. However, while Philippe le Chancelier and Eudes de Châteauroux did not utilize the terms in their sermons against the Albigensians, Jacques de Vitry did use them and referred to the Albigensian crusade as a 'pilgrimage' in his writings, as did others.[134] The question is not simple, as there is some variation in the use of terms by the crusade preachers. This variation could be the consequence of a great many things, among them the date of the text and the circumstances, the audience, the intent of the preacher, and personal style.

Jacques's reference to the 'pilgrimage' against the Albigensian heretics is from *c.* 1213/15, whereas Philippe's and Eudes's crusade sermons are dated over a decade later, to 1226. Although Jacques's reference comes from a hagiographic source and not a sermon, there is no reason to assume that he did not use the term in his crusade preaching against the Albigensians, a task which he received in the same year when he was compiling the *Vita Mariae Oigniacensis*.[135] Jacques uses both the terms 'pilgrimage' and 'signed with the cross' concurrently in the *Vita*. He uses the term 'signed with the cross' in a form common when it first appeared, split into two words, *cruce signatus*.[136] Later, when the term became established, it usually appeared as a compound word. This form, *crucesignatus*, is used in those crusade sermons of Jacques which were written down in the

[134] Jacques de Vitry, Troyes, MS 401, fol. 67ᵛᵇ; Jacques de Vitry, *Vita Maria Oigniacensi*, cap. IX (82), *AASS*, v, 565; Tyerman, *The Crusades*, pp. 163–65. Tyerman also points out that the apologists of the 'Livonian Crusade' described the crusaders as pilgrims or 'the militia of pilgrims' at the beginning of the thirteenth century.

[135] Jacques de Vitry was commissioned to preach the cross in 1213 against the Albigensian heretics. He wrote the *Vita Mariae Oigniacensis* shortly after Marie d'Oignies's death, in 1213–15. Jacques de Vitry, *Historia Occidentalis*, ed. by Hinnebusch, pp. 5–9.

[136] In the *AASS* edition of the *Vita* there appears also the form 'Cruce-signatus'. This spelling with the hyphen is not used in the manuscripts. Jacques de Vitry, Troyes, MS 401, fol. 49ᵛᵃ, fol. 67ᵛᵇ; Jacques de Vitry, *Vita Maria Oigniacensi, AASS*, v, 565.

1230s. The early form used in the *Vita* would conform to the development of the term suggested by Michael Markowski.[137]

In 1226, when Philippe and Eudes preached against the Albigensians, the circumstances had altered from those of a decade earlier: the initial success of the years 1209–15, during the period when Jacques first preached the crusade against the heretics and wrote the *Vita*, had been reversed after a revolt had initiated a gradual expulsion of the crusaders from the lands they had won. This forced Louis VIII to take action in Languedoc. Throughout the conflict, the papacy remained cautious with its terminology. Pope Innocent III and his successor Honorius III refrained from using the term 'pilgrimage' in the Albigensian context, which may have influenced Philippe's and Eudes's choice of words.[138]

At the beginning of the thirteenth century, the term *crucesignatus* became more popular and steadily superseded other terms in the different crusading texts. The term 'pilgrim' was always an ambiguous one, as it was unclear whether it referred to a crusader or simply to a pilgrim. To avoid confusion between the two meanings of the word, medieval writers had often used various other terms for the crusader through the twelfth century. The term *crucesignatus* appears to have developed during the latter half of that century, and during the pontificate of Innocent III it was finally adopted by the papacy and used in official crusading tracts. In the Fourth Lateran Council in 1215, Innocent III utilized the term *crucesignatus* publicly for the first time, after which the term became more common than alternative terms used to refer to crusaders. At the same time, the theme of service was increasingly emphasized by the papacy. This service was something the *crucesignati* owed to God.[139] The lack of references to pilgrims or pilgrimage in some of the crusade model sermons of the thirteenth century, which were all written after the Fourth Lateran Council, would seem to be part of the general development of crusading terminology, rather than a direct result of changes in 'crusading realities'.

This is not to say that there was no change in the shape or emphasis of the crusade movement, or that the changing goals and targets of the crusades did not have any impact on the development of the terminology. *Crucesignatus* became the preferred term when referring to the crusader in many kinds of crusading texts during the thirteenth century, which avoided the ambiguity of the

---

[137] Markowski, '*Crucesignatus*'. Jacques de Vitry, *Vita Maria Oigniacensi*, *AASS*, v, 547, 565. This development had begun already during the late twelfth century; see Tyerman, *God's War*, pp. 375–76.

[138] Rist, *Papacy and Crusading in Europe*, pp. 90–91.

[139] Markowski, '*Crucesignatus*'.

term 'pilgrim'. The use of different euphemistic terms such as 'service', 'journey', or 'business of the cross' gave flexibility with regard to the different targets of the crusades, and were thus used in different situations.[140]

However, I do agree with Caroline Smith that the theme of pilgrimage developed during the thirteenth century and was used rather differently than earlier by some of the preachers. This development was slow and was influenced by many things, one of which may have been that the crusades were directed to many areas which did not possess traditional Christian holy sites. Smith has suggested that the crusader 'pilgrim's status was defined by his disposition rather than by his destination' during the thirteenth century.[141] This observation appears accurate in some accounts of the sermon material. Humbert de Romans, for example, did not discuss holy places in his sermon for the crusader pilgrims, but emphasized holy intentions.[142] The most striking difference is perhaps the fact that Humbert did not mention the Holy Sepulchre at all in a sermon intended especially for the crusading pilgrims, and this was the most important site in the Holy Land for Christian pilgrims and the ideological landmark for the crusaders throughout the crusading period.[143]

In the manual *De predicatione sancte crucis* Humbert de Romans did, however, discuss quite specifically the sanctity of the Holy Land and made clear that the crusade there was well and truly a pilgrimage. Humbert urged the crusade preachers to emphasize the devotional dimension of crusading in their sermons by demonstrating that the crusaders would participate in an expedition which was directed to the holiest of all places. The Holy Land was the place where mankind was created, where the patriarchs had lived and died, and where the apostles had followed Christ. Christ himself had been born in the Holy Land, not in Africa or in Europe, and there he was nursed and baptized, there he preached, fought the devil, and worked miracles, and there he suffered, was buried, and resurrected, before his final ascent to heaven. Humbert drew a comparison, in the manual written in the latter half of the 1260s, between famous pilgrims — such as Helena, Paula, and Jerome — and the crusading pilgrims.[144]

---

[140] Tyerman, *God's War*, p. 376.

[141] Smith, *Crusading in the Age of Joinville*, p. 78.

[142] Humbert de Romans, 'Ad peregrinos crucesignatos', *CPI*, p. 212; Smith, *Crusading in the Age of Joinville*, p. 78.

[143] Morris, *Sepulchre of Christ and the Medieval West*, p. 277.

[144] Humbert de Romans, *De predicatione sancte crucis*, cap. xiiij, De deuotione habenda ad terram sanctam; see also, for example, cap. iv, Quare crux imponitur peregrinantibus in subsidium terre sancte.

Guibert de Tournai, who did not utilize the theme of pilgrimage to the same extent as Jacques de Vitry and Humbert de Romans, did nonetheless mention in his crusade sermon the Holy Sepulchre as a special place that the crusaders would want to visit to honour the Lord.[145] Humbert may have deliberately avoided mentioning any specific sites or holy places in his crusade model sermon. Humbert's models are abbreviated versions of sermons that needed further elaboration by the preacher who wanted to use them. Humbert may have wished to leave the question of the destination of the pilgrimage open. The preacher utilizing the model could incorporate a reference to a holy shrine or explain the holiness of a particular place where the particular crusade which he was preaching would be directed. The preachers using his manual, on the other hand, needed to emphasize the sanctity of the Holy Land when preaching a crusade there, and portray the crusaders as pilgrims on a very special pilgrimage.

The 'spiritual geography' of the crusade model sermons was different from conventional geography. Holiness could also be created or connected to the region where the crusades were directed. The Languedoc region in southern France was, for example, associated with the Holy Land in the crusade sermons. Philippe le Chancelier viewed both places, Languedoc and the Holy Land, as 'promised lands' in his sermons. These regions belonged to the Christians and were important for the spiritual well-being of the whole of Christendom.[146] In the same way, the region inhabited by the Lucera Muslims in Apulia was considered to be holy and was compared to the Holy Land by Eudes de Châteauroux. The Lucera Muslims were described as polluters of holy ecclesiastical lands, just as the Muslims were depicted as polluting the tomb of Christ in the Holy Land.[147] These associations made crusades to places other than the Holy Land holy wars, and made it possible to consider the crusaders to these regions as pilgrims also. The Albigensian crusaders or those fighting against the Lucera Muslims pursued the good of Christendom out of love for God and for their fellow Christians. They tried to liberate the Christian holy lands. Thus their purposes were holy and they could be regarded as pilgrims, obtaining the same

---

[145] Guibert de Tournai, 'Ad crucesignatos et crucesignandos sermo primus', *CPI*, 180: 'Glorificatur enim Christi sepulcrum, quando ex amore et devotione crucem assumunt, ut videant illud et honorent ipsum'.

[146] Philippe le Chancelier, 'Sermo de eodem, quomodo apparuit potentia Dei', Avranches, MS 132, fol. 250ʳᵃ; Maier, 'Crisis, Liturgy and the Crusade', p. 654.

[147] Eudes de Châteauroux, 'Sermo de rebellione Sarracenorum Lucherie in Apulia', *CR*, p. 378.

benefits and undertaking the same obligations as the crusader pilgrims to the Holy Land.

The Narrow Path

How did the authors use the theme of pilgrimage to guide the participants of the expeditions to 'true' crusading? What kind of behavioural norms were adopted into crusade ideology from the pilgrimage tradition? The preachers' use of the theme of pilgrimage varies in the sermons. Humbert de Romans, for example, gave some cursory instructions in his sermon *ad peregrinos cruces-ignatos*, while Jacques de Vitry went into specifics in his two sermons for the pilgrims and the crusaders. Both Humbert and Jacques concerned themselves with the conduct of the crusader pilgrims. The preachers advised the crusaders to take the utmost care on their journey, ensuring that their conduct was appropriate to the excellence of their pilgrimage. Humbert underlined that the crusaders ought to make the pilgrimage in a proper, dignified manner. Above all, the crusaders needed to remember that their journey was a sacred one.[148] Jacques warned that there were some Christians who had left for the Holy Land as pilgrims, as crusaders, or as settlers who had changed their whereabouts but not their ways. The pilgrims and the crusaders needed to avoid these worldly Christians and reject their example. 'True' pilgrims and crusaders were mindful that they were on a holy journey, and act accordingly.[149]

Jacques de Vitry's two sermons for the pilgrims are full of detailed instructions on how the Christians ought to act on their journey. These were well suited as advice for both pilgrims and crusaders. The sermons may have been preached in one form or another during the Fifth Crusade or the preparations for the expedition. The sermons may initially have had different crusading audiences. Parts of the first sermon may originally have been preached to an audience of mixed groups of lay people, many of whom may have been common people, including non-combatants. This is indicated by its easily comprehensible language and simple themes, some taken from everyday life, as well as regular utilization of exempla.[150]

---

[148] Humbert de Romans, 'Ad peregrinos crucesignatos', *CPI*, p. 212: 'Notandum autem quod quanto peregrinatio ista est maioris prerogative, tanto peregrini isti maiorem curam debent apponere, ut eam debito modo et digno faciant. Proinde debent eam facere sancte, ut impleatur in eorum via'.

[149] Jacques de Vitry, 'Ad peregrines. Thema sumpta ex Zacharias ultimo', *JVSP*, p. 98.

[150] Jacques de Vitry, 'Ad peregrinos, thema sumpta ex epistola ad Galathas iii', *JVSP*,

We know from Jacques's own letters, which he dispatched from the Fifth Crusade, that he preached the crusade to non-combatants both in Europe, in Genoa before leaving for the East in 1216, and in the Levant, in Acre, Tyre, Sidon, Beirut, Byblos, the fortress Chastel-Blanc, and Tortosa, after arriving there in 1216–17 and before the crusade truly got under way.[151] On these occasions, when Jacques preached to noble knights and soldiers as well as to women, children, and other non-combatants, either separately or all mixed in one group, he may have preferred to use the terms 'pilgrim' and 'pilgrimage'. This ensured that no one in the audience was excluded from becoming a pilgrim and all had access to the movement.[152] However, it needs to be noted that Jacques used the term 'pilgrim' often in the crusading context and made no apparent distinction between the fighting men and the non-combatants when he used the term.

Parts of Jacques's second sermon for the pilgrims may have been delivered to an audience of ecclesiastics. The themes presented in the sermon are more sophisticated than in the first sermon. The focus is on the ideology of life as a pilgrimage. The pilgrims are described as students of pilgrimage ready to learn the lessons.[153] These themes would have been well suited for a scholarly and ecclesiastical audience.[154] As Jessalynn Bird has suggested, this sermon may have been preached to Jacques's companions and fellow crusading clerics, bishops and trained theologians who, like him, participated in the Fifth Crusade.[155]

In his first sermon for the pilgrims, Jacques portrayed Abraham as the model which the participants of the pilgrimage should follow. Abraham was the 'first

---

pp. 88–94; Birch, 'Jacques de Vitry and the Ideology of Pilgrimage', esp. p. 82. The sermon contains material which connects it to the Fifth Crusade, and it could have been preached sometime between the years 1214 and 1221. There may have been many so-called non-combatants among the lay groups in the audience, together with soldiers and knights. The non-combatants were common people who wanted to participate in the crusades but were not fit enough or were not regarded by others as able enough to take part in the battles.

[151] Jacques de Vitry, *Epistola*, I–II, ed. by Huygens, pp. 76–77, pp. 83–89.

[152] There were large groups of non-combatant crusaders among the army of the Fifth Crusade. The non-combatant participants were often described as pilgrims rather than *crucesignati* when they participated in crusades. Common people participating in the crusades were often described in veiled terms in the crusade texts, such as *pedites, mediocres, juniores*, and particularly *peregrini*. Tyerman, 'Who Went on Crusades to the Holy Land?', p. 22.

[153] Jacques de Vitry, 'Ad peregrinos. Thema sumpta ex Zacharias ultimo', *JVSP*, p. 94.

[154] Birch, 'Jacques de Vitry and the Ideology of Pilgrimage', pp. 88–89.

[155] *JVSP*, p. 84.

pilgrim', his voluntary exile was an example of pilgrimage, and his actions and attitude were to be imitated by all Christian pilgrims. Jacques used the conventional argument, utilized by many crusade preachers of the thirteenth century, explaining that the crusaders and pilgrims had to leave everything behind, like Abraham, when they went on their journey.[156] Another model for the crusader pilgrims in the sermon was Christ, whose family was compelled to flee to Egypt, an example which Eudes de Châteauroux also referred to in his crusade sermon from the Seventh Crusade.[157]

Abraham's wanderings and the land of Egypt were themes used in various medieval texts promoting or describing pilgrimages. Guibert de Tournai also referred to Egypt in his sermon for the pilgrims.[158] However, Jacques's extensive utilization of this theme seems to point to the exceptional destination of the Fifth Crusade. The Fifth Crusade was the first major expedition directed to Egypt for strategic reasons, rather than to the Holy Land, which probably caused some controversy during the journey. Some members of the army may have been disappointed with the decision, as the Holy Land was most likely the destination that most of them had in mind when they took the cross. Jacques was involved in the decision making when Damietta in Egypt was agreed upon as the main target. He explained and defended this decision in a letter to Pope Honorius III in September 1218. The letter contains similarities with the sermon for the pilgrims in the references to Egypt.[159] These arguments may have been put forward by Jacques in a sermon meant for the crusading pilgrims during the expedition. Jacques may have wanted to explain the decision to the participants and comfort those who had wanted to visit Jerusalem, but who were now forced to go elsewhere.[160]

In his sermons for the pilgrims and crusaders, Jacques explained how the participants ought to behave away from home. Making the journey in itself was

[156] See, for example, Jacques de Vitry, 'Ad peregrinos, thema sumpta ex epistola ad Galathas iii', *JVSP*, p. 89. Gen. 12. 1–2, 10.

[157] Jacques de Vitry, 'Ad peregrinos, thema sumpta ex epistola ad Galathas iii', *JVSP*, p. 89; Eudes de Châteauroux, 'De sancto Georgio', *UEE*, ii, 702.

[158] Dyas, *Pilgrimage in Medieval English Literature*, esp. pp. 5, 12, 15–22, 76–78. Guibert de Tournai, 'Ad peregrinos', Assisi, MS 501, fol. 130ʳ.

[159] Jacques de Vitry, *Epistola*, IV, ed. by Huygens, pp. 101–04; Jacques de Vitry, 'Ad peregrinos, thema sumpta ex epistola ad Galathas iii', *JVSP*, p. 89. See also Jacques de Vitry, *Epistola*, V, ed. by Huygens, pp. 117–18, Jacques de Vitry, 'Ad peregrinos. Thema sumpta ex Zacharias ultimo', *JVSP*, p. 99.

[160] *JVSP*, p. 84.

not enough for the participants to earn their reward. A pilgrimage was a penitential journey which purified the participants, but this purification would happen only through earnest spiritual repentance, suffering, and heavy labour.[161] The path of the pilgrim was narrow and straight, and they should not deviate from it, neither to the left nor to the right.[162] To stay on the right path the crusaders and pilgrims needed to be cautious about who they associated with during the pilgrimage and who their crusading companions were. Crusaders and pilgrims might encounter dangerous people on their journey — bad men and evil women, particularly prostitutes, who could misguide, corrupt, tempt, and rob them.[163] In the service of Christ, as crusaders, as pilgrims, or as members of the military orders, moderation and modesty were required. The pilgrims and the crusaders, Jacques notes, should wear only plain clothes. Jacques pointed out that the travellers should not carry too much money with them, for this would only tempt thieves to rob them.[164]

Pilgrimage was a time of penitence and abstinence, which meant that the participants ought to make the journey humbly, modestly, and chastely. Pilgrims and crusaders should not indulge themselves in carnal pleasures. In Jacques's opinion it was safer for the crusaders to sleep with demons than with prostitutes, for the sign of the cross would put the evil spirits to flight, but evil women were like a thorn in the foot or a nail in the eye.[165] By giving in to carnal

[161] Jacques de Vitry, 'Ad peregrinos, thema sumpta ex epistola ad Galathas iii', *JVSP*, p. 90.

[162] Jacques de Vitry, 'Ad peregrinos, thema sumpta ex epistola ad Galathas iii', *JVSP*, p. 90; Jacques quoted Bernard of Clairvaux in his first sermon urging the pilgrims and crusaders not to lapse into bad behaviour during their voyage. Bernard of Clairvaux, *Sermones de tempore*, in *PL*, CLXXXIII, col. 183.

[163] Jacques de Vitry, 'Ad peregrinos. Thema sumpta ex Zacharias ultimo', *JVSP*, pp. 97–98.

[164] Jacques de Vitry, 'Ad peregrinos, thema sumpta ex epistola ad Galathas iii', *JVSP*, p. 90: 'Vos autem scitis quod peregrinus leves vestes assumit. Non oneratur superfluis. Monetam non recisam, non factam, non falsam accipit. Peram habet et baculum, dietam non retardat libenter, pecuniam suam latronibus non ostendat'. There were robbers and bandits lurking on the pilgrims' route to the Holy Land, and many kinds of hustlers awaiting their arrival there, so they might cheat the pilgrims by demanding immoderate charges for accommodation and various other schemes, as Jacques reports in his *Historia orientalis*. Jacques de Vitry, *Historia orientalis*, LXXIII, ed. by Donnadieu, p. 292: 'Postquam autem in hospitiorum immoderato pretio et mercimoniis et concambio et aliis multimodis negotiationibus circumvenientes et depauperantes peregrinos in immensum ditati sunt tunc demum'. This description is so vivid that it may be the result of a swindle of pilgrims that Jacques himself witnessed while acting as the Bishop of Acre.

[165] Jacques de Vitry, 'Ad peregrinos. Thema sumpta ex Zacharias ultimo', *JVSP*, p. 98: 'Multas enim in hospitiis invenietis meretrices et malas mulieres quibus insidiantur incautis et in male remunerant hospites suos, velud mus in pera, serpens in sinu, et ignis in gremio, spina in

desires, the crusaders would ruin everything. Only a fool or a madman would lose his reward for a brief spell of carnal delight. Such an act would be akin to a farmer who had worked all year on his fields, but who set his harvest on fire after gathering it.[166] The 'true' crusaders should not give in to temptations and should eschew the company of prostitutes, for all implication of carnal sin was to be avoided during the pilgrimage.

Jean de Joinville's historical account of the Seventh Crusade indicates that there were some concerns with regard to sexual purity during the expeditions, or with the conduct of the knights under their command, which the army leaders feared might stain their own reputation as crusader pilgrims. Jean explains that he placed his bed in the crusaders' tent so that everyone who entered the tent could see him lying there. He did this so as to avoid any suspicions of consorting with women, so no one could doubt his decency or chastity while he was on the pilgrimage.[167] The leaders of the crusade army also tried to find ways to cope with knights who did not follow the rules and had sexual relations with prostitutes during the crusade. Jean says that one knight was caught in a brothel. According to the custom of the Holy Land, he was given a choice: the knight could either walk through the crusade host, wearing only his undershirt and dragged by the prostitute with a rope tied around his genitals, or he could give up his horse and armour and be expelled from the host. The latter alternative was the one the knight chose.[168]

The Liminality of the Crusader Pilgrims

Jean de Joinville clearly regarded the Seventh Crusade as a pilgrimage, as did many other participants in the expedition. Jean's decision to take the pil-

---

pede, clavus in oculo. Tutius autem esset dormire inter demones qui signo crucis fugantur quam prope huiusmodi pessimas mulieres quibus ebriis insidiantur'.

[166] Jacques de Vitry, 'Ad peregrinos. Thema sumpta ex Zacharias ultimo', *JVSP*, p. 99: 'Valde autem fatuus est et vecors qui pro modico delectatione carnali vel aliquo alio peccato tantos labores amittit. Sicut agricola qui per annum in messe sua laboravit et collectis segetibus ignem apponit. Si igitur diabolus temptat vos de peccato respondeatis suggerenti, "Vade retro sathana!"'

[167] Jean de Joinville, *Vie de Saint Louis*, ed. by Monfrin, p. 248: 'Mon lit estoit fait en mon paveillon en tel maniere que nul ne pooit entrer ens que il ne me veist gesir en mon lit; et ce fesoie je pour oster toutes mescreances de femmes'.

[168] Jean de Joinville, *Vie de Saint Louis*, ed. by Monfrin, p. 250: 'Tout premier vous dirons d'un chevalier qui fu pris au bordel, au quel l'en parti un jeu, selonc les usages du païs. Le jeu parti fu tel, ou que la ribaude le menroit par l'ost en chemise, une corde liee aus genetaires, ou il pedroit son cheval et s'armeure, et le chaceroit l'en de l'ost'.

grim's symbols, the staff and the purse, in a separate ritual before leaving for the crusade has been categorized as 'late', perhaps old-fashioned behaviour by Jonathan Riley-Smith.[169] However, when Louis IX departed for the Seventh Crusade, he too received the pilgrim's insignia. Louis's departure was a spectacle, where the people of France could express their sorrow and shed their tears on account of the departure of the king and the crusading army. Eudes de Châteauroux gave the king the pilgrim's staff and purse and the oriflamme in a separate ceremony at Saint-Denis in 1248. Later, Louis set out barefoot from Paris in the company of his wife and his brothers and their wives in a great procession, in front of a large crowd of people, and left for the crusade.[170] Louis IX performed a similar ritual departure when leaving for the Eighth Crusade in 1270, receiving the pilgrim's insignia and the oriflamme once more at Saint-Denis.[171]

It seems that the link between the crusades and the pilgrimages remained close all through the thirteenth century. Different sources, both lay and ecclesiastical, portray the crusades as pilgrimages. The famous poet Rutebeuf, for example, appears to have accepted the idea that the crusades were highly valued pilgrimages. He had no difficulty in viewing Louis IX's second crusade as 'paramount among all pilgrimages', even though the expedition was not directed to the Holy Land or any major holy site, but to Tunisia.[172]

Before leaving for the journeys many crusaders would go through different kinds of acts of purification and rites of separation. The crusade preachers advised those participating in the crusade expeditions to lay aside their ordinary lives and leave behind their fatherlands, homes, families, and friends.[173] The

---

[169] Riley-Smith, *The First Crusaders*, p. 81; Smith, *Crusading in the Age of Joinville*, p. 115.

[170] Le Goff, *Saint Louis*, pp. 184–88, 381; Folda, *Crusader Art in the Holy Land*, p. 236.

[171] Le Goff, *Saint Louis*, p. 294. Jean de Joinville also took the pilgrim's insignia as he set out for the Seventh Crusade, also barefoot, and carefully portrayed the whole campaign in terms of a pilgrimage in his *Vie de Saint Louis*. Smith, *Crusading in the Age of Joinville*, pp. 114–15.

[172] Rutebeuf, 'La Voie de Tunes', ed. by Faral and Bastin, p. 465: 'Plus ainme Dieu que home qui emprent teil voiage | Qui est li souverains de tout pelerinage: | Le cors mettre a essil et meir passeir a nage | Por amor de celui qui le fist a s'ymage'. For this and other thirteenth-century sources, see Smith, *Crusading in the Age of Joinville*, pp. 76–82.

[173] Jacques de Vitry, 'Sermo ad crucesignatos vel -signandos', *CPI*, p. 98; Eudes de Châteauroux, 'Sermo in conversione sancti Pauli et exhortation ad assumendam crucem', *CPI*, pp. 132, 136; Guibert de Tournai, 'Ad crucesignatos et crucesignandos sermo tertius', *CPI*, p. 202. As Jacques de Vitry put it, 'true sons' would consider their father's fatherland their own — that is, the Holy Land. Jacques de Vitry, 'Sermo ad crucesignatos vel -signandos', *CPI*, p. 88: 'qui veri filii sunt patriam patris sui suam reputant patriam'.

spiritual preparations for the journey and for the inevitable separation often took a ritual form. Common crusaders would often visit a local shrine, or the shrine of a favourite saint, before leaving for the expeditions, where they might be given the pilgrim's staff and purse, or they might change their clothing for a pilgrim's humble dress before leaving, or there could be a procession held by the townspeople and the departing crusaders in the town, where the separation of the *crucesignati* from their homes was publicly grieved and celebrated.[174] These visitations and rituals marked the parting of the crusaders from their ordinary lives, which were put on hold or cast aside as the crusading journey began. This placed the crusaders, in a sense, in a liminal situation.[175]

The concept of 'liminality' has been associated with medieval pilgrimages by some modern scholars, most notably Victor and Edith Turner.[176] This anthropological concept was first introduced by Arnold van Gennep in 1908, and since the Turners' study has been both criticized and utilized by various scholars.[177] In his *Les Rites de passage* van Gennep made a distinction between three different types of rites, subcategories or stages that led to a change of an individual's or group's social status. These were *rites of separation*, *transition rites*, and *rites of incorporation*. In the first stage a break from the old status was made; the second stage was the transition period, also called a liminal period; in the third stage, the process was completed and a new status was gained, and the individual or the group was reincorporated through rites of incorporation, or postliminal rites.[178]

Victor and Edith Turner claimed in their study that the pilgrimages were a 'liminoid phenomenon'. According to their interpretation the pilgrims were freed from the rules of the social structure as they took part in the pilgrimages. The pilgrims followed the precepts of community, equality, simplicity, and poverty. Their liminality and their distance from previous social identities created a strong sense of *communitas*.[179] Although many of the arguments and conclusions of the Turners' study have been contested, particularly the

---

[174] Housley, *Fighting for the Cross*, pp. 76–79.

[175] Liminality is usually associated with pilgrims' journeys in medieval studies. In crusade studies the liminality of the crusaders is not discussed. For an exception, see Lloyd, 'Crusader Knights and the Land Market in the Thirteenth Century', esp. p. 119 n. 2.

[176] Turner and Turner, *Image and Pilgrimage in Christian Culture*.

[177] Van Gennep, *The Rites of Passage*.

[178] Van Gennep, *The Rites of Passage*, pp. 10–11; Thomassen, 'The Uses and Meanings of Liminality'; See also Dickson, 'Rite de Passage?', esp. p. 323.

[179] Turner and Turner, *Image and Pilgrimage in Christian Culture*, pp. 252–53.

pilgrims' alleged freedom from social structures, the concept of liminality has been adopted by several historians and its utility has been acknowledged.[180]

Liminality also appears useful to a certain extent in the crusading context, although a crusade was not a rite of passage in the anthropological sense. From the moment of making the crusade vow to the time of fulfilling the vow or redeeming the vow, or to the moment of death, the crusader was, in a sense, in a state of liminality.[181] The preparations for departure and the celebrations of the separation were part of the break in which the crusaders voluntarily gave up their old life. According to Eudes de Châteauroux, those who took the cross 'rejected' and 'adjured' themselves by leaving behind their loved ones and placing themselves in mortal danger, so that they might afterwards ascend to heaven.[182] The crusaders disassociated themselves from their ordinary lives and entered an abnormal period of life, when certain roles and rules might differ, and which would reach its climax in the end of the crusading journey.

The crusaders' liminal situation was also reflected in their legal status and in the privileges of the cross. The *crucesignati* were in between lay and religious persons, or common pilgrims and 'special' pilgrims. The crusaders had many rights and privileges. Some of these they had inherited from the pilgrimage tradition, and some were created to respond to the particular needs of the crusader. The crusaders, like the pilgrims, might enjoy the hospitality of religious houses along their travelling route. They could also, like the pilgrims, travel through any Christian lands without interference. The crusaders had other special privileges as well: their wives and children, as well as their properties and possessions, were placed under the protection of the Church.[183] Like clergy, the crusaders could also be judged in ecclesiastical courts rather than the secular courts.

---

[180] Giles Constable has, for example, admitted that the concept helps to understand 'the temporary types of medieval religious life, such as pilgrimages, crusades, and periods of eremitical retreat'. Constable, *The Reformation of the Twelfth Century*, pp. 21–22; Bynum, *Holy Feast and Holy Fast*, p. 280. See also Katajala-Peltomaa, 'Gender and Spheres of Interaction', pp. 168–70; Dubisch, *In a Different Place*, pp. esp. 37–47. For a recent discussion on the concept of 'liminality', see especially Thomassen, 'The Uses and Meanings of Liminality'.

[181] Simon Lloyd has described the crusader as a 'liminal being'. Lloyd, 'Crusader Knights and the Land Market in the Thirteenth Century', p. 119 n. 2.

[182] Eudes de Châteauroux, 'Sermo ad invitandum ad crucem', *CPI*, p. 170: 'Assumentes enim crucem se abnegant, id est abiurant, se mortis periculo exponendo, suos eos derelinquendo, sua ea consumendo, tollentes crucem suam, ut postmodum a cruce portentur in celum quasi quodam vehiculo'.

[183] Muldoon, 'Crusading and Canon Law', esp. p. 46.

The crusade preachers' insistence on true contrition and sincere piety from those who had been signed with the cross may also reflect the problems which the abuses of the privileges of the cross had caused. The crusader's privileges also attracted those who did not want to participate in the crusades. People could try to avoid undesired law suits or they might hope to get more lenient justice from the ecclesiastical court, or they might want to escape the paying off of debts or interest from their loans or to collect the crusading subsidies for themselves.[184] The papacy fought against these violations of the crusader's privileges by putting pressure on all those who had taken the cross so that they would either go on the expeditions or redeem their vows with money. The papacy was also prepared to revoke the privileges from those people who had, for example, committed serious crimes and taken the cross so that they could escape the punishment of the secular courts.[185]

Regulating the Emotions

The theme of pilgrimage provided for the crusade preachers material with which they could guide the crusader pilgrims' inward emotions as well as their outward appearance. By utilizing the pilgrimage tradition, the authors of the model sermons gave advice about the emotional state of mind that the participants in crusades should adopt. According to the preachers, the crusader pilgrims' journey was hindered by obstacles, and it was important that they suffered along the way. This, however, ought not to depress the crusaders. The participants of the special pilgrimage should not be grief-stricken or unhappy. On the contrary, the crusaders should be delighted and they should express their happiness. In his second sermon for the crusader pilgrims, Jacques de Vitry stressed that their task, although laborious and full of suffering, should be a joyful one.[186]

Humbert de Romans also agreed that the crusaders' sacred pilgrimage should be performed joyfully. He made a distinction between different kinds of pilgrimages: the pilgrimage of man in this world, the 'general pilgrimage', and 'the pilgrimage of prerogative excellence', that is, the crusaders' journey.[187]

---

[184] Brundage, *Medieval Canon Law and the Crusader*, pp. 159–87.

[185] Brundage, *Medieval Canon Law and the Crusader*, pp. 188–89.

[186] Jacques de Vitry, 'Ad peregrinos. Thema sumpta ex Zacharias ultimo', *JVSP*, pp. 94–95: 'Peregrinatio autem dicitur festum eo quod cum gaudio laborare debemus in Domini servitio'. He used the feast of Tabernacles as an example of a pilgrimage, as did Eudes de Châteauroux in his crusade sermon. Eudes de Châteauroux, 'De sancto Georgio', *UEE*, II, 700–705, esp. p. 703.

[187] Humbert de Romans, 'Ad peregrinos crucesignatos', *CPI*, p. 212: 'Alia est peregrinatio

According to Humbert, the crusaders' pilgrimage surpassed the other pilgrimages in merit, because this was a journey made for Christ, while ordinary pilgrimages were made for the saints, and because the participants were exposing themselves to death on this journey, whereas they merely exposed themselves to labour on the other pilgrimages. The crusade-pilgrimage was also
superior to other pilgrimages because it was made for the good of the whole
of Christendom, while other pilgrimages were merely done for the individual
pilgrim's benefit.[188] This was also a journey that gave the crusader pilgrims the
plenary indulgence.[189]

The pilgrimage tradition provided models for the eating and drinking habits
of the participants in crusades. These questions had some importance and were
taken into consideration by the crusade ideologists and the spiritual leaders of
the expeditions. Already during the First and the Second Crusades, the crusaders' eating habits were supervised and at times restricted. During the First
Crusade, before attacking Antioch, the crusaders fasted for three days, which
was also mentioned by Humbert de Romans in his preaching manual.[190] Later,
before an assault on Jerusalem was carried out in 1099, the crusaders went
through multiple collective penitential observances: fasting, almsgiving, praying, confession, communion, and a barefoot march around the city in a procession.[191] In 1147, during the Second Crusade, Pedro Pitões advised the crusaders
to be temperate in their eating, but still recommended that the flesh should be
satisfied, so that it could serve in 'the good works' that the crusaders were about
to do, that is, in the coming battle. The crusaders of the Second Crusade might
have, according to the report of the bishop's sermon, a certain amount of satisfaction: they could indulge themselves in carnal pleasures, provided they did
not 'burst forth into disgraceful iniquity'.[192]

prerogative excellentie, scilicet crucesignatorum, que in multis precellit alias peregrinationes
Christianas'.

[188] Humbert de Romans, 'Ad peregrinos crucesignatos', *CPI*, p. 212: 'Alie enim fiunt propter aliquem sanctum, ista autem propter sanctum sanctorum, scilicet Christum, specialiter. Item
in aliis exponunt se homines labori, in ista autem exponunt se morti, et hoc in casibus multis'.

[189] Humbert de Romans, *De predicatione sancte crucis*, cap. xiiij, De deuotione habenda ad
terram sanctam.

[190] Humbert de Romans, *De predicatione sancte crucis*, cap. xl, De historia Anthiocena ad
idem.

[191] Brundage, 'Prostitution, Miscegenation and Sexual Purity in the First Crusade', esp.
p. 59.

[192] 'De expugnatione Lyxbonensi', ed. and trans. by David, pp. 76–77: 'Sit vobis inter cetera
temperatio gule, et ut breviter dicam, satietur caro ut in bono opera famulari nobis sufficiat.

Overeating and drunkenness were considered disgraceful iniquities. The temptation was particularly dangerous for those who were travelling and tired. In his sermon for the pilgrims and the crusaders, Jacques de Vitry warned that weary and thirsty travellers should not drink wine excessively, and above all they should not get intoxicated.[193] They should eat moderately with the intent to refresh and nourish themselves. Excessive eating or drinking was not behaviour suitable for pilgrims and crusaders.[194]

Fasting was an important part of the crusades and pilgrimages. It was promoted in different crusade model sermons by several of the authors.[195] Pilgrims often went through ritual purification before reaching a holy shrine, which included fasting, or they might begin fasting at the outset of their journey.[196] On the crusading campaigns fasting was part of the spiritual purification that was needed in different situations. The penitential observances that the first crusaders went through became 'standard crusading procedure' after the First Crusade, during the preparations for battle.[197]

The lack of genuine desire to fast could be regarded as a reason for a crusading defeat. Eudes de Châteauroux discussed the connection between fasting, feasting, and crusading disaster in his crusade sermon for the anniversary of Robert d'Artois, preached sometime during the Seventh Crusade after the defeat at Mansurah in 1250. Eudes built the sermon on the biblical passage from Zacharias, where God gave the Israelites advice about fasting.[198] The sons

---

[...] Sit itaque vobis ars quedam satiari, ne unusquisque per satietatem carnis ad iniquitatem prorumpat turpitudinis'.

[193] Jacques de Vitry, 'Ad peregrinos. Thema sumpta ex Zacharias ultimo', *JVSP*, p. 97: 'Ebrius autem non tam bibit vinum quam bibitur a vino vel absorbetur [...]. Multos quidem vidi peregrinos qui fatigati ex itinere usque ad ebrietatem bibebant, et alii licet non sitiant dum socios bibere vident ipsi absque ulla neccesitate bibere conantur ne forte decipiantur'.

[194] Jacques de Vitry, 'Ad peregrinos. Thema sumpta ex Zacharias ultimo', *JVSP*, p. 98: 'Manducare igitur et bibere oportet ad corporis refectionem, non ad superfluitatem'.

[195] Philippe le Chancelier, 'Sermo scolaribus inter Epiphaniam et Purificationem', Avranches, MS 132, fols 249ᵛᵇ–250ʳᵃ; Roger of Salisbury, '*Ascendente* Ihesu *in naviculam*, et cetera', *PCHL*, p. 229; Eudes de Châteauroux, 'Sermo de eodem anniversario', *PCHL*, pp. 240–41.

[196] Finucane, *Miracles and Pilgrims*, p. 48.

[197] Brundage, 'Prostitution, Miscegenation and Sexual Purity', p. 59. Jacques de Vitry, 'Sermo ad fratres militaris insignitos charactere militiae Christi', Troyes, MS 228, fol. 132ᵛᵇ. Jacques de Vitry also made it clear, in a sermon for the brothers of the military orders, that the knights should take time to do 'spiritual exercises', which included fasting, so that they could go securely into battle.

[198] Eudes de Châteauroux, 'Sermo de eodem anniversario', *PCHL*, p. 240: 'Et *dicit Dominus*

of Israel ought to have coped with adversities by fasting and lamenting. When this was not fully understood, God rebuked the Israelites. Eudes interpreted this reproach as condemnation of spiritual insincerity and linked it to the crusading disaster. Some men, like the Israelites, expressed superficial piety. Their fasting was not for God and they were not motivated by love or charity: these men fasted and feasted for themselves out of selfish reasons and for them the Lord could say, 'non curo'.[199]

God did not care for false, external expressions of piety, but sought genuine feelings of devotion from the crusaders, pilgrims, and supporters of the movement. This requirement was demanded by several of the authors of the crusade model sermons in various ways. Philippe le Chancelier insisted that displays of piety and penitential exercises needed to reflect sincere internal emotions and ought not to be outward, hypocritical gestures. Those who bent their knees and greeted God insincerely while praying tried to appease God, but in fact offended him with their sins.[200] Philippe urged the ecclesiastics to be joyful when they supported the crusade movement by fasting. They should not dramatize their sufferings and disfigure their faces while they fasted, for these were signs of insincerity.[201]

In his sermon for the pilgrims, Jacques de Vitry underlined that the pilgrims were not travelling for their own delight. They should not stay more than one night in any one place. The pilgrims were not on a journey out of curiosity to see the sights, but they were travelling for penitential reasons.[202] At first glance, this passage might be taken as a piece of advice solely intended for the pilgrims

---

exercituum, "Ieiunium quarti et ieiunium quinti et ieiunium septimi et ieiunium decimi erit domui Iude in gaudium et letitiam et in sollempnitates preclaras". Zach. 8. 19.

[199] Eudes de Châteauroux, 'Sermo de eodem anniversario', *PCHL*, p. 240: '*Cum ieiunaveritis et plangetis in quinto et septimo mensa per hos septuaginta annos, nunquid ieiunium ieiunastis mihi et cum comedistis et bibistis, nunquid non vobis comedistis et vobismet bibistis?* quasi dicat de ieiuniis vestris et comestionibus "non curo" quia vobismetipsis ieiunastis non pauperibus quos fame periclitari vidistis et eis non subvenistis'. Zach. 7. 5–6.

[200] Philippe le Chancelier, 'Sermo in die veneris infra octabas Assumptionis beate Virginis', Avranches, MS 132, fol. 244rb: 'Alii genua flectunt et false salutant, ut yipocrite qui flectunt genua in orationibus ut placare videantur et peccatis suis offendunt eum'. Transcribed by Maier and Bériou.

[201] Philippe le Chancelier, 'Sermo de eodem, quomodo apparuit potentia Dei', Avranches, MS 132, fol. 250rb. Mt. 6. 16.

[202] Jacques de Vitry, 'Ad peregrinos, thema sumpta ex epistola ad Galathas iii', *JVSP*, p. 90: 'Non moratur in villa si potest nisi una nocte. Prefigit in animo certum locum ad quem tendat, non delectatur aspectu pulchrarum rerum. Non multum gaudet donec ad propriam revertatur'.

visiting the holy places, but this is not the case, as the crusaders also hoped to see and to honour the holy places during the expeditions. Eudes de Châteauroux and King Louis IX, for example, found time to visit local shrines in the Holy Land during the Seventh Crusade. In 1251, they made a joint pilgrimage to Nazareth and travelled to Cana and Mount Tabor. Louis expressed his devotion by alighting from his horse when they first saw Nazareth from afar. The king worshipped God on bended knees and continued forward to the city in this manner. In Nazareth, Louis fasted on bread and water and attended Mass — which was celebrated by Eudes in the Church of the Annunciation — and heard a sermon delivered by the legate.[203] These were personal pilgrimages made by the king and the legate during the collective crusading pilgrimage. Such personal pilgrimages could be made by the participants of the crusade expeditions, which would render 'spiritual fulfilment' for them even if the crusade campaigns were unsuccessful. Similar journeys were made by Thibaud de Champagne and Richard of Cornwall in 1239 and 1241, during the Barons' Crusade.[204]

The close link between crusading and pilgrimage also encouraged the crusaders to burden their bodies and undergo physical trials that were part of the penitential journey of a pilgrim. Jacques de Vitry and Guibert de Tournai utilized this dimension of crusading in their sermons, reminding Christians that as they had sinned with all of their limbs, so they needed to do satisfaction by using all of their limbs, and that there was merit in the roughness of a pilgrimage.[205] If their feet ached from travelling, the pilgrim-crusaders should recall that Christ's feet had been pierced with nails.[206] Louis IX appears to have accepted these ideals presented by the crusade preachers, as he wore a hairshirt under his clothes while visiting the holy places, which was a sign of his humility and penitent frame of mind.[207]

---

[203] Geoffroy de Beaulieu, *Vita Ludovici noni*, ed. by Bouquet, esp. p. 14. Folda, *Crusader Art in the Holy Land*, pp. 248–49; Smith, *Crusading in the Age of Joinville*, pp. 115–16.

[204] Smith, *Crusading in the Age of Joinville*, p. 116.

[205] Guibert de Tournai, 'Ad crucesignatos et crucesignandos sermo tertius', *CPI*, pp. 204–07. Guibert follows closely Jacques de Vitry's example. Jacques viewed the pilgrimage as one representation of the *imitatio Christi*. The pilgrims should bear in mind the sufferings of Christ as they suffered their own hardships during the journey. Jacques emphasizes that the pilgrims had a chance to suffer as Christ had suffered. They could sweat for their tribulations as Christ had done on his way to the cross. Jacques de Vitry, 'Ad peregrinos, thema sumpta ex epistola ad Galathas iii', *JVSP*, pp. 90, 92.

[206] Guibert de Tournai, 'Ad crucesignatos et crucesignandos sermo tertius', *CPI*, pp. 204–07.

[207] Folda, *Crusader Art in the Holy Land*, p. 249.

During the Seventh Crusade, fasting was part of the crusaders' everyday life, even in extreme situations. Jean de Joinville tells in his *Vie de Saint Louis* that the crusaders did not eat fish during Lent, except burbots, even though they were pressed by the enemy army at the time.[208] Strict observance of the diet was also expected from the crusaders while in captivity. Jean reports that after the disaster of Mansurah, when the crusaders were prisoners of the enemy, he accidently ate meat on Lent Friday. After Jean was informed what day it was by a worried fellow crusader, he quickly pushed aside his plate. Later, Eudes de Châteauroux absolved Jean from all blame, as he had not done the deed knowingly.[209]

After the defeat at Mansurah, Eudes de Châteauroux explained in the *Sermo de eodem anniversario* how Christians should piously feast and fast so that it was pleasing to God. He drew extensive moral implications from these actions by using biblical quotations. Optimal feasting, according to Eudes, was that where true judgement, mercy, and compassion to every man were expressed.[210] Fasting was abstention from wickedness: desire not to oppress the widow, the orphan, the stranger, the poor, and not to plot evil in one's heart against one's brother.[211] This was not just a question of proper diet for the crusaders, but a way of finding an appropriate spiritual outlook on the journey and a way for the crusaders to express their religious devotion to God.

In the sermon, Eudes acknowledged that men were selfish creatures and that 'money subdues everything' in the world, but he warned Christians not to be indifferent to the divine law or uninterested in what pleases God, for punishment for these transgressions was severe. The biblical disasters occurred because

---

[208] Jean de Joinville, *Vie de Saint Louis*, ed. by Monfrin, p. 144: 'Nous ne mangions nulz poissons en l'ost tout le quaresme mez que bourbetes, et les bourbetes manjoient les gens mors, pour ce que ce sont glous poissons'.

[209] Jean de Joinville, *Vie de Saint Louis*, ed. by Monfrin, p. 160. Jean was so mortified over the mishap that he made sure that he fasted on bread and water every Friday at Lent thereafter. This steadfastness allegedly irritated Eudes de Châteauroux, but Jean fails to specify why. The only reason given is that Jean was the only great magnate left in the crusade army and who remained with the king in the Holy Land as others returned home. Jean de Joinville, *Vie de Saint Louis*, ed. by Monfrin, p. 160.

[210] Eudes de Châteauroux, 'Sermo de eodem anniversario', *PCHL*, p. 240: '*Hec dicit Dominus exercituum dicens, "Iudicium verum iudicate et misericordiam et miserationes facite unusquisque cum fratre suo." Hoc est convivium optimum et valde delectabile*'. Zach. 7. 9.

[211] Eudes de Châteauroux, 'Sermo de eodem anniversario', *PCHL*, p. 240: '*Et viduam et pupillum et advenam et pauperem nolite calumpniari, et malum vir fratri suo non cogitet in corde suo. Hoc est ieiunium bonum et salutare abstinere a talibus*'. Zach. 7. 10.

of deafness and stony-heartedness.[212] God's anger was manifested in the ancient disasters, as it was expressed also in the current crusading disaster of 1250. But sincerity, pious observance of God's will, and love of peace and truth would transform the sorrow and misery of Christians into joy and happiness, as promised by the prophet Zacharias.[213]

Eudes's *Sermo de eodem anniversario* may well have been preached to an audience of ecclesiastics in Acre, as suggested by Cole, d'Avray, and Riley-Smith. This would explain the heavy use of scriptural exegesis and cautious handling of theologically difficult questions.[214] The anniversary for those who died at Mansurah would occur each year in the time of Lent or shortly beforehand, which would partly explain the use of the theme of fasting in Eudes's sermon.[215] However, there were also other reasons why this was a well-suited theme for a crusade sermon, particularly one discussing crusading defeat. The catastrophe of Mansurah was a consequence of the sins of Christians, not just the sins of the crusaders, but also the rest of the Christian faithful. Those who refused to fast or those who fasted insincerely were 'bad crusaders' who had not deserved to win. The sins of Christians and their insincerity were causes for the failure, but they could now, after the defeat, demonstrate their true repentance, renounce all their sins, and show their spiritual sincerity by fasting. In this way God's anger could be placated and again successful crusades could be waged against the Saracens.

The Community of Crusaders

Women and Children

Women and children belonged together with the old and the infirm in the large group of 'non-combatants' in the crusade movement. The crusade expeditions were generally regarded as masculine military service suitable for healthy, adult males. Women and children's participation in the expeditions was criticized and discouraged throughout the twelfth century: they were meant to be left behind, and their duty was to stay at home and wait for the return of the fight-

---

[212] Eudes de Châteauroux, 'Sermo de eodem anniversario', *PCHL*, p. 241: 'pecuniam que domat omnia'.

[213] Eudes de Châteauroux, 'Sermo de eodem anniversario', *PCHL*, pp. 240–43. Zach. 8. 19.

[214] Cole, d'Avray, and Riley-Smith, 'Application of Theology to Current Affairs', p. 231; Tamminen, 'The Test of Friendship', p. 226.

[215] Cole, d'Avray, and Riley-Smith, 'Application of Theology to Current Affairs', p. 238.

ing men.[216] Women and children were considered 'anti'-crusaders by some of the authors of the sermons. Modern scholars have tended to follow the same track when viewing the crusade sermon material or examining women's participation in the crusading campaigns.[217] Were women and children merely crusading obstacles, or could they too be regarded as crusaders who had the right to participate in the movement and who could be considered 'true' crusaders?

Through the twelfth and thirteenth centuries the papacy attempted to restrict women's participation in the campaigns. For example, crusade preachers were instructed to encourage women to redeem their vows with money.[218] In 1260 the papal legate in Acre, Tommaso d'Agni, sent a letter to the Frisians advising them not to let women take part in the expeditions. According to Tommaso, women's participation would only lead to fornication and adultery.[219] Nonetheless, both women and children did participate in crusades. Married and unmarried women, the old and the young, all took part, and children were born during the expeditions. Jean Tristan, the son of Louis IX, is perhaps the best-known crusade baby, born in 1250 in Damietta, then held by the Christians, three days after the king had been captured by the enemy.[220]

Women and children also had important, at times recognized, tasks during the crusades: they and the other non-combatants helped in various ways by building fortifications, tending the sick, guarding the camp, and carrying and

[216] Rousseau, 'Home Front and Battlefield', esp. p. 39.

[217] See, for example, Tyerman, *The Invention of the Crusades*, pp. 75–76; *CPI*, p. 65; Siberry, *Criticism of Crusading*, pp. 45–46; Holt, 'Feminine Sexuality and the Crusades'.

[218] X 3.34.8, *Corpus Iuris Canonici*; Siberry, *Criticism of Crusading*, pp. 45–46.

[219] 'Menkonis Chronicon', ed. by Pertz, MGH, SS, 23, p. 549: 'Attendentes siquidem ex accessu mulierum Frisie ad has partes pro devotione vel subsidio terre sancte, pro locorum nimia distantia et pro multis aliis casibus, qui offerunt se in via, multa pericula provenire, cum contingat frequentius instigante humani generis inimico, quod cum aliquibus earum, prout fertur, adulteria et fornicationes a peregrinis in via et navibus committantur'. See also Siberry, *Criticism of Crusading*, p. 46.

[220] Jean was called Tristan, 'sadness', because of the dire situation in which he was born. Jean Tristan also accompanied his father twenty years later on the Eighth Crusade, that is, the second crusade of Louis IX to Tunisia, on which both Jean Tristan and Louis IX died. Jordan, *Louis IX and the Challenge of the Crusade*, p. 188 n. 45, p. 217. Another famous crusade baby was captured by Muslim thieves in 1191 and brought to Saladin, according to the chronicler Bahā' al-Dīn. However, the three-month-old infant was returned unharmed to its mother in a demonstration of the sultan's clemency. Bahā' al-Dīn Ibn Shaddād, *The Rare and Excellent History of Saladin*, trans. by Richards, pp. 145–48; Housley, *Fighting for the Cross*, p. 117.

throwing stones.[221] The scope of the participation of the women and children is, however, unclear due to the nature of our sources, which give us very little evidence from which to draw any conclusions.[222] The ages of those who participated in crusades are seldom revealed. Some of the key words are also unclear in meaning. For instance, the word *pueri* could mean children or boys, but it was also used to define social status, to mean low social class rather than youth.[223]

The problem with women crusaders, from the clerical point of view, was their susceptibility to sin and their tendency to lead others into sin, that is, the crusading men. The prevailing medieval clerical view was that women were a danger and a temptation to the morality and chastity of men. Many of the authors of the crusade sermons reiterate this view in their various writings and model sermons. The feminine sex was regarded as defective, weaker than the male sex, and more likely to give in to carnal pleasures. This clerical antipathy towards women is a commonplace in the Middle Ages, but it would be a misconception to label all the authors of the crusade sermons misogynists. These Paris-educated preachers appear to have shared a common dedication to pastoral care and reform. In this pastoral context, the authors often profess a note of compassion for women, whom they try earnestly to guide and advise. Some of the preachers, after hearing the confessions of women, learned to appreciate the difficulties that they faced in a patriarchal society. Federico Visconti,

---

[221] 'Gesta Obsidionis Damiatae', *QBSS*, p. 111. See also Powell, *Anatomy of a Crusade*, p. 162.

[222] The question of age and the concept of childhood are altogether problematic issues in medieval studies. There have traditionally been two approaches to childhood in historical research: one that considers the concept purely a modern invention, and the other that accepts that childhood existed also in medieval thought and that it is in a sense a natural occurrence. What childhood meant in the Middle Ages and the age when it ended varied greatly in different parts of Europe, with males and females, and in different social classes. As a rule, marriage was usually regarded as the threshold of maturity. The canonical age of marriage for girls was twelve, whereas boys reached this mark at the age of fourteen. However, noblewomen might be married as young as seven years old, and common women often married much later, after working many years for their dowry. Hodgson, *Women, Crusading and the Holy Land*, p. 55.

[223] The term *iuvenes* could also indicate youths, young men or women, but in crusade chronicles it appears to have had several meanings: it might, for instance, indicate that the crusading *iuvenes* were combatants who had not yet established themselves. A *iuvenis* could also be a famed knight of mature age. In the social sense the term appears to have referred to someone with a reputation for bravery and an illustrious but non-princely background. The same seems to be the case with the word *adolescens*, which could point to a youth or a minor, but in the crusading context also to an adult knight who was in the process of changing his status. Kostick, *The Social Structure of the First Crusade*, pp. 187–212, esp. pp. 201, 209.

for example, noted that men used Eve's fall to sin as a pretext for reproaching women.[224]

It would also be a mistake to assume that the authors of the crusade model sermons disregarded women and children, or declined to preach the cross to them, or avoided signing them. In a letter written in Palestine in 1216–17, Jacques de Vitry explains how he had stayed for many days in the city of Beirut and preached there, signing 'all, both women and men, even children' with the cross.[225] Jacques did not hesitate to make the women or children crusaders, although his use of the word 'even' when he refers to the signed children suggests that this practice was not wholly conventional.

The fundamental question with regard to women and children crusaders is the nature of their intended participation. How, then, did crusader preachers conceptualize the contribution of women and children? Pope Innocent III's new policy with regard to crusading women has usually been interpreted by modern scholars as a twofold approach, aiming firstly to raise more funds through commutation of crusade vows, and secondly to obtain further military assistance for the Holy Land. Wealthy women could hire mercenaries to accompany them on crusades.[226] Innocent III, however, appears also to have wanted to get everyone more involved in the recovery of the Holy Land. Innocent wanted all Christians to partake in the movement: everybody had obligations, and everyone was to have benefits.[227]

One of Eudes de Châteauroux's crusade sermons challenges the usual presumption of modern scholars with regard to the participation of women and

[224] Murray, 'Archbishop and Mendicants', esp. pp. 35–36. For Guibert de Tournai's and Humbert de Romans's model sermons intended for women, see Casagrande, *Prediche alle donne del secolo XIII*. For Jacques de Vitry's, see, for example, Longere, 'Deux sermons de Jacques de Vitry'. See also Longere, 'La Femme dans la théologie pastorale'. For Jacques de Vitry's and Guibert de Tournai's views, see also d'Avray and Tausche, 'Marriage Sermons in *ad status* Collections of the Central Middle Ages'. See also Ferruolo, 'Preaching to the Clergy and Laity in Early Thirteenth-Century France', esp. pp. 19–20; Brett, *Humbert of Romans*, pp. 66–71; Farmer, *Surviving Poverty in Medieval Paris*, pp. 105–35.

[225] Jacques de Vitry, *Epistola*, II, ed. by Huygens, p. 92: 'Postquam autem aliquot diebus moram feci in civitate Berithi et eis verbum dei predicavi, omnibus signatis tam mulieribus quam viris et etiam parvulis, signato domino civitatis cum militibus eius'. Jacques appears also to have signed with the cross 'the lord of the city', Jean d'Ibelin.

[226] Derbes and Sandona, 'Amazons and Crusaders', esp. p. 207.

[227] Pope Innocent III decreed in the encyclical *Quia maior* of 1213 that anyone who so wished might take the cross, except the religious who had vowed otherwise. Innocentius III, *Quia maior*, in *PL*, CCXVI, cols 817–22.

children. Eudes's crusade sermon was delivered during the feast of St George, possibly in 1246 or 1248, for an audience of crusaders of the Seventh Crusade.[228] In the sermon, Eudes justifies and defends the personal participation of both women and children, using biblical examples. His sermon indicates that there was some criticism of the involvement of these groups while Louis IX's first crusade was in preparation. According to Eudes, many people did not want children, relatives, or friends to follow them on a pilgrimage or into a religious order.[229] Eudes refutes this opinion, showing that these critics did not understand religious reform and were not like the great leaders of the Old Testament.

Eudes viewed the upcoming crusade as a pilgrimage to the earthly and the celestial Jerusalem. According to Eudes, it was easier to bear the burden of this pilgrimage together than alone: Christians should journey in groups. Further, Eudes notes, children could also be taken to the expedition, just as Moses had taken the children when the Israelites travelled from Sinai to the Promised Land. Moses was afraid that the Israelites' love for their children would make them turn back before the journey was completed. The Israelites had grumbled about God and yearned for 'the onion and garlic' that they used to eat in Egypt. According to Eudes's interpretation, Moses decided that the children should also be taken along and they too should travel to the Holy Land, so as to avoid complications.[230] Noah was another example used by the legate. Noah had taken his wife, his sons, and his sons' wives with him to the ark during the Flood.[231] Lot also took his wife and daughters with him when he fled from Sodom, another example used by Eudes in the sermon to convince his audience that the non-combatants, particularly wives and children, both sons and daughters, could be taken to the expeditions with the crusading men.[232]

Being the legate of the Seventh Crusade, Eudes de Châteauroux's support for the participation of women and children is significant. This was not just an opinion of one crusade preacher, but the view of the spiritual leader of the

[228] See Appendix V.

[229] Eudes de Châteauroux, 'De sancto Georgio', *UEE*, ɪɪ, 702: 'Sunt enim quamplurimi qui nolunt quod parvuli sui, consanguinei vel amici, sequentur eos in religionem vel peregrinacionem'.

[230] Eudes de Châteauroux, 'De sancto Georgio', *UEE*, ɪɪ, 702: 'Sic debemus parvulos nostros nobiscum ducere, ut Moyses parvulos suos et pecora. Timebat enim ne amore parvulorum redirent, ex quo propter amorem cepum et alliorum redire voluerunt'. Num. 11. 1–5, 32. 26.

[231] Eudes de Châteauroux, 'De sancto Georgio', *UEE*, ɪɪ, 702: 'Non sunt sicut Noe qui ingressus est archam cum uxore et filiis et uxoribus filiorum'. Gen. 7. 7.

[232] Eudes de Châteauroux, 'De sancto Georgio', *UEE*, ɪɪ, 702: 'Et Loth exiuit cum uxore et filiabus de Sodomis'. Gen. 19. 15–17.

whole expedition. Eudes's apology for the women and children's participation may suggest that Louis IX's intention from the start was to occupy and populate the land that the crusaders would conquer. Louis's crusade seems to have had additional goals, over and above the liberation of the Holy Land and defending Christendom, such as a permanent occupation of Egypt and an attempt to populate the conquered land.[233] Clearly such a colonization would have required the presence of the non-combatants, especially women. Children's participation would have also removed the potential obstacle created by the pain of separation from one's children.

The early dating of Eudes's crusade sermon, the year 1246, calls into question whether plans such as this had been made by then. It is unclear when the leaders of the Seventh Crusade decided that the expedition would be directed to Damietta. 'The Egyptian strategy' was by now an established crusading scheme that needed no particular justification and which could have been the plan all along. The main contingent of the army set out from Aigues Mortes in August 1248. Damietta may have been selected as the first target of the crusade to Egypt in the war council held in Cyprus in 1249, as reported by Jean de Joinville.[234] The claim that Alexandria was the real target and the army was carried by a storm near Damietta seems contrived.[235] It is also debatable whether Louis IX had in mind a permanent occupation of all or parts of Egypt from the start, or whether he was first planning to conquer cities so as to have a 'bargaining counter' by which Jerusalem could be saved.[236]

Even if the intent was to occupy Egypt as early as 1248, when the crusading army set sail from France, May 1246, a suggested year for Eudes's crusade sermon, seems too early for him to have known of a planned occupation and settlement of the conquered land. Louis IX himself took the cross in December 1244, and it took him some time to convince his subjects of the necessity to go on a crusade.[237] During the years 1245–48, when the preparations were made for the expedition, Louis IX and Eudes de Châteauroux were heavily involved in the raising of funds for the crusade.[238] Papal attention was divided, and few

---

[233] Louis IX brought with him to Egypt ploughs and other farming equipment by which the soil could be cultivated. *The Seventh Crusade*, trans. by Jackson, pp. 69, 92.

[234] Jean de Joinville, *Vie de Saint Louis*, ed. by Monfrin, pp. 88–91.

[235] Both Alexandria and Cairo were discussed as possible targets, according to Jean. Jean de Joinville, *Vie de Saint Louis*, ed. by Monfrin, pp. 88–91.

[236] *The Seventh Crusade*, trans. by Jackson, p. 71.

[237] Tyerman, *God's War*, pp. 770–75.

[238] Tyerman, *God's War*, pp. 773–82.

resources came from outside the Kingdom of France. There were crusades against Frederick II, the Mongols had devastated Hungary, and the Greeks were threatening Constantinople: thus the papal-imperial struggle and the defence of the Latin Empire, as well as the Mongol threat, were all consuming resources and men at the same time that Louis IX's crusade was in the making.[239] Given this situation, it would have been strange for the legate of the expedition to preach a crusade sermon that encouraged and defended the personal participation of non-combatants, thus denying Louis funds from their vow redemptions. There are two ways to solve this incongruity in the dating and the content of the sermon.

One possibility is that Eudes wanted to promote the participation of the women and children independently, without any regard for Louis's plans to occupy land and without any particular concern for the consequences this might have on the funding of the crusade. The apology in the sermon may simply reflect the legate's own opinions and visions of crusading. Eudes views the coming journey as a pilgrimage and makes repeated references in the sermon to the earthly and celestial Jerusalem, which may indicate that by the time the sermon was preached the destination of the crusade was still unclear, Jerusalem still being one of the options. However, references to Jerusalem were not uncommon in crusade propaganda for other crusades than those specifically directed to the Holy Land.[240]

The other possibility is to date the crusade sermon to a later year, to May 1248. As Alexis Charansonnet has acknowledged, the dating of Eudes's first sermon for the feast of St George is difficult, and the year 1246 is suggested on the basis that other possible dates are more unlikely.[241] However, the year 1248 cannot be ruled out. Charansonnet has expressed puzzlement over Eudes's enthusiasm to recruit women and children,[242] but if the sermon is dated to the year 1248, it can be viewed as the same kind of sermon for the crusaders that the *Sermo ad invitandum ad accipiendum crucem et ad confortandum crucesignatos* was, a sermon from 1248 that focuses on giving guidance and comfort to those who have already taken the cross and are about to leave for the Seventh

[239] For the rival crusades, see *The Seventh Crusade*, trans. by Jackson, pp. 49–62.

[240] See above, pp. 40–43.

[241] *UEE*, I, 119–27, esp. p. 120 n. 94. The possible years for the sermon seem to be 1246, 1247, and 1248. However, the year 1247 seems the most unlikely, given the situation at the time in the Kingdom of France with the barons' revolt against the clergy and Eudes's involvement in opposing the revolt. See above, p. 29 n. 90.

[242] *UEE*, I, 126–27.

Crusade, in addition to trying to recruit new crusaders, an aim common to most crusade sermons.

This would make the apology for the participation of the women and children in the sermon less peculiar. We know that once Louis IX's decision to go on the crusade had been made public and his appeals to his subjects to join him had taken effect, between the years 1245 and 1248, there was great crusading fervour in different parts of France. Furthermore, despite the initial reluctance and the competing crusades, both the French clergy and the laity signed up for the crusade in large numbers. Amongst the *crucesignati* there were groups of artisans, peasants, and other non-combatants.[243] In his sermon Eudes may be justifying the existence of these large groups of non-combatant crusaders, including women and children, who had already taken the cross with the intention of going. The legate may also be reacting to criticism from within the army, aggravated by the fact that such groups were about to set out for the crusade rather than redeeming their vows and staying at home.

The commutation and redemption of crusade vows was a disputed matter all through the thirteenth century. During the preparations for the Seventh Crusade, a scandal arose over the vow redemptions. In Frisia a false crusade preacher collected the money from the vow redemptions for himself. After the scandal, in March 1248, Innocent IV ordered the French bishops to apply sterner standards with the vow redemptions. The Bishop of Paris was to inspect and approve all vow redemptions.[244] However, the collectors of crusading funds in France complained that the weak and the feeble were unable to make the long journey to Paris to make their vow redemptions there, and it would be better if the collectors could make the decisions about the redemptions and the amount of the payment required on the spot.[245]

During the actual campaign in 1251, a popular movement in France called the Shepherds' Crusade also developed. This movement was born after the defeat at Mansurah and started as an attempt to aid Louis IX's crusade but turned into violence against the clergy. The anticlericalism of the crusade may

---

[243] Tyerman, *God's War*, pp. 775–76.

[244] Maier, *Preaching the Crusades*, p. 141.

[245] 'Triennis et biennis decimal ab anno mccxlviii collecta', ed. by Bouquet, esp. p. 540: 'Cum imbecilles crucesignati et debiles, ac alias ad pugnandum inutiles, transmitti praecipiantur ad reverendum patrem episcopum Parisiensem, cui votorum suorum redemptio a domino papa committitur, ut a votis suis, satisfactione praehabita, ab ipso episcopo absolvantur, et aliqui sint qui propter imbecillitatem et debilitatem ad ipsum accedere personaliter non possint pro redemptione votorum suorum'. See also Maier, *Preaching the Crusades*, pp. 141, 149.

have been a reaction against the papal policy of redeeming and commuting crusade vows. This policy was regarded by the 'shepherds' as a reason for the failure of the Egyptian expedition.[246] There appears to have been resentment and disappointment over the vow redemptions in different parts of France, both during the preparations for the Seventh Crusade and during the expedition, particularly among young shepherds, peasants, women, and children, who were described as the participants in the crusade, that is the non-combatants, who were usually instructed to redeem their vows and stay at home.

If Eudes's crusade sermon for the feast of St George is from 1248 rather than 1246, the sermon might be viewed in this context. In these circumstances Eudes may have considered it more practical to allow those non-combatants who did not want to redeem their vows with money, but wished to take part in Louis IX's crusade, to go ahead with their plans and not to attempt to force them to make vow redemptions. If this is the case, the sermon would be less about recruitment than about advising those who had already taken the cross and defending the presence of the non-combatants in the crusade host with the hope of creating unity between the different groups in the army. By May 1248, Louis IX's crusading scheme and the intent to occupy the land which the crusaders might seize would most likely have shaped into a plan, since the departure was only a few months away. Hence the participation of the non-combatant crusaders, the women and the children, would have been easier to accept for those in charge of the logistics of the crusade army, that is, the noble leaders, who were traditionally against the participation of the non-combatants.

The dating and the specific circumstances of Eudes's sermon for the feast of St George are debatable and they are likely to remain so, but the message is clear. The legate of the Seventh Crusade viewed the journey as a pilgrimage, in which women and children were entitled to take part. In fact, by joining the expedition the children could be considered to be following the example of Christ. Eudes reminded his audience in the sermon that Jesus himself was only twelve years old when he went on the journey to Jerusalem.[247] The children who joined the crusade could be interpreted as imitating the young Christ, just as the rest of the crusaders were emulating other episodes of his earthly life. This was the children's version of the *imitatio Christi*, which gave justification to their crusading and refuted the critics' claims.

Eudes appears to have wanted to create cohesion in the crusading force with his crusade sermon. He explained to the crusaders that their pilgrimage, their

---

[246] *The Seventh Crusade*, trans. by Jackson, pp. 179–80.

[247] Eudes de Châteauroux, 'De sancto Georgio', *UEE*, ii, 702. Lk. 2. 42–43.

journey to Jerusalem, ought to be made in the company of others, in a group which was united in their religion. The legate wished to build a strong sense of solidarity; for this reason he created an image of people merged together in their love for Christ, in their common intent, and in their mutual destination. Thus, the non-combatants, women and children, ought to be taken on the journey. Travelling together was safer and more pleasant; the burden of pilgrimage was easier to bear when it was shared.[248]

It is also important the bear in mind that Eudes's sermon for the feast of St George, whichever year we date it to, is a model sermon. This has been reworked and edited later on, and it was incorporated into the sermon collections made in Eudes's own scriptorium some fifteen or twenty years later. Eudes did not want to erase the apology on behalf of women and children's participation when the initial circumstances of the 1240s had changed, but the apology is represented in the model sermon that crusade preachers could use when promoting the crusades. This is how Eudes, an experienced crusade preacher, a former legate of an expedition, and a cardinal of the Roman Church, wished the crusade preachers to respond to questions about the participation of women and children in crusades or pilgrimages, and how he suggested the preachers should explain the nature of these journeys to their audiences in the 1260s and during the later period.

Eudes also encouraged the participation of non-noble participants in the Seventh Crusade in another sermon from 1248. Eudes explained in this sermon what others should do when they saw 'the older deer', the crusaders, leave for their journey. 'The young deer' should follow them 'in person' if possible, or if they were unable to leave they should at least participate in crusading 'in heart'.[249] Eudes used the biblical metaphor of the deer from Genesis throughout his model sermon.[250] The references to older and younger deer appear to

---

[248] Eudes de Châteauroux, 'De sancto Georgio', *UEE*, ii, 700–702, esp. p. 702.

[249] Eudes de Châteauroux, 'Ad invitandum ad accipiendum crucem et ad confortandum crucesignatos', *UEE*, ii, 736; *CPI*, p. 158.

[250] Eudes builds the sermon on Jacob's words to his son Nephtali: '*Nephtali, a hart let loose, and giving words of beauty*'. Gen. 49. 21. This sermon may have been first delivered in France before the departure of Louis IX on his first crusade to Egypt in 1248. There are passages in the sermon that seem to indicate an imminent departure on a crusade. Eudes mentions crusaders 'who will soon travel across the sea', comparing them to the first crusaders, the nobles who left France and conquered Antioch and Jerusalem. He also bids farewell to those staying behind, which would point to his own departure on the first crusade of Louis IX. Eudes de Châteauroux, 'Ad invitandum ad accipiendum crucem et ad confortandum crucesignatos', *UEE*, ii, 734, 736; *CPI*, pp. 154, 158.

point to social status, the *iuniores* being the common people who ought to follow the example provided by the *maiores*, that is, the king and the nobility. The metaphor was well suited to explain how the weaker and poorer people could participate in the crusade movement. If prevented from leaving by circumstances such as poverty, age, gender, or health, they could participate in the movement in spirit and offer perceptible aid in the form of prayers or financial support. However, the overriding aim was to include the *iuniores* among the actual participants in the expedition.[251]

Expulsions of Improper Crusaders

There is evidence that Eudes de Châteauroux's views were shared by women and children, many of whom regarded themselves as fit to take part in the Seventh Crusade. A famous passenger list has survived from the crusade that proves that women did not just accompany their husbands or parents on the expedition, but left by themselves in considerable numbers and without chaperons. The passenger list of the ship *St Victor* indicates that several women were travelling from Messina to Acre in 1250.[252]

On the *St Victor* there were 453 crusaders, of which 42 were women. Fifteen of these were accompanied by their husbands, one travelled with her father, two with their brothers, twenty-two had no male travelling companions, while the circumstances of two are unknown. There was also one father and a married couple travelling with their sons.[253] The original destination of the ship was Damietta in Egypt, not the Holy Land. The ship had to change course after Louis IX's crusade to Egypt had failed. It is difficult to know the specific intentions of the women or the children travelling on the ship. All the passengers on the list are generally referred to as *peregrini*. It is probable that many of the women and the children were travelling as pilgrims or as new settlers to the East.[254]

---

[251] Eudes de Châteauroux, 'Sermo ad invitandum ad accipiendum crucem et ad confortandum crucesignatos', *CPI*, p. 158: 'Sed vos alii, quid deberetis facere? Deberetis facere sicut faciunt iuniores cervi: quando vident maiores cervos iter arripere, vadunt post eos et eos sequuntur. Sic deberetis et vos facere, et si non vultis eos sequi corpore, saltem corde et oratione et subsidio debetis eos sequi, et si non modo saltem in alio passagio'.

[252] Kedar, 'The Passenger List of a Crusader Ship'.

[253] Kedar, 'The Passenger List of a Crusader Ship'.

[254] Kedar, 'The Passenger List of a Crusader Ship', pp. 268–69. For more information on the failure of the Seventh Crusade and on other aspects of the crusade, see *The Seventh Crusade*, trans. by Jackson.

It is, however, unclear how far the other authors of the crusade model sermons shared Eudes's opinions. Some may have had their reservations. Jacques de Vitry, for example, persuaded his close friend, Marie d'Oignies, not to take part in the Albigensian Crusade, although she wanted to go to Languedoc at the beginning of the 1210s. In the *Vita Mariae Oigniacensis*, Jacques says that Marie saw two crusading visions, after which she was so full of zeal for the crusade that he hardly managed to restrain her from joining in the campaign.[255] Jacques and his companions would not have succeeded in persuading Marie to abandon her plans without reminding her that there was 'a chance of scandalizing her nearest ones' by taking part in the crusade. When Jacques laughingly asked Marie what she would do if she got to the Languedoc region, Marie replied, 'I would honour my Lord there by confessing his name where all the impious have rejected him with blasphemy'.[256]

Marie d'Oignies's intentions appear to have been mildly amusing to Jacques. Her decision to leave would have set a bad example to her followers and friends, and possibly tempt other women to do the same, or lead others to sin, as Jacques's use of the term *scandalum* suggests.[257] It may also have been suspected that it would bring discredit to the newly born Beguine movement. However, Marie's reply seems to have made an impression on Jacques. The simple argument of honouring the Lord where others dishonoured him was further proof of her extraordinary piety, which should be admired by all, if not imitated.

Marie's revelations could also be used in the promotion of the crusade against the Albigensian heretics. Jacques took full advantage of the visions of

[255] Jacques de Vitry, *Vita Maria Oigniacensi*, *AASS*, v, 565. According to Jacques, Marie saw the first vision three years before the Albigensian Crusade was launched, in which heavenly crosses appeared in the sky, and another after Marie had heard of men killed by the Albigensians, in which she saw angels carrying the souls of those killed 'immediately to the joys of heaven without purgatory': 'Quando autem sancti Christi Martyres, qui zelo Crucifixi a longinquis partibus, ut Christi dedecus vindicarent, devenerant ad locum qui dicitur Mons-gaudii, ibidemque ab inimicis Crucis Christi interfecti sunt; ipsa, licet per tanta terrarum spatia remota esset, vidit sanctos Angelos gratulantes, et interfectorum animas absque aliquo purgatorio ad superna gaudia deferentes'.

[256] Jacques de Vitry, *Vita Maria Oigniacensi*, *AASS*, v, 565: 'Unde tantum hujus peregrinationis concepit ardorem, quod vix retineri posset, si sine scandalo proximorum aliquo modo id peragere valeret. Cumque quasi ridendo ab ea quaereremus, quid illic si pervenisset faceret; saltem ajebat illa, Dominum meum honorarem, illic nomen ejus confitendo, ubi toties impii abnegaverunt eum blasphemando'.

[257] The medieval term *scandalum* had connotations of 'sin' — scandal was something which led others either directly or as a consequence to sin. Thomas Aquinas, *Summa Theologiae*, secunda pars secundae, q. 43; For the term, see also Throop, *Criticism of the Crusade*, p. 70.

Marie in the *Vita*, using them to justify and promote the Albigensian Crusade while in the process of recording her saintly life. The propaganda value of these visions did not go unnoticed by other crusade preachers. In the *De predicatione sancte crucis*, Humbert de Romans also recounts the story. The mystic revelations served as evidence of the divine will set against the impious heretics in Languedoc. From so far away and even before the crusade had begun, Marie was able to see what would happen and feel the heavenly concerns of Christ. These visions gave explicit justification for the crusade. Marie's apparition seemed to promise direct ascent to heaven for all those who died at the hands of the heretics. The crusaders needed not worry about purgatory, for all of their sins had been forgiven. Hence if any had doubts about crusading against fellow Christians, these doubts could be set aside, for God wished to suppress the heresy of the Albigensians and would reward his servants abundantly.[258]

The sexuality of the women participating in the expeditions cast doubts on the purity of the army. A particular problem was the prostitutes who appeared to take part in all the major crusading campaigns. The expulsions of improper crusaders, 'the lewd women', became something of a standard course of action during the crusading period.[259] Humbert de Romans referred to these expulsions in his *De predicatione sancte crucis* and included an excerpt from Fulcher de Chartres's *Historia Hierosolymitana* describing the capture of Antioch. Crusade preachers could use this story in their sermons while promoting the crusades or explaining how moral questions related to the expeditions should be dealt with.[260]

During the siege of Antioch the crusade army suffered from various difficulties, and the leaders of the expedition decided to drive out all the crusading women from the army, both unmarried and married, so as to avoid sexual licentiousness and impurity, which were thought to have angered God. After

---

[258] Humbert de Romans, *De predicatione sancte crucis*, cap. xliij, De diuersis legendis sanctorum; Jacques de Vitry, *Vita Maria Oigniacensi*, *AASS*, v, 565.

[259] Robert de Clari, *La Prise de Constantinople*, ed. by Hopf, p. 58: 'Et quemanda on que on quesist et que on ostast toutes les foles femmes de l'ost, et que on les envoiast bien loins ens de l'ost. Et on si fist; que on les mist toutes en une nef; si les envoia on bien loins de l'ost'. Jacques de Vitry, *Epistola*, V, ed. by Huygens, pp. 117–18; 'Gesta Obsidionis Damiatae', *QBSS*, pp. 81–82; Jean de Joinville, *Vie de Saint Louis*, ed. by Monfrin, p. 84: 'Le commun peuple se prist aus foles femmes, dont il avint que le roy donna congié a tout plein de ses gens quant nous revenimes de prison. Et je li demandé pour quoi il avoit ce fait, et il me dit que il avoit trouvé de certein que au giet d'une pierre menue entour son paveillon tenoient cil leur bordiaus a qui il avoit donné congié, et ou temps du plus grant meschief que l'ost eust onques esté'. Tamminen, 'Crusading in the Margins?', esp. pp. 151–52.

[260] Humbert de Romans, *De predicatione sancte crucis*, cap. xl.

the expulsion the crusaders were able to conquer Antioch with the help of Christ himself.[261] Humbert de Romans's passage from Fulcher's *Historia Hierosolymitana* clearly reflects the concerns that the ecclesiastics might have with women's participation in the expeditions. The problem-solving method which the crusaders utilized in 1098 would be an appropriate way to solve similar problems during the thirteenth century, as suggested by the incorporation of the story into the manual.

The Old and the Sick

There were also old men and women who wanted to take part in the crusades, as well as those who were about to die from illness, age, or for some other reason, who were signed with the cross on their deathbed.[262] Pope Urban II appears to have discouraged the participation of these groups of Christians. According to one version of Urban's Clermont sermon, the pope declared that 'the old and the weak, who are unable to use arms' were not to take part in the expeditions.[263] Eudes's feast day sermon for St George gives an interesting perspective on this subject as well. In the sermon, Eudes used a motif of different seasons of the year and different liturgical feasts to explain crusading. Metaphorically speaking this kind of spiritual conversion or a pilgrimage to Jerusalem happened three times a year: during Easter, which is in the springtime, that is, during childhood, during Pentecost, which is in the summer, the age of youth, and during the feast of Tabernacles, which is in the autumn, the days of maturity.[264]

These are the age groups — children, youths, and adults — who should make the journey to Jerusalem, according to Eudes. After these periods of life comes old age. People should not travel to Jerusalem during this 'winter season', for in old age people are hardly ever converted to the Lord.[265] Eudes viewed the

[261] Humbert de Romans, *De predicatione sancte crucis*, cap. xl. Compare to Fulcher's account of the siege of Antioch, in Fulcher de Chartres, *Historia Hierosolymitana*, lib. I, cap. XV, ed. by Hagenmeyer, p. 223. See also Brundage, 'Prostitution, Miscegenation and Sexual Purity in the First Crusade', p. 59.

[262] *CPI*, p. 63.

[263] Robert the Monk, *Historia Iherosolimitana*, in *RHC Occ.*, iii, 729.

[264] Eudes de Châteauroux, 'De sancto Georgio', *UEE*, ii, 703: 'Et ter in anno: in Pascha, hoc est in pueritia; Pascha enim est in vere. Et in Penthecoste, id est in iuventute que est quasi estas. Et in Cenofegia, que est in autupno, hoc est in senectute in qua homo debet esse maturus'.

[265] Eudes de Châteauroux, 'De sancto Georgio', *UEE*, ii, 703: 'Non precipiebatur autem quod in hieme ascenderent in Iherusalem, quia in senio uix aut nunquam homines ad Dominum convertuntur'.

pilgrimage to Jerusalem, and the Seventh Crusade, as a journey of spiritual conversion. It meant the abandonment of old ways and the renunciation of former
sins. For the elderly, this appeared too late. Eudes maintained in the sermon
that it was commonly said that everyone, 'whether living or dead', should visit
Jerusalem, but surely whoever wants to climb up to Jerusalem has to set out on
the journey alive, so as to be able to arrive dead.[266]

In his crusade sermon, Eudes encouraged the personal participation of all
people in the expeditions, that is, of all ages except the elderly. The old were
not supposed to take part in the actual journeys, because for them the proper
time for such ventures had passed. Eudes's opinion may have been influenced
by Louis IX's crusading plans. If the sermon is from 1248, it may reflect the
king's intentions to occupy and populate the lands conquered during the crusade. Unlike women and children, old people could contribute little to these
plans. The old and the dying were unsuitable as new settlers, for they would die
too soon, from the conqueror's point of view. By contrast, the women and the
children were essential for populating newly acquired territories, as in them lay
the prospects for future generations.

During the thirteenth century, the papacy encouraged the signing of the
aged and the mortally ill with the cross. These crusaders, particularly those who
were very advanced in years or very ill, or already bedridden when taking the
cross, were not expected to make the journey in practice, but to redeem their
vows. Pope Innocent IV advised the crusade preachers to focus their attention
on those who were about to die. In the First Council of Lyons in 1245, it was
stipulated that the prelates should try to persuade the faithful to leave something in their testaments for the aid of the Holy Land or the Latin Empire,
from which they would earn 'a special indulgence'.[267] This appeared to be a good
deal both for those responsible for the financing of the crusades and for those
who were about to die. The crusade preachers could expect the dying to invest
a good portion or all of their funds in the vow redemptions, for they could not
personally profit any longer from their wealth. The dying would also seize the

---

[266] Eudes de Châteauroux, 'De sancto Georgio', *UEE*, ii, 703: 'Vulgo dicitur quod oportet
ut quilibet eat in Iherusalem, aut vivus aut mortuus. Sed certe oportet ut qui vult ad hanc
Iherusalem ascendere, ut vivus iter arripiat, et sic poterit mortuus pervenire'.

[267] 'Admonitio praelatorum ad populum sibi commissum', *COD*, p. 272: 'quatenus sin-
guli vestrum fideles populos vestrae curae commissos in vestris praedicationibus, vel quando
poenitentiam ipsis iniungitis, piis monitis inducatis, concessa super hoc, prout expedire videri-
tis indulgentia speciali, ut in testamentis, quae pro tempore fecerint, aliquid in Terrae sanctae
vel imperii Romaniae subsidium pro suorum peccaminum remissione relinquant'. *CPI*, p. 63;
Maier, *Preaching the Crusades*, pp. 145–47.

opportunity to earn full pardon for all their sins before dying, and thus hope to avoid purgatory or hell.[268]

There were some difficulties with this policy. Wills in which funds were bequeathed for the aid of the Holy Land left the relatives of the 'deathbed crusader' bitter. The heirs resented the loss of part or all of their inheritance. There may also have been problems caused by the sudden recuperation of the crusader who had been assumed to be mortally ill but who returned to health and could not redeem his vow with the promised sum — this at least according to Matthew Paris. Matthew describes the ill feelings caused by the vow redemptions with a story that the Bishop of Lincoln, Robert Grosseteste, on his own deathbed condemned the practice of signing the sick, the old, and the dying. According to Matthew, Grosseteste criticized this kind of trading — the pope was selling crosses as the Jews once sold the sheep and the oxen in the Temple.[269] Whether or not we can take this as an accurate account of Robert Grosseteste's last speech,[270] it seems clear that the business of the vow redemptions caused irritation, and the testaments of dying crusaders were one particular reason for a rancour over papal policy.

Jacques de Vitry discussed these issues in a roundabout way in his second crusade sermon. While previously mentioning in the sermon that the non-combatants — wives, children, and parents — could profit from the crusades, he goes on to assure the audience that those who would perhaps die before fulfilling their crusade vows would nonetheless also receive their reward.[271] This appears to be a message intended especially for the aged and the sick *crucesignati*, those about to die. Jacques wanted to confirm that the dying could also take the cross and gain the crusade indulgence, even if they died before departure. Those about to die could leave a contribution in their wills for the aid of the Holy Land, and thus redeem their vows with money when they passed

---

[268] *CPI*, p. 63.

[269] Matthew Paris, *Chronica majora*, ed. by Luard, p. 405: 'novimus Papam fratribus Praedicatoribus et Minoribus praecepisse ut morituris assistentes, quos inquirant diligenter, persuadeant urgenter ut condant testamenta sua ad commodum et subsidium Terrae Sanctae, et crucem assumant, ut cum convaluerint subsantiolas eorum emungant, vel si moriantur ab executoribus tantum [recipiatur] vel extorqueatur. Cruce quoque signatos personis laicis, sicut quondam in templo oves et boves venundari consueverunt, vendit apporiandos'. John 2. 14–15. Siberry, *Criticism of Crusading*, pp. 150–51; Maier, *Preaching the Crusades*, pp. 147–49.

[270] Modern scholars have expressed different views about the truthfulness of Robert Grosseteste's last speech. See Siberry, *Criticism of Crusading*, pp. 150–52; Maier, *Preaching the Crusades*, pp. 147–49.

[271] Jacques de Vitry, 'Item sermo ad crucesignatos vel -signandos', *CPI*, p. 116.

away. If this contribution was large enough in comparison to their wealth, they could earn the indulgence and be freed from their sins.

Jacques seems careful with his wording, perhaps because his views did not yet have official papal backing in the 1230s. *Crucesignati* who could not fulfil their vows and go on crusades because they died before departure were not to be blamed. Those who died from sickness, old age, or by accident — prematurely, from the crusade preacher's point of view — would not be deprived of their reward, as they had taken the cross out of devotion with the intention of going and with a contrite heart. For them the resolution — the decision to take the cross and the intention of going — equalled the deed itself.[272]

Jacques appears to stress that for the mortally ill and aged the decision to become crusaders should be the same as for the rest of the 'true' crusaders. The old and the sick should take the cross out of love for Christ and at least have the intention of going. They ought not become crusaders with the sole intention of helping themselves with their money. These *crucesignati* should not be motivated by selfish reasons, such as trying to escape death, purgatory, or hell simply by donating wealth. The intent was as important for these crusaders as it was for any other crusader. If they were not cured, if they did not gain strength or did not recover health sufficiently to travel, but died, this was not their fault, but the decision of God, and they would receive the crusade indulgence because of their testamentary provisions.

Harmonious Crusading

In the manual *De predicatione sancte crucis*, Humbert de Romans portrayed the crusade expedition as a journey on which people held together and stood by each other. Humbert wanted crusade preachers using his handbook to depict the crusade as a harmonious journey in which the rich participants willingly helped the poor ones. Humbert acknowledged that the crusade was a difficult and tiresome undertaking, but presented different themes and circumstances that would bring consolation for the participants. The crusaders could find comfort in the 'joy of conscience' and the 'security of salvation' as they no longer had

---

[272] Jacques de Vitry, 'Item sermo ad crucesignatos vel -signandos', *CPI*, p. 116: 'Multos insuper lucratus est Dominus qui signum crucis accipientes ex cordis contriti devotione se ipsos voto solempni Domino obligaverunt, unde licet preventi sint morte, quia per eos non stetit. Confidimus in Domino quod tam sancte voluntatis non privabuntur premio: talis enim voluntas pro facto reputatur in ipsis'.

the burden of their sins on their conscience, and they could be confident that they would get their reward, the crusader's indulgence, and earn salvation.[273]

Humbert emphasized the communal aspects of the crusade-pilgrimages. The crusaders would find consolation in the 'good company' of others. They would create a fellowship, where no one was alone. There would always be others around, on the right or on the left. There would be people singing, people bringing back news and rumours, people playing, and people helping and comforting others. The great magnates, the nobles, the ecclesiastics, and the 'good men' would journey together, achieving a harmonious society, where the rich would aid the poor, the strong would help the weak, and the *maiores* would not oppress the *minores*. There would be no envy, no disagreement, no injury, but all would have only one mind, to serve Christ.[274] This was the idealized image of the crusade-pilgrimage that Humbert wanted the crusade preachers who used his manual to impress upon their audiences.

These images of social harmony and the ideological premises of collective support and redistribution of wealth created equality among the different participants of the crusades. The emphasis on poverty, the apology on behalf of the paupers' participation, and the appeal to redistribute funds smoothed the differences between the rich and the poor in the crusading context. Ideologically the social relations among the participants of the crusade movement were more ambiguous and more equal than in normal circumstances. Here, the liminality of crusading seems to surface. The rich and the powerful ought not to show their high position in the social hierarchy while on the crusade, but they should demote themselves and express their humility and poverty. The poor, on the other hand, could be regarded to have a higher status in the movement than in ordinary circumstances, as their state of poverty was an ideological requirement for all the ideal crusaders.

---

[273] Humbert de Romans, *De predicatione sancte crucis*, cap. xxvi, De nouem que faciunt consolationem huiusmodi peregrinorum. See also *PCHL*, p. 212.

[274] Humbert de Romans, *De predicatione sancte crucis*, cap. xxvi: 'Tercium est societas bona. Sicut enim solitudo est peregrino occasio tristicie. ita bona societas cum alij precedunt alij subsequuntur. alij sunt a dextris. alij sunt a sinistris. alij cantant. alij rumores referunt. alij ludunt. alij alios iuuant. alij alios confortant. et similia. solent esse ad magnam consolationem. que autem potest esse melior societas quam crucesignatorum peregrinantium. in qua sunt tot magnates, tot nobiles, tot clerici. tot boni viri. tanta multitudo populi societas in quam. in qua diuites subueniunt pauperibus. fortes debiles. maiores non grauant minores. sed mutuo se iuuant inuicem omnes. Societas in qua non est inuidia. non est discordia. non sit inuicem iniuria. sed omnes uno animo sunt in seruitio Ihesu Cristi'.

The crusades were regarded by the crusade preachers as special pilgrimages. The close link between crusades and pilgrimages made it possible for women and children to take part in the actual campaigns. Women were as free to set out on pilgrimages as men were. Ideologically and legally they had every right to participate in a spiritual, penitential exercise.[275] The women and the children could take part in military ventures, which in ordinary circumstances they could not. Women and children participated together with adult male crusaders in the expeditions, and at times women even seem to have been involved in the fighting, either alongside the men or in their absence.

Together the rich and the poor, the weak and the powerful, the lesser folk and the nobles, the women, the children, and the men would create a *communitas*, to use Turner's controversial term,[276] or perhaps more aptly, a *societas*, to adopt Humbert de Romans's term.[277] The different social groups would enjoy each other's company and comfort each other during the crusade-pilgrimage. They would 'walk together, cross the sea together, pitch tents together, attack the enemies of Christ together, and be prepared to fulfil the will of God together'.[278] The collective journey and the shared objectives, the common dedication to Christ, and the concerted action against the enemy, as well as the common status of the *crucesignati*, united the crusaders and brought the different social groups inside the army closer to each other. This formed, at least ideologically and in the opinion of a crusade propagandist, Humbert de Romans, a strong sense of togetherness. The leaders of this special *societas* were the angels. The society of crusaders would also receive the aid of the saints and the prayers of the Church.[279]

Turner's concepts of liminality and *communitas* are useful to a certain extent in understanding the crusader's journey. However, the view that the pilgrims, or in this context the crusaders, would have been freed from social structures while participating in the pilgrimage is untenable. Humbert's image of *societas* has similarities to Turner's *communitas*, but the crusade was not a journey where the distance from social identities at home would lead to homogenization of

---

[275] Hodgson, *Women, Crusading and the Holy Land*, pp. 40–41.

[276] For the concepts of liminality, *communitas*, anti-structure, see Turner, *The Ritual Process*; Turner and Turner, *Image and Pilgrimage in Christian Culture*.

[277] Humbert de Romans, *De predicatione sancte crucis*, cap. xxvi.

[278] Humbert de Romans, *De predicatione sancte crucis*, cap. xxvi: 'simul ambulare. simul transfretare. simul tentoria collocare. simul Christi hostes inuadere. simul paratos esse ad exequendum Domini voluntatem'.

[279] Humbert de Romans, *De predicatione sancte crucis*, cap. xxvi.

status or to an 'anti-structure' as conceived by Turner. The social order was as valid during the crusading journey as it was at home: the kings and princes led the crusade armies, the knights fought against the enemies with their weapons, the ecclesiastics dealt with spiritual questions, and the common people followed the lead of and obeyed the decisions made by their superiors. However, the crusading journey does appear to have drawn all these different crusaders closer to one another and smoothed the differences between the social groups.

Conclusions

THE FEATURES OF THE TRUE CRUSADER

T his book has focused on the construction of the 'true' crusader in the crusade model sermons and preaching manuals of the thirteenth century. The purpose has been to explore how the ideal crusader was created, what features were regarded as important for the crusaders, and why these features were emphasized in crusade ideology. The thirty-six crusade model sermons and the two crusade preaching manuals examined in this study diverge in many ways from one another. The messages and the themes in the sermons differ, the length and the structure vary, the intentions of the authors may be dissimilar, and the intended audiences or the initial circumstances when the sermons were first preached different.

As a whole the crusade model sermons and the preaching manuals must be viewed as didactic texts that were written to inform the preachers utilizing them of different aspects of the crusade movement and to offer help for the crusade preachers in the construction of sermons. The authors of the models conveyed messages that they thought were important for understanding the movement, for justifying the expeditions, and for promoting the crusades, and which should therefore be understood by the preachers utilizing the models and communicated to the Christian audience hearing the sermons.

Some of the crusade model sermons may be linked to specific circumstances, such as the sermons of Philippe le Chancelier, Eudes de Châteauroux, and Federico Visconti. These sermons may be examined to a certain extent in the historical context in which they were originally preached. Eudes's sermons from the Seventh Crusade, for example, present an invaluable view for modern scholars to observe how crusade preachers delivered sermons during the expeditions and how they reacted to changing circumstances. However, all the sermons I examined are model sermons; thus they have been reworked and edited. Even if we are able to place the sermons into a historical context, or to link them to some particular situation during the expeditions or promotion of a specific campaign, the original sermons have been processed and revised and made into model sermons.

The authors of the model sermons utilized different methods while trying to guide the common preachers in their task, at the same time trying to provide examples for the promotion of crusades and messages meant to be communicated to the crusaders. The authors used exempla, distinctions, and comparisons. They structured their sermons in various ways and made the most of their own high education and their talent as skilled preachers, combining classical citations with contemporary politics or biblical quotations with secular stories.

This study has shown that many of the authors of the model sermons prepared the crusade preachers so that they could give guidance to both the *crucesignandi* and the *crucesignati* on how they should behave and think when they joined the movement or while they participated in the campaigns. The actions and the attitude of the participants in the movement were considered in several of the crusade model sermons and in the crusade preaching manuals. With the concept of the 'true' crusader — by explaining how ideal crusading was carried out — people's perceptions of crusades could be governed and the behaviour of the crusaders could be controlled by the preachers.

The authors of the crusade sermons do not speak with one voice, as the model sermons offer various views and opinions about the crusades and the crusaders. There is nonetheless some uniformity in the crusading messages expressed by the eight authors included. All of the crusade preachers studied here agreed that the crusades were fought for God and Christ and that this was God's will. Certain features and themes are consistent in the crusade sermons. The crusades are portrayed as penitential journeys, in which consequences of sins are discussed and their renouncement promoted.

The preachers represent crusading as following Christ, expressing one's love and devotion to him. The crusades are also depicted as holy wars similar to the wars fought by the Israelites. In the construction of the 'true' crusader, four uniform ideological features are manifested in the crusade model sermons: penitential, mimetic, pious, and soldierly features. These different features may be combined together in the model sermons or utilized in different ways. There are also certain exceptions: the soldierly features are, for example, non-existent in the crusade model sermon of Roger of Salisbury.

The four features highlight different aspects of ideal crusading. With the theme of piousness, for example, the crusaders' emotions and motivations could be directed. The crusaders were urged to love Christ and to express true reverence and obedience to God, that is, to show crusading piety. The four features of crusading converged in the model sermons in the idea of comprehensive conversion. The authors of the crusade sermons describe crusading for the 'true' crusaders as something that ought not to be halfhearted or careless under any circumstances. The ideal crusader did not join the movement on a whim, nor did he or she participate in the campaigns impassively. Becoming an ideal crusader involved a complete transformation from sinner to true servant of Christ.

The crusades provided for the participants of the movement a chance of a lifetime, but it also required a lifelong commitment from them. The authors of the crusade model sermons demanded from the crusaders true penitence and moral reform. The penitential theme is one of the most important and most consistently used themes in the thirteenth-century crusade model sermons. The penitential features of crusading are repeatedly utilized by the preachers in the construction of the 'true' crusader. This theme continues through all the different phases of the crusader's journey and even beyond crusading. From beginning to end it was important for the crusaders to express remorse and consider themselves penitents.

The authors of the crusade model sermons wanted the crusade preachers to explain crusading in their sermons with the theme of repentance. Prospective crusaders were urged to take the cross for penitential reasons, because of their sins. In the act of taking the cross true contrition had to be demonstrated. The ideal crusaders would show to everyone that they had sinned, that they regretted having sinned, and that they wanted to lay aside the burden of their sins. After this public display of remorse the crusaders ought to confess all their sins to priests with a contrite heart. This was an important phase in the construction of the 'true' crusader, since insincerity at this point could block the crusader's path to salvation and might lead to crusading failure later on during the expedition. Thus sincerity had considerable relevance for both the individuals taking the cross and for the crusade ideologists who wanted the crusades to succeed.

Many of the authors of the crusade model sermons took note of the outer expressions of true penitence in their sermons. The clothing, the eating, and the manner in which the journey was conducted should correspond to the crusaders' penitent and pious attitude, for 'true' crusaders showed their humility and renounced all extravagance, abandoning luxuries and vanities. However, the authors emphasized that the inner composition of the crusader's mind was more important. Insincere expressions of piety and remorse were futile or even damaging, as insincerity could anger God.

The penitential theme was also enclosed in other prominent themes in crusade ideology, such as pilgrimage or suffering, and was closely connected to important crusading concepts such as the crusade indulgence and crusading martyrdom. The ideal crusaders were on a similar penitential journey to the pilgrims. The crusaders ought to search for suffering, so as to purge themselves of their sins like true penitents. Only those who were truly contrite would gain the crusade indulgence, while those who suffered most and sacrificed themselves for God might be regarded as crusading martyrs. In some of the crusade model sermons the penitential theme supersedes all others; even the references to crusading may be secondary, as for example in the crusade model sermon of Roger of Salisbury.

The crusade preachers did not cease to fight against the sins of the crusaders after signing them with the cross. This aspect of crusade preaching is often overlooked by modern scholars. The task of a crusade preacher was not fulfilled once people were made crusaders, as the crusaders needed guidance on many different aspects of their journey. In particular, those preachers who participated in the expeditions themselves needed to offer advice and moral guidance, to comfort and to instruct the participants of the expeditions during the actual journeys. The authors of the crusade model sermons encouraged the crusaders to reform their ways, for the taking of the cross did not free them from sins committed as crusaders or sins committed after the crusading expeditions had begun.

The crusade model sermons that appear to have been preached to crusaders during the expeditions show an acute concern about the sins crusaders might commit. The theme *peccatis exigentibus hominum*, which was used by many of the preachers to explain crusading disaster, was not a mere literary device utilized only when confronted with crusading failure. Also, the urgent appeals for true penitence and renouncement of sins were not meant solely for the *crucesignandi*, that is, for recruiting purposes; the crusaders were encouraged time and again to repent their sins and to reform their ways during the actual campaigns. The authors of the model sermons sought to cleanse the crusaders from their sins, so as to avoid a repeat of past crusading failures.

The preachers attempted to have control over the actions of the crusaders to maintain high morale and discipline in the crusade army and to keep the crusaders spiritually clean while the expeditions were carried out. The crusaders' fight against inner enemies, the vices and the temptations of the devil, was as important as the fight against external enemies. In this internal struggle against their invisible enemies the crusaders could also be victorious, even if their physical journey failed and they were not victorious in the fight against their visible enemies.

Many different themes and models were utilized in the crusade sermons to guide the crusaders to comprehensive conversion. The ideal crusaders who had gone through moral rebirth were described as 'spiritually angels'. The authors of the crusade model sermons did not need to invent a new ethical code of conduct for the ideal crusaders, but they could utilize the existing Christian ideals. The angelic features of the 'true' crusaders could be attained by following closely the examples of Christ, the Old Testament patriarchs and kings, and the New Testament apostles, martyrs, and saints. Accordingly, the crusaders were instructed to imitate various biblical and saintly figures.

In this study I have argued against the opinions of some modern scholars who have played down the importance of the theme of *imitatio Christi* in crusade ideology and propaganda. My conclusion is quite the contrary — imitation of Christ was an important theme of crusading rhetoric. In fact, this theme appears as the most important of all those used by the authors of the crusade sermons of the thirteenth century when they instructed the crusaders about conduct. The theme of *imitatio Christi* provided for the preachers an ideological 'tool box', whence they could select various different instruments. In the crusading context the imitation of Christ could be conceived as meaning following Christ into battle, or it could mean following Christ's footsteps by going to the Holy Land and literally walking where he had walked, or it could mean following Christ's teachings or emulating his sufferings. The authors utilized the theme in many different ways as they explained crusading in their sermons.

With the concept of *imitatio Christi* the preachers could guide the crusaders through different stages of the crusading journey. The *crucesignandi* could be urged to imitate the love of Christ as they took the cross. With the example of Christ's infinite love, Christians could be inspired to take the cross, that is, to love as Christ had loved and to show similar devotion to Christ and Christians as Christ had shown for them. Alternatively, the crusaders' initial motivations could be remoulded to correspond with the ideological foundations of the crusade movement, as ideal crusaders were counselled to be motivated by love and devotion rather than by hatred. With the theme of *imitatio Christi* the pious, devout features of ideal crusading might be best explained to the crusaders.

The *crucesignati* could also be guided with the concept of *imitatio Christi*. Crusaders participating in the campaigns were to be instructed not to seek revenge or kill their enemies in a state of anger. Ideal crusaders did not wage war out of hatred, for they burned with love of God and Christ. This burning love could turn into zeal for God. The zealous 'true' crusaders might kill their enemies out of love for Christ, because God wanted it so. Their burning zeal was an emotion similar to righteous anger, through which the ideal crusaders could be conceived as instruments of God's wrath and justice that were wreaked upon his enemies.

The participants of crusades were also advised by the authors of the model sermons to imitate many different characteristics of Christ, to adopt his way of life or to follow his teachings while taking part in the campaigns or supporting the movement from the home front. The ideal crusaders were encouraged to emulate Christ's humility, poverty, simplicity, and love. If they followed Christ's example in all things, the crusaders could not wander off the penitential path or relapse into vice, for Christ had no vices, only virtues.

The imitation of the sufferings of Christ was represented as particularly important for the 'true' crusaders in the model sermons. Through such imitation, the participants of crusades could prove that they were 'true' crusaders. The ideal crusaders would go through tribulations and seek out suffering, thus acquiring further merit that would enable them to build a closer relationship with Christ. The 'true' crusaders, who suffered voluntarily for Christ's sake, showed their love and compassion for him. They would be able to find Christ, 'wear his skin on the outside', and hold him in their hearts by taking part in the Passion of Christ. The truest of the crusaders were also prepared to imitate Christ's sacrifice on the cross and die for him. This ultimate emulation was a sign of true commitment and devotion that would make the ideal crusaders Christ's special friends.

The crusaders were also guided to ideal crusading with models and examples which were taken from other traditions and from other contexts than the biblical one. The pilgrimage tradition and the feudal system provided many established rules and codes of conduct that some crusade preachers found applicable in their sermons. In particular, those authors of the model sermons who themselves participated in major crusade expeditions to distant destinations found the pilgrimage theme suitable for guiding the crusaders. It was a theme that appears to have had continuing significance in thirteenth-century crusade propaganda and ideology, contrary to some scholarly views.

Jacques de Vitry, Humbert de Romans, and Eudes de Châteauroux used the theme of pilgrimage in their model sermons when explaining to the crusaders how they ought to behave during the journey. The modesty, humility, and contrition of the pilgrims and the acts of purification that belonged to the pilgrimage tradition were traits and courses of action that the 'true' crusaders should follow. The crusade preachers also utilized features of the feudal system, such as lordship, vassalage, loyalty, and devotion, while explaining to the crusaders the call for military service, requiring of the crusaders similar faith and loyalty to God as that of good vassals to their lords.

The authors of the crusade model sermons portrayed the crusades as devotional enterprises, where all the participants should openly express their deep devotion to God. When examining the construction of the ideal crusader, the soldierly features appear, perhaps surprisingly as we are dealing with military ventures, the least significant for the authors of the crusade model sermons. This is explained by the heavy emphasis on spiritual values in thirteenth-century crusade propaganda and ideology. The authors of the crusade sermons represent the ideal crusaders as spiritual soldiers, as God's warriors, whose virtues were priestly virtues — the love of Christ, the practice of charitable works or penitential exercises, or the demonstration of pious devotion to God.

The military skills of the crusaders, the strength of the armies, or the number of the crusaders are inconsequential for the crusade preachers. These aspects could even be considered harmful in the creation of the ideal crusader, for trust in physical strength might suggest, at least to some of the authors of the sermons, a lack of devotion or failure to reach the spiritual standards of ideal crusading. The soldierly features are utilized in the construction of the 'true' crusader as an explanation of the defensive nature of crusading. The ideal crusaders fought with physical weapons so they could liberate the patrimony of Christ, or the occupied lands of the Christians, and so protect the true faith, the Church, or the weak and the innocent who were persecuted and oppressed. The 'true' crusaders reacted against aggression, and their military measures were protective and responsive: the crusaders themselves were not aggressive or belligerent.

Piety and a love of God would also make the crusaders good soldiers. The authors wanted the crusade preachers who used their models or manuals to underline the zeal of the crusaders in their sermons and to stress the need to stay firm and committed to the cause. The pious determination of the crusaders would make them good warriors in a holy war. They would fight vigorously and bravely against their enemies, neither wishing to return home too early nor trying to escape possible death. The soldierly features of the 'true' crusaders would be demonstrated when they burned with the love of God, wanting only to fight for him and to conquer his enemies. This zeal would make the crusaders true soldiers of God.

The authors of the crusade model sermons express many different views of the crusades and depict many different kinds of 'true' crusaders. The intentions of the authors and the various audiences of the crusade sermons obviously had an influence on the different views. The boundaries of crusading seem to be most blurred in the sermons preached initially to ecclesiastical audiences. In Philippe le Chancelier's crusade sermons, for example, the ecclesiastics are for the most part regarded as supporters of the movement who could help the crusaders from the home front. They could give financial aid for the crusaders or spiritual support for the soldiers and against their enemies from afar. The ecclesiastics could thus actively participate in the crusade movement without being signed with the cross.

Philippe also appears to have hoped that the ecclesiastics would assist in the promotion of the crusades, that is, that they would preach the cross. The crusade preachers could gain the crusade indulgence from these services. Some of the religious could also take the cross, which would be an example for others to follow. These ecclesiastics would then be signed with the cross and go on the expeditions. In Philippe's crusade sermons these different ways of ecclesiastical participation create some confusion with regard to ideal crusading. The distinction between the participants of the expeditions and the supporters of the movement — between the 'true' crusaders and the 'true' supporters — is rather hazy. There are similarly blurred boundaries in the crusade model sermons of Federico Visconti and Roger of Salisbury, where the participation of the ecclesiastics is also discussed or the crusaders' and penitents' actions guided. It is nonetheless clear that the crusaders, the penitents, and the supporters of the movement needed to be pious, contrite, and sincere in order to be considered 'true' crusaders or truly penitent.

The authors of the crusade sermons represent the crusades as a movement in which all Christians could and should take part. Different kinds of crusaders could also be regarded as 'true' crusaders. The ecclesiastics are portrayed as a significant group of crusaders, whose input is needed and who could be conceived as 'true' crusaders, if they acted accordingly during the journeys. The participation of the poor is also defended in some of the model sermons. The poor were potentially even better crusaders than the rich, for the paupers took part in the expeditions humbly, in the state of modesty and poverty in which the journeys ought to be taken.

The participation of women and children is also specifically defended in one of the crusade sermons. The evidence of this sermon, preached by the legate of the Seventh Crusade, suggests that the critical views expressed by modern scholars on the crusading of women and children should also be reassessed. The sermon writers' criticism of the participation of women and children in the crusades is not as one-dimensional or unambiguous as often put forward, but more nuanced. Women were regarded in the sermons as impediments and in the crusading context as a threat to the purity of crusading men, but women and even children could also be regarded as 'true' crusaders and their participation in the campaigns might be supported, even by high-ranking ecclesiastics such as Eudes de Châteauroux.

There are many different kinds of 'true' crusaders represented in the sermons and various groups whose participation is not only defended but also encouraged. Gender, status, descent, wealth, or profession did not determine who could be considered a 'true' crusader. Their young age did not mean that the children were deprived of the chance to go crusading. However, in one of the sermons old age was regarded as a handicap that might prevent participation in expeditions. The old were encouraged to give financial aid for the crusade movement rather than go on campaigns. There were also other groups, such as townspeople, whose crusading efforts were viewed negatively in some of the sources.

The different kinds of 'true' crusaders presented often seem to reflect the intentions of the crusade preachers and the possible audiences of the original sermons. When praising the efforts of the knights and condemning the townspeople, it is likely that the knights were in the audience of the initial crusade sermon and the intention of the preacher was to stir up crusading enthusiasm among this particular group, rather than the townsfolk. When calling the clergy the 'other high mountains' who participated in the crusades, it was this group that made up the audience and whose aid was being requested.

The crusaders were in many ways in an exceptional, 'liminal' situation. After making the crusade vow, those signed with the cross gave up their old life, separated themselves from normal society, and began a crusading journey. The *crucesignati* were between the making of the vow and the fulfilling of the vow. They were pilgrims on the road to both the earthly Jerusalem and the heavenly Jerusalem, travellers between the two destinations. The crusaders were former sinners on the way to redemption, fighting against internal as well as external enemies, and waging a war in both the visible and the invisible world. Many of the crusaders were also members of the laity, but as crusaders they were regarded as having a religious calling, obliged to follow rules similar to those followed by the clergy and privileged with the same advantages as the servants of the Church or pilgrims. The ideal crusaders bore the stigmata of Christ on their bodies and in their hearts. The 'true' crusaders were physically suffering the tribulations of Christ on their own bodies, but at the same time they were 'spiritually angels', guided by love and charity, freed from the burden of temporal sins — between humanity and deity.

'True' crusading also created some social ambiguity, a form of equality between all the participants of the movement. The rules and the roles of ordinary life could differ in the crusading context. The nobles and the rich were instructed to downgrade themselves in the crusade model sermons: while taking part in the crusades, they should redistribute their wealth, disregard their position, forget about their nobility, and show humility and modesty. The poor crusaders, on the other hand, were upgraded to a higher status and applauded for attaining one of the standards of ideal crusading by being poor. Women and children also gained a certain degree of equality, just by being allowed to take part in the campaigns with the adult male participants.

The rapprochement of different groups of crusaders was influenced by both practical and ideological causes. The different social groups came into close contact with each other during the crusade expeditions: they made their voyages together across the sea in ships, they journeyed overland together to the intended destinations, they camped together during the expeditions, and they fought together against the common enemy. These practical reasons, the close and inevitable contact between the different groups, decreased the gulf between the social groups. The authors of the crusade model sermons also wanted to create harmony between the different groups within the army. The participants of the expeditions all shared a common status, a common goal, and a common devotion to Christ. The crusade preachers were guided by the authors of the model sermons to emphasize the cohesion of the crusade host and were urged to build a sense of solidarity in their sermons. The special *societas* of crusaders, led by angels and saints, would fight against the enemies of God and move together towards salvation. Ideologically all of the crusaders, whatever their social origin or the group to which they belonged, were the *electi*, chosen by God and redeemed by Christ. Together the *crucesignati* would form an invincible force that fought only for God.

The various kinds of participants could create peculiarities and different 'levels' of ideal crusading, which may be observed particularly when examining the rewards and the merits of crusading. A *crucesignatus* who took the cross on his deathbed with the sole intention of redeeming the vow immediately afterwards or after dying could be conceived a 'true' crusader if he was motivated by the love of God and was sincerely penitent. The reward for this redemption would depend on the amount which the crusader was willing to pay in proportion to his wealth. This kind of crusader could earn the crusade indulgence or a partial indulgence without ever leaving his bed. On the other hand, a *crucesignatus* who took part in an expedition personally, but for the wrong reasons or in an improper manner, could ideologically be regarded as a 'bad' crusader rather than a 'true' one, even if this crusader travelled a long way with the army.

The amount of merit that the crusaders could gain through crusading was equivalent to the amount of suffering they were willing to endure for Christ's sake. A 'true' crusader who redeemed his vow and stayed at home and a 'true' crusader who suffered deeply during the journey could both gain the crusade indulgence, but they would earn a different amount of merit from crusading. Those 'true' crusaders who were prepared to suffer the most, who could prove their loyalty and love by first suffering and then dying for Christ during the expeditions, might be regarded as the 'truest' of the crusaders. These crusaders would receive the love and the special friendship of Christ. Those crusaders who died during the expeditions from sickness or of hunger could also be regarded as having exceptional merit, while the ideal crusaders who died in battle were the purest of all.

The comprehensive conversion promoted by many of the authors of the crusade model sermons might mean, in ideal cases, 'permanent' liminality for the crusaders or, more accurately, indissoluble change. The authors urged the sinners to reform their ways fully and commit themselves to the service of God. For some of the 'true' crusaders this would mean withdrawal from the ordinary world and mundane life for good. Some crusaders would stay in the service of Christ in the Holy Land and fight against the enemies of God even after a crusade campaign was over and their vows had been fulfilled. Some crusaders would join the military orders or other monastic institutions, where they could continue to seek God and serve Christ through contemplation, abstinence, and works of mercy. Others would try to compensate for the living of a worldly life after a crusade by continuing to do works of penance and by seeking further indulgences, or even another crusade indulgence, as Louis IX did. These ideal crusaders would persevere and would stay on the chosen path until the end. They were deprived of crusading martyrdom, but they would be living up to the highest standards of 'true' crusading as put forth by the crusade preachers.

APPENDICES

Appendix I. Crusade Preaching Manual

Manuscripts/Editions used in this study	Incipit/ Thema	Date	Audience/ Place	Occasion/ Context
Oxford, Balliol College, MS 167/ R *QBSS*, pp. 1–26	Brevis ordinacio de predicacione sancte crucis laicis facienda *etc.*	*c.* 1216	crusade preachers/ crusaders England	crusade preaching crusades to the Holy Land/ crusades

Appendix II. Crusade Model Sermons of Philippe le Chancelier

Manuscripts/Editions used in this study	Incipit/Thema
Avranches, MS 132, fols 248va–250ra	Sermo scolaribus inter Epiphaniam et Purificationem tempore quo rex Ludovicus assumpsit crucem in Albigenses, de dolore et signis doloris eccles sancte matris nostre et infirmitate et causis doloris et remediis contra dolore et quid sit clipeum levare
Avranches, MS 132, fols 250ra–251ra	Sermo de eodem, quomodo apparuit potentia Dei et sapientia et bonitas in eo quod mutavit voluntatem regis et principum prius contradicentium ad assumendum crucem, quod factum est per tria suffragia supradicta, scilicet elemosinam, ieiunium et orationem, et nota v psalmos qui intitulantur ab oratione
Avranches, MS 132, fols 251ra–252vb	Sermo de eodem, de gaudio quod rex et principes assumpserunt crucem; quod sic altare et que oblationes et quomodo concordant que facta sunt in Purificatione
Avranches, MS 132, fols 272rb–273vb	*Dicit Dominus ad Moysen: Dic Aaron: Tolle virgam tuam et extende manum super aquas Egypti et super fluvios et rivos et super paludes et omnes lacus ut vertantur in sanguinem, et sit cruor in universa terra Egypti, tam in ligneis va quam in saxeis. Elevans ergo virgam* etc.
Avranches, MS 132, fols 243ra–244vb	Sermo in die veneris infra octabas Assumptionis beate Virginis apud Sanctu Victorem in processione pro rege Ludovico quando erat ante Avinionem, quomodo tota spes nostra debet esse in cruce et beata Virgine et quomodo Christus multiplex pependit pro nobis ut nos ad simile provocaret

Appendix III. Crusade Model Sermons of Jacques de Vitry

Manuscripts/Editions used in this study	Incipit/Thema
Troyes, MS 228, fols 148rb–149rb *CPI*, Sermo I, pp. 82–99	Sermo ad crucesignatos vel -signandos
Troyes, MS 228, fols 149rb–151va *CPI*, Sermo II, pp. 100–127	Item sermo ad crucesignatos vel signandos
Troyes MS 228, fols 151rb–152va *JVSP*, Sermo 49, pp. 88–94	Ad peregrinos, thema sumpta ex epistola ad Galathas iii
Troyes MS 228, fols 152va–154rb *JVSP*, Sermo 50, pp. 94–102	Ad peregrinos. Thema sumpta ex Zacharias ultimo

e	Audience/Place	Occasion/Context
-2.2.1226 ible date: .1226	University community in Paris	Second Sunday of Epiphany Other occasions: feast day of the Conversion of St Paul Albigensian Crusade (1209–29)
-2.2.1226 ible date: .1226	University community in Paris	Third Sunday of Epiphany Other occasions: feast day of the Conversion of St Paul Albigensian Crusade (1209–29)
-2.2.1226 ible date: l226	University community in Paris	Candlemas Other occasions: for preaching at councils of prelates and princes Albigensian Crusade (1209–29)
.1226	King Louis VIII and the crusaders at Bourges	King Louis VIII took the cross Other occasions: feast day of the Exaltation of the Cross; Feast day of the Invention of the Cross; Feast days of the Virgin; sermons for the lepers Albigensian Crusade (1209–29)
.1226	Paris townspeople procession at Saint-Victor in Paris	Friday after the feast of the Assumption of the Virgin procession held to support the crusaders besieging Avignon Albigensian Crusade (1209–29)

e	Audience/Place	Occasion/Context
)–40	Crusaders and intending crusaders	Crusades (Fifth Crusade, 1217–21)
)–40	Crusaders and intending crusaders	Crusades (Fifth Crusade, 1217–21)
)–40	Crusaders and pilgrims	Crusades and pilgrimages (Fifth Crusade, 1217–21)
)–40	Crusaders and pilgrims	Crusades and pilgrimages (Fifth Crusade, 1217–21)

Appendix IV. Crusade Model Sermon of Roger of Salisbury

Manuscripts/Editions used in this study	Incipit/Thema
PCHL, Appendix B, pp. 227–31	*Ascendente* Ihesu *in naviculam*, et cetera. Istud poste[esse thema ad crucesignatos vel in die Parasceves

Appendix V. Crusade Model Sermons of Eudes de Châteauroux

Manuscripts/Editions used in this study	Incipit/Thema
Arras MS 876 [olim 137], fols 88vb–90rb	Sermo contra hereticos de Albigensibus partibus
Roma, AGOP, MS XIV, 35, fols 27rb–28rb *CPI*, Sermo IV, pp. 160–65 *UEE*, Sermo 2, ii, 697–99	Sermo de cruce et de invitatione ad crucem
UEE, Sermo 3, ii, 700–705	De sancto Georgio
Roma, Bibl. Angelica, MS 157, fols 137vb–140ra *CPI*, Sermo I, pp. 128–43 *UEE*, Sermo 8, ii, 721–28	Sermo in conversione sancti Pauli et exhortatio ad assumendam crucem
UEE, Sermo 9, ii, 729–32	Sermo in festo reliquiarum (sancte capelle regis Francie)
Roma, AGOP, MS XIV, 35, fols 22vb–23vb *UEE*, Sermo 10, ii, 733–36 *CPI*, Sermo III, pp. 152–59	Sermo ad invitandum ad accipiendum crucem et ad confortandum crucesignatos
UEE, Sermo 11, ii, 737–41	De sancto Georgio sermo
UEE, Sermo 12, ii, 742–46	Sermo in festo sanctarum reliquiarum
UEE, Sermo 13, ii, 747–49	Sermo de sancto Georgio
Arras, MS 876 [olim 137], fols 159va–161ra *PCHL*, Appendix D, pp. 236–39 *UEE*, Sermo 14, ii, 750–56	Sermo in anniversario Roberti comitis Attrabatens et aliorum nobilium qui interfecti fuerant a Sarracenis apud Mansoram in Egipto

ate	Audience/Place	Occasion/Context
44–47	Crusaders England	Crusades on Good Friday Other occasions: fourth Sunday after the octave of Epiphany

ate	Audience/Place	Occasion/Context
26	University community in Paris?	Albigensian Crusade (1209–29)
tober 1245	At the Parliament of King Louis IX in Paris	Convened to organize Louis IX's first crusade Seventh Crusade (1248–54)
.4.1246/1248?	France crusaders and intending crusaders	Feast of St George Seventh Crusade (1248–54)
1.1248?	Crusaders and intending crusaders	Feast day of the Conversion of St Paul Seventh Crusade (1248–54)
4.1248	Louis IX, nobility, ecclesiastics, many noble crusaders	Dedication of Sainte-Chapelle Seventh Crusade (1248–54)
5.1248?	Crusaders and intending crusaders	Seventh Crusade (1248–54)
4. 1249	Crusaders at Cyprus	Feast of St George Seventh Crusade (1248–54)
9. 1249	Crusaders in Damietta	Feast of the holy relics Seventh Crusade (1248–54)
4. 1250	Crusaders in Damietta	Feast of St George Seventh Crusade (1248–54)
.1251?	Crusaders in the Holy Land (mainly French audience?)	Anniversary sermon for Robert d'Artois and the other nobles Seventh Crusade (1248–54)

continued on the following page

Crusade Model Sermons of Eudes de Châteauroux (cont.)

Manuscripts/Editions used in this study	Incipit/Thema
Arras, MS 876 [olim 137], fols 161ra–162ra *PCHL*, Appendix D, pp. 240–43 *UEE*, Sermo 15, II, 757–61	Sermo in eodem anniversario
UEE, Sermo 16, II, 762–66	Sermo in festo sanctarum reliquiarum
Roma, AGOP, MS XIV, 35, fols 21va–22vb *CPI*, Sermo II, pp. 144–51 *UEE*, Sermo 23, II, 820–24	Sermo de invitatione ad crucem
Arras, MS 876 [olim 137], fols 108rb–109rb *CR*, Sermon 1, pp. 376–79	Sermo de rebellione Sarracenorum Lucherie in Ap.
Arras, MS 876 [olim 137], fols 109rb–110va *CR*, Sermon 2, pp. 379–82	Sermo de rebellione Sarracenorum Lucherie
Arras, MS 876[olim 137], fols 110va–111vb *CR*, Sermon 3, pp. 382–85	Sermo de rebellione Sarracenorum Lucherie
Roma, AGOP, MS XIV, 35, fols 26ra–27rb *CPI*, Sermo V, pp. 166–75 *UEE*, Sermo 49, II, 980–85	Sermo ad invitandum ad crucem

ate	Audience/Place	Occasion/Context
..1251, 1252, 53, 1254?	Crusaders in the Holy Land (clerical audience?)	Anniversary sermon for Robert d'Artois and the other nobles
		Seventh Crusade (1248–54)
51	Crusaders in the Holy Land	Feast of the Holy Relics
		Seventh Crusade (1248–54)
60	Crusaders and intending crusaders; esp. the nobility	Crusade against the Mongols
bruary 1268 – gust 1269	Crusaders and intending crusaders audience: curia, (King Charles of Anjou?)	Crusade against the Lucera Muslims
bruary 1268 – gust 1269	Crusaders and intending crusaders	Crusade against the Lucera Muslims
bruary 1268 – gust 1269	Crusaders and intending crusaders	Crusade against the Lucera Muslims
tumn 1268	Crusaders and intending crusaders Italy	Crusade against the Ghibellins?

BIBLIOGRAPHY

Manuscripts

Aberdeen, Aberdeen University Library, MS 22, <http://www.abdn.ac.uk/bestiary/translat/22r.hti> [accessed November 2012]

Arras, Médiathèque d'Arras, MS 876 [olim 137]

Assisi, Biblioteca del Sacro Convento, MS 501

Avranches, Bibliothèque municipale d'Avranches, [Hôtel de Ville], MS 132

Città del Vaticano, Archivum Secretum Vaticanum, Reg. Vat. 5

Firenze, Biblioteca Medicea-Laurenziana [BML], MS Plut. 33 sin. 1

Oxford, Balliol College, MS 167

Paris, Bibliothèque nationale de France [BnF], MS latin 14470

Paris, Bibliothèque nationale de France [BnF], MS latin 17509

Paris, Bibliothèque nationale de France [BnF], MS nouv. ac. lat. 999

Roma, Biblioteca Angelica, MS 157

Roma, Santa Sabina, Archivio Generale dell'Ordine dei Predicatori [AGOP], MS XIV, 34

Roma, Santa Sabina, Archivio Generale dell'Ordine dei Predicatori [AGOP], MS XIV, 35

Troyes, Médiathèque de l'Agglomération Troyenne, MS 27-2

Troyes, Médiathèque de l'Agglomération Troyenne, MS 228

Troyes, Médiathèque de l'Agglomération Troyenne, MS 401

Troyes, Médiathèque de l'Agglomération Troyenne, MS 1099

Troyes, Médiathèque de l'Agglomération Troyenne, MS 1504

Primary Sources

Albertus Magnus, *Commentarii in IV Sententiarum*, in *Opera omnia*, ed. by Augusti Borgnet, vol. XXX (Paris: Apud Ludovicum Vives, 1894)

Alexander III, *Cor nostrum*, in *Patrologiae Cursus Completus. Series Latina*, ed. by Jacques-Paul Migne, 221 vols (Paris: Garnier, 1844–64), CCXXI, cols 1294–96

Alexander Minorita, *Expositio in Apocalypsim*, ed. by Alois Wachtel, Monumenta Germaniae Historica, Quellen zur Geistesgeschichte des Mittelalters, 1 (Weimar: Hermann Böhlaus Nachfolger, 1955)

Ambrosius Mediolanensis, *De officiis ministrorum*, in *Patrologiae Cursus Completus. Series Latina*, ed. by Jacques-Paul Migne, 221 vols (Paris: Garnier, 1844–64), XVI, cols 23–184

Analecta Novissima Spicilegii Solesmensis, altera continuatio, ed. by Jean-Baptiste Pitra, vol. II (Tusculana, 1888)

'Andreae Ungari description victoriae a Karolo Provinciae comite reportatae', ed. by Georg Waitz, in Monumenta Germaniae Historica, Scriptores, 26 (Hannover: Hahn, 1882), pp. 559–80

'Anonymi de Innocentio IV. P. M. antichristo libellus', in *Fratris Arnoldi Ord. Praed. De Correctione Ecclesiae Epistola*, ed. by Eduardus Winkelmann (Berlin: E. S. Mittler et Filii, 1865), pp. 20–22

Anonymi Gesta Francorum et aliorum Hierosolymitanorum, ed. by Heinrich Hagenmeyer (Heidelberg: Winter, 1890)

'Aspidis ova ruperant', in *Acta imperii inedita, seculi XIII*, ed. by Eduard Winkelmann (Innsbruck: Wagner, 1885), II, 717–21

Augustinus, *Epistola XLVII*, in *Patrologiae Cursus Completus. Series Latina*, ed. by Jacques-Paul Migne, 221 vols (Paris: Garnier, 1844–64), XXXIII, cols 184–87

——, *Sermo CCCXVI*, in *Patrologiae Cursus Completus. Series Latina*, ed. by Jacques-Paul Migne, 221 vols (Paris: Garnier, 1844–64), XXXVIII, col. 1432

Bacon, Roger, *Opus Majus*, ed. by John Henry Bridges, *The 'Opus Majus' of Roger Bacon* (Oxford: Clarendon Press, 1897)

Bahā' al-Dīn Ibn Shaddād, *The Rare and Excellent History of Saladin*, trans. by D. S. Richards (Aldershot: Ashgate, 2001)

Baldric de Dol, *Historia Ierosolimitana*, in *Gesta Dei per Francos, sive Orientalium expeditionum et regni Francorum Hierosolymitani historia*, ed. by Jacques Bongars, vol. I (Hanoviae: Typis Wechelianus, 1611), pp. 84–138

Bernard of Clairvaux, *De consideratione ad Eugenium papam*, in *S. Bernardi Opera*, vol. III, *Tractatus et Opuscula*, ed. by Jean Leclercq and Henri Rochais (Roma: Editiones Cistercienses, 1963), pp. 393–493

——, *De laude novae militiae*, in *S. Bernardi Opera*, vol. III, *Tractatus et Opuscula*, ed. by Jean Leclercq and Henri Rochais (Roma: Editiones Cistercienses, 1963), pp. 213–39

——, *Epistolae*, in *Patrologiae Cursus Completus. Series Latina*, ed. by Jacques-Paul Migne, 221 vols (Paris: Garnier, 1844–64), vol. CLXXXII

——, *Sermones de tempore*, in *Patrologiae Cursus Completus. Series Latina*, ed. by Jacques-Paul Migne, 221 vols (Paris: Garnier, 1844–64), vol. CLXXXIII

Bernold von Konstanz, *Chronicon*, ed. by Georg Heinrich Pertz, in Monumenta Germaniae Historica, Scriptores, 5 (Hannover: Hahn, 1882), pp. 385–467

Biblia Sacra Iuxta Vulgatam Clementinam, <http://vulsearch.sf.net/html> [accessed November 2012]

Biblia Sacra Iuxta Vulgatam Versionem, ed. by R. Weber, vols I–II (Stuttgart: Württembergische Bibelanstalt, 1969)

Bonaventura, *Epistola de imitatione Christi*, in *Doctoris Seraphici S. Bonaventurae, Opera Omnia*, vol. VIII (Florentiam: Ad Claras Aquas, Quaracchi, 1898), pp. 499–503

'Brevis ordinacio de predicacione' = 'Ordinacio de predicacione S. Crucis in Anglia', ed. by Reinhold Röhricht, *Quinti belli sacri scriptores minores* (Geneva: J.-G. Fick, 1879), pp. 1–26

Caesarius von Heisterbach, *Homiliae*, ed. by Johann Andreas Coppenstein, *Fasciculus Moralitatis Venerabilis Fr. Caesarii Heisterbacensis*, vol. III (Coloniae: Apud Petrum Henningium, 1615)

Calendar of Entries in the Papal Register Relating to Great Britain and Ireland: Papal Letters, ed. by W. H. Bliss, vol. XIX (London: Her Majesty's Stationery Office, 1893)

Cartulaire de l'abbaye de Saint-Père de Chartres, ed. by M. Guérard, vol. II (Paris: De l'Imprimerie de Crapelet, 1840)

Catalogue général des bibliothèques publiques de France, vol. XIII (Paris: Librairie Plon, 1891)

Chapotin, Marie-Dominique, *Histoire des Dominicains de la Province de France* (Rouen: Cagniard, 1898)

'Chronica Regiae Coloniensis Continuatio prima', ed. by Georg Waitz, in Monumenta Germaniae Historica, Scriptores, 24 (Hannover: Hahn, 1879), pp. 1–20

Die Chronik von Karl dem Grossen und Roland: Der lateinische Pseudo-Turpin in den Handschriften aus Aachen und Andernach, ed. by Hans-Wilhelm Klein (Munich: W. Fink, 1986)

Conciliorum Oecumenicorum Decreta, ed. by Joseph Alberigo (Freiburg: Herder, 1962)

Corpus Inscriptionum Crucesignatorum Terrae Sanctae, ed. by Sabino de Sandoli (Jerusalem: Studium Biblicum Franciscanum, 1973)

Corpus Iuris Canonici Emendatum et Notis Illustratum. Gregorii XIII. pont. max. iussu editum (Roma: In aedibus Populi Romani, 1582)

Crusaders as Conquerors: The Chronicle of Morea, trans. by Harold E. Lurier (New York: Columbia University Press 1964)

'De expugnatione Lyxbonensi', ed. and trans. by Charles W. David, *The Conquest of Lisbon* (New York: Columbia University Press, 1936)

'De Oneribus Prophetarum', ed. by Oswald Holder-Egger, in 'Italienische Prophetieen des 13. Jahrhunderts. III.', *Neues Archiv der Gesellschaft für Ältere Deutsche Geschichtskunde*, 33 (1908), 95–188

Dubois, Pierre, *De recuperatione Terre Sancte*, ed. and trans. by Walther Brandt, *The Recovery of the Holy Land* (New York: Columbia University Press, 1956)

Ekkehard von Aura, *Hierosolymita*, in *Recueil des Historiens des Croisades: Historiens Occidentaux*, 16 vols (Paris: Académie des Inscriptions et Belles-Lettres, 1844–1906), vol. V, 11–40

Étienne de Bourbon, 'Quod passio et crux letificant, maxime in morte', ed. by A. Lecoy de La Marche, *Anecdotes historiques: Légendes et apologues tirés du recueil inédit d'Étienne de Bourbon* (Paris: Librairie Renouard, 1877), p. 91

Eudes de Châteauroux, 'Appendix D', ed. by Penny J. Cole, *The Preaching of the Crusades to the Holy Land, 1095–1270* (Cambridge, MA: Medieval Academy of America, 1991), pp. 235–43

——, 'Odonis Episcopi Tusculani ad Innocentium IV. Papam', ed. by Luc d'Achéry, *Spicilegium sive Collectio Veterum Aliquot Scriptorium qui in Galliae Bibliothecis Delituerant*, vol. III (Paris: Apud Montalant, 1723), pp. 624–28

——, Sermones I–V, ed. by Christoph T. Maier, *Crusade Propaganda and Ideology: Model Sermons for the Preaching of the Cross* (Cambridge: Cambridge University Press, 2000), pp. 128–75

——, Sermones 1–3, ed. by Christoph T. Maier, 'Crusade and Rhetoric against the Muslim Colony of Lucera: Eudes of Châteauroux's *Sermones de Rebellione Sarracenorum Lucherie in Apulia', Journal of Medieval History*, 21 (1995), 376–85

——, Sermones 2–3, 7–16, 23, 41–45, 49, ed. by Alexis Charansonnet, 'L'Université, l'Eglise et l'Etat dans les sermons du cardinal Eudes de Châteauroux (1190?–1273)', vol. II (unpublished doctoral dissertation, Université de Lyon 2 — Louis Lumière, 2001), pp. 697–705, 721–66, 820–24, 980–85

Die Exempla aus den Sermones feriales et communes des Jakob von Vitry, ed. by Joseph Greven (Heidelberg: Winter, 1914)

Fasti Ecclesiae Anglicanae, 1066–1300, ed. by Diana E. Greenway, vols 4, 7 <http://www.british-history.ac.uk/search/series/fasti-ecclesiae> [accessed June 2016]

Federico Visconti, Sermones XXVI–XXVII, LXXX, ed. by Nicole Bériou and Isabelle le Masne de Chermont, *Les Sermons et la visite pastorale de Federico Visconti archévêque de Pise (1253–1277)* (Roma: École Française de Rome, 2001), pp. 543–55, 932–41

Fulcher de Chartres, *Historia Hierosolymitana*, ed. by Heinrich Hagenmeyer (Heidelberg: Winter, 1913)

Fuller, Thomas, *The Historie of the Holy Warre* (Cambridge: Thomas Buck, 1639)

Geoffroi de Charny, *Livre de chevalerie*, ed. and trans. by Richard W. Kaeuper and Elspeth Kennedy, *The Book of Chivalry of Geoffroi de Charny: Text, Context, and Translation* (Philadelphia: University of Pennsylvania Press, 1996)

Geoffroy de Beaulieu, *Vita Ludovici noni*, in *Recueil des Historiens des Gaules et de la France*, ed. by Martin Bouquet, 24 vols (Paris: Palmé, 1840–1904), XX, 2–27

Gregorius VIII, *Audita tremendi*, in *Patrologiae Cursus Completus. Series Latina*, ed. by Jacques-Paul Migne, 221 vols (Paris: Garnier, 1844–64), CCII, cols 1541–42

Gregorius IX, *Les Registres de Grégoire IX: Recueil des bulles de ce pape publiées ou analysées d'après les manuscrits originaux du Vatican*, ed. by Lucien Auvray, 4 vols (Paris: Librairie Thorin et Fils, 1844–96)

Guibert de Nogent, *Gesta Dei per Francos*, in *Recueil des Historiens des Croisades: Historiens Occidentaux*, 16 vols (Paris: Académie des Inscriptions et Belles-Lettres, 1844–1906), vol. IV

Guibert de Tournai, *Collectio de scandalis ecclesiae*, ed. by Bernhard Autbert Stroick, *Archivum Franciscanum Historicum*, 24 (1931), 33–62

——, *Eruditio regum et principum*, ed. by Alphonse de Poorter, *Le Traité Eruditio regum et principum de Guibert de Tournai* (Louvain: Institut Supérieur de Philosophie de l'Université, 1914)

——, Sermones I–III, ed. by Christoph T. Maier, *Crusade Propaganda and Ideology: Model Sermons for the Preaching of the Cross* (Cambridge: Cambridge University Press, 2000), pp. 176–209

——, *Tractatus de Pace*, ed. by Ephrem Longpré, *Tractatus de Pace. Auctore fr. Gilberto de Tornaco*, vol. VI (Firenze: Ad Claras Aquas, Quaracchi, 1925)

Hieronymus, *Epistolae*, in *Patrologiae Cursus Completus. Series Latina*, ed. by Jacques-Paul Migne, 221 vols (Paris: Garnier, 1844–64), vol. xxii

——, *Liber interpretationis Hebraicorum nominum*, ed. by Paul de Lagarde, *Opera*, i.1, Corpus Christianorum, Series Latina, 72 (Turnhout: Brepols 1959)

Historia de Expeditione Friderici Imperatoris, ed. by Ansbertus Austriensis and Josef Dobrowsky (Prague: Mayregg, 1827)

Historiae Francorum Scriptores, ed. by André Duchesne, vol. v (Paris: Cramoisy, 1649)

Honorius III, 'Ad Pelagium', in *Recueil des Historiens des Gaules et de la France*, ed. by Martin Bouquet, 24 vols (Paris: Palmé, 1840–1904), xix, 690–91

Hostiensis, *Summa aurea, ad vetustissimos codices summa fide diligentiaque nunc primum collate*, Liber III (Venetiis: Apud Iacobum Vitalem 1574)

Humbert de Romans, *De eruditione praedicatorum*, ed. by Marguerin de la Bigne, *Maxima Bibliotheca Veterum Patrum*, vol. xxv (Lugduni: Apud Anissonios, 1677)

——, 'De Modo prompte cudendi', in *Maxima bibliotheca veterum patrum*, ed. by M. de la Bigne, vol. xxv (Lugduni: Apud Anissonios, 1677), pp. 456–567

——, *De predicatione sancte crucis*, ed. by Kurt Villads Jensen <http://www.jggj.dk/saracenos.htm> [accessed July 2008 – November 2016]

——, *De predicatione sancte crucis*, ed. by Peter Wagner, *Tractatus solemnis fratris Humberti quondam magistri generalis ordinis predicatorum. De predicatione sancte crucis* (Nuremburg, 1495)

——, *Opusculum tripartitum*, ed. by Edward Brown, *Appendix ad Fasciculus rerum expetendarum et fugiendarum*, vol. ii (London, 1690), pp. 191–98

——, Sermones I–IV, ed. by Christoph T. Maier, *Crusade Propaganda and Ideology: Model Sermons for the Preaching of the Cross* (Cambridge: Cambridge University Press, 2000), pp. 210–29

Innocentius III, *Opera omnia*, in *Patrologiae Cursus Completus. Series Latina*, ed. by Jacques-Paul Migne, 221 vols (Paris: Garnier, 1844–64), vol. ccxiv

——, *Pope Innocent III, Between God and Man: Six Sermons on the Priestly Office*, trans. and introd. by Corinne J. Vause and Frank C. Gardiner (Washington, DC: Catholic University of America Press, 2004)

——, *Quia maior*, in *Patrologiae Cursus Completus. Series Latina*, ed. by Jacques-Paul Migne, 221 vols (Paris: Garnier, 1844–64), ccxvi, cols 817–21

——, *Regestorum sive epistolarum*, in *Patrologiae Cursus Completus. Series Latina*, ed. by Jacques-Paul Migne, 221 vols (Paris: Garnier, 1844–64), vol. ccxv

Innocentius IV, *Les Registres d'Innocent IV. publiés ou analysés d'après les manuscrits originaux du Vatican et de la Bibliothèque Nationale*, ed. by Élie Berger, 4 vols (Paris: E. Thorin, 1884–1921)

'Itinerarium Peregrinorum et Gesta Regis Ricardi', ed. by William Stubbs, *Chronicles and Memorials of Reign of Richard I: Itinerarium Peregrinorum et gesta regis Ricardi, auctore, ut videtur, Ricardo canonico Sanctae Trinitatis Londoniensis* (London: Longman, 1864)

'Iuxta vaticinium Ysaie', in *Acta imperii inedita, seculi XIII*, ed. by Eduard Winkelmann (Innsbruck: Wagner, 1885), ii, 709–17

Jacopo da Varazze, *Legenda Aurea*, ed. by Giovanni Paolo Maggioni (Firenze: Edizioni del Galluzzo, 1998)

Jacques de Vitry, 'Eadem dominica thema sumptum de Epistola Philip. 2', in *Reverendissimi D. Iacobi de Vitriaco, Sermones in epistolas et evangelia dominicalia totius anni*, ed. by Damianus a Ligno (Antverpiae: In aedibus viduae, 1575) pp. 316–21

——, *Epistola*, ed. by R. B. C. Huygens, *Lettres de Jacques de Vitry, 1160/70–1240, évêque de Saint-Jean d'Acre* (Leiden: Brill, 1960)

——, *Historia*, ed. by Franciscus Moschus, *Iacobi de Vitriaco, libri duo, quorum prior Orientalis sive Hierosolymitanae, alter Occidentalis historiae nomine inscribitur* (Douai: Balthasar Beller, 1597)

——, *Historia Occidentalis*, ed. by Jonh Frederick Hinnebusch, *The Historia Occidentalis of Jacques de Vitry* (Fribourg: University Press Fribourg, 1972)

——, *Historia orientalis*, ed. by Jean Donnadieu, *Jacques de Vitry. Histoire orientale* (Turnhout: Brepols, 2008)

——, Sermones I–II, ed. by Christoph T. Maier, *Crusade Propaganda and Ideology: Model Sermons for the Preaching of the Cross* (Cambridge: Cambridge University Press, 2000), pp. 82–127

——, Sermones 49–50, ed. by Jessalynn Bird, 'James of Vitry's Sermons to Pilgrims', *Essays in Medieval Studies*, 25 (2008), 88–102

——, 'Sermo XXXVII', in *Analecta novissima: spicilegii solesmensis altera continuatio*, ed. by Jean-Baptiste Pitra, vol. II (Paris: Tusculana, 1888) pp. 405–14

——, *Vita Maria Oigniacensi in Naurcensis Belgii diocecesi*, ed. by Danile Papebroeck, in *Acta Sanctorum quotquot toto orbe coluntur, vel a catholicis scriptoribus celebrantur, quae ex Latinis & Graecis, aliarumque gentium antiquis monumentis*, vol. V (Paris, 1867)

Jean de Joinville, *Vie de Saint Louis*, ed. by Jacques Monfrin (Paris: Dunod, 1995)

Jean d'Ibelin, *Le Livre des Assises*, ed. by Peter W. Edbury, *John of Ibelin, Le Livre des Assises* (Leiden: Brill, 2003)

Joachim of Fiore, *Liber Concordiae novi ac veteris Testamenti* (Venetiis: Simonem de Luere, 1519)

Joinville and Villehardouin, Chronicles of the Crusades, trans. by Caroline Smith (London: Penguin, 2008)

Die Kreuzzugsbriefe aus den Jahren 1088–1000, ed. by Heinrich Hagenmeyer (Innsbruck: Verlag der Wagner'schen Universitäts Buchhandlung, 1901)

Layettes du trésor des chartes: de l'année 1224 à l'année 1246, ed. by M. Alexandre Teulet (Paris: H. Plon, 1866)

Magister Thadeus, *Ystoria de desolatione et conculcatione civitatis Acconensis et tocius terre sancte*, ed. by R. B. C. Huygens (Turnhout: Brepols, 2004)

Matthew Paris, *Chronica majora*, ed. by Henry Richards Luard, *Matthaei Parisiensis, monachi sancti Albani, Chronica Majora*, vol. III (London: Longman, 1876)

——, *Chronica majora, Additamenta*, ed. by Henry Richards Luard, *Matthaei Parisiensis, monachi sancti Albani, Chronica Majora*, vol. VI (London: Longman, 1882)

——, *Historia Anglorum*, ed. by Frederic Madden, vol. III (London: Longman, 1869)

'Menkonis Chronicon', ed. by Georg Heinrich Pertz, in Monumenta Germaniae Historica, Scriptores, 23 (Hannover: Hahn, 1874), pp. 523–61

Notices et Documents publiés pour la Société de l'histoire de France à l'occasion du cinquantième anniversaire de sa fondation, ed. by Paul Riant (Paris: Librairie Renouard, 1884)

Odo Rigaldus, *The Register of Eudes of Rouen*, trans. by Sidney M. Brown, ed. by Jeremiah F. O'Sullivan (New York: Columbia University Press, 1964)

Oliver von Paderborn, *Epistola salutaris regi Babilonis conscripta*, ed. by Hermann Hoogeweg, *Die Schriften des Kölner Domscholasters, späteren Bischofs von Paderborn und Kardinal-Bischofs von S. Sabina Oliverus* (Tübingen: Gedruckt für den Literarischen Verein in Stuttgart, 1894)

——, *Historia Damiatina*, ed. by Hermann Hoogeweg, *Die Schriften des Kölner Domscholasters, späteren Bischofs von Paderborn und Kardinal-Bischofs von S. Sabina Oliverus* (Tübingen: Gedruckt für den Literarischen Verein in Stuttgart, 1894)

Peter the Chanter, *Pierre le Chantre: Summa de sacramnetis et de animae consiliis*, ed. by Jean-Albert Dugauquier, Analecta Mediaevalia Namurcensia, 4, 7, 11, 16, 21 (Louvain: Éditions Nauwelaerts & Lille: Librairie Giard, 1954–67)

Philippe le Chancelier, *Philippi Cancellarii Parisiensis, Summa de bono*, ed. by Nicolai Wicki, 2 vols (Bern: Editiones Francke, 1985)

Primat, *Chronique de Primat traduite par Jean du Vignau*, in *Recueil des Historiens des Gaules et de la France*, ed. by Martin Bouquet, 24 vols (Paris: Palmé, 1840–1904), XXIII, 1–106

'Prophetia filii Agap', ed. by Reinhold Röhricht, *Quinti belli sacri scriptores minores* (Geneva: J.-G. Fick, 1879), pp. 214–22

'Protocoll der Commission zu Anagni', ed. by Franz Ehrle, *Das Evangelium aeternum und die Commission zu Anagni* (Berlin: Archiv für Literatur- und Kirchengeschichte des Mittelalters, 1885)

Raoul de Caen, *Gesta Tancredi*, trans. by Bernard S. Bachrach and David S. Bachrach, *Gesta Tancredi of Ralph of Caen. A History of the Normans on the First Crusade* (Farnham: Ashgate, 2005)

Raymond d'Aguilers, *Historia Francorum qui ceperunt Iherusalem*, in *Recueil des Historiens des Croisades: Historiens Occidentaux*, 16 vols (Paris: Académie des Inscriptions et Belles-Lettres, 1844–1906), vol. III, 231–309

Rishanger, Willelmi, *Chronica et Annales*, ed. by Henry Thomas Riley (London: Longman, 1865)

Robert de Clari, *La Prise de Constantinople*, ed. by Charles Hopf, *Chroniques gréco-romanes* (Berlin: Weidmann, 1873)

Robert de Courçon, *De usura*, ed. by Georges Lefèvre, *Le traité 'De usura' de Robert de Courçon*, vol. X (Lille: Au siège de l'Université, 1902)

Robert the Monk, *Historia Iherosolimitana*, in *Recueil des Historiens des Croisades: Historiens Occidentaux*, 16 vols (Paris: Académie des Inscriptions et Belles-Lettres, 1844–1906), vol. III, 717–882

Roger of Salisbury, 'Appendix B', ed. by Penny J. Cole, *The Preaching of the Crusades to the Holy Land, 1095–1270* (Cambridge, MA: Medieval Academy of America, 1991), pp. 227–31

Roger of Wendover, *Flores Historiarum*, ed. by Henricus O. Coxe, *Rogeri de Wendover, Chronica, sive Flores Historiarum*, vols ii, iv (London: Sumptibus Societatis, 1841)

Rutebeuf, 'La Voie de Tunes', ed. by Edmond Faral and Julia Bastin, in *Oeuvres complètes de Rutebeuf* (Paris: Èditions A. et J. Picard, 1959), pp. 460–68

Salimbene di Adam, *Cronica Fratris Salimbene de Adam*, ed. by Ferdinando Bernini, *Salimbene de Adam. Chronica*, 2 vols (Bari: Gius. Laterza & Figli, 1942)

——, *Cronica fratris Salimbene de Adam ordinis Minorum*, ed. by Oswald Holder-Egger, Monumenta Germaniae Historica, Scriptores, 32 (Hannover: Hahn, 1874)

'Salvator saeculi', ed. by Lucas Wadding, *Annales Minorum*, vol. iii (Roma: Typis Rochi Bernabo, 1732)

The Seventh Crusade, 1244–1254: Sources and Documents, trans. by Peter Jackson (Farnham: Ashgate, 2009)

'Sibilla Erithea Babilonica', ed. by Oswald Holder-Egger, in 'Italienische Prophetieen des 13. Jahrhunderts. II.', *Neues Archiv der Gesellschaft für Ältere Deutsche Geschichtskunde*, 30 (1905), 321–86

'Super Prophetas' [Super Esaiam], in *Abbatis Joachim Florensis Scriptum super Esaiam Prophetam* (Venetiis: Lazaro de Soardis, 1517)

Tertullianus, *De Idololatria*, ed. by Augustus Reifferscheid and Georgius Wissowa, Corpus Scriptorum Ecclesiasticorum Latinorum, 20 (Wien: F. Tempsky, 1890)

Thesaurus novus anecdotorum, ed. by Edmond Martène and Ursin Durand, vol. i (Paris: F. Delaulne, 1717)

Thomas Aquinas, *Doctoris Angelici Divi Thomae Aquinatis Opera Omnia*, ed. by Stanislas Edouard Frette (Paris: Apud Ludovicum Vives, 1875)

——, *Summa Theologiae*, <http://www.corpusthomisticum.org/sth3034.html> [accessed July 2010 – April 2012]

Thomas de Cantimpré, *Bonum Universale de Apibus*, ed. by Georgii Colvenerius, *Thomae Cantimpratensis miraculorum, et exemplorum memorabilium sui temporis libri duo* (Douai: Balthasar Beller, 1605)

Thomas de Chobham, *Summa de arte praedicandi*, ed. by Franco Morenzoni, Corpus Christianorum Continuatio Mediaevalis, 82 (Turnhout: Brepols, 1988)

Traduction des chroniques de Rigord et Guillaume le Breton: Collection de mémoires relatifs à l'histoire de France, ed. by Francois Guizot, vol. xi (Paris: J.-L.-J. Brière, 1825)

'Triennis et biennis decimal ab anno mccxlviii collecta', in *Recueil des Historiens des Gaules et de la France*, ed. by Martin Bouquet, 24 vols (Paris: Palmé, 1840–1904), xxi, 533–40

Villani, Giovanni, *Chronica*, ed. by Ignazio Moutier, *Cronica di Giovanni Villani*, vol. ii (Firenze: Magheri, 1823)

Secondary Studies

Abulafia, David, *Frederick II: A Medieval Emperor* (London: Penguin, 1988; repr. London: Pimlico, 2002)

Allen, Peter L., *The Wages of Sin: Sex and Disease, Past and Present* (Chicago: University of Chicago Press, 2000)

Alphandéry, Paul, *La Chrétienté et l'idée de croisade*, ed. by Alphonse Dupront, 2 vols (Paris: Albin Michel, 1954–59)

Andrea, Alfred J., *Contemporary Sources for the Fourth Crusade* (Leiden: Brill, 2000)

Baldwin, John W., *Masters, Princes and Merchants: The Social Views of Peter the Chanter and his Circle*, 2 vols (Princeton, NJ: Princeton University Press, 1970)

Barber, Malcolm, 'The Crusade of the Shepherds in 1251', in *Proceedings of the Tenth Annual Meeting of the Western Society for French History*, ed. by John Sweets (Kansas: University of Kansas Press, 1984), pp. 1–23

Bataillon, Louis-Jacques, 'Sermons rédigés, sermons reports (xiiie siècle)', in *La Prédication au xiiie siècle en France et Italie* (Aldershot: Ashgate, 1993), pp. 69–86

Baudry, L., 'Wibert de Tournai', *Revue d'histoire franciscaine*, 5 (1928), 23–61

Behrman, David, '*Volumina vilissima*: A Sermon of Eudes de Châteauroux on the Jews and their Talmud', in *Le Brûlement du Talmud à Paris, 1242–1244*, ed. by Gilbert Dahan and Elie Nicolas (Paris: Éditions du Cerf, 1999), pp. 191–209

Belleville, Linda L., '"Imitate Me, Just as I Imitate Christ": Discipleship in the Corinthian Correspondence', in *Patterns of Discipleship in the New Testament*, ed. by Richard N. Longenecker (Grand Rapids, MI: Eerdmans, 1996), pp. 120–42

Bériou, Nicole, *L'Avènement des maîtres de la Parole*, 2 vols (Paris: Institut d'Études Augustiniennes, 1998

——, 'Philippe le Chancelier', in *Dictionnaire de Spiritualité*, vol. xii (Paris: Beauchesne, 1984), pp. 1289–97

——, 'La Predication de croisade de Philippe le Chancelier et d'Eudes de Châteauroux en 1226', *Cahiers de Fanjeaux*, 32, *La Prédication en Pays d'Oc (xiie – début xve s.)* (1997), 85–109

Bériou, Nicole, and Isabelle le Masne de Chermont, *Les Sermons et la visite pastorale de Federico Visconti archévêque de Pise (1253–1277)* (Rome: École Française de Rome, 2001)

Bériou, Nicole, and François-Olivier Touati, *Voluntate Dei leprosus: Les Lépreux entre conversion et exclusion aux xiie et xiiie siècles* (Spoleto: Centro italiano studi sull'alto medioevo, 1991)

Betz, Hans Dieter, *Nachfolge und Nachahmung Jesu Christi in Neuen Testament*, Beiträge zur Historischen Theologie (Tübingen: J. C. B. Mohr, 1967)

Birch, Debra, 'Jacques de Vitry and the Ideology of Pilgrimage', in *Pilgrimage Explored*, ed. by Jennifer Stopford (York: York Medieval Press, 1999), pp. 79–93

Bird, Jessalynn, 'The Construction of Orthodoxy and the (De)construction of Heretical Attacks on the Eucharist in *Pastoralia* from Peter the Chanter's Circle in Paris', in *Texts and the Repression of Medieval Heresy*, ed. by Caterina Bruschi and Peter Biller (York: York Medieval Press 2002), pp. 45–61

——, 'Crusade and Conversion after the Fourth Lateran Council (1215): Oliver of Paderborn's and James of Vitry's Missions to Muslims Reconsidered', *Essays in Medieval Studies*, 21 (2005), 23–47

——, 'Heresy, Crusade and Reform in the Circle of Peter the Chanter, c. 1187 – c. 1240' (unpublished doctoral dissertation, University of Oxford, 2001)

——, 'The *Historia Orientalis* of Jacques de Vitry: Visual and Written Commentaries as Evidence of a Text's Audience, Reception, and Utilization', *Essays in Medieval Studies*, 20 (2003), 56–74

——, 'Innocent III, Peter the Chanter's Circle, and the Crusade Indulgence: Theory, Implementation, and Aftermath', in *Innocenzo III: Urbs et Orbis, Atti del Congresso Internazionale Roma, 9–15 settembre 1998*, ed. by Andrea Sommerlechner, vols i–ii (Roma: Società romana di storia patria, 2003), i, 504–24

——, 'James of Vitry's Sermons to Pilgrims', *Essays in Medieval Studies*, 25 (2008), 81–113

——, 'Paris Masters and the Justification of the Albigensian Crusade', *Crusades*, 6 (2007), 117–55

——, 'Reform or Crusade? Anti-Usury and Crusade Preaching During the Pontificate of Innocent III', in *Pope Innocent III and his World*, ed. by John C. Moore (Aldershot: Ashgate, 1999), pp. 165–85

——, 'The Victorines, Peter the Chanter's Circle, and the Crusade: Two Unpublished Crusading Appeals in Paris, Bibliothèque Nationale, Ms. Latin 11470', *Medieval Sermon Studies*, 48 (2004), 5–28

Bloch, Marc, *Feudal Society*, vol. i, trans. by L. A. Manyon (London: Routledge, 1989)

Bolton, Brenda, *Innocent III: Studies on Papal Authority and Pastoral Care* (Aldershot: Ashgate, 1995)

——, '*Paupertas Christi*: Old Wealth and New Poverty in the Twelfth Century', in *Studies in Church History*, vol. xiv, *Renaissance and Renewal in Christian History*, ed. by Derek Baker (Oxford: Basil Blackwell, 1977), pp. 95–103

Boutaric, Edgard, *Saint Louis et Alphonse de Poitiers* (Paris: Henry Plon, 1870)

Boyle, Leonard E., 'The Inter-Conciliar Period 1179–1215 and the Beginnigs of Pastoral Manuals', in *Miscellanea Rolando Bandinelli Papa Alessandro III*, ed. by Filippo Liotta (Siena: Academia Senese degli Intronati, 1986), pp. 43–56

Bradbury, Jim, *Capetians: Kings of France, 987–1328* (London: Continuum, 2007)

Bray, Jennifer, 'The Mohammetan and Idolatry', in *Studies in Church History*, vol. xxi, *Persecution and Toleration*, ed. by W. J. Sheils (Oxford: Basil Blackwell, 1984), pp. 89–98

Brenk, Beat, 'The Sainte-Chapelle as a Capetian Political Program', in *Artistic Integration in Gothic Buildings*, ed. by Virginia Chieffo Raguin (Toronto: University of Toronto Press, 1995), pp. 195–213

Brentano, Robert, *Two Churches: England and Italy in the Thirteenth Century* (Berkeley: University of California Press, 1968)

Brett, E. T., *Humbert of Romans: His Life and Views of Thirteenth-Century Society* (Wetteren: Pontifical Institute of Mediaeval Studies, 1984)

Brodman, James, *Charity & Religion in Medieval Europe* (Washington, DC: Catholic University of America Press, 2009)

Brundage, James, 'The Crusader's Wife: A Canonistic Quandary', *Studia Gratiana*, 12 (1967), 425–41

——, 'Humbert of Romans and the Legitimacy of Crusader Conquests', in *The Horns of Hattin*, ed. by Benjamin Z. Kedar (London: Ashgate, 1992), pp. 302–13

——, *Medieval Canon Law and the Crusader* (Madison: University of Wisconsin Press, 1969)

——, 'Prostitution, Miscegenation and Sexual Purity in the First Crusade', in *Crusade and Settlement: Papers Read at the First Conference of the Society for the Study of the Crusades and the Latin East and Presented to R. C. Smail*, ed. by Peter W. Edbury (Cardiff: University College Cardiff Press, 1985), pp. 57–65

——, 'Voluntary Martyrs and Canon Law: The Case of the First Crusaders', *Cristianesimo nella storia*, 27.1 (2006), 143–60

Bynum, Carolyn Walker, *Holy Feast and Holy Fast: The Religious Significance of Food to Medieval Women* (Berkeley: University of California Press, 1987)

Carolus-Barré, Louis, 'Un recueil épistolaire composé à Saint-Denis sur la Croisade (1270–1271), *Comptes-rendus des séances de l'Académie des Inscriptions et Belles-Lettres*, 110.4 (1966), 555–68

Casagrande, Carla, *Prediche alle donne del secolo XIII* (Milano: Bompiani, 1978)

Charansonnet, Alexis, 'L'Évolution de la predication du cardinal Eudes de Châteauroux (1190?–1273): Une approche statistique', in *De l'homelie au sermon: Histoire de la prédication médiévale*, ed. by Jacqueline Hamesse and Xavier Hermand (Louvain-la-Neuve: Université Catholique de Louvain, 1993), pp. 103–42

——, 'L'Université, l'Eglise et l'Etat dans les sermons du cardinal Eudes de Châteauroux (1190?–1273)' (unpublished doctoral dissertation, Université de Lyon 2 — Louis Lumière, 2001)

Charland, Thomas M., *Artes praedicandi: Contribution à l'histoire de la rhétorique au Moyen Âge* (Paris: Publications de l'Institut d'études médiévales d'Ottawa VII, 1936)

Chazan, Robert, *European Jewry and the First Crusade* (Berkeley: University of California Press, 1987)

——, *Medieval Jewry in Northern France: A Political and Social History* (Baltimore: Johns Hopkins University Press, 1973)

Christiani, Emilio, 'L'arcivescovo Federico Visconti, Pisa e la Sardegna', in *Les Sermons et la visite pastorale de Federico Visconti archévêque de Pise (1253–1277)*, ed. by Nicole Bériou and Isabelle le Masne de Chermont (Roma: École Française de Rome, 2001), pp. 9–23

Cole, Penny, 'Humbert of Romans and the Crusade', in *The Experience of Crusading*, vol. I, *Western Approaches*, ed. by Marcus Bull and Norman Housley (New York: Cambridge University Press, 2003), pp. 157–74

——, *The Preaching of the Crusades to the Holy Land, 1095–1270* (Cambridge, MA: Medieval Academy of America, 1991)

Cole, Penny, David d'Avray, and Jonathan Riley-Smith, 'Application of Theology to Current Affairs: Memorial Sermons on the Dead of Mansurah and on Innocent IV', *Historical Research*, 63 (1990), 227–47

Constable, Giles, *Crusaders and Crusading in the Twelfth Century* (Farnham: Ashgate, 2008)

——, 'The Historiography of the Crusades', in *The Crusades from the Perspective of Byzantium and the Muslim World*, ed. by A. E. Laiou and R. P. Mottahedeh (Washington, DC: Dumbarton Oaks Research Library, 2001), pp. 1–22

——, *The Reformation of the Twelfth Century* (Cambridge: Cambridge University Press, 1996)

——, *Three Studies in Medieval Religious and Social Thought: The Interpretation of Mary and Martha; The Ideal of the Imitation of Christ; The Orders of Society* (Cambridge: Cambridge University Press, 1995)

Cowdrey, H. E. J., 'Martyrdom and the First Crusade', in *The Crusades and Latin Monasticism, 11ᵗʰ–12ᵗʰ Centuries* (Aldershot: Ashgate, 1999), pp. 45–56

——, 'Pope Gregory VII and Martyrdom', in *Dei gesta per Francos: Crusade Studies in Honour of Jean Richard*, ed. by Michel Balard, Benjamin Z. Kedar, and Jonathan Riley-Smith (Aldershot: Ashgate, 2001), pp. 3–11

——, 'Pope Urban II's Preaching of the First Crusade', *History*, 55 (1970), 177–88

Curta, Florin, and Jace Stuckey, 'Charlemagne in Medieval East Central Europe (ca. 800 to ca. 1200)', *Canadian Slavonic Papers*, 53.2–4 (2011), 181–208

Daniel, Norman, *Islam and the West: The Making of an Image* (Edinburgh: Edinburgh University Press, 1960)

d'Avray, David L., *Death and the Prince: Memorial Preaching before 1350* (Oxford: Clarendon Press, 1994)

——, 'Method in the Study of Medieval Sermons', in *Modern Questions about Medieval Sermons*, ed. by Nicole Bériou and David d'Avray (Spoleto: Centro Italiano di Studi sull'alto Medioevo, 1994), pp. 3–29

——, *The Preaching of the Friars: Sermons Diffused from Paris before 1300* (Oxford: Clarendon Press, 1985)

d'Avray, David L., and Martin Tausche, 'Marriage Sermons in *ad status* Collections of the Central Middle Ages', *Archives d'histoire doctrinale et littéraire du moyen âge*, 47 (1980), 71–119

Delaruelle, Étienne, *L'Idée de croisade au moyen âge* (Torino: Bottega d'Erasmo, 1980)

Derbes, Aisne, and Mark Sandona, 'Amazons and Crusaders: The *Histoire Universelle* in Flanders and the Holy Land', in *France and the Holy Land: Frankish Culture at the End of the Crusades*, ed. by Daniel H. Weiss and Lisa Mahoney (Baltimore: Johns Hopkins University Press, 2004), pp. 187–229

Dernbecher, Christine, *'Deus et virum suum diligens': Zur Rolle und Bedeutung der Frau im Umfeld Kreuzzüge* (St Ingbert: Röhrig, 2003)

Deschamps, Paul, 'Combats de cavalerie et épisodes des Croisades dans les peintures murales du XIIᵉ et du XIIIᵉ siècle', *Orientalia christiana periodica*, 13 (1947), 454–74

Dickson, Gary, *The Children's Crusade: Medieval History, Modern Mythistory* (Houndmills: Palgrave Macmillan, 2008)

——, *Religious Enthusiasm in the Medieval West* (Aldershot: Ashgate, 2000)

——, '*Rite de Passage*? The Children's Crusade and Medieval Childhood', *Journal of the History of Childhood and Youth*, 2.3 (2009), 315–22

Dubisch, Jill, *In a Different Place: Pilgrimage, Gender, and Politics at a Greek Island Shrine* (Princeton: Princeton University Press, 1995)

Dunbabin, Jean, 'The Maccabees as Exemplars in the Tenth and Eleventh Centuries', in *Studies in Church History*, vol. IV, *The Bible in the Medieval World: Essays in Memory of Beryl Smalley*, ed. by K. Walsh and D. Wood (Oxford: Basil Blackwell, 1985), pp. 31–41

Dupront, Alphonse, *Du Sacré: Croisades et pèlerinages. Images et languages* (Paris: Èditions Gallimard, 1987)

Dyas, Dee, *Pilgrimage in Medieval English Literature, 700–1500* (Cambridge: D. S. Brewer, 2001)

Earl, Douglas S., 'Joshua and the Crusades', in *Holy War in the Bible: Christian and Old Testament Problem*, ed. by Heath A. Thomas (Downers Grove, IL: InterVarsity Press, 2013), pp. 19–44

Egger, Christoph, '*The Growling of the Lion and the Humming of the Fly*: Gregory the Great and Innocent III', in *Pope, Church and City*, ed. by Frances Andrews, Christoph Egger, and Constance M. Rousseau (Leiden: Brill, 2004), pp. 13–46

Erdmann, Carl, *Die Entstehung des Kreuzzugsgedankens* (Darmstadt: Wissenschaftliche Buchgesellschaft, 1965)

Evans, Michael R., '"A Far from Aristocratic Affair": Poor and Non-combatant Crusaders from the Midlands, c.1160–1300', *Midland History*, 21 (1996), 23–36

——, '"Unfit to Bear Arms": The Gendering of Arms and Armour in Accounts of Women on Crusade', in *Gendering the Crusades*, ed. by Susan Edgington and Sarah Lambert (Cardiff: University of Wales Press, 2001), pp. 45–58

Farmer, Sharon, *Surviving Poverty in Medieval Paris: Gender, Ideology, and the Daily Lives of the Poor* (Ithaca, NY: Cornell University Press, 2005)

Ferreiro, Alberto, 'Simon Magus, Dogs, and Simon Peter', in *The Devil, Heresy & Witchcraft in the Middle Ages*, ed. by Alberto Ferreiro (Leiden: Brill, 1998), pp. 45–89

Ferruolo, Stephen C., 'Preaching to the Clergy and Laity in Early Thirteenth-Century France: Jacques of Vitry's *Sermones ad status*', in *Proceedings of the Twelfth Annual Meeting of the Western Society for French History*, ed. by John F. Sweets (Lawrence: University of Kansas, 1985), pp. 12–22

Field, Sean, 'Gilbert of Tournai's Letter to Isabelle of France: An Edition of the Complete Text', *Mediaeval Studies*, 65 (2003), 57–97

Finucane, Ronald, *Miracles and Pilgrims: Popular Beliefs in Medieval England* (London: J. M. Dent, 1977; repr. New York: St. Martin's Press, 1995)

——, *Soldiers of Faith: Crusaders and Muslims at War* (London: Dent, 1983)

Flori, Jean, 'Ideology and Motivations in the First Crusade', in *The Palgrave Advances in the Crusades*, ed. by Helen J. Nicholson (Basingstoke: Palgrave Macmillan, 2005), pp. 15–36

——, *Pierre l'Ermite et la Première Croisade* (Paris: Fayard, 1999)

Folda, Jaroslav, *Crusader Art in the Holy Land: From the Third Crusade to the Fall of Acre* (Cambridge: Cambridge University Press, 2005)

Fonnesberg-Schmidt, Iben, *Popes and the Baltic Crusades, 1147–1254*, vol. XXVI of *Northern World* (Boston: Brill, 2007)

Forey, Alan, 'The Crusading Vows of the English King Henry III', *Durham University Journal*, 65 (1973), 229–47

Forni, Alberto, 'La "Nouvelle Prédication" des disciples de Foulques de Neuilly: Intentions, techniques et réactions', in *Faire croire: Modalités de la diffusion et de la recep-*

tion des messages religieux du XIIe au XVe siècle (Roma: École Française de Rome, 1981), pp. 19–37

France, John, *The Crusades and the Expansion of Catholic Christendom, 1000–1714* (New York: Routledge, 2005)

Frolow, Anatole, *La Relique de la Vraie Croix: Recherches sur le développement d'un culte* (Paris: Institut Francais d'etudes Byzantines, 1961)

Funk, Philipp, *Jakob von Vitry: Leben und Werke* (Leipzig: Beiträge zur Kulturgeschichte des Mittelalters und der Renaissance, 1909)

Gaposchkin, M. Cecilia, 'Louis IX, Crusade and the Promise of Joshua in the Holy Land', *Journal of Medieval History*, 34 (2008), 245–74

——, *The Making of Saint Louis: Kingship, Sanctity, and Crusade in the Later Middle Ages* (Ithaca, NY: Cornell University Press, 2008)

——, 'The Place of the Crusades in the Sanctification of Saint Louis', in *Crusades: Medieval Worlds in Conflict*, ed. by Thomas F. Madden, James L. Naus, and Vincent Ryan (Farnham: Ashgate, 2010), pp. 195–209

Gasnault, Marie-Claire, 'Jacques de Vitry: Sermon aux gens mariés', in *Prêcher d'Exemples: Récits de prédicateurs du Moyen Age*, ed. by Jean-Claude Schmitt (Paris: Stock, 1985), pp. 41–67

Geldsetzer, Sabine, *Frauen auf Kreuzzügen* (Darmstadt: Wissenschaftliche Buchgesellschaft, 2003)

Gennep, Arnold van, *The Rites of Passage* (London: Routledge, 1960; repr. 2004); orig. *Les Rites de passage* (Paris: Nourry, 1908)

Gerstel, Sharon E. J., 'Art and Identity in the Medieval Morea', in *The Crusades from the Perspective of Byzantium and the Muslim World*, ed. by A. E. Laiou and R. P. Mottahedeh (Washington, DC: Dumbarton Oaks Research Library, 2001), pp. 263–85

Gervers, Michael, ed., *The Second Crusade and the Cistercians* (New York: St. Martin's Press, 1992)

Ghellinck, Joseph de, 'Imitari, Imitatio', *Bulletin du Cange: Archivum Latinitatis Medii Aevi*, 15 (1940), 151–59

Gilson, Etienne, 'Michel Menot et la technique du sermon médiéval', *Revue d'histoire franciscaine*, 2 (1925), 301–60; reprinted in Etienne Gilson, *Les Idées et les lettres* (Paris: J. Vrin, 1932)

Golubovich, Girolamo, *Biblioteca Bio-Bibliografica della Terra Santa e dell'Oriente Francescano*, vol. I (Firenze: Quaracchi, 1906)

Gottlob, Adolf, *Kreuzablass und Almosenablass* (Stuttgart: Verlag von Ferdinand Enke, 1906)

——, *Die päpstlichen Kreuzzugs-Steuern des 13. Jahrhunderts* (Heiligenstadt: F. W. Cordier, 1892)

Grousset, René, *Histoire des croisades et du royaume franc de Jérusalem*, 3 vols (Paris: Plon, 1934–36)

Haendler, Gert, *Epochen karolingischer Theologie: eine Untersuchung über die karolingischen Gutachten zum byzantinischen Bilderstreit* (Berlin: Evang. Verl.–Anst., 1958)

Hagenmeyer, Heinrich, *Peter der Eremite: Ein Kritischer Beitrag zur Geschichte des Ersten Kreuzzuges* (Leipzig: Otto Harrassowitz, 1879)

Hamilton, Bernard, *The Latin Church in the Crusader States* (London: Variorum Publications, 1980)

——, 'Women in the Crusader States: The Queens of Jerusalem (1100–1190)', in *Studies in Church History, Subsidia 1: Medieval Women*, ed. by Derek Baker (Oxford: Basil Blackwell, 1978), pp. 143–47

Hanska, Jussi, *'And the Rich Man also died; and He was buried in Hell': The Social Ethos in Mendicant Sermons* (Helsinki: Finnish Historical Society, 1997)

——, *Strategies of Sanity and Survival: Religious Responses to Natural Disasters in the Middle Ages* (Helsinki: Finnish Literature Society, 2002)

Hehl, Ernst-Dieter, 'Was ist eigentlich ein Kreuzzug?', *Historische Zeitschrift*, 259 (1994), 297–336

Henderson, John, *Piety and Charity in Late Medieval Florence* (Chicago: University of Chicago Press, 1997)

Hess, Richard S., 'Achan and Achor: Names and Wordplay in Joshua 7', *Hebrew Annual Review*, 14 (1994), 89–98

——, 'Reflections on Translating Joshua', in *Translating the Bible: Problems and Prospects*, ed. by Stanley Porter and Richard S. Hess (Sheffield: Sheffield Academic Press, 1999), pp. 125–42

Hodgson, Natasha R., *Women, Crusading and the Holy Land in Historical Narrative* (Woodbridge: Boydell Press, 2007)

Holdsworth, Christopher, 'An "Airier Aristocracy": The Saints at War: *The Prothero Lecture*', *Transactions of the Royal Historical Society*, 6 (1996), 103–22

Holt, Andrew, 'Feminine Sexuality and the Crusades', in *Sexuality in the Middle Ages and Early Modern Times*, ed. by Albrecht Classen (Berlin: de Gruyter, 2008), pp. 449–70

Hoogeweg, Hermann, 'Die Kreuzpredigt des Jahres 1224 in Deutschland mit besonderer Rücksicht auf die Erzdiözese Köln', *Deutsche Zeitschrift für Geschichtswissenschaft*, 4 (1890), 54–74

——, *Die Schriften des Kölner Domscholasters, späteren Bischofs von Paderborn und Kardinal-Bischofs von S. Sabina Oliverus* (Tübingen: Gedruckt für den Literarischen Verein in Stuttgart 1894)

Houser, Roland E., *The Cardinal Virtues: Aquinas, Albert, and Philip the Chancellor* (Toronto: Pontifical Institute of Mediaeval Studies, 2004)

Housley, Norman, *Contesting the Crusades* (Malden, MA: Blackwell Publishing, 2006)

——, *Fighting for the Cross: Crusading to the Holy Land* (New Haven, CT: Yale University Press, 2008)

——, *The Later Crusades, 1274–1580: From Lyons to Alcazar* (Oxford: Oxford University Press, 1992)

——, 'Review: Crusade Propaganda and Ideology: Model Sermons for the Preaching of the Cross by Christoph Maier', *English Historical Review*, 115.463 (2000), 939–40

Hughes, Kevin, *Constructing Antichrist: Paul, Biblical Commentary, and the Development of Doctrine in the Early Middle Ages* (Washington, DC: Catholic University of America Press, 2005)

Iozzelli, Fortunato, *Odo da Châteauroux: Politica e religione nei sermoni inediti* (Padova: Bottega d'Erasmo, 1994)

Jackson, Peter, 'The Crisis in the Holy Land in 1260', *English Historical Review*, 95.376 (1980), 481–513

——, 'The Crusade against the Mongols (1241)', *Journal of Ecclesiastical History*, 42 (1991), 1–18

——, *The Mongols and the West* (Harlow: Pearson, Longman, 2005)

Jansen, Katherine, *The Making of the Magdalen: Preaching and Popular Devotion in the Later Middle Ages* (Princeton, NJ: Princeton University Press, 2001)

Jordan, Alyce, *Visualizing Kingship in the Windows of the Sainte-Chapelle* (Turnhout: Brepols, 2002)

Jordan, William Chester, *The French Monarchy and the Jews: From Philip Augustus to the Last Capetians* (Philadelphia: University of Pennsylvania Press, 1989)

——, *Louis IX and the Challenge of the Crusade: A Study in Rulership* (Princeton, NJ: Princeton University Press, 1979)

Jotischky, Andrew, *Crusading and the Crusader States* (Harlow: Pearson Education, 2004)

Kantorowicz, Ernst H., *Kaiser Friedrich der Zweite* (Berlin: Georg Bondi, 1927)

——, *The King's Two Bodies: A Study in Mediaeval Political Theology* (Princeton: Princeton University Press, 1957; repr. 1997)

Katajala-Peltomaa, Sari, 'Gender and Spheres of Interaction: Devotional Practices in Fourteenth-Century Canonisation Processes' (unpublished doctoral dissertation, University of Tampere, 2006)

Katzir, Yael, 'The Conquest of Jerusalem, 1099 and 1187: Historical Memory and Religious Typology', in *The Meeting of Two Worlds: Cultural Exchange between East and West during the Period of the Crusades*, ed. by Vladimir P. Goss (Kalamazoo: Medieval Institute Publications, 1986), pp. 103–13

Kedar, Benjamin Z., 'The Passenger List of a Crusader Ship, 1250: Towards the History of Popular Element on the Seventh Crusade', *Studi Medievali*, 12 (1972), 267–79

Kelly, Samantha, *New Solomon: Robert of Naples (1309–1343) and Fourteenth-Century Kingship* (Leiden: Brill, 2003)

Kennan, Elizabeth, 'Innocent III and the First Political Crusade: A Comment on the Limitations of Papal Power', *Traditio*, 27 (1971), 231–49

Kostick, Conor, *The Social Structure of the First Crusade* (Leiden: Brill, 2008)

Lawrence, Clifford Hugh, *Medieval Monasticism: Forms of Religious Life in Western Europe in the Middle Ages* (London: Longman, 1984)

Lecoy de la Marche, A., 'La Prédication de la croisade au treizième siècle', *Revue des questions historiques*, 48 (1890), 5–28

Le Goff, Jacques, *The Birth of Purgatory*, trans. by A. Goldhammer (London: Scolar Press, 1984); orig. *La Naissance du Purgatoire* (Paris: Editions Gallimard, 1981)

——, *L'Imaginaire médiéval* (Paris: Editions Gallimard, 1985)

——, *Marchands et banquiers du Moyen Âge* (Paris: Presses universitaires de France, 1956)

——, *Saint Louis* (Paris: Éditions Gallimard, 1996)

——, 'Saint Louis, croisé idéal?', *Notre histoire*, no. 20 (1986), 42–47

Leopold, Antony, *How to Recover the Holy Land* (Aldershot: Ashgate, 2000)

Lerner, Robert E., 'Frederick II, Alive, Aloft, and Allayed, in Franciscan-Joachite Eschatology', in *The Use and Abuse of Eschatology in the Middle Ages*, ed. by Werner Verbeke, Daniel Verhelst, and Andries Welkenhuysen (Leuven: Leuven University Press, 1988), pp. 359–84

——, 'The Medieval Return to the Thousand-Year Sabbath', in *The Apocalypse in the Middle Ages*, ed. by Richard K. Emmerson and Bernard McGinn (Ithaca, NY: Cornell University Press, 1992), pp. 51–71

Lewis, Robert E., ed., *Middle English Dictionary* (Ann Arbor: University of Michigan Press, 1989)

Little, Lester K., 'Pride Goes before Avarice: Social Change and the Vices in Latin Christendom', *American Historical Review*, 76.1 (1971), 16–49

Lloyd, Simon, 'Crusader Knights and the Land Market in the Thirteenth Century', in *Thirteenth-Century England*, vol. II, *Proceedings of the Newcastle upon Tyne Conference 1987*, ed. by Peter R. Coss and Simon D. Lloyd (Woodbridge: Boydell Press, 1988), pp. 119–36

——, *English Society and the Crusade, 1216–1307* (Oxford: Clarendon Press, 1988)

Longere, Jean, 'Deux sermons de Jacques de Vitry († 1240), *Ad servos et ancillas*', in *La Femme au moyen-âge*, ed. by Michel Rouche and Jean Heuclin (Mauberge: Actes du colloque Mauberge, 1990), pp. 261–97

——, 'La Femme dans la théologie pastorale', *Cahiers de Fanjeaux*, 23, *La Femme dans la vie religieuse du Languedoc* (1988), 127–52

Lopez, Robert S., *The Commercial Revolution of the Middle Ages, 950–1350* (Cambridge: Cambridge University Press, 1976)

Loud, G. A., *Crusade of Frederick Barbarossa* (Farnham: Ashgate, 2010)

——, 'Frederick II's War with the Church, 1239–1250', in *Studies in Church History*, vol. XXX, *Martyrs and Martyrologies*, ed. by Diana Wood (Oxford: Basil Blackwell, 1993), pp. 141–52

Lower, Michael, *The Barons' Crusade: A Call to Arms and its Consequences* (Philadelphia: University of Pennsylvania Press, 2005)

——, 'The Burning at Mont-Aimé: Thibaut of Champagne's Preparations for the Barons' Crusade of 1239', *Journal of Medieval History*, 29 (2003), 95–108

——, 'Louis IX, Charles of Anjou, and the Tunis Crusade of 1270', in *Crusades: Medieval Worlds in Conflict*, ed. by Thomas F. Madden, James L. Naus, and Vincent Ryan (Farnham: Ashgate, 2010), pp. 173–93

Maccarrone, Michele, *Vicarius Christi: Storia del Titolo Papale* (Roma: Facultas Theologica Pontificii Athenaei Lateranensis, 1952)

MacGregor, James B., 'The First Crusade in Late Medieval *Exempla*', *The Historian*, 68.1 (2006), 29–48

——, 'The Ministry of Gerold d'Avranches: Warrior-Saints and Knightly Piety on the Eve of the First Crusade', *Journal of Medieval History*, 29 (2003), 219–37

Maier, Christoph T., 'Crisis, Liturgy and the Crusade in the Twelfth and Thirteenth Centuries', *Journal of Ecclesiastical History*, 48 (1997), 628–57

——, 'Crusade and Rhetoric against the Muslim Colony of Lucera: Eudes of Châteauroux's *Sermones de Rebellione Sarracenorum Lucherie in Apulia*', *Journal of Medieval History*, 21 (1995), 343–85

——, *Crusade Propaganda and Ideology: Model Sermons for the Preaching of the Cross* (Cambridge: Cambridge University Press, 2000)

——, 'Mass, the Eucharist and the Cross: Innocent III and the Relocation of the Crusade', in *Pope Innocent III and his World*, ed. by John C. Moore (Aldershot: Ashgate, 1999), pp. 351–60

——, *Preaching the Crusades: Mendicant Friars and the Cross in the Thirteenth Century* (Cambridge: Cambridge University Press, 1994)

——, 'The Roles of Women in the Crusade Movement', *Journal of Medieval History*, 30 (2004), 61–82

Markowski, Michael, '*Crucesignatus*: Its Origins and Early Usage', *Journal of Medieval History*, 10 (1984), 157–65

——, 'Peter of Blois and the Conception of the Third Crusade', in *The Horns of Hattin*, ed. by Benjamin Z. Kedar (London: Ashgate, 1992), pp. 261–69

——, 'Richard Lionheart: Bad King, Bad Crusader?' *Journal of Medieval History*, 23 (1997), 351–65

Markus, R. A., 'Saint Augustine's Views on the "Just War"', in *Studies in Church History*, vol. xx, *The Church and War*, ed. by W. J. Sheils (Oxford: Basil Blackwell, 1983), pp. 1–13

Martini, Giuseppe, 'Innocenzo III ed il finanziamento delle crociate', *Archivio della R. deputazione romana di storia patria*, 67 (1944), 309–35

Mattox, John Mark, *St. Augustine and the Theory of Just War* (London: Continuum, 2006)

Matzke, John E., 'Contributions to the History of the Legend of Saint George, with Special Reference to the Sources of the French, German and Anglo-Saxon Metrical Versions', *Publications of the Modern Language Association*, 17.4 (1902), 464–535

Mayer, Hans E., *Geschichte der Kreuzzüge* (Stuttgart: Kohlhammer, 1965)

McCluskey, Colleen, 'The Roots of Ethical Voluntarism', *Vivarium*, 39.2 (2001), 185–208

McDonnel, Ernest W., *The Beguines and Beghards in Medieval Culture* (New Brunswick: Rutgers University Press, 1954)

Menache, Sophia, *The Vox Dei: Communication in the Middle Ages* (New York: Oxford University Press, 1990)

Miller, T. S., 'What's in a Name? Clerical Representations of the Parisian Beguines (1200–1328)', *Journal of Medieval History*, 33 (2007), 60–86

Moore, John C., *Pope Innocent III (1160/61–1216): To Root Up and to Plant* (Leiden: Brill, 2003)

Morris, Colin, 'A Hermit Goes to War: Peter and the Origins of the First Crusade', in *Studies in Church History*, vol. xxii, *Monks, Hermits and the Ascetic Tradition*, ed. by W. J. Sheils (Oxford: Basil Blackwell, 1985), pp. 79–107

——, 'Martyrs on the Field of Battle before and during the First Crusade', in *Studies in Church History*, vol. XXX, *Martyrs and Martyrologies*, ed. by Diana Wood (Oxford: Basil Blackwell, 1993), pp. 93–104

——, 'Peter the Hermit and the Chroniclers', in *The First Crusade: Origins and Impact*, ed. by Jonathan Phillips (Manchester: Manchester University Press, 1997), pp. 21–34

——, 'Propaganda for War: The Dissemination of the Crusading Ideal in the Twelfth Century', in *Church History*, vol. XX, *The Church and War*, ed. by W. J. Sheils (Oxford: Basil Blackwell, 1983), pp. 79–101

——, *Sepulchre of Christ and the Medieval West: From the Beginning to 1600* (Oxford: Oxford University Press, 2005)

Morris, David, 'The Historiography of the *Super Prophetas* (also known as *Super Esaiam*) of Pseudo-Joachim of Fiore', *Oliviana: Mouvements et dissidences spirituels XIIIᵉ–XIVᵉ siècles*, 4 (2012), <http://oliviana.revues.org/512> [accessed 2016]

Morton, Nicholas, 'The Defence of the Holy Land and the Memory of the Maccabees', *Journal of Medieval History*, 36 (2010), 275–93

Muessig, Carolyn, 'Audience and Preacher: *Ad Status* Sermons and Social Classification', in *Preacher, Sermon and Audience in the Middle Ages*, ed. by Carolyn Muessig (Leiden: Brill, 2002), pp. 255–76

——, 'Les Sermons de Jacques de Vitry sur les cathares', *Cahiers de Fanjeaux*, 32, *La Prédication en Pays d'Oc (XIIᵉ – début XVᵉ s.)* (1997), 69–83

Muldoon, James, 'Crusading and Canon Law', in *The Palgrave Advances in the Crusades*, ed. by Helen J. Nicholson (Basingstoke: Palgrave Macmillan, 2005), pp. 37–57

Munro, Dana C., 'The Speech of Pope Urban II at Clermont, 1095', *American Historical Review*, 11.2 (1906), 231–42

Murray, Alexander, 'Archbishop and Mendicants in Thirteenth-Century Pisa', in *Stellung und Wirksamkeit der Bettelorden in der städtischen Gesellschaft*, ed. by Kaspar Elm (Berlin: Duncker & Humblot, 1981), pp. 19–75

——, 'Religion among the Poor in Thirteenth-Century France: The Testimony of Humbert de Romans', *Traditio*, 30 (1974), 285–324

——, *Suicide in the Middle Ages* (Oxford: Oxford University Press, 1998)

Newhauser, Richard, ed., *The Seven Deadly Sins: From Communities to Individuals* (Leiden: Brill, 2007)

Nicol, David, 'Crusades and the Unity of Christendom', in *The Meeting of Two Worlds: Cultural Exchange between East and West during the Period of the Crusades*, ed. by Vladimir P. Goss (Kalamazoo: Medieval Institute Publications, 1986), pp. 169–80

Paulus, Nikolaus, *Geschichte des Ablasses im Mittelalter vom Ursprunge bis zur Mitte des 14. Jahrhunderts*, vol. III (Paderborn: Ferdinand Schöningh, 1923)

Pincikowski, Scott E., *Bodies of Pain: Suffering in the Works of Hartmann von Aue* (New York: Routledge, 2002)

Plummer, Robert L., *Paul's Understanding of the Church's Mission* (Milton Keynes: Paternoster, 2006)

Porges, Walter, 'The Clergy, the Poor, and the Non-combatants on the First Crusade', *Speculum*, 21.1 (1946), 1–23

Powell, James M., *Anatomy of a Crusade, 1213–1221* (Philadelphia: University of Pennsylvania Press, 1986)

——, 'The Role of Women in the Fifth Crusade', in *The Horns of Hattin*, ed. by Benjamin Z. Kedar (London: Ashgate, 1992), pp. 294–301

Pryor, John, ed., *Logistics of Warfare in the Age of the Crusades* (Aldershot: Ashgate, 2006)

Purcell, Maureen, *Papal Crusading Policy: The Chief Instruments of Papal Crusading Policy and Crusade to the Holy Land from the Loss of Jerusalem to the Fall of Acre, 1244–1291* (Leiden: Brill, 1975)

Purkis, William J., *Crusading Spirituality in the Holy Land and Iberia, c. 1095–c.1187* (Woodbridge: Boydell Press, 2008)

——, 'Elite and Popular Perceptions of *Imitatio Christi* in Twelfth-Century Crusade Spirituality', in *Studies in Church History*, vol. XLII, *Elite and Popular Religion*, ed. by Kate Cooper and Jeremy Gregory (Woodbridge: Boydell Press, 2006), pp. 55–64

——, 'Stigmata on the First Crusade', in *Studies in Church History*, vol. XLI, *Signs, Wonders, Miracles: Representation of Divine Power in the Life of the Church*, ed. by Kate Cooper and Jeremy Gregory (Woodbridge: Boydell Press, 2005), pp. 99–108

Queller, Donald E., and Thomas F. Madden, eds, *The Fourth Crusade: The Conquest of Constantinople* (Philadelphia: University of Pennsylvania Press, 1997)

Raedts, Peter, 'The Children's Crusade of 1212', *Journal of Medieval History*, 3 (1977), 282–89

Ranke, Leopold von, *Weltgeschichte*, vol. VIII (Leipzig: Duncker – Humblot, 1887)

Rawcliffe, Carol, *Leprosy in Medieval England* (Woodbridge: Boydell Press, 2006)

Reeves, Marjorie, *The Influence of Prophecy in the Later Middle Ages: A Study in Joachimism* (Oxford: Clarendon Press, 1969)

Reynolds, Susan, *Fiefs and Vassals: The Medieval Evidence Reinterpreted* (Oxford: Clarendon Press, 1994)

Richard, Jean, 'La Fondation d'une eglise latine en orient par saint Louis: Damiette', *Bibliothèque de l'École des Chartes*, 120 (1962), 39–54

Richard, Jean, *Histoire des croisades* (Paris: Librairie Arthème Fayard 1996)

Riley-Smith, Jonathan, *The Crusades, Christianity, and Islam* (New York: Columbia University Press, 2008)

——, *The Crusades: A History*, 2nd edn (London: Continuum, 2005)

——, 'Crusading as an Act of Love', *History*, 65 (1980), 177–91

——, 'The Crusading Movement and Historians', in *The Oxford Illustrated History of the Crusades*, ed. by Jonathan Riley-Smith (Oxford: Oxford University Press, 1995), pp. 1–12

——, 'Death on the First Crusade', in *The End of Strife*, ed. by David Loades (Edinburgh: T. & T. Clark, 1984), pp. 14–31

——, 'Early Crusaders to the East and the Costs of Crusading, 1095–1130', in *Cross Cultural Convergences in the Crusader Period: Essays Presented to Aryeh Grabois on his Sixty-Fifth Birthday*, ed. by Michael Goodich, Sophie Menache, and Sylvia Schein (New York: Peter Lang, 1999), pp. 237–57

——, *The First Crusade and the Idea of Crusading* (1986; repr. London: Continuum, 2003)

——, *The First Crusaders, 1095–1131* (Cambridge: Cambridge University Press, 1997)

——, *What Were the Crusades?* (London: Macmillan, 1977)

Rist, Rebecca, *Papacy and Crusading in Europe, 1198–1245* (London: Continuum, 2009)

Roberts, Phyllis, 'The *Ars Praedicandi* and the Medieval Sermon', in *Preacher, Sermon and Audience in the Middle Ages*, ed. by Carolyn Muessig (Leiden: Brill, 2002), pp. 41–62

Roest, Bert, *Franciscan Literature of Religious Instruction Before the Coincil of Trent* (Leiden: Brill, 2004)

Roos, Lena, '"God Wants It!": The Ideology of Martyrdom of the Hebrew Crusade Chronicles and its Jewish and Christian Background' (unpublished doctoral dissertation, Uppsala University, 2003)

Roscher, H., *Papst Innocenz III. und die Kreuzzüge* (Göttingen: Vandenhoeck & Ruprecht, 1969)

Rousseau, Constance M., 'Home Front and Battlefield: The Gendering of Papal Crusading Policy (1095–1221)', in *Gendering the Crusades*, ed. by Susan Edgington and Sarah Lambert (Cardiff: University of Wales Press, 2001), pp. 31–44

Runciman, Steven, *A History of the Crusades*, 3 vols (Cambridge: Cambridge University Press, 1951–54)

——, *The Sicilian Vespers* (1958; repr. Cambridge: Cambridge University Press, 1995)

Ruotsala, Antti, *Europeans and Mongols in the Middle of the Thirteenth Century: Encountering the Other* (Helsinki: Finnish Academy of Science and Letters, 2001)

Rusconi, Roberto, 'De la predication à la confession: Transmission et contrôle de modèles de comportement au XIIIe siècle', in *Fraire croire: Modalités de la diffusion et de la reception des messages religieux du XIIe au XVe siècle* (Roma: École Française de Rome, 1981), pp. 67–85

Russell, Frederick H., *The Just War in the Middle Ages* (Cambridge: Cambridge University Press, 1975)

Röhricht, Reinhold, 'Die Kreuzpredigten gegen den Islam: Ein Beitrag zur Geschichte der christlichen Predigt im 12. und 13. Jahrhundert', *Zeitschrift für Kirchengeschichte*, 6 (1884), 550–72

Sanders, Boykin, 'Imitating Paul: 1 Cor. 4:16', *Harvard Theological Review*, 74.4 (1981), 353–63

Sandor, Monica, 'Jacques de Vitry: Biography', in *De l'homelie au sermon: Histoire de la prédication médiévale*, ed. by Jacqueline Hamesse and Xavier Hermand (Louvain-la-Neuve: Université Catholique de Louvain, 1993), pp. 53–59

Schein, Sylvia, *Gateway to the Heavenly City: Crusader Jerusalem and the Catholic West (1099–1187)* (Aldershot: Ashgate, 2005)

Schenk, Jochen, *Templar Families: Landowning Families and the Order of the Temple in France, c. 1120–1307* (Cambridge: Cambridge University Press, 2012)

Schneyer, Johannes Baptist, *Repertorium der lateinischen Sermones des Mittelalters*, 11 vols (Münster: Aschendorffsche Verlagsbuchhandlung, 1969–90)

Shaffern, Robert W., 'Images, Jurisdiction, and the Treasury of Merit', *Journal of Medieval History*, 22 (1996), 237–47

——, *The Penitents' Treasury: Indulgences in Latin Christendom, 1175–1375* (Scranton: University of Scranton Press, 2007)

Siberry, Elizabeth, *Criticism of Crusading, 1095–1274* (Oxford: Clarendon Press, 1985)

Smith, Caroline, *Crusading in the Age of Joinville* (Aldershot: Ashgate, 2006)

——, 'Martyrdom and Crusading in the Thirteenth Century: Remembering the Dead of Louis IX's Crusades', *Al-Masāq*, 15 (2003), 189–96

Sommerlechner, Andrea, ed., *Innocenzo III: Urbs et Orbis, Atti del Congresso Internazionale Roma, 9–15 settembre 1998*, vols I–II (Roma: Società romana di storia patria, 2003)

Strayer, Joseph Reese, *The Albigensian Crusades* (New York: Dial Press, 1971; repr. Ann Arbor: University of Michigan Press, 1992)

Stroick, Bernhard A., *Verfasser und Quellen der Collectio de Scandalis Ecclesiae*, Reformschrift des fr. Gilbert von Tournay, O.F.M. zum II. Konzil von Lyon, 1274 (Firenze: Quaracchi, 1930)

Stuckey, Jace, 'Charlemagne: The Making of an Image, 1100–1300' (unpublished doctoral dissertation, University of Florida, 2006)

Sumption, Jonathan, *The Albigensian Crusade* (1978; repr. London: Faber and Faber, 1999)

Tamminen, Miikka, 'The Crusader's Stigmata: True Crusading and the Wounds of Christ in the Crusade Ideology of the 13th Century', in *Infirmity in Antiquity and the Middle Ages*, ed. by Christian Krötzl, Katariina Mustakkallio, and Jenni Kuuliala (Farnham: Ashgate 2015), pp. 103–17

——, 'Crusading in the Margins? Women and Children in the Crusade Model Sermon of the Thirteenth Century', in *Religious Participation in Ancient and Medieval Societies*, ed. by Sari Katajala-Peltomaa and Ville Vuolanto (Roma: Acta Instituti Romani Finlandiae, 2013), pp. 145–58

——, 'The Test of Friendship: *Amicitia* in the Crusade Ideology of the Thirteenth Century', in *De Amicitia: Friendship and Social Networks in Antiquity and the Middle Ages*, ed. by Katariina Mustakallio and Christian Krötzl (Roma: Acta Instituti Romani Finlandiae, 2010), pp. 213–29

——, 'Who Deserves the Crown of Martyrdom? Martyrs in the Crusade Ideology of Jacques de Vitry (1160/70–1240)', in *On Old Age: Approaching Death in Antiquity and the Middle Ages*, ed. by Christian Krötzl and Katariina Mustakallio (Turnhout: Brepols, 2011), pp. 293–313

Tanner, Heather J., 'In His Brothers' Shadow: The Crusading Career and Reputation of Eustace III of Boulogne', in *The Crusades: Other Experiences, Alternate Perspectives*, ed. by Khalil I. Semaan (Binghamton, NY: Global Academic Publishing, Binghamton University, 2003), pp. 83–99

Taylor, Julie Anne, 'Muslim–Christian Relations in Medieval Southern Italy', *Muslim World*, 97 (2007), 190–99

——, *Muslims in Medieval Italy: The Colony at Lucera* (Lanham: Lexington Books, 2003)

Taylor, Philip M., *Munitations of the Mind: A History of Propaganda* (Manchester: Manchester University Press, 2003)

Thomassen, Bjørn, 'The Uses and Meanings of Liminality', *International Political Anthropology*, 2.1 (2009), 5–27

Throop, Palmer A., *Criticism of the Crusade: A Study of Public Opinion and Crusade Propaganda* (Philadelphia: Porcupine Press, 1975)

——, 'Criticism of Papal Crusade Policy in Old French and Provencal', *Speculum*, 13.4 (1938), 379–412

Throop, Susanna, *Crusading as an Act of Vengeance, 1095–1216* (Farnham: Ashgate, 2011)

——, 'Zeal, Anger and Vengeance: The Emotional Rhetoric of Crusading', in *Vengeance in the Middle Ages: Emotion, Religion, and Feud*, ed. by Susanna Throop and Paul Hyams (Farnham: Ashgate, 2010), pp. 177–201

Tierney, Brian, *Origins of Papal Infallibility, 1150–1350: A Study on the Concepts of Infallibility, Sovereignty and Tradition in the Middle Ages* (Leiden: Brill, 1972)

Tinsley, Ernest J., *The Imitation of God in Christ: An Essay on the Biblical Basis of Christian Spirituality* (London: S.C.M. Press, 1960)

Tolan, John V., *Saracens: Islam in the Medieval European Imagination* (New York: Columbia University Press, 2002)

Traill, David A., 'Philip the Chancellor and the Heresy Inquisition in Northern France, 1235–1236', *Viator*, 37 (2006), 241–54

Trotter, David A., *Medieval French Literature and the Crusades (1100–1300)* (Geneva: Librairie Droz S. A., 1988)

——, ed., *Multilingualism in Later Medieval Britain* (Cambridge: D. S. Brewer, 2000)

Tugwell, Simon, '*De huiusmodi sermonibus texitur omnis recta predicatio*: Changing Attitudes towards the Word of God', in *De l'homelie au sermon: Histoire de la prédication médiévale*, ed. by Jacqueline Hamesse and Xavier Hermand (Louvain-la-Neuve: Université Catholique de Louvain, 1993), pp. 159–68

Turner, Victor, *The Ritual Process: Structure and Anti-structure* (New Brunswick: Aldine Transaction, 1969)

Turner, Victor, and Edith Turner, *Image and Pilgrimage in Christian Culture* (New York: Columbia University Press, 1978)

Tyerman, Christopher: *The Crusades* (New York: Sterling Publishing, 2009)

——, *England and the Crusades, 1095–1588* (Chicago: University of Chicago Press, 1988)

——, *Fighting for Christendom* (Oxford: Oxford University Press, 2004)

——, *God's War: A New History of the Crusades* (London: Penguin Books, 2007)

——, 'The Holy Land and the Crusades of the Thirteenth and Fourteenth Centuries', in *Crusade and Settlement: Papers Read at the First Conference of the Society for the Study of the Crusades and the Latin East and Presented to R. C. Smail*, ed. by Peter W. Edbury (Cardiff: University College Cardiff Press, 1985), pp. 105–12

——, *The Invention of the Crusades* (Houndmills: MacMillan Press, 1998)

——, 'Who Went on Crusades to the Holy Land?', in *The Horns of Hattin*, ed. by Benjamin Z. Kedar (London: Ashgate, 1992), pp. 13–26

Van Der Nat, P. G., 'Observations on Tertullian's Treatise on Idolatry', *Vigiliae Christianae*, 17.2 (1963), 71–84

Vauchez, André, 'Les Origines de l'hérésie cathare en Languedoc, d'après un sermon de l'archevêque de Pise Federico Visconti († 1277)', in *Società, istituzioni, spiritualità:*

Studi in onore di Cinzio Violante, vol. II (Spoleto: Centro Italiano di Studi sull'alto medievo, 1994), pp. 1023–36

——, 'Prosélytisme et action antihérétique en milieu féminin au XIIIᵉ siècle: La Vie de Marie d'Oignies († 1213) par Jacques de Vitry,' in *Propagande et contre-propagande religieuses*, ed. by Jacques Marx (Brussel: Editions de l'Universitaire, 1987), pp. 95–110

——, *La Sainteté en Occident aux derniers siècles du Moyen Âge (1198–1431)* (Roma: École Française de Rome, 1981)

Wakefield, Walter L., and Austin P. Evans, *Heresies of the High Middle Ages* (New York: Columbia University Press, 1991)

Weiler, Björn K. U., *Henry III of England and the Staufen Empire, 1216–1272* (Wood-bridge: Boydell Press, 2006)

Whalen, Brett Edward, *Dominion of God: Christendom and Apocalypse in the Middle Ages* (Cambridge, MA: Harvard University Press, 2009)

Wolff, Robert Lee, 'The Latin Empire of Constantinople, 1204–1311', in *A History of the Crusades*, ed. by Kenneth M. Setton, vol. II, *The Later Crusades, 1189–1311*, ed. by R. L. Wolff and H. W. Hazard (Philadelphia: University of Wisconsin Press, 1962), pp. 187–235

Wolfram, G., 'Kreuzpredigt und Kreuzlied', *Zeitschrift für deutsches Alterthum und deutsche Litteratur*, 30 (1886), 89–132

Wood, Diana, *Medieval Economic Thought* (New York: Cambridge University Press, 2002)

Index of Manuscripts

General Index

Aaron, biblical priest: 69, 69 n. 90,
    69 n. 92, 118
Absalom, biblical figure: 68
Abraham, biblical patriarch: 66, 246–47
Achor, *Achan*, biblical figure: 53–54,
    54 n. 31, 54 n. 33, 55, 55 n. 34, 56–57,
    57 n. 41, 57 n. 42, 57 n. 43, 58,
    58 n. 44, 58 n. 45, 59, 64, 66
Acre: 6, 15, 73, 124 n. 126, 125 n. 129,
    156, 160 n. 258, 185 n. 348, 189,
    217, 218 n. 57, 246, 248 n. 164, 259,
    260, 269
Adam, biblical figure: 145
age, old age: 229, 230 n. 91, 259–60,
    272–75, 287
Ai: 45–46, 50–52, 52 n. 25, 53, 54, 58–59
Aigues Mortes: 264
Albertus Magnus: 15, 15 n. 42, 167,
    168 n. 284
Alexander the Great: 174
Alexander III, Pope: 204 n. 5
Alexander IV, Pope: 26 n. 77, 51, 51 n. 22,
    80, 213 n. 39, 214
Alexander Minorita: 80, 80 n. 137
Alexandria: 240, 264, 264 n. 235
Alphonse de Poitiers: 161, 201, 201 n. 409
Amalek, Amalekites, biblical figure, biblical
    people: 67, 67 n. 78, 70
Ambrose of Milan: 223
Andrew, St: 173, 218–19
angel of Revelation (the sixth angel): 77–80,
    80 n. 137, 81

Antichrist: 75, 75 n. 113–14, 76, 76 n. 115,
    80, 83, 83 n.149, 84–86
'anti'-crusaders: 73, 93, 105, 108, 149, 152,
    206, 208, 210–12, 260
Antioch: 75, 157, 172–73, 173 n. 303, 190,
    254, 268 n. 250, 271–72, 272 n. 261
Ark of the Covenant: 48–50
Augustine of Hippo: 65 n. 72, 87, 92,
    92 n. 5, 93, 175, 191 n. 367
avarice: 52, 55, 58–59, 93, 124, 156, 176,
    178, 187, 212–13, 217, 219

Baldric de Dol: 93 n. 6
Baldwin I, King of Jerusalem: 46 n. 6, 60,
Baldwin II, Latin Emperor of
    Constantinople: 47
Beirut: 246, 262
Benevento, battle of 1266: 56
Bériou, Nicole: 12–13, 14 n. 38
Bernard of Clairvaux: 10, 10 n. 23, 109,
    120, 120 n. 108, 197, 248 n. 162
Bernold von Konstanz: 134 n. 163
Bertrand de la Tour: 53 n. 25
Bird, Jessalynn: 13–14, 31, 246
Boaz, biblical figure: 185
Bohemond of Taranto: 75 n. 113
Bonaventure: 80, 127, 167
Boniface de Montferrat: 163 n. 127
Bouchard d'Avesnes: 177 n. 317
Bourges: 30, 136, 170, 221–22, 222 n. 68
Byblos: 246

SERMO: STUDIES ON PATRISTIC, MEDIEVAL, AND REFORMATION SERMONS AND PREACHING

All volumes in this series are evaluated by an Editorial Board, strictly on academic grounds, based on reports prepared by referees who have been commissioned by virtue of their specialism in the appropriate field. The Board ensures that the screening is done independently and without conflicts of interest. The definitive texts supplied by authors are also subject to review by the Board before being approved for publication. Further, the volumes are copyedited to conform to the publisher's stylebook and to the best international academic standards in the field.

Titles in Series

Ruth Horie, *Perceptions of Ecclesia: Church and Soul in Medieval Dedication Sermons* (2006)

A Repertorium of Middle English Prose Sermons, ed. by Veronica O'Mara and Suzanne Paul, 4 vols (2007)

Constructing the Medieval Sermon, ed. by Roger Andersson (2008)

Alan John Fletcher, *Late Medieval Popular Preaching in Britain and Ireland: Texts, Studies, and Interpretations* (2009)

Kimberly A. Rivers, *Preaching the Memory of Virtue and Vice: Memory, Images, and Preaching in the Late Middle Ages* (2010)

Holly Johnson, *The Grammar of Good Friday: Macaronic Sermons of Late Medieval England* (2012)

The Last Judgement in Medieval Preaching, ed. by Thom Mertens, Maria Sherwood-Smith, Michael Mecklenburg, and Hans-Jochen Schiewer (2013)

Preaching the Word in Manuscript and Print in Late Medieval England: Essays in Honour of Susan Powell, ed. by Martha W. Driver and Veronica O'Mara (2013)

Preaching and Political Society: From Late Antiquity to the End of the Middle Ages / Depuis l'Antiquité tardive jusqu'à la fin du Moyen Âge, ed. by Franco Morenzoni (2013)

Sermo Doctorum: Compilers, Preachers, and their Audiences in the Early Medieval West, ed. by Maximilian Diesenberger, Yitzhak Hen, and Marianne Pollheimer (2013)

From Words to Deeds: The Effectiveness of Preaching in the Late Middle Ages, ed. by Maria Giuseppina Muzzarelli (2014)

Yuichi Akae, *A Mendicant Sermon Collection from Composition to Reception: The* Novum opus dominicale *of John Waldeby, OESA* (2015)

Siegfried Wenzel, *The Sermons of William Peraldus: An Appraisal* (2017)

In Preparation

Christian, Jewish, and Muslim Preaching in the Mediterranean and Europe: Identities and Interfaith Encounters, ed. by Linda G. Jones and Adrienne Dupont-Hamy